Historical Viewpoints

Historical Viewpoints

Notable Articles from
American Heritage

THIRD EDITION

Volume Two
Since 1865

Editor

John A. Garraty

Columbia University

Harper & Row, Publishers

New York   Hagerstown   Philadelphia   San Francisco   London

Sponsoring Editor: John Greenman
Special Projects Editor: Mary Lou Mosher
Project Editor: Claudia Kohner
Designer: T. R. Funderburk
Senior Production Manager: Kewal K. Sharma
Photo Researcher: Myra Schachne
Compositor: Maryland Linotype Composition Co., Inc.
Printer and Binder: The Murray Printing Company

Cover: Fourth of July celebration, Washington, D.C., 1976. McNamee, Woodfin Camp.

All articles have appeared in *American Heritage, The Magazine of History,* some under different titles.

Historical Viewpoints, Third Edition, Volume Two Since 1865

Library of Congress Cataloging in Publication Data

Garraty, John Arthur, Date-   comp.
    Historical viewpoints.

    CONTENTS: v. 1. to 1877.—v. 2. Since 1865.
    1. United States—History—Addresses, essays,
lectures. I. American heritage. II. Title.
E178.6.G37 1979   973   78-23787
ISBN 0-06-042272-6 (v. 1)
ISBN 0-06-042273-4 (v. 2)

Acknowledgments

"Why They Impeached Andrew Johnson," by David Herbert Donald, © 1956 by American Heritage Publishing Co., Inc.

"Ride-in: A Century of Protest Begins," by Alan F. Westin, © 1962 by American Heritage Publishing Co., Inc.

"Mississippi: The Past That Has Not Died," from *The Past That Would Not Die* by Walter Lord. Copyright © 1965 by Walter Lord. Reprinted by permission of Harper & Row, Publishers, Inc.

"Reluctant Conquerors: American Army Officers and the Plains Indians," by Thomas C. Leonard, © 1976 by American Heritage Publishing Co., Inc.

"Andrew Carnegie: Captain of Industry," © 1960 by Robert L. Heilbroner. Reprinted by permission.

"The Diaspora in America: A Study of Jewish Immigration," by David Boroff, © 1966 by American Heritage Publishing Co., Inc.

"The Immigrant: White and Black," by Bernard A. Weisberger, © 1970 by American Heritage Publishing Co., Inc.

"The Age of the Bosses," by William V. Shannon, © 1969 by American Heritage Publishing Co., Inc.

"Two Early Critics of Industrial America," © 1967 by Robert L. Beisner. Reprinted by permission.

"The Myth of the Happy Yeoman," from *The Age of Reform* by Richard Hofstadter. Copyright © 1955. Reprinted by permission of Alfred A. Knopf, Inc.

"Economic Reform and the Sherman Antitrust Act," © 1960 by Thurman Arnold. Reprinted by permission.

"Was Bryan a Reformer?," by John A. Garraty, © 1961 by American Heritage Publishing Co., Inc.

"Jane Addams: Urban Crusader," by Anne Firor Scott, © 1960 by American Heritage Publishing Co., Inc.

"Consumer Protection: The Pure Food and Drugs Act," by Gerald H. Carson, © 1956 by American Heritage Publishing Co., Inc. Reprinted by permission of Collins-Knowlton-Wing, Inc.

"The Fight for Women's Suffrage: An Interview with Alice Paul," by Robert S. Gallagher, © 1974 by American Heritage Publishing Co., Inc.

"The Needless War with Spain," by William L. Leuchtenburg, © 1957 by American Heritage Publishing Co., Inc.

"The Enemies of Empire," © 1960 by Harold A. Larrabee. Reprinted by permission.

"Woodrow Wilson and the League of Nations," by Thomas A. Bailey, © 1957 by American Heritage Publishing Co., Inc.

"Pearl Harbor: Who Blundered?," by Col. T. N. Dupuy, © 1962 by American Heritage Publishing Co., Inc.

"The Cold War," © 1977 by Charles L. Mee, Jr. Reprinted by permission.

"The Causes of the Great Crash," by John Kenneth Galbraith, © 1958 by American Heritage Publishing Co., Inc.

"The Poor in the Great Depression," by David J. Rothman, © 1972 by American Heritage Publishing Co., Inc.

"The Place of Franklin D. Roosevelt in History," by Allan Nevins, © 1965 by American Heritage Publishing Co., Inc.

"The American City: Continuity and Change," by Daniel P. Moynihan, © 1969 by American Heritage Publishing Co., Inc.

"The American Farm: Change and Revolution," © 1978 by Richard Rhodes. Originally published in The American Heritage Magazine. Reprinted by permission.

"Lyndon B. Johnson and Vietnam," © 1976 by Larry L. King. Reprinted by permission.

"Modern American Society," by John Brooks. Copyright © 1970 by John Brooks. Reprinted by permission of Harold Ober Associates Incorporated.

"America: Experiment or Destiny?," © 1977 by Dr. Arthur M. Schlesinger, Jr. Reprinted by permission.

Picture Credits

Contents

Introduction

This third edition has been inspired by the encouraging reception afforded the two earlier editions of *Historical Viewpoints* and by the fact that interesting new articles continue to appear in *American Heritage*. This edition contains ten new essays. I have included these new selections because they seemed better suited to current historical interests and because they present fresh points of view. I have also restored one essay, Colonel Dupuy's "Pearl Harbor: Who Blundered?" that I left out of the second edition. I had mistakenly thought that the subject had lost some of its appeal. A large number of users of the book took the trouble to inform me that they thought the change unfortunate and to urge that I include it in this edition.

There are almost as many kinds of history as there are historians. In addition to the differences between political history and the social, economic, and cultural varieties, the discipline lends itself to such classifications as analytical, narrative, statistical, impressionistic, local, comparative, philosophical, and synthetic. Often the distinctions between one and another kind of history are overemphasized. No one can write good political history without some consideration of social, economic, and cultural questions; narrative history requires analysis to be meaningful; impressionistic treatments of past events are, in a way, statistical histories based on very tiny samples. Nevertheless, the types exist and serve different purposes. Each focuses on part of the total human experience and sees it from a particular perspective; each, when well done, adds its own contribution to the total record.

It is therefore foolish to argue that any one historical approach is inherently better than all the others. Some are perhaps more generally useful (that is, more interesting to a wider segment of the population) or more suggestive at a particular time and place than others, but the distinctions are like those between a miniature and a mural, a sonnet and an epic poem. No one would suggest that "The Moonlight Sonata" was a waste of Beethoven's time because he was capable of producing the *Choral* symphony, or that Mozart should not have written "Eine Kleine Nachtmusik" because he had within him *Don Giovanni*. In the same way a monograph or an article of twenty pages can be as well worth doing and as satisfying to read as Edward Gibbon's *Decline and Fall of the Roman Empire*.

The most useless and confusing distinction commonly drawn between varieties of history is that separating "scholarly" from "popular" history. These terms came into existence during the latter half of the nineteenth century. Before that time, all history was popular in the sense that those who wrote it, viewing themselves as possessors of special information acquired through scholarship or through having observed firsthand the events they described, aimed to transmit that knowledge to anyone interested in the subject. But when history became "scientific" and professionalized, historians began to write primarily for other historians. They assumed that nonspecialists had no interest in their work or were incapable of understanding it, and even argued that to write history for the general reader was to prostitute one's talents. Therefore, although with many notable exceptions, the best-trained and most intelligent historians tended to forswear the task of transmitting their scholarly findings to ordinary readers.

Of course popular history continued to be written and read, but most of it was produced by amateurs. Its quality varied greatly. The scholarly prejudice against "popularizers" had a solid basis in fact. Too often popular history was—and still is—shallow, error-ridden, out of date before publication, a mere rehash of already written books, an exasperating mixture, as one critic has said, of "something we all knew before" and "something which is not so." Much of it was written by journalists and novelists who often lacked the patience, the professional skills, and the knowledge of sources that are as necessary for the writing of good history as narrative power, imagination, and lucidity of style.

It was chiefly with the hope of encouraging professional historians to broaden their perspectives that, beginning in the 1930's, a group of historians led by Professor Allan Nevins of Columbia University began to think of founding a general circulation magazine of American history. Their aim was a magazine in which solidly researched and significant articles would be presented in a way that would interest and educate readers who were not professional students of the past. Nevins himself, one of the great historians of the twentieth century, epitomized the combination they sought to produce. He was a prodigious scholar, author of dozens of learned volumes, and trainer of literally hundreds of graduate students, but he was also a fluent and graceful writer whose work was widely read and appreciated. Nevins' books won Pulitzer Prizes as well as academic renown.

The example provided by Nevins and a few other outstanding historians of his generation, such as Samuel Eliot Morison, undoubtedly influenced the gradual revival of concern for popular history that has occurred in recent times on the part of professional academic scholars. So did the increasing sophistication of the general reading public, which made it less difficult for these experts to write this type of history without sacrificing their intellectual standards. In any case, in

1954 the Nevins group—the Society of American Historians—joined the American Association for State and Local History in sponsoring the hardcover magazine they had envisioned: *American Heritage*.

The success of *American Heritage* was rapid and substantial. It achieved a wide circulation, and the best professional historians began to publish in its pages. Its articles, at their best, have been authoritative, interesting, significant, and a pleasure to read. They have ranged over the whole course of American history from the pre-colonial era to the present, and have dealt with every aspect of American development from politics to painting and from economics to architecture.

The present selection from among the hundreds of essays and book excerpts that have appeared in *American Heritage* since 1954 does not pretend to offer "the best" of these articles, although any such collection would undoubtedly include many of those I have chosen. It seeks rather to provide a balanced assortment of articles to supplement and enrich general college courses in American history. Keeping in mind the structure of these courses and the topics they tend to emphasize, I have reprinted here articles which, in my opinion, will add depth and breadth to the student's understanding.

This is—by definition—popular history, but it is also history written by experts. The articles differ in purpose and approach. Some present new findings, some reexamine old questions from a fresh point of view, others magisterially distill and synthesize masses of facts and ideas. From the total, readers may extract, along with the specifics of the individual essays, a sense of the variety and richness of historical literature. They will observe how forty-odd historians (and not all of them academic scholars) have faced the task of presenting knowledge not to other historians alone but to an audience of intelligent and interested general readers.

Since most of the students enrolled in college history courses are not specialists—even those who intend to become professional historians stand at the very beginning of their training—this approach seems to me ideally adapted to their needs. Many, though by no means all, of the subjects treated in these essays have also been covered in articles in professional historical periodicals, often written by the same historians. But as here presented, without sacrifice of intellectual standards, the material is not so much easier to grasp as it is more meaningful. Details are clearly related to larger issues; historical characters are delineated in the round, not presented as stick figures or automatons; too much previous knowledge is not assumed. I once read the draft of an essay on the history of the Arabs which contained the sentence, "The life and philosophy of Mohammed are well-known," and which then went on to other less universally understood topics. Such essays no doubt have their place, but that place is not in collections designed for beginners, whatever the subject.

Finally, I believe that at least some of the essays I have included here illustrate the truth that history is, at its best, an art as well as a science. After all, the ancients gave history its own Muse, Clio. From reading the following pages, I hope and expect that students will come to realize that history is a form of literature, that it can be *enjoyed,* not merely assimilated. Even those who see college history courses exclusively as training grounds for future professionals surely will not object if their students enjoy these readings while they learn.

Needless to say, I hope the book will serve even better than its predecessors the needs and interests of students of American history.

John A. Garraty

Historical Viewpoints

Part One
Reconstruction and Race Relations

David Herbert Donald

WHY THEY IMPEACHED ANDREW JOHNSON

The story of Presidential Reconstruction begun by Randall and Current in the last essay [see "How Lincoln Would Have Rebuilt the Union" in Volume One] is completed in this one by David Herbert Donald, Charles Warren Professor of American History at Harvard University. Lincoln's approach to restoring the Union was cautious, practical, thoughtful—humane in every sense of the word. Because of his assassination, however, the evaluation of his policy has to be a study in the might-have-beens of history. The Reconstruction policy of his successor, Andrew Johnson, superficially similar to Lincoln's, was reckless, impractical, emotional, and politically absurd. While historians have differed in evaluating his purposes, they have been in unanimous agreement that his management of the problem was inept and that his policy was a total failure.

Professor Donald's essay provides an extended character study of Johnson, and it is not an attractive portrait. Donald believes that Johnson "threw away a magnificent opportunity" to smooth and speed the return of the Confederate states to a harmonious place in the Union. But he also shows how difficult Johnson's task was and to how great an extent southern white opinion was set against the full acceptance of black equality. Donald, a former student of James G. Randall, is best known for his revision and expansion of Randall's *The Civil War and Reconstruction,* and for his own Pulitzer Prize winning biography of the Massachusetts senator *Charles Sumner.*

Reconstruction after the Civil War posed some of the most discouraging problems that have ever faced American statesmen. The South was prostrate. Its defeated soldiers straggled homeward through a countryside desolated by war. Southern soil was untilled and exhausted; southern factories and railroads were worn out. The four billion dollars of southern capital invested in Negro slaves was wiped out by advancing Union armies, "the most stupendous act of sequestration in the history of Anglo-American jurisprudence." The white inhabitants of eleven states had somehow to be reclaimed from rebellion and restored to a firm loyalty to the United States. Their four million former slaves had simultaneously to be guided into a proper use of their new-found freedom.

For the victorious Union government there was no time for reflection. Immediate decisions had to be made. Thousands of destitute whites and Negroes had to be fed before long-range plans of rebuilding the southern economy could be drafted. Some kind of government had to be established in these former Confederate states, to preserve order and to direct the work of restoration.

A score of intricate questions must be answered: Should the defeated southerners be punished or pardoned? How should genuinely loyal southern Unionists be rewarded? What was to be the social, economic, and political status of the now free Negroes? What civil rights did they have? Ought they to have the ballot? Should they be given a freehold of property? Was Reconstruction to be controlled by the national government, or should the southern states work out their own salvation? If the federal government supervised the process, should the President or the Congress be in control?

Intricate as were the problems, in early April, 1865, they did not seem insuperable. President Abraham Lincoln was winning the peace as he had already won the war. He was careful to keep every detail of Reconstruction in his own hands; unwilling to be committed to any "exclusive, and inflexible plan," he was working out a pragmatic program of restoration not, perhaps, entirely satisfactory to any group, but reasonably acceptable to all sections. With his enormous prestige as commander of the victorious North and as victor in the 1864 election, he was able to promise freedom to the Negro, charity to the southern white, security to the North.

The blighting of these auspicious beginnings is one of the saddest stories in American history. The reconciliation of the sections, which seemed so imminent in 1865, was delayed for more than ten years. Northern magnanimity toward a fallen foe curdled into bitter distrust. Southern whites rejected moderate leaders, and inveterate racists spoke for the new South. The Negro, after serving as a political pawn for a decade, was relegated to a second-class citizenship, from which he is yet struggling to emerge. Rarely has democratic government so completely failed as during the Reconstruction decade.

The responsibility for this collapse of American statesmanship is, of course, complex. History is not a tale of deep-dyed villains or pure-as-snow heroes. Part of the blame must fall upon ex-Confederates who refused to recognize that the war was over: part upon freedmen who confused liberty with license and the ballot box with the lunch pail; part upon northern antislavery extremists who identified patriotism with loyalty to the Republican party; part upon the land speculators, treasury grafters, and railroad promoters who were unwilling to have a genuine peace lest it end their looting of the public till.

Yet these divisive forces were not bound to triumph. Their success was due to the failure of constructive statesmanship that could channel the magnanimous feelings shared by most Americans into a positive program of reconstruction. President Andrew Johnson was called upon for positive leadership, and he did not meet the challenge.

Andrew Johnson's greatest weakness was his insensitivity to public opinion. In contrast to Lincoln, who said, "Public opinion in this country is everything," Johnson made a career of battling the popular will. A poor white, a runaway tailor's apprentice, a self-educated Tennessee politician, Johnson was a living defiance to the dominant southern belief that leadership belonged to the plantation aristocracy.

As senator from Tennessee, he defied the sentiment of his section in 1861 and refused to join the secessionist movement. When Lincoln later appointed him military governor of occupied Tennessee, Johnson found Nashville "a furnace of treason," but he braved social ostracism and threats of assassination and discharged his duties with boldness and efficiency.

Such a man was temperamentally unable to understand the northern mood in 1865, much less to yield to it. For four years the northern people had been whipped into wartime frenzy by propaganda tales of Confederate atrocities. The assassination of Lincoln by a southern sympathizer confirmed their belief in southern brutality and heartlessness. Few northerners felt vindictive toward the South, but most felt that the rebellion they had crushed must never rise again. Johnson ignored this postwar psychosis gripping the North and plunged ahead with his program of rapidly restoring the southern states to the Union. In May, 1865, without any previous preparation of public opinion, he issued a proclamation of amnesty, granting forgiveness to nearly all the millions of former rebels and welcoming them back into peaceful fraternity. Some few Confederate leaders were excluded from his general amnesty, but even they could secure pardon by special petition. For weeks the White House corridors were thronged with ex-Confederate statesmen and former southern generals who daily received presidential forgiveness.

Ignoring public opinion by pardoning the former Confederates, Johnson actually entrusted the formation of new governments in the South to them. The provisional governments established by the President proceeded, with a good deal of reluctance, to rescind their secession ordinances, to abolish slavery, and to repudiate the Confederate debt. Then, with far more enthusiasm, they turned to electing governors, representatives, and senators. By December, 1865, the southern states had their delegations in Washington waiting for admission by Congress. Alexander H. Stephens, once vice president of the Con-

A Harper's Weekly *cartoon depicts Johnson (left) and Thaddeus Stevens as engineers committed to a collision course.*

federacy, was chosen senator from Georgia; not one of the North Carolina delegation could take a loyalty oath; and all of South Carolina's congressmen had ''either held office under the Confederate States, or been in the army, or countenanced in some way the Rebellion.''

Johnson himself was appalled, ''There seems in many of the elections something like defiance, which is all out of place at this time.'' Yet on December 5 he strongly urged the Congress to seat these southern representatives ''and thereby complete the work of reconstruction.'' But the southern states were omitted from the roll call.

Such open defiance of northern opinion was dangerous under the best of circumstances, but in Johnson's case it was little more than suicidal. The President seemed not to realize the weakness of his position. He was the representative of no major interest and had no genuine political following. He had been considered for the vice presidency in 1864 because, as a southerner and a former slaveholder, he could lend plausibility to the Republican pretension that the old parties were dead and that Lincoln was the nominee of a new, nonsectional National Union party.

A political accident, the new Vice President did little to endear himself to his countrymen. At Lincoln's second inauguration Johnson appeared before the Senate in an obviously inebriated state and made a long, intemperate harangue about his plebeian origins and his hard-won success. President, Cabinet, and senators were humiliated by the shameful display, and Charles Sumner felt that ''the Senate should call upon him to resign.'' Historians now know that Andrew Johnson was not a heavy drinker. At the time of his inaugural display, he was just recovering from a severe attack of typhoid fever. Feeling ill just before he entered the Senate chamber, he asked for some liquor to steady his nerves, and either his weakened condition or abnormal sensitivity to alcohol betrayed him.

Lincoln reassured Republicans who were worried over the affair: "I have known Andy for many years; he made a bad slip the other day, but you need not be scared. Andy ain't a drunkard." Never again was Andrew Johnson seen under the influence of alcohol, but his reformation came too late. His performance on March 4, 1865, seriously undermined his political usefulness and permitted his opponents to discredit him as a pothouse politician. Johnson was catapulted into the presidency by John Wilkes Booth's bullet. From the outset his position was weak, but it was not necessarily untenable. The President's chronic lack of discretion made it so. Where common sense dictated that a chief executive in so disadvantageous a position should act with great caution, Johnson proceeded to imitate Old Hickory, Andrew Jackson, his political idol. If Congress crossed his will, he did not hesitate to defy it. Was he not "the Tribune of the People"?

Sure of his rectitude, Johnson was indifferent to prudence. He never learned that the President of the United States cannot afford to be a quarreler. Apprenticed in the rough-and-tumble politics of frontier Tennessee, where orators exchanged violent personalities, crude humor, and bitter denunciations, Johnson continued to make stump speeches from the White House. All too often he spoke extemporaneously, and he permitted hecklers in his audience to draw from him angry charges against his critics.

On Washington's birthday in 1866, against the advice of his more sober advisers, the President made an impromptu address to justify his Reconstruction policy. "I fought traitors and treason in the South," he told the crowd; "now when I turn around, and at the other end of the line find men—I care not by what name you call them— who will stand opposed to the restoration of the Union of these States, I am free to say to you that I am still in the field."

During the "great applause" which followed, a nameless voice shouted, "Give us the names at the other end. . . . Who are they?"

"You ask me who they are," Johnson retorted. "I say Thaddeus Stevens of Pennsylvania is one; I say Mr. Sumner is another; and Wendell Phillips is another." Applause urged him to continue. "Are those who want to destroy our institutions . . . not satisfied with the blood that has been shed? . . . Does not the blood of Lincoln appease the vengeance and wrath of the opponents of this government?"

The President's remarks were as untrue as they were impolitic. Not only was it manifestly false to assert that the leading Republican in the House and the most conspicuous Republican in the Senate were opposed to "the fundamental principles of this government" or that they had been responsible for Lincoln's assassination; it was incredible political folly to impute such actions to men with whom the President had to work daily. But Andrew Johnson never learned that the President of the United States must function as a party leader.

There was a temperamental coldness about this plain-featured, grave man that kept him from easy, intimate relations with even his political supporters. His massive head, dark, luxuriant hair, deep-set and piercing eyes, and cleft square chin seemed to Charles Dickens to indicate "courage, watchfulness, and certainly strength of purpose," but his was a grim face, with "no genial sunlight in it." The coldness and reserve that marked Johnson's public associations doubtless stemmed from a deep-seated feeling of insecurity; this self-educated tailor whose wife had taught him how to write could never expose himself by letting down his guard and relaxing.

Johnson knew none of the arts of managing men, and he seemed unaware that face-saving is important for a politician. When he became President, Johnson was besieged by advisers of all political complexions. To each he listened gravely and non-committally, raising no questions and by his silence seeming to give consent. With Radical Senator Sumner, already intent upon giving the freedmen both homesteads and the ballot, he had repeated interviews during the first month of his presidency. "His manner has been excellent, & even sympathetic," Sumner reported triumphantly. With Chief Justice Salmon P. Chase, Sumner urged Johnson to support immediate Negro suffrage and found the President was "well-disposed, & sees the rights & necessities of the case." In the middle of May, 1865, Sumner reassured a Republican caucus that the President was a true Radical; he had listened repeatedly to the Senator and had told him "there is no difference between us." Before the end of the month the rug was pulled from under Sumner's feet. Johnson issued his proclamation for the reconstruction of North Carolina, making no provisions for Negro suffrage. Sumner first learned about it through the newspapers.

While he was making up his mind, Johnson appeared silently receptive to all ideas; when he had made a decision, his mind was immovably closed, and he defended his course with all the obstinacy of a weak man. In December, alarmed by Johnson's Reconstruction proclamations, Sumner again sought an interview with the President. "No longer sympathetic, or even kindly," Sumner found, "he was harsh, petulant, and unreasonable." The Senator was depressed by Johnson's "prejudice, ignorance, and perversity" on the Negro suffrage issue. Far from listening amiably to Sumner's argument that the South was still torn by violence and not yet ready for readmission, Johnson attacked him with cheap analogies. "Are there no murders in Massachusetts?" the President asked.

"Unhappily yes," Sumner replied, "sometimes."

"Are there no assaults in Boston? Do not men there sometimes knock each other down, so that the police is obliged to interfere?"

"Unhappily yes."

"Would you consent that Massachusetts, on this account, should be excluded from Congress?" Johnson triumphantly queried. In the excitement the President unconsciously used Sumner's hat, which the Senator had placed on the floor beside his chair, as a spittoon!

Had Johnson been as resolute in action as he was in argument, he might conceivably have carried much of his party with him on his Reconstruction program. Promptness, publicity, and persuasion could have created a presidential following. Instead Johnson boggled. Though he talked boastfully of "kicking out" officers who failed to support his plan, he was slow to act. His own Cabinet, from the very beginning, contained members who disagreed with him, and his secretary of war, Edwin M. Stanton, was openly in league with the Republican elements most hostile to the President. For more than two years he impotently hoped that Stanton would resign; then in 1867, after Congress had passed the Tenure of Office Act, he tried to oust the Secretary. This belated firmness, against the letter of the law, led directly to Johnson's impeachment trial.

Instead of working with his party leaders and building up political support among Republicans, Johnson in 1866 undertook to organize his friends into a new party. In August a convention of white southerners, northern Democrats, moderate Republicans, and presidential appointees assembled in Philadelphia to endorse Johnson's policy. Union General Darius Couch of Massachusetts marched arm in arm down the convention aisle with Governor James L. Orr of South Carolina, to symbolize the states reunited under Johnson's rule. The convention produced fervid oratory, a dignified statement of principles —but not much else. Like most third-party reformist movements it lacked local support and grass-roots organization.

Johnson himself was unable to breathe life into his stillborn third party. Deciding to take his case to the people, he accepted an invitation to speak at a great Chicago memorial honoring Stephen A. Douglas. When his special train left Washington on August 28 for a "swing around the circle," the President was accompanied by a few Cabinet members who shared his views and by the war heroes Grant and Farragut.

At first all went well. There were some calculated political snubs to the President, but he managed at Philadelphia, New York, and Albany to present his ideas soberly and cogently to the people. But Johnson's friends were worried lest his tongue again get out of control. "In all frankness," a senator wrote him, do not "allow the excitement of the moment to draw from you any *extemporaneous speeches*."

At St. Louis, when a Radical voice shouted that Johnson was a "Judas," the President flamed up in rage. "There was a Judas and he was one of the twelve apostles," he retorted. ". . . The twelve apostles had a Christ. . . . If I have played the Judas, who has been my Christ that I have played the Judas with? Was it Thad Stevens? Was it Wendell Phillips? Was it Charles Sumner?" Over mingled hisses and applause, he shouted, "These are the men that stop and compare themselves with the Saviour; and everybody that differs with them . . . is to be denounced as a Judas."

Johnson had played into his enemies' hands. His Radical foes denounced him as a "trickster," a "culprit," a man "touched with insanity, corrupted with lust, stimulated with drink." More serious in consequence was the reaction of northern moderates, such as James Russell Lowell, who wrote, "What an anti-Johnson lecturer we have in Johnson! Sumner has been right about the *cuss* from the first. . . ."

The fall elections were an overwhelming repudiation of the President and his Reconstruction policy.

Johnson's want of political sagacity strengthened the very elements in the Republican party which he most feared. In 1865 the Republicans had no clearly defined attitude toward Reconstruction. Moderates like Gideon Welles and Orville Browning wanted to see the southern states restored with a minimum of restrictions; Radicals like Sumner and Stevens demanded that the entire southern social system be revolutionized. Some Republicans were passionately concerned with the plight of the freedmen; others were more interested in maintaining the high tariff and land grant legislation enacted during the war. Many thought mostly of keeping themselves in office, and many genuinely believed, with Sumner, that "the Republican party, in its objects, is identical with country and with mankind." These diverse elements came slowly to adopt the idea of harsh Reconstruction, but Johnson's stubborn persistency in his policy left them no alternative. Every step the President took seemed to provide "a new encouragement to (1) the rebels at the South, (2) the Democrats at the North and (3) the discontented elements everywhere." Not many Republicans would agree with Sumner that Johnson's program was "a defiance to God and Truth," but there was genuine concern that the victory won by the war was being frittered away.

The provisional governments established by the President in the South seemed to be dubiously loyal. They were reluctant to rescind their secession ordinances and to repudiate the Confederate debt, and they chose high-ranking ex-Confederates to represent them in Congress. Northerners were even more alarmed when these southern governments began to legislate upon the Negro's civil rights. Some laws were necessary—in order to give former slaves the right to marry, to hold property, to sue and be sued, and the like—but the Johnson legislatures went far beyond these immediate needs. South Carolina, for example, enacted that no Negro could pursue the trade "of an artisan, mechanic, or shopkeeper, or any other trade or employment besides that of husbandry" without a special license. Alabama provided that "any stubborn or refractory servants" or "servants who loiter away their time" should be fined $50 and, if they could not pay, be hired out for six months' labor. Mississippi ordered that every Negro under eighteen years of age who was an orphan or not supported by his parents must be apprenticed to some white person, preferably the former owner of the slave. Such southern laws indicated a determination to keep the Negro in a state of peonage.

It was impossible to expect a newly emancipated race to be content with such a limping freedom. The thousands of Negroes who had served in the Union armies and had helped conquer their former Confederate masters were not willing to abandon their new-found liberty. In rural areas southern whites kept these Negroes under control through the Ku Klux Klan. But in southern cities white hegemony was less secure, and racial friction erupted in mob violence. In May, 1866, a quarrel between a Memphis Negro and a white teamster led to a riot in which the

JOHNSON'S LOVE FOR THE SOLDIER.

Black Soldier—Massa, I come for my Bounty of $300, under the bill signed by President Johnson.

Johnson Paymaster, All right, my brave man, here is your money.

White Soldier—I come for the EXTRA bounty of $100 which Congress voted to me.

Johnson Paymaster, I am very sorry, but the President says the brave black troops must be paid first.

This cartoon is an example of the virulence of the attacks on Johnson by his enemies.

city police and the poor whites raided the Negro quarters and burned and killed promiscuously. Far more serious was the disturbance in New Orleans two months later. The Republican party in Louisiana was split into pro-Johnson conservatives and Negro suffrage advocates. The latter group determined to hold a constitutional convention, of dubious legality, in New Orleans, in order to secure the ballot for the freedmen and the offices for themselves. Through imbecility in the War Department, the Federal troops occupying the city were left without orders, and the mayor of New Orleans, strongly opposed to Negro equality, had the responsibility for preserving order. There were acts of provocation on both sides, and finally, on July 30, a procession of Negroes marching toward the convention hall was attacked.

"A shot was fired . . . by a policeman, or some colored man in the procession," General Philip Sheridan reported. "This led to other shots, and a rush after the procession. On arrival at the front of the Institute [where the convention met], there was some throwing of brick-bats by both sides. The police . . . were vigorously marched to the scene of disorder. The procession entered the Institute with the flag, about six or eight remaining outside. A row occurred between a policeman and one of these colored men, and a shot was again fired by one of the parties, which led to an indiscriminate firing on the building, through the windows, by the policemen.

"This had been going on for a short time, when a white flag was displayed from the windows of the Institute, whereupon the firing ceased and the police rushed into the building. . . . The policemen opened an indiscriminate fire upon the audience until they had emptied their revolvers, when they retired, and those inside barricaded the doors. The door was broken in, and the firing again commenced when many of the colored and white people either escaped out of the door, or were passed out by the policemen inside, but as they came out, the policemen who formed the circle nearest the building fired upon them, and they were again fired upon by the citizens that formed the outer circle.''

Thirty-seven Negroes and three of their white friends were killed; 119 Negroes and seventeen of their white sympathizers were wounded. Of their assailants, ten were wounded and but one killed. President Johnson was, of course, horrified by these outbreaks, but the Memphis and New Orleans riots, together with the Black Codes, afforded a devastating illustration of how the President's policy actually operated. The southern states, it was clear, were not going to protect the Negroes' basic rights. They were only grudgingly going to accept the results of the war. Yet, with Johnson's blessing, these same states were expecting a stronger voice in Congress than ever. Before 1860, southern representation in Congress had been based upon the white population plus three fifths of the slaves; now the Negroes, though not permitted to vote, were to be counted like all other citizens, and southern states would be entitled to at least nine additional congressmen. Joining with the northern Copperheads, the southerners could easily regain at the next presidential election all that had been lost on the Civil War battlefield.

It was this political exigency, not misguided sentimentality nor vindictiveness, which united Republicans in opposition to the President.

Johnson's defenders have pictured Radical Reconstruction as the work of a fanatical minority, led by Sumner and Stevens, who drove their reluctant colleagues into adopting coercive measures against the South. In fact, every major piece of Radical legislation was adopted by the nearly unanimous vote of the entire Republican membership of Congress. Andrew Johnson had left them no other choice. Because he insisted upon rushing Confederate-dominated states back into the Union, Republicans moved to disqualify Confederate leaders under the Fourteenth Amendment. When, through Johnson's urging, the southern states rejected that amendment, the Republicans in Congress unwillingly came to see Negro suffrage as the only counterweight against Democratic majorities in the South. With the Reconstruction Acts of 1867 the way was open for a true Radical program toward the South, harsh and thorough.

Andrew Johnson became a cipher in the White House, futilely disapproving bills which were promptly passed over his veto. Through his failure to reckon with public opinion, his unwillingness to recognize his weak position, his inability to functon as a party leader, he had sacrificed all influence with the party which had elected him and had turned over its control to Radicals vindictively opposed to his policies. In March, 1868, Andrew Johnson was summoned before the Senate of the United States to be tried on eleven accusations of high crimes and misdemeanors. By a narrow margin the Senate failed to convict him, and historians have dismissed the charges as flimsy and false. Yet perhaps before the bar of history itself Andrew Johnson must be impeached with an even graver charge—that through political ineptitude he threw away a magnificent opportunity.

Alan F. Westin

RIDE-IN: A CENTURY OF PROTEST BEGINS

The last quarter of the nineteenth century—after the federal government relaxed its pressure on the southern states to deal fairly with their black citizens—has been called "the nadir" of the history of black Americans after emancipation. Some historians argue that the low point came somewhat later, during the early twentieth century, but few would disagree with the thesis that the period in question was indeed disastrous for American blacks. Although never really treated decently (in the North as well as in the South), they had made important gains during Reconstruction; the Fourteenth and Fifteenth Amendments "guaranteed" their political and civil rights, and Congress passed stiff laws protecting these rights, including the Civil Rights Act of 1875, which outlawed discrimination in places of public accommodation.

After the so-called Compromise of 1877, however, these gains were gradually stripped away by a combination of southern pressure, northern indifference, and a series of crippling legal interpretations by the Supreme Court. In this essay Professor Alan F. Westin of Columbia University, an expert on constitutional history, describes one of the first and most significant of the Supreme Court decisions of the era, one which emasculated the Civil Rights Act of 1875. His story reads in some ways like an account of the civil rights struggles of the 1950's and 1960's, but with the terrible difference that freedom and justice were in this instance the losers, not the winners of the fight.

It began one day early in January when a Negro named Robert Fox stepped aboard a streetcar in Louisville, Kentucky, dropped his coin into the fare box, and sat down in the white section of the car. Ordered to move, he refused, and the driver threw him off the car. Shortly after, Fox filed a charge of assault and battery against the streetcar company in the federal district court, claiming that separate seating policies were illegal and the driver's actions were therefore improper. The district judge instructed the jury that under federal law common carriers must serve all passengers equally without regard to race. So instructed, the jury found the company rules to be invalid and awarded damages of fifteen dollars (plus $72.80 in legal costs) to Mr. Fox.

Immediately there was sharp criticism of the Fox decision from the city and state administrations, both Democratic; the company defied the court's ruling and continued segregated seating. After several meetings with local federal officials and white attorneys co-operating with them, Louisville Negro leaders decided to launch a full-scale "ride-in." At 7 P.M. on May 12, a young Negro boy boarded a streetcar near the Willard Hotel, walked past the driver, and took a seat among the white passengers. The driver, under new company regulations, did not attempt to throw him off but simply stopped the car, lit a cigar, and refused to proceed until the Negro moved to "his place." While the governor, the Louisville chief of police, and other prominent citizens looked on from the sidewalks, a large crowd which included an increasingly noisy mob of jeering white teen-agers gathered around the streetcar.

Before long, there were shouts of "Put him out!" "Hit him!" "Kick him!" "Hang him!" Several white youths climbed into the car and began yelling insults in the face of the young Negro rider. He refused to answer—or to move. The youths dragged him from his seat, pulled him off the car, and began to beat him. Only when the Negro started to defend himself did the city police intervene: they arrested him for disturbing the peace and took him to jail.

This time the trial was held in Louisville city court, not the federal court. The magistrate ruled that streetcar companies were not under any obligation to treat Negroes exactly as they treated whites, and that any federal measures purporting to create such obligations would be "clearly invalid" under the constitutions of Kentucky and the United States. The defendant was fined, and the judge delivered a warning to Louisville Negroes that further ride-ins would be punished.

But the ride-in campaign was not halted that easily. In the following days, streetcar after streetcar was entered by Negroes who took seats in the white section. Now the drivers got off the cars entirely. On several occasions, the Negro riders drove the cars themselves, to the sound of cheers from Negro spectators. Then violence erupted. Bands of white youths and men began to throw Negro riders off the cars: windows were broken, cars were overturned, and for a time a general race riot threatened. Moderate Kentucky newspapers and many community leaders deplored the fighting; the Republican candidate for

governor denounced the streetcar company's segregation policies and
blamed the violence on Democratic encouragement of white extremists.

By this time, newspapers across the country were carrying reports
of the conflict, and many editorials denounced the seating regulations.
In Louisville, federal marshals and the United States attorney backed
the rights of the Negro riders and stated that federal court action
would be taken if necessary. There were even rumors that the President
might send troops.

Under these threats, the streetcar company capitulated. Soon, all
the city transit companies declared that ''it was useless to try to resist
or evade the enforcement by the United States authorities of the claim
of Negroes to ride in the cars.'' To ''avoid serious collisions,'' the
company would thereafter allow all passengers to sit where they
chose. Although a few disturbances took place in the following months,
and some white intransigents boycotted the streetcars, mixed seating became a common practice. The Kentucky press soon pointed with
pride to the spirit of conciliation and harmony which prevailed in
travel facilities within the city, calling it a model for good race
relations. Never again would Louisville streetcars be segregated.

The event may have a familiar ring, but it should not, for it
occurred almost one hundred years ago, in 1871. The streetcars were
horse-drawn. The President who considered ordering troops to Louisville was ex-General Grant, not ex-General Eisenhower. The Republican
gubernatorial candidate who supported the Negro riders, John
Marshall Harlan, was not a post-World War II leader of the G.O.P.
but a former slaveholder from one of Kentucky's oldest and most
famous political families. And the ''new'' Negroes who waged this
ride-in were not members of the Congress of Racial Equality and the
National Association for the Advancement of Colored People, or
followers of Dr. Martin Luther King, but former slaves who were
fighting for civil rights in their own time, and with widespread success.

And yet these dramatic sit-ins, ride-ins, and walk-ins of the 1870's
are almost unknown to the American public today. The standard
American histories do not mention them, providing only thumbnail
references to ''bayonet-enforced'' racial contacts during Reconstruction. Most commentators view the Negro's resort to direct action as
an invention of the last decade. Clearly, then, it is time that the civil-
rights struggle of the 1870's and 1880's was rescued from newspaper
files and court archives, not only because it is historically important
but also because it has compelling relevance for our own era.

Contrary to common assumptions today, no state in the Union during the 1870's, including those south of the Mason-Dixon line, required
separation of whites and Negroes in places of public accommodation.
Admission and arrangement policies were up to individual owners.
In the North and West, many theatres, hotels, restaurants, and public
carriers served Negro patrons without hesitation or discrimination.
Some accepted Negroes only in second-class accommodations, such as
smoking cars on railroads or balconies in theatres, where they sat
among whites who did not have first-class tickets. Other northern and

An 1875 Harper's Weekly *cartoon bore the caption, "Shall We Withdraw Our Troops?"*

western establishments, especially the more exclusive ones, refused Negro patronage entirely.

The situation was similar in the large cities of the southern and border states. Many establishments admitted Negroes to second-class facilities. Some gave first-class service to those of privileged social status—government officials, army officers, newspapermen, and clergymen. On the other hand, many places of public accommodation, particularly in the rural areas and smaller cities of the South, were closed to Negroes whatever their wealth or status.

From 1865 through the early 1880's, the general trend in the nation was toward wider acceptance of Negro patronage. The federal Civil Rights Act of 1866, with its guarantee to Negroes of ''equal benefit of the laws,'' had set off a flurry of enforcement suits—for denying berths to Negroes on a Washington-New York train; for refusing to sell theatre tickets to Negroes in Boston; and for barring Negro women from the waiting rooms and parlor cars of railroads in Virginia, Illinois, and California. Ratification of the Fourteenth Amendment in 1868 had spurred more challenges. Three northern states, and two southern states under Reconstruction regimes, passed laws making it a crime for owners of public-accommodation businesses to discriminate. Most state and federal court rulings on these laws between 1865 and 1880 held in favor of Negro rights, and the rulings built up a steady pressure on owners to relax racial bars.

Nevertheless, instances of exclusion and segregation continued throughout the 1870's. To settle the issue once and for all (thereby

Cartoonist Thomas Nast mocked the provision of the Civil Rights Act of 1875 that allowed blacks to collect $500 from those who barred them from places of public accommodation.

reaping the lasting appreciation of the Negro voters), congressional Republicans led by Senator Charles Sumner pressed for a federal statute making discrimination in public accommodations a crime. Democrats and conservative Republicans warned in the congressional debates that such a law would trespass on the reserved powers of the states and reminded the Sumner supporters that recent Supreme Court decisions had taken a narrow view of federal power under the Civil War amendments.

After a series of legislative compromises, however, Sumner's forces were able to enact the statute; on March 1, 1875, "An Act to Protect all Citizens in their Civil and Legal Rights" went into effect. "It is essential to just government," the preamble stated, that the nation "recognize the equality of all men before the law, and . . . it is the duty of government in its dealings with the people to mete out equal and exact justice to all, of whatever nativity, race, color, or persuasion, religious or political . . ."

Section 1 of the act declared that "All persons within the jurisdiction of the United States shall be entitled to the full and equal enjoyment of the accommodations . . . of inns, public conveyances on land or water, theaters and other places of public amusement; subject only to the conditions and limitations established by law, and applicable alike to citizens of every race or color. . . ." Section 2 provided that any person violating the act could be sued in federal district court for a penalty of $500, could be fined $500 to $1,000, or could be imprisoned from thirty days to one year. (A separate section forbade racial discrimination in the selection of juries.)

Reaction to the law was swift. Two Negro men were admitted to the dress circle of Macauley's Theatre in Louisville and sat through the performance without incident. In Washington, Negroes were served

for the first time at the bar of the Willard Hotel, and a Negro broke
the color line when he was seated at McVicker's Theatre in Chicago.
But in other instances, Negroes were rejected despite "Sumner's law."
Several hotels in Chattanooga turned in their licenses, became private
boardinghouses, and accepted whites only. Restaurants and barber
shops in Richmond turned away Negro customers.

Suits challenging refusals were filed en masse throughout the country. Perhaps a hundred were decided in the federal district courts during the late 1870's and early 1880's. Federal judges in Pennsylvania,
Texas, Maryland, and Kentucky, among others, held the law to be
constitutional and ruled in favor of Negro complainants. In North
Carolina, New Jersey, and California, however, district judges held
the law invalid. And when other courts in New York, Tennessee,
Missouri, and Kansas put the issue to the federal circuit judges, the
judges divided on the question, and the matter was certified to the
United States Supreme Court.

But the Supreme Court did not exactly rush to make its ruling.
Though two cases testing the 1875 act reached it in 1876 and a third
in 1877, the Justices simply held them on their docket. In 1879, the
Attorney General filed a brief defending the constitutionality of the
law, but still the Court reached no decisions. In 1880, three additional cases were filed, but two years elapsed before the Solicitor General presented a fresh brief supporting the statute. It was not until
late in 1883 that the Supreme Court passed upon the 1875 act, in
what became famous as the *Civil Rights Cases* ruling. True, the Court
was badly behind in its work in this period, but clearly the Justices
chose to let the civil-rights cases "ripen" for almost eight years.

When they finally came to grips with the issue, six separate test
suits were involved. The most celebrated had arisen in New York
City in November of 1879. Edwin Booth, the famous tragedian and
brother of John Wilkes Booth, had opened a special Thanksgiving
week engagement at the Grand Opera House. After playing *Hamlet*,
Othello, and *Richelieu* to packed houses, he was scheduled to perform
Victor Hugo's *Ruy Blas* at the Saturday matinee on November 22.

One person who had decided to see Booth that Saturday was William R. Davis, Jr., who was later described in the press as a tall,
handsome, and well-spoken Negro of twenty-six. He was the business
agent of the *Progressive-American*, a Negro weekly published in New
York City. At 10 o'clock Saturday morning, Davis' girl friend ("a
bright octoroon, almost white," as the press put it), purchased two
reserved seats at the box office of the Grand Opera House. At 1:30 P.M.,
Davis and his lady presented themselves at the theatre, only to be
told by the doorkeeper, Samuel Singleton, that "these tickets are
no good." If he would step out to the box office, Singleton told Davis,
his money would be refunded.

It is unlikely that Davis was surprised by Singleton's action, for
this was not the first time he had encountered such difficulties. Shortly
after the passage of the 1875 act, Davis had been refused a ticket to
the dress circle of Booth's Theatre in New York. He had sworn out a

In this cartoon Leslie's Weekly *praised theatres that flaunted the 1875 law and refused to sell Negroes tickets.*

warrant against the ticket seller, but the failure of his witnesses to appear at the grand jury proceedings had led to a dismissal of the complaint. This earlier episode, as well as Davis' activity as a Negro journalist, made it probable that this appearance at the Opera House in 1879 was a deliberate test of the management's discriminatory policies.

Though Davis walked out of the lobby at Singleton's request, he did not turn in his tickets for a refund. Instead, he summoned a young white boy standing near the theatre, gave him a dollar (plus a dime for his trouble), and had him purchase two more tickets. When Davis and his companion presented these to Singleton, only the lady was allowed to pass. Again Davis was told that his ticket was "no good." When he now refused to move out of the doorway, Singleton called a policeman and asked that Davis be escorted off the theatre property. The officer told Davis that the Messrs. Poole and Donnelly, the managers of the Opera House, did not admit colored persons. "Perhaps the managers do not," Davis retorted, "but the laws of the country [do]."

The following Monday, November 24, Davis filed a criminal complaint; on December 9, this time with witnesses in abundance, Singleton was indicted in what the press described as the first criminal proceeding under the 1875 act to go to trial in New York. When the case opened on January 14, 1880, Singleton's counsel argued that the 1875 law was unconstitutional. "It interferes," he said, "with the right of the State of New York to provide the means under which citizens of the State have the power to control and protect their rights in respect to their private property." The assistant United States attorney replied that such a conception of states' rights had been "exploded and superseded long ago." It was unthinkable, he declared, that "the United States could not extend to one citizen of

New York a right which the State itself gave to others of its citizens—
the right of admission to places of public amusement.''

The presiding judge decided to take the constitutional challenge
under advisement and referred it to the circuit court, for consideration at its February term. This left the decision up to Justice Samuel
Blatchford of the Supreme Court, who was assigned to the circuit court
for New York, and District Judge William Choate. The two judges
reached opposite conclusions and certified the question to the United
States Supreme Court.

Davis' case, under the title of *United States v. Singleton,* reached
the Supreme Court in 1880. Already lodged on the Court's docket
were four similar criminal prosecutions under the act of 1875. *U.S. v.
Stanley* involved the refusal of Murray Stanley in 1875 to serve a
meal at his hotel in Topeka, Kansas, to a Negro, Bird Gee. *U.S. v.
Nichols* presented the refusal in 1876 of Samuel Nichols, owner of
the Nichols House in Jefferson City, Missouri, to accept a Negro
named W. H. R. Agee as a guest. *U.S. v. Ryan* involved the conduct
of Michael Ryan, doorkeeper of Maguire's Theatre in San Francisco,
in denying a Negro named George M. Tyler entry to the dress circle
on January 4, 1876. In *U.S. v. Hamilton,* James Hamilton, a conductor
on the Nashville, Chattanooga, and St. Louis Railroad, had on April
21, 1879, denied a Negro woman with a first-class ticket access to the
ladies' car.

There was a fifth case, with a somewhat different setting. On the
evening of May 22, 1879, Mrs. Sallie J. Robinson, a twenty-eight-year-
old Negro, purchased two first-class tickets at Grand Junction, Tennessee, for a trip to Lynchburg, Virginia, on the Memphis and
Charleston Railroad. Shortly after midnight she and her nephew,
Joseph C. Robinson, described as a young Negro ''of light complexion,
light hair, and light blue eyes,'' boarded the train and started into
the parlor car. The conductor, C. W. Reagin, held Mrs. Robinson
back (''bruising her arm and jerking her roughly around,'' she
alleged) and pushed her into the smoker.

A few minutes later, when Joseph informed the conductor that
he was Mrs. Robinson's nephew and was a Negro, the conductor looked
surprised. In that case, he said, they could go into the parlor car at
the next stop. The Robinsons finished the ride in the parlor car but
filed complaints with the railroad about their treatment and then
sued for $500 under the 1875 act. At the trial, Reagin testified that he
had thought Joseph to be a white man with a colored woman, and his
experience was that such associations were ''for illicit purposes.''

Counsel for the Robinsons objected to Reagin's testimony, on the
ground that his actions were based on race and constituted no defense. Admitting the constitutionality of the 1875 law for purposes
of the trial, the railroad contended that the action of its conductor
did not fall within the statute. The district judge ruled that the
motive for excluding persons was the decisive issue under the act:
if the jury believed that the conductor had acted because he thought
Mrs. Robinson ''a prostitute travelling with her paramour,'' whether

"well or ill-founded" in that assumption, the exclusion was not because of race and the railroad was not liable. The jury found for the railroad, and the Robinsons appealed.

These, with William Davis' suit against the doorkeeper of New York's Grand Opera House, were the six cases to which the Supreme Court finally turned in 1882. The Justices were presented with a learned and eloquent brief for the United States submitted by Solicitor General Samuel F. Phillips, who reviewed the leading cases, described the history of the Civil War amendments to the Constitution, and stressed the importance to the rights of citizens of equal access to public accommodation. Four times since 1865, Phillips noted, civil-rights legislation had been enacted by a Congress filled with men who had fought in the Civil War and had written the war amendments. These men understood that "every rootlet of slavery has an individual vitality, and, to its minutest hair, should be anxiously followed and plucked up. . . ." They also knew that if the federal government allowed Negroes to be denied accommodation "by persons who notably were sensitive registers of local public opinion," then "what upon yesterday was only 'fact' will become 'doctrine' tomorrow."

The Supreme Court Justices who considered Phillips' brief and the six test cases were uncommonly talented, among them being Chief Justice Morrison R. Waite, a man underrated today; Joseph P. Bradley, that Court's most powerful intellect; and Stephen J. Field, a *laissez-faire* interpreter of American constitutional law. John Marshall Harlan, the youngest man on the Court, had already started on the course which was to mark him as the most frequent and passionate dissenter in the Gilded Age.

As a whole, the Court might have appeared to be one which would have looked favorably on the 1875 act. All were Republicans except Justice Field, and he was a Democrat appointed by Abraham Lincoln. All except Justice Harlan, who was the Court's only southerner, had made their careers primarily in the northern and western states. Without exception, all had supported the Northern cause in the war, and none had any hostility toward Negroes as a class.

Yet on the afternoon of October 15, 1883, Justice Bradley announced that the Court found Sections 1 and 2 of the Civil Rights Act of 1875 to be unconstitutional. (This disposed of five of the cases; the sixth, *U.S. v. Hamilton*, was denied review on a procedural point.) There was added irony in the fact that Bradley delivered the majority opinion for eight of the Justices. A one-time Whig, Bradley had struggled for a North-South compromise in the darkening months of 1860–61, then had swung to a strong Unionist position after the firing on Fort Sumter. He had run for Congress on the Lincoln ticket in 1862 and in 1868 headed the New Jersey electors for Grant. When the Thirteenth and Fourteenth Amendments were adopted, he had given them firm support, and his appointment to the Supreme Court by Grant in 1870 had drawn no criticism from friends of the Negro, as had the appointment of John Marshall Harlan seven years later.

Bradley's opinion had a tightly reasoned simplicity. The Thirteenth Amendment forbade slavery and involuntary servitude, he noted, but protection against the restoration of bondage could not be stretched to cover federal regulation of "social" discriminations such as those dealt with in the 1875 statute. As for the Fourteenth Amendment, that was addressed only to deprivations of rights by the *states;* it did not encompass *private* acts of discrimination. Thus there was no source of constitutional authority for "Sumner's law"; it had to be regarded as an unwarranted invasion of an area under state jurisdiction. Even as a matter of policy, Bradley argued, the intention of the war amendments to aid the newly freed Negro had to have some limits. At some point, the Negro must cease to be "the special favorite of the law" and take on "the rank of a mere citizen."

At the Atlanta Opera House on the evening of the Court's decision, the end man of Haverly's Minstrels interrupted the performance to announce the ruling. The entire orchestra and dress circle audience rose and cheered. Negroes sitting in the balcony kept their seats, "stunned," according to one newspaper account. A short time earlier, a Negro denied entrance to the dress circle had filed charges against the Opera House management under the 1875 act. Now his case—their case—was dead.

Of all the nine Justices, only John Marshall Harlan, a Kentuckian and a former slaveholder, announced that he dissented from the

Justice John Marshall Harlan wrote the dissenting opinion on the Civil Rights Cases.

ruling. He promised to give a full opinion soon.

Justice Harlan's progress from a supporter of slavery to a civil-rights dissenter makes a fascinating chronicle. Like Bradley, he had entered politics as a Whig and had tried to find a middle road between secessionist Democrats and antislavery Republicans. Like Bradley, he became a Unionist after the firing on Fort Sumter. But there the parallels ended. Although Harlan entered the Union Army, he was totally opposed to freeing the slaves, and his distaste for Lincoln and the Radicals was complete. Between 1863 and 1868, he led the Conservative party in Kentucky, a third-party movement which supported the war but opposed pro-Negro and civil-rights measures as "flagrant invasions of property rights and local government."

By 1868, however, Harlan had become a Republican. The resounding defeat of the Conservatives in the 1867 state elections convinced him that a third party had no future in Kentucky. His antimonopoly views and his general ideas about economic progress conflicted directly with state Democratic policies, and when the Republicans nominated his former field commander, Ulysses S. Grant, for President, in 1868, Harlan was one of the substantial number of Conservatives who joined the G.O.P.

His views on Negro rights also changed at this time. The wave of vigilante activities against white Republicans and Negroes that swept Kentucky in 1868–70, with whippings and murders by the scores, convinced Harlan that federal guarantees were essential. He watched Negroes in Kentucky moving with dignity and skill toward useful citizenship, and his devout Presbyterianism led him to adopt a "brotherhood-of-man" outlook in keeping with his church's national position. Perhaps he may have been influenced by his wife, Mallie, whose parents were New England abolitionists. As a realistic Republican politician, he was also aware that 60,000 Kentucky Negroes would become voters in 1870.

Thus a "new" John Harlan took the stump as Republican gubernatorial candidate in 1871, the year of the Louisville streetcar ride-ins. He opened his rallies by confessing that he had formerly been anti-Negro. But "I have lived long enough," he said, "to feel that the most perfect despotism that ever existed on this earth was the institution of African slavery." The war amendments were necessary "to place it beyond the power of any State to interfere with . . . the results of the war. . . ." The South should stop agitating the race issue, and should turn to rebuilding itself on progressive lines. When the Democrats laughed at "Harlan the Chameleon" and read quotations from his earlier anti-Negro speeches, Harlan replied: "Let it be said that I am right rather than consistent."

Harlan soon became an influential figure in the Republican party and, when President Rutherford B. Hayes decided to appoint a southern Republican to the Supreme Court in 1877, he was a logical choice. Even then, the Negro issue rose to shake Harlan's life again. His confirmation was held up because of doubts by some senators as to his "real" civil-rights views. Only after Harlan produced his speeches between 1871 and 1877 and party leaders supported his firmness on the question was he approved.

Once on the Supreme Court, Harlan could have swung back to a conservative position on civil rights. Instead, he became one of his generation's most intense and uncompromising defenders of the Negro. Perhaps his was the psychology of the convert who defends his new faith more passionately, even more combatively, than the born believer. Harlan liked to think that he had changed because he knew the South and realized that any relaxation of federal protection of the rights of Negroes would encourage the "white irreconcilables" first to acts of discrimination and then to violence, which would destroy all hope of accommodation between the races.

When Harlan sat down in October of 1883 to write his dissent in the *Civil Rights Cases,* he hoped to set off a cannon of protest. But he simply could not get his thoughts on paper. He worked late into the night, and even rose from half-sleep to write down ideas that he was afraid would elude him in the morning. "It was a trying time for him," his wife observed. "In point of years, he was much the youngest man on the Bench; and standing alone, as he did in regard to a decision which the whole nation was anxiously awaiting, he felt that . . . he must speak not only forcibly but wisely." After weeks of drafting and discarding, Harlan seemed to reach a dead end. The dissent would not "write." It was at this point that Mrs. Harlan contributed a dramatic touch to the history of the *Civil Rights Cases.*

When the Harlans had moved to Washington in 1877, the Justice had acquired from a collector the inkstand which Chief Justice Roger Taney had used in writing all his opinions. Harlan was fond of showing this to guests and remarking that "it was the very inkstand from which the infamous *Dred Scott* opinion was written." Early in the 1880's, however, a niece of Taney's, who was engaged in collecting her uncle's effects, visited the Harlans. When she saw the inkstand she asked Harlan for it, and the Justice agreed. The next morning Mrs. Harlan, noting her husband's reluctance to part with his most prized possession, quietly arranged to have the inkstand "lost." She hid it away, and Harlan was forced to make an embarrassed excuse to Taney's niece.

Now, on a Sunday morning, probably early in November of 1883, after Harlan had spent a sleepless night working on his dissent, Mallie Harlan remembered the inkstand. While the Justice was at church, she retrieved it from its hiding place, filled it with a fresh supply of ink and pen points, and placed it on the blotter of his desk. When her husband returned from church, she told him, with an air of mystery, that he would find something special in his study. Harlan was overjoyed to recover his symbolic antique. Mrs. Harlan's gesture was successful, for as she relates:

> The memory of the historic part that Taney's inkstand had played in the Dred Scott decision, in temporarily tightening the shackles of slavery upon the negro race in those ante-bellum days,

seemed, that morning, to act like magic in clarifying my husband's thoughts in regard to the law . . . intended by Sumner to protect the recently emancipated slaves in the enjoyment of equal 'civil rights.' His pen fairly flew on that day and, with the running start he then got, he soon finished his dissent.

How directly the recollection of Dred Scott pervaded Harlan's dissent is apparent to anyone who reads the opinion. He began by noting that the pre-Civil War Supreme Court had upheld congressional laws forbidding individuals to interfere with recovery of fugitive slaves. To strike down the act of 1875 meant that "the rights of freedom and American citizenship cannot receive from the Nation that efficient protection which heretofore was unhesitatingly accorded to slavery and the rights of masters."

Harlan argued that the Civil Rights Act of 1875 was constitutional on any one of several grounds. The Thirteenth Amendment had already been held to guarantee "universal civil freedom"; Harlan stated that barring Negroes from facilities licensed by the state and under legal obligation to serve all persons without discrimination restored a major disability of slavery days and violated that civil freedom. As for the Fourteenth Amendment, its central purpose had been to extend national citizenship to the Negro, reversing the precedent upheld in the Dred Scott decision; its final section gave Congress power to pass appropriate legislation to enforce that affirmative grant as well as to enforce the section barring any state action which might deny liberty or equality. Now, the Supreme Court was deciding what legislation was appropriate and necessary for those purposes, although that decision properly belonged to Congress.

Even under the "State action" clause of the Fourteenth Amendment, Harlan continued, the 1875 act was constitutional; it was well established that "railroad corporations, keepers of inns and managers of places of public accommodation are agents or instrumentalities of the State." Finally, Harlan attacked the unwillingness of the Court's majority to uphold the public-carrier section of the act under Congress' power to regulate interstate trips. That was exactly what was involved in Mrs. Robinson's case against the Memphis and Charleston Railroad, he reminded his colleagues; it had not been true before that Congress had had to cite the section of the Constitution on which it relied.

In his peroration, Harlan replied to Bradley's comment that Negroes had been made "a special favorite of the law." The war amendments had been passed not to "favor" the Negro, he declared, but to include him as "part of the people for whose welfare and happiness government is ordained."

Today, it is the colored race which is denied, by corporations and individuals wielding public authority, rights fundamental in their freedom and citizenship. At some future time, it may be that some other race will fall under the ban of race discrimination. If the constitutional amendments be enforced, according to the intent with which, as I conceive, they were adopted, there cannot be in this republic, any class of human beings in practical subjection to another class. . . .

The *Civil Rights Cases* ruling did two things. First, it destroyed the delicate balance of federal guarantee, Negro protest, and private enlightenment which was producing a steadily widening area of peacefully integrated public facilities in the North and South during the 1870's and early 1880's. Second, it had an immediate and profound effect on national and state politics as they related to the Negro. By denying Congress power to protect the Negro's rights to equal treatment, the Supreme Court wiped the issue of civil rights from the Republican party's agenda of national responsibility. At the same time, those southern political leaders who saw anti-Negro politics as the most promising avenue to power could now rally the "poor whites" to the banner of segregation.

If the Supreme Court had stopped with the *Civil Rights Cases* of 1883, the situation of Negroes would have been bad but not impossible. Even in the South, there was no immediate imposition of segregation in public facilities. During the late 1880's, Negroes could be found sharing places with whites in many southern restaurants, streetcars, and theatres. But increasingly, Democratic and Populist politicians found the Negro an irresistible target. As Solicitor General Phillips had warned the Supreme Court, what had been tolerated as the "fact" of discrimination was now being translated into "doctrine": between 1887 and 1891, eight southern states passed laws requiring railroads to separate all white and Negro passengers. The Supreme Court upheld these laws in the 1896 case of *Plessy v. Ferguson*. Then in the Berea College case of 1906, it upheld laws forbidding private schools to educate Negro and white children together. Both decisions aroused Harlan's bitter dissent. In the next fifteen or twenty years, the chalk line of Jim Crow was drawn across virtually every area of public contact in the South.

Today, as this line is slowly and painfully being erased, we may do well to reflect on what might have been in the South if the Civil Rights Act of 1875 had been upheld, in whole or in part. Perhaps everything would have been the same. Perhaps forces at work between 1883 and 1940 were too powerful for a Supreme Court to hold in check. Perhaps "Sumner's law" was greatly premature. Yet it is difficult to believe that total, state-enforced segregation was inevitable in the South after the 1880's. If in these decades the Supreme Court had taken the same *laissez-faire* attitude toward race relations as it took toward economic affairs, voluntary integration would have survived as a countertradition to Jim Crow and might have made the transition of the 1950's less painful than it was. At the very least, one cannot help thinking that Harlan was a better sociologist than his colleagues and a better southerner than the "irreconcilables." American constitutional history has a richer ring to it because of the protest that John Marshall Harlan finally put down on paper from Roger Taney's inkwell in 1883.

Walter Lord

MISSISSIPPI: THE PAST THAT HAS NOT DIED

The situation that southern blacks and their white supporters
had to contend with after the Civil War, a situation that had
much to do with the frustration of President Johnson's policies
and which helped to produce the Supreme Court decisions in the
Civil Rights Cases and in *Plessy v. Ferguson,* is described in the
following essay by Walter Lord.

This is a case study—a very useful historical approach that
seeks, by examining one part of a subject, to throw light on the
whole. The main advantages of the case study method are that it
concentrates on a more easily mastered body of materials and
permits the use of details and examples that in a broader
treatment would have to be sacrificed to avoid excessive length.
The disadvantages lie chiefly in the inevitable loss of perspective,
and in the not always correct assumption that the case chosen
is entirely typical. The effect is like looking at a distant landscape
through a telescope or at a piece of tissue under a microscope.
Elements that would be lost to the "normal" view are brought
sharply into focus, but the image of the total object is lost or
distorted.

Lord's essay on Mississippi after the Civil War is a fine example
of the intelligent use of the case study. His selection of
Mississippi, home of the most intransigent foes of Negro equality
but also a region where blacks exercised considerable power during
Reconstruction, produces undoubtedly a heightening effect that
is somewhat at variance with the whole truth, but it brings out
very clearly all the problems of the postwar South and the
"solutions" found for them in the late nineteenth century. Mr.
Lord is best known for his "you are there" style of history, first
developed in his popular book, *A Night to Remember,* the story
of the sinking of the liner *Titanic.* However, he makes relatively
little use of that technique in this essay, thus demonstrating
that he is a sound analytical historian as well as a graphic
storyteller.

Splinters flew in every direction as the northern troops hacked apart the chairs and tables of Edward McGehee, one of the wealthiest cotton planters in Wilkinson County, Mississippi. It was October 5, 1864, and Colonel E. D. Osband's men were simply acting on the philosophy expressed by General Sherman when he told a group of protesting Mississippians, "It is our duty to destroy, not build up; therefore do not look to us to help you."

Soon the work was done, the house in flames, and Edward McGehee left contemplating his only remaining possession—a gracefully carved grand piano. It was no comfort to Mr. McGehee, once the owner of hundreds of Negro slaves, that these deeds were done by a company of stern, efficient Negro soldiers.

Ruin upon ruin, the destruction continued for six more gruelling months of war. By the end, Mississippi seemed but a forest of chimneys. The whole town of Okolona could be bought for $5,000. There was not a fence left within miles of Corinth, not a clock running in Natchez. The capital, Jackson, was in ashes—the Confederate Hotel as complete a wreck as the cause it honored.

The first visitors from the North were stunned. Approaching old Charles Langworthy's home near Aberdeen, a man from Chicago recalled spending two pleasant weeks there back in 1855. Greeting the owner, the visitor quickly asked after Mr. Langworthy's five boys and two girls.

"Where is John, your oldest son?"

"Killed at Shiloh."

"Where is William?"

"Died of smallpox in the Army."

"And the other boys?"

"All were killed. . . ."

The Langworthy daughters came forward, dripping with mourning. Not only were their brothers gone; both also had lost their husbands in the service.

The incident was all too typical. Mississippi had sent 78,000 into the fight; only 28,000 came back. Whole companies were wiped out— the Vicksburg Cadets marched off 123 strong; only six returned. One legacy of this sacrifice was 10,000 orphans.

Nor were those who returned always able to play their full part. Surgery was not one of the happier aspects of the Civil War. Empty sleeves flapped everywhere. At a town meeting in Aberdeen a visitor noticed that one hundred of the three hundred men present had lost either an arm or a leg. It is not surprising that in the first year after the war Mississippi spent one fifth of its entire revenue for artificial limbs.

Painfully, the people of the state struggled to live again. Nearly everyone was wiped out. The greatest source of wealth—436,000 slaves worth over 218 million dollars—had vanished with Emancipation. The farm animals that meant so much to a rural people had been carried off—one out of every three mules gone. Most of the cotton was confiscated as Confederate property; any that escaped was mercilessly

*D. H. Euyett painted this water color of
the ruins of Jackson, Mississippi, in 1863,
shortly after Sherman took the state's capital.*

taxed by Washington. Land values crashed—on December 13, 1865, alone, the Vicksburg *Herald* advertised forty-eight plantations for sale or lease. After five years of war Mississippi tumbled from the nation's fifth state in per capital wealth to the very bottom of the list.

"My children, I am a ruined man," Thomas Dabney told his daughters one evening in November, 1866. In happier days Mr. Dabney had endorsed some notes. At the time there seemed little danger— the risk was good and Dabney was the wealthy owner of Burleigh, a fabulous plantation near the town of Raymond. But now times had changed, and the sheriff was downstairs.

Ultimately, Burleigh was auctioned off, and Dabney managed to buy it back only by consigning his cotton crop for years to come. Meanwhile, the family had nothing—even the "loyal" Negro servants had vanished. As the once pampered Dabney girls faced the novel prospect of housework, it looked like a major victory for General Sherman's perhaps apocryphal boast that he would force every southern woman to the washtub.

But this time the General had met his match. "He shall never bring my daughters to the washtub," Dabney thundered. "I'll do the washing myself!" And he did. Dabney was now seventy years old, but for the next two years he scrubbed away, grimly satisfied that here at least he was foiling the hated Yankee.

There were other consolations too, as the people of Mississippi struggled to recover. There was relief that the war was over—whatever their original feelings, most Mississippians were heartily sick of destruction. There was also hope that the state could get back into the Union rather painlessly; President Andrew Johnson had decided to carry on Lincoln's lenient plans for restoration. Best of all, there was the land. Mississippi's towns might lie in ruins, but her match-less asset was the soil itself. If only cotton could get going again . . .

But that was the problem. If the key to prosperity was cotton, the key to cotton had always been slaves—and there weren't any slaves any more. Over 380,000 freedmen aimlessly roamed the state, nearly all of them at loose ends, living where they chose, eating off the federal troops. The former owners had no influence. Most Negroes felt this was what freedom meant—no work. And there were plenty of people around the Union Army camps who advised them not to go back to their old masters. There were even rumors that Washington soon would be dividing up the plantations—forty acres and a mule for everyone.

Actually Washington was never more at cross-purposes. President Johnson suffered from being a states' rights Democrat from Tennessee, and as his prestige waned so did the chances for his lenient program. The Radical Republicans in Congress were winning control over na-tional policy, but beyond a thirst for revenge, they had no clear-cut plans at all. As late as October, 1865, the Radical leader Thaddeus Stevens was asking his friend Charles Sumner if he knew of any good books on how the Russians freed their serfs.

The Negroes themselves could be of very little help in solving their problems. Over ninety-five per cent were illiterate. In the old days it had been illegal to teach the slaves to read or write, and now they were hopelessly ignorant. Few had any idea of citizenship, law, suffrage, or responsibility. Hauled before a court for stealing a bag of corn, one ex-slave happily camping on Jefferson Davis' plantation was asked if he wanted a jury trial.

"What's that?" was all he could say.

The whites felt cornered and helpless. For years they had done as they wanted with these people, and now the tables were turned. They were generally outnumbered, and in the rich cotton areas the margin seemed appalling—Bolivar County was eighty-seven per cent Negro; Issaquena County had 7,000 Negroes, only 600 whites.

But most frightening of all to white Mississippi residents were the Negro troops. When the United States Army's XVI Corps went home in August, 1865, 9,122 of the 10,193 Union soldiers still in the state were Negroes. Their mere presence seemed to invite the most hideous trouble. In Jackson, Major Barnes, commanding the 5th U.S. Colored Infantry, urged the local Negroes to defend their rights even to the "click of the pistol and at the point of the bayonet."

And incidents did happen. William Wilkinson was murdered at Lauderdale Springs by five of his former slaves for selling his planta-tion—they claimed it was rightfully theirs by Christmas. This sort of bloodshed was rare, but it was enough to set off the whites.

Terror bred fantastic rumors. The Natchez *Courier* warned that the county's Negroes were supposed to rise on New Year's Day. In Yazoo City the date was Christmas. The Brandon *Republican* set no date but reported, "They are evidently preparing something and it behooves us to be on the alert and prepare for the worst." There was nothing to any of these reports, but each rumor hardened the feelings of the whites.

They soon developed a fierce callousness toward the Negro, no matter how harmless he might be. On a quiet Sunday afternoon in Natchez an elderly freedman protested to a small white boy raiding his turnip patch. The boy shot him dead, and that was that. In Vicksburg the *Herald* complained that the town's children were hitting innocent bystanders when using their ''nigger shooters.''

Nor was it just the specter of Negro supremacy that aroused white Mississippians—Negro equality was just as bad. ''God damn your soul, get off this boat!'' raged the captain of the Memphis–Vicksburg packet on Christmas morning, 1865. The greeting was directed at a Negro couple who had dared ask for first-class passage. As their luggage was pitched ashore, the captain turned back to his work muttering, ''They can't force their damned nigger equality on me.''

Even when the principle of equality was acknowledged, the practice must have mystified the beneficiaries. ''Take off your hat, you black scoundrel, or I'll cut your throat,'' a Mississippi state legislator yelled at his former slave; later he explained, ''Sam, you've got just the same rights as a white man now, but not a bit better, and if you come into my room again without taking off your hat, I'll shoot you.''

The case of Negro suffrage showed that even token equality was too much for whites to stomach. In 1865 President Johnson—already fearing for his generous Reconstruction program—urged William L. Sharkey, a former Mississippi Chief Justice whom the President had appointed as provisional governor, to make some gesture toward Negro enfranchisement. It might allay congressional doubts, for instance, if Mississippi gave the vote to those who could read the Constitution and write their names and who owned at least $250 in property—perhaps five per cent of the Negro population. Governor Sharkey couldn't have been less interested.

But the greatest anathema was Negro education. It was not so much a question of integrated schools; it was a question of any schools at all. At Oxford an angry band drove off the missionary assigned to the local freedmen's school, even though he was a southern man. At Okolona someone fired four shots at Dr. Lacy, the old Episcopal minister who was trying to teach the town's young Negroes.

''If any man from the North comes down here expecting to hold and maintain radical or abolitionist sentiments,'' warned the *Nation's* correspondent, ''let him expect to be shot down from *behind* the first time he leaves his home.'' Visitors were shocked by the sheer violence of the state's reaction. Lulled by a carefully cultivated tradition of moonlight and magnolias, they forgot that life in Mississippi had always been closer to the frontier than the Tidewater, indeed had been a true frontier as late as the 1830's.

Harder to explain was the stream of contradictory assurances that soon became so familiar. Negroes? ''The southern people are really their best friends,'' a planter told author John T. Trowbridge in 1865. ''We're the only ones that understand them,'' someone explained to Whitelaw Reid, another visitor. Just give the southerners time, begged the sympathetic editor of *DeBow's Review:* "If let alone to manage affairs in their own way, and with their intimate knowledge of Negro character, everything possible will be done in good time for the social, physical, and political advancement of the race."

There was also an odd element of fantasy in it all—almost as if the war hadn't been lost . . . in fact, as if Mississippi were dealing with Washington as an equal. When Whitelaw Reid doubted that Congress would seat the ex-Confederates who swept Mississippi's first postwar election of 1865, his listeners scoffed at the very thought. Of course they would be seated—"because of the tremendous pressure we can bring to bear." The Natchez *Courier* agreed: "The State of Mississippi still stands in all its grand individuality. Massachusetts has no more right to dictate to us now about our internal laws than she had five years ago—nor has she half the power. . . ."

Occasionally a voice of doubt was raised, but the moderates seemed, in the *Nation*'s words, "somewhat bewildered . . . bullied . . . humbugged." Usually they could be quickly silenced. When one Mississippi planter suggested in August, 1865, that the Negroes might be trained to use their rights, his companion shot back the clincher that was also getting familiar: "They'll be wanting to marry your daughters next."

And this was the heart of the matter. To the ordinary white Mississippian, political equality automatically led to social equality, which in turn automatically led to race-mixing. It was inevitable—and unthinkable. To a people brought up to believe that Negroes were genetically inferior—after all, that was why they were slaves—the mere hint of "mongrelization" was appalling. And all the more so in view of the homage paid the white southern woman. It was she who had sacrificed so much, whose purity, in fact, carried on the whole system. She was everything.

Of course there were other factors too. Cotton planters didn't want their field hands getting out of line; the red-neck farmers worried about Negroes taking their bread. Yet these were areas where something might be worked out; but there could be no compromise—not an inch—on anything that might open the door to race-mixing. Emancipation made absolutely no difference. "A monkey with his tail off," explained the Natchez *Courier*, "is a monkey still."

It didn't matter that the position was illogical. Northerners might snigger that if the Negro was so backward, why might he advance so far? Other visitors might wonder about the high percentage of Negroes with white blood—surely race-mixing must have once been all right with somebody. None of this made any difference. So in November, 1865, it was easy for the Jackson *Daily News* to lecture the state's first postwar government: "We must keep the ex-slave in a position of inferiority. We must pass such laws as will make him *feel* his inferiority."

Mississippi's new government understood. Under President Johnson's generous terms the state had freed the slaves but done little else.

A new constitution had been drafted—but it seemed pretty much along prewar lines. A new state legislature had been chosen—but it featured many old leaders. A new governor had been elected—but he was Benjamin G. Humphreys, an outstanding Confederate general who hadn't even been pardoned yet. On November 20, 1865, Governor Humphreys set the tone of things in a message to the legislature: "Under the pressure of federal bayonets, urged on by the misdirected sympathies of the world, the people of Mississippi have abolished the institution of slavery. The Negro is free, whether we like it or not; we must realize that fact now and forever. To be free, however, does not make him a citizen, or entitle him to social or political equality with the white man."

A series of laws, later known as the Black Code, swiftly put the Negro in his place. He was allowed to marry, own property, sue and be sued, even testify if he was a party—but that was all. No Negro could vote, keep firearms, rent a home outside town, ride in a first-class railroad car with whites, or "make insulting gestures." Any unemployed Negro over eighteen was declared a vagrant, fined $50, and turned over to whoever paid up. Any unsupported Negro under eighteen could be apprenticed out. If he tried to run away, "the master or mistress" (the law easily slipped back into ante-bellum language) had the right to pursue and recapture.

Reaction was not long in coming. "We tell the white men of Mississippi," exploded the Chicago *Tribune* on December 1, "that the men of the North will convert the state of Mississippi into a frog pond before they will allow any such laws to disgrace one foot of soil in which the bones of our soldiers sleep and over which the flag of freedom waves."

Northern fury grew as other southern states followed Mississippi's lead with Black Codes of their own. Finally, in 1867 Congress threw out President Johnson's Reconstruction program and launched a far harsher one of its own. The Confederate-dominated state governments were scrapped, and the South was divided into five military districts, each under martial law. Negroes were given the vote, new constitutional conventions held. No state could get back into the Union until Congress approved its new government . . . until it granted Negro suffrage . . . until it ratified the Fourteenth Amendment, guaranteeing the people of every state (among other things) "equal protection of the laws."

Mississippi eventually knuckled under, but only after three more years of rear-guard defiance. By 1870, however, the state was "reconstructed," and by 1873 the local Radical Republicans were riding high. The electorate was fifty-seven per cent Negro—mostly illiterate and easily controlled. The legislature boasted sixty-four Negroes and twenty-four carpetbaggers. The Speaker of the House, the lieutenant governor, the superintendent of education were all Negroes. The new Reconstruction governor himself was an ex-Union officer—General Adelbert Ames, a remote, tactless New Englander who stayed away from Mississippi for protracted periods.

It would later be argued that this state government turned in an impressive performance, and indeed there were many bright spots. The Negro legislators included at least fifteen well-educated, conscientious clergymen. The carpetbaggers were often solid middle westerners who had come not to loot but to farm. The Negro troops had all been withdrawn, and only a token force of federals remained— for instance, 59 at Natchez, 129 at Vicksburg, about 700 men altogether. The state debt never got out of hand. There was little stealing —the only major case involved the carpetbag treasurer of the state hospital in Natchez who took $7,251.81. And all the while important things were being accomplished—war-damaged bridges repaired, northern innovations like free hospitals established, courts expanded to take care of freedmen, and a public-school system launched.

All this was done, but it would take the perspective of a century to appreciate it. At the time the white people of Mississippi felt only bitterness. They didn't care if most of the troops were gone; one blue uniform was too many. They didn't know about worthy projects; they only knew taxes on land had soared 1,300 per cent in five years. They didn't notice that most key officials were honest; in their frayed poverty, they only saw any sign of waste: why, the state contingency fund even paid for Governor Ames' bedpan. And perhaps most important, they knew little about the conscientious work of many Negroes in top-level positions; they only knew their own county, where they were in daily contact, and that was often appalling.

Negro sheriffs, clerks, and magistrates thrashed about in confusion and ignorance. In Warren County the sheriff couldn't write a simple return. In Issaquena County not one member of the board of supervisors—responsible for handling the county's business—could read a contract. There wasn't a justice of the peace in Madison County who could write a summons.

Petty corruption spread everywhere, often induced by light-fingered whites. Hinds County ran up a bigger printing bill in nine months than the whole state paid in 1866–67. The Wilkinson County board of supervisors shelled out $1,500 for three bridges—containing four, eight, and twenty planks respectively. Vicksburg's Republican candidate for mayor staggered under twenty-three indictments. Nor were the dethroned Democrats entirely innocent. An officer in Vicksburg's clean-government group was caught charging the city $500 to move a safe from the river to the courthouse.

Little matter—it was all the same to most of white Mississippi. Reconstruction was to blame, and that meant the Negroes. Free voting and the shadow of federal bayonets might make them invulnerable to ordinary political tactics, but there were other ways. . . .

The shifting seasons merged into one long blur of desperate violence. There was the sunny October morning when Thomas Dabney's daughters heard a hail of shots and watched a Negro's riderless horse race across the Burleigh lawn . . . the starlit winter night in Monroe County when carpetbagger A. P. Huggins knelt on a lonely road as the K.K.K. delivered seventy-five lashes with a stirrup strap . . . the

Entitled Reconstruction, *or "A White Man's Government," this 1868 Currier and Ives cartoon summed up Northern liberals' simplistic view of the Southern dilemma.*

bright March day when the Meridian courthouse erupted in rifle fire and the Radical judge fell dead on his bench. . . .

"Life is not sacred as it is in the North," wrote correspondent Charles Nordhoff:

> Everybody goes armed, and every trifling dispute is ended with the pistol. The respectable people of the State do not discourage the practice of carrying arms as they should, they are astonishingly tolerant of acts which would arouse a Northern community to the utmost, and I believe that to this may be ascribed all that is bad in Mississippi—to an almost total lack of a right opinion; a willingness to see men take the law into their own hands; and, what is still worse, to let them openly defy the laws, without losing, apparently, the respect of the community.

In this atmosphere there was no hope for a man with the "wrong" attitude, whatever his credentials. At Aberdeen the town teacher, Dr. Ebart, had an impeccable southern background, but he favored Negro schools, and that was the end of his job. The pressure was too much. The white Republicans soon melted away. Many crossed over to the Democratic fold; others fled north; only a few stood by the helpless mass of Negroes. The moderates, who might have been a third force, seemed mesmerized by the fury of the blast. "The quiet, sensible and orderly people," mused Charles Nordhoff, "seem to have almost entirely resigned the power and supremacy which belong to them."

This was the picture by 1875, when, with state and local elections scheduled, the Democrats decided that the time had come formally to recapture control. A skillfully conceived strategy—to be known as the Mississippi Plan and later to be copied throughout the South—took care of the two chief obstacles: the Negro majority and federal bayonets.

"We are determined to have an honest election if we have to stuff the ballot box to get it," shouted one Democratic leader, and this was only a small part of the plan. Newspaper notices warned Negroes that they would be thrown off their land if they voted the Republican ticket. Democratic "rifle clubs," usually sporting conspicuous red shirts, drilled endlessly near Negro sections. In Hinds, Lowndes, and other counties, cannon appeared and "salutes" were fired near Republican rallies.

The Negro voters got the message, but the Democrats still faced the danger of federal intervention. The trick here was not to let things go too far, and the Democratic campaign chairman, General J. Z. George, proved a past master at the art of intimidation by indirection. Still, it was a delicate tightrope. The embattled Governor Ames was calling Washington for help, and the slightest slip might bring in the federals. . . .

A crash of rifle fire scattered the 1,200 Negroes swarming around the Republican barbecue at the little town of Clinton on September 4, 1875. Here and there men fell—not all of them black. Two young white hecklers were cut down by return fire as they scurried from the scene. It seemed that Negroes too could feel strongly about elections. Wholesale shooting began, and for days undeclared war raged around Clinton. On September 8 Governor Ames appealed to General Grant for troops to restore peace and supervise the coming elections. The whole future of Mississippi hung in the balance. A nod from the President, and all of General George's strategy would fall apart.

Grant looked the other way. "The whole public are tired out with these annual autumnal outbreaks in the South," the President sighed, "and the great majority are ready now to condemn any interference on the part of the government." Word was passed to Governor Ames through Attorney General Pierrepont to try harder, to exhaust his own resources before calling on Washington for aid.

It was really not Grant's fault. The country was indeed tired of Reconstruction, and the President was but echoing the national mood. Most people had never been for Negro civil rights in the first place. Freedom, yes; but that didn't necessarily mean all the privileges of citizenship. At the end of the war only six northern states let Negroes vote, and in 1867 the District of Columbia rejected Negro suffrage 7,337 to 36. Nor did anyone feel the Fourteenth Amendment had much to do with education. In fact, stalwart Union states like New York, Pennsylvania, and Ohio all had segregated schools. Congress itself set up a segregated school system in Washington only weeks after approving the Fourteenth Amendment.

These feelings were rising to the surface, now that the initial exhilaration of winning the war was over. Other forces were at work too: the implacable Thaddeus Stevens had died . . . anti-Grant liberals were happy to attack everything about the Administration, including Reconstruction . . . northern investors were anxious to resume "normal" relations with the South . . . the nation's eyes were turning to fresh, exciting visions in the Far West.

The new mood showed itself in various ways. Congress had indeed passed the Civil Rights Act of 1875 (protecting the Negro in public places like trains and restaurants), but it was the dying gasp of a lame-duck session. Besides, it was a shaky victory. A school integration provision had been defeated; also a "force bill" giving the measure teeth. Even more significant, the Supreme Court was now nibbling away at the earlier Reconstruction Acts. And in the background came a steady chorus from the press, "Let the South solve its own problems." The President understood and gave the nation its way.

The Silver Cornet Band led the Jackson victory parade to General George's house on election night, November 2, 1875. The returns were rolling in, and huge Democratic majorities were piling up: Morton, 233 to 17 . . . Deasonville, 181 to 0 . . . Yazoo County, 4,052 to 7. In the end the Democrats carried sixty-two of the state's seventy-four counties. In the time-honored fashion of all political leaders everywhere, General George gave full credit to the rank and file "for the redemption of our common mother, Mississippi." Governor Ames was a practical man. Exactly 146 days later, in exchange for the withdrawal by Democrats of a set of impeachment charges, he resigned his office, packed his bags, and left the state forever. In the word of the times, Mississippi had been "redeemed."

To Mississippi's Negroes redemption meant a loss of power but not the trappings. The men now running the state came from the old cotton-planting gentry, who got along well with their former slaves. Some of these leaders, like Lucius Quintus Cincinnatus Lamar, were far more interested in corporation law than in eight-cent cotton, but they still had a tradition of *noblesse oblige* and gave the Negroes considerable leeway—as long as they were "good."

This arrangement was further cemented by a sort of gentlemen's agreement with Washington after the presidential election of 1876. The South accepted Hayes' dubious claims to the Presidency, and in return the Republicans adopted Grant's hands-off attitude as the new administration line. The last troops were withdrawn, and the old Confederacy was left free to work out its own problems. But at the same time it was always understood that the Negroes would retain at least their surface gains. The redemption leaders happily agreed. In fact, the Jackson *Clarion* had accepted the obligation on the very morning after the great 1875 victory. Observing that Negroes had helped make the triumph possible, the paper declared that the state must now "carry out in good faith the pledges of equal and even justice to them and theirs in which they placed their confidence."

So the Negroes continued to vote and often held minor offices. Nor were they barred from most public places. The two races drank at the same bars and ate at the same restaurants, though at separate tables. In Jackson, Angelo's Hall echoed with Negro laughter one week, white the next. And when life was done, both races could rest together in Greenwood Cemetery.

With the Negro's role settled, Mississippi's redemption government launched a massive economy wave. The conservative landowning leaders had been hit hardest by the staggering taxes of Reconstruction, and now they were determined to end all that. State expenditures were slashed from $1,430,000 in 1875 to $518,000 in 1876. Teachers' salaries alone fell from $55.47 a month in 1875 to $29.19 the following year.

In a way it was all justifiable. Mississippi remained wretchedly poor. In 1877 the state's per capita wealth was only $286, compared to a $1,086 average in the northern states. Even as late as 1890 there were only forty-six banks in the state, with combined cash assets of but $635,000. The war had wiped out Mississippi, and there just seemed no way to get going again. In those days the idea of federal recovery aid was unknown—between 1865 and 1875 Washington spent 21 million dollars on public works in Massachusetts and New York, only $185,000 in Mississippi and Arkansas.

Still, whatever the justification, Mississippi paid a high price for her sweeping economies. Letting roads disintegrate meant even more stagnant communities. Appropriating merely $5,392 a year for health meant the end of nearly all services. Spending only $2 a head on schoolchildren (against $20 in Massachusetts) meant mounting illiteracy and a new generation utterly untrained to advance in life.

Nor was cost-cutting a viable solution to the state's problems. Despite all the economies, conditions continued to slide. From the mid-seventies to the early nineties cotton sagged from 11 cents to 5.8 cents a pound. Field hands' pay fell from $15 to $12 a month . . . when there was any cash at all. More often there was the share-cropping system, which saw little money ever change hands. Yet the plantation owners themselves were certainly not getting rich. Under a vicious system of liens, they mortgaged their future crops for months or even years ahead to get the tools and supplies needed for tomorrow.

Everything seemed to conspire against Mississippi. While crop prices fell, the farmer's costs soared. Freight rates rigged in the East increased his shipping charges. Combinations like the jute-bagging trust raised the cost of his supplies. High tariffs added more to his burden. Creditors insisted that he plant only cotton; shackled to a one-crop system, his land quickly eroded. Even nature joined the conspiracy—a flood, freeze, or drought usually came along to spoil the few otherwise good years. Whether holding out in some paint-peeled mansion or hanging on in the squalor of a dog-trot cabin, most Mississippians knew only the bitterest poverty.

The state's landed leaders proved utterly unable to cope with the situation. They came from the lowlands—the cotton belt that had run everything in prewar days. They owed their authority to an odd combination of ante-bellum nostalgia and redemption heroics—certainly not new ideas. They easily took to the laissez-faire views of eastern business—tax concessions, hard money, railroad grabs like the Texas-Pacific. They shied away from new panaceas like government regulation and flexible currency. Their most lustrous figure, L. Q. C. Lamar, shuddered at the Greenback movement's "boundless, bottomless, and brainless schemes."

Such men neither understood nor even liked the up-country farmers who scratched away at the red clay hills to the east. Desperately these red-necks—along with a growing number of poor white tenants all over the state—turned to new and more radical sources of hope: the Farmers' Alliance and later the Populists.

And all the while they smouldered with growing hate—hatred for the Yankee banks and railroads that squeezed them so tightly . . . hatred for the Black Belt leaders who seemed to care so little . . . and, above all, hatred for the Negroes to whose level they were sinking so fast.

Jim Crow laws began to sprout . . . the first in twenty years. In 1888 Mississippi became the first state to have segregated waiting rooms. In 1890 Jackson extended the racial barrier beyond death by establishing a separate cemetery for Negroes. The rules grew ever more strict as the margin narrowed between white and colored living standards. If race was all the whites might have left, that was all the more reason to guard this sacred heritage. Woe to the Negro who flirted with crossing the line.

Lynchings multiplied at a fearful rate—nobody knows how many, for the press handled the incidents as casually as the weather. "Four Negroes were lynched at Grenada last week," remarked the Raymond *Gazette* on July 18, 1885, "also one at Oxford." That was the whole item.

With Mississippi in this mood, it certainly didn't help matters when the big landowners met the red-neck challenge with thousands of Negro votes from the black counties they controlled. A weird political duel, utterly lacking in logic or principle, developed as the eighties wore on. The old conservative leaders represented traditional white supremacy, yet relied on Negro votes to hold their power. The mass of poor whites had much in common with the Negro, yet fought him as a mortal enemy. The remaining Republicans in the state stood for the Negro's freedom, yet deserted him as a hopeless handicap. No wonder the Negro himself soon lost interest. Untrained in politics anyhow, he found Mississippi's brand far too confusing. Usually he just sold his vote to the highest bidder or was thrust aside while someone else cast it for him.

The situation proved too sordid to last. In 1890 a special convention assembled in Jackson to draw up a new state constitution. The solution, most people felt, was to take away the Negro's vote. Even the Black Belt leaders now agreed—the advantage Negro suffrage gave them was outweighed by the cost (usually a dollar a vote) and the ever-haunting possibility that the Negroes might some day decide to go back into politics for themselves. It was, of course, a little odd to keep Negroes from casting votes in order to stop white people from stealing them, but nobody worried too much about that. A far greater problem was how to do it. The Fifteenth Amendment specifically stated that the right to vote should not be abridged on account of color.

Clearly, the trick was to frame a set of qualifications that would technically apply to everybody but actually eliminate the Negro without touching the white. A poll tax alone was not enough—it might discourage more whites than Negroes. Nor would a literacy test do— there were thousands of good white voters who couldn't even write their names. In the end the convention came up with a series of devices which were, in the words of one delegate, "a monument to the resourcefulness of the human mind."

Most important were the new qualifications: all voters had to be able to read any section of the state constitution, or understand it when read to him, or give it a reasonable interpretation. This, of course, dumped the final decision into the lap of the examining registrar . . . who would know exactly what to do.

Reregistration began immediately. In 1885 over 1,600 Negroes had qualified in Panola County; by 1896 the figure stood at 114. The same thing happened everywhere: in Coahoma County only four per cent of its once-eligible Negroes now could vote; in De Soto, only five per cent; in Tunica, two per cent. Loyal Mississippians held their breath— how would the nation react to this giant wink at the Fifteenth Amendment?

They need not have worried. The White House was in friendly hands—first under the conservative Grover Cleveland, later under the benign William McKinley. Congress was no threat either—in 1894 it repealed most of the remaining civil rights laws. The western Populists were bitter at the Negroes for sticking by their old masters. The southern progressives felt that white solidarity would weld all classes more closely together. Eastern liberals recalled the reactionary leaders who had engineered Reconstruction—and found it easy to sympathize with Mississippi. And above all, there was the American mood—a moment of bursting national pride and pious imperialism. As the liberal *Atlantic Monthly* noted with gentle irony: "If the stronger and cleverer race is free to impose its will upon the 'new-caught sullen peoples' on the other side of the globe, why not in South Carolina and Mississippi?"

The Supreme Court added its blessing in 1898. In *Williams v. Mississippi* the justices solemnly declared there was no reason to suppose that the state's new voting qualifications were aimed especially at Negroes. . . .

As the new century dawned, it was clear that the Negro—stripped of his gains, abandoned by the courts, and rejected by the country— was in a highly vulnerable position. And for the Negro in Mississippi —the state which had invented the Black Code in 1865, pioneered the "Mississippi Plan" in 1875, and led the way to disenfranchisement in 1890—the future looked bleak indeed. . . .

Thomas C. Leonard

RELUCTANT CONQUERORS: AMERICAN ARMY OFFICERS AND THE PLAINS INDIANS

The post-Civil War decades saw the tragic completion of the
destruction of the cultures of the American Indian that began
when Columbus first set foot in the New World. Previously, at least
some of the tribes that inhabited what was to become the United
States had been able to maintain their cultural integrity more or
less intact by falling back before the white juggernaut into the
western wilderness. After 1865 further retreat became impossible
and in a few years the free Indians were crushed and the
survivors compelled to settle on reservations where their
conquerors expected them to become "civilized Americans."

The role of the Army in the destruction of the Indians has
frequently been described. What is unique about Thomas C.
Leonard's treatment of the subject is its focus on the thoughts and
feelings of the soldiers rather than on their deeds—on their
appreciation of the Indians, not on their efforts to exterminate
them. That professional soldiers should respect a foe so clever, so
steadfast, so courageous, so dignified in defeat is not difficult to
understand. Yet Leonard does not over-simplify or romanticize the
reactions of the American military to the Indians and their way
of life. His essay presents a complex and fascinating picture of a
part of American history usually depicted in grossly over-simplified
terms. Professor Leonard, who teaches at the University of
California at Berkeley, is the author of *Above the Battle: War-
Making in America from Appomatox to Versailles.*

The white man's peace at Appomattox in 1865 meant war for the Plains Indians. In the next quarter century six and a half million settlers moved west of the Missouri River, upsetting a precarious balance that had existed between two million earlier pioneers and their hundred thousand "hostile" red neighbors. The industrial energy that had flowed into the Civil War now pushed rail lines across traditional hunting grounds. Some twenty-five thousand soldiers were sent west to meet insistent demands for protection coming from stockmen and miners spread out between the Staked Plains of Texas and the Montana lands watered by the Powder, Bighorn, and Yellowstone rivers.

It is ironic that the men who carried the wounds of the struggle to maintain the union of their own society now were ordered to dismember the culture of the native Americans. These Indian fighters today have been knocked out of that false gallery of heroes created by western novels and movies. On the centennial of the Battle of the Little Bighorn a granite mountain outside of Custer, South Dakota, is being carved into the shape of the Sioux warrier leader Crazy Horse. Times have changed, and a second look at the Army's Indian fighters is in order. They have a complex story to tell, one filled with an ambivalence about their enemy as well as about the civilians who sent them to fight.

The officer corps did not relish their double assignment of pushing Indians back from lands claimed by whites and, for good measure, "redeeming" native Americans from "barbarism"—for Christian civilization. In the letter books and official reports that these men kept so meticulously on the frontier there is a continual lament: civilian officials and opinion makers only cut budgets and issued contradictory directions. The rules of war demanded restraint and a fine regard for the enemy's rights, but it seemed as if the same civilians who interpreted these rules wanted quick work on the battlefield. The United States government itself broke the treaties that promised the Indians land, yet expected the Army to keep the peace through mutual trust.

At the same time that western settlers were clamoring for protection, their land grabs were provoking Indian retaliation. Not incidentally, army officers endured the torture of the annual congressional debate over how much their pay should be cut and seethed as western bankers charged 12 to 40 per cent to convert their government paper into the coin they needed on the frontier. "Friends" of the Indian—with their talk of a "conquest by kindness"—were a special annoyance. Eastern philanthropists like Edward A. Lawrence damned the officers when blood was shed and were among those who chillingly approved the "swift retribution" meted out to General Custer by the Sioux. Frontier forts rarely had the long, timbered stockades beloved by Hollywood set designers—but perhaps many officers longed for a massive wall, high enough to repel civilians as well as Indians.

By 1870 General William T. Sherman doubted he could fight with honor on the plains; from the west and the east, he wrote, "we are placed between two fires." But Sherman may have been envied by another proud Civil War hero, General Philip H. Sheridan, who mused

William Tecumseh Sherman, commander of the Army from 1869–1883.

upon a shattered reputation as he watched whole frontier towns—wanting the extermination of Indians—turn out to hang him in effigy.

To officers so provoked, action seemed the thing to sweep away the complications of the Indian problem; to strike at the red man again and again appeared not only the quickest way to dry up civilian complaints but the just way to punish an incomprehensibly wild enemy. Sheridan pleaded with Sherman for authority to act upon the appalling reports that crossed his desk each week:

> Since 1862 at least 800 men, women, and children have been murdered within the limits of my present command, in the most fiendish manner; the men usually scalped and mutilated, their [he omits the word] cut off and placed in their mouth; women ravished sometimes fifty and sixty times in succession, then killed and scalped, sticks stuck in their persons, before and after death.

Sheridan said it was now a question of who was to remain alive in his district, red or white. As for himself: "I have made my choice." It was, in fact, Sheridan who first enunciated the judgment that would

Starting in 1867, Philip Henry Sheridan was responsible for Indian campaigns in the West. In 1883, he succeeded Sherman as Army commander in chief.

become the epitaph of so many native Americans: ''The only good Indians I ever saw were dead.''

Sheridan's choice, made in passion, proved extraordinarily complicated to carry out, for the fact is that the Indian fighters were troubled by various kinds of respect for their enemy. In the first place, no commander in the West could conceal his admiration for the red man's fighting skill. ''Experience of late years,'' one reported to his colleagues, ''has most conclusively shown that our cavalry cannot cope with the Indian man for man.'' Though these seasoned veterans and heroes reported a very favorable official casualty ratio, in more candid moments they pronounced that Indian fighting was the most difficult combat American soldiers had ever faced.

It followed that so high an estimate of the enemy's ability undermined the Army's pride in its own competence. Sheridan berated the inefficiency that made campaigns in the West ''a series of forlorn hopes,'' and Sherman wrote in so many words to the Secretary of War what had silently haunted his fellow officers: ''. . . it seems to be impossible to force Indians to fight at a disadvantage in their own country. Their sagacity and skill surpasses that of the white race.'' It further followed that victory against such valiant opponents was bittersweet. Both Sheridan and Sherman confessed to pity and compassion for the native Americans they had set out to destroy. As Sheridan wrote:

> We took away their country and their means of support, broke up their mode of living, their habits of life, introduced disease and decay among them and it was for this and against this they made war. Could anyone expect less?

Few officers escaped a sort of wistful appreciation of their primitive enemy in what they took to be his insatiable appetite for war—and not a few admired precisely this unrestrained aggressiveness. Indeed, peaceful assimilation seemed not good enough for the Indians. One of Sheridan's favorite generals sought a large audience to explain the temptations of the Indian culture:

> To me, Indian life, with its attendant ceremonies, mysteries, and forms, is a book of unceasing interest. Grant that some of its pages are frightful, and, if possible, to be avoided, yet the attraction is none the weaker. Study him, fight him, civilize him if you can, he remains still the object of your curiosity, a type of man peculiar and undefined, subjecting himself to no known law of civilization, contending determinedly against all efforts to win him from his chosen mode of life.
>
> If I were an Indian, I often think I would greatly prefer to cast my lot among those of my people who adhered to the free open plains rather than submit to the confined limits of a reservation, there to be the recipient of the blessed benefits of civilization, with its vices thrown in without stint or measure.

Two years after he published this gratuitous advice, General George A. Custer met the object of his interest for the last time at the Little Bighorn.

General Nelson A. Miles, one of the officers who chased the Sioux after Custer's fall, had a personal reason for revenge: an Indian had taken a pointblank shot at him during an awkward moment in a peace parley. But Miles's reflections show the remarkable extent to which men like him overcame their anger with the enemy. The general spoke of the Indian's ''courage, skill, sagacity, endurance, fortitude, and self-sacrifice of a high order'' and of ''the dignity, hospitality, and gentleness of his demeanor toward strangers and toward his fellow savages.'' Miles was inclined to think that lapses from this standard meant only that Indians had ''degenerated through contact with the white man.'' Writing on this subject, he did not show the personal arrogance and pride that was the despair of his military superiors. Miles viewed Custer's fall in 1876 as a chastising message for the nation's centennial. He quoted Longfellow: ''. . . say that our broken

A drawing of the Battle of Little Bighorn by Amos Bad Heart Bull,
an Oglala Sioux. Crazy Horse and Sitting Bull
are mounted before their warriors.

faith / wrought all this ruin and scathe, / In the Year of a Hundred
Years.''

Miles was not an eccentric in the sympathies he expressed. Colonel
John Gibbon, for example, the man who discovered the mutilated
bodies of the soldiers who had fallen with Custer at the Little Bighorn,
seemed, during his subsequent chase of the Sioux, more angry at the
''human ghouls'' in the Army who had disturbed some Sioux graves
than at the warriors who had killed his colleagues. Such desecrations,
he thundered, ''impress one with the conviction that in war barbarism
stands upon a level only a little lower than our boasted civilization.''
By Gibbon's lights, the record of white hostility and treachery would
force any man to fight: ''Thus would the savage in us come to the
surface under the oppression which we know the Indian suffers.'' Like
so many Indian fighters who addressed the perennial ''Indian question,'' Gibbon raised more questions about his own culture than he
answered about his enemy's.

To these soldiers the courage and bearing of the red man suggested
a purer way of life before the coming of the white man, and the military
frequently searched for Greek and Roman analogies to suggest the
virtues of its enemies. Heathens though they were, they had nobility.

Even the Indians' faults might be excused by their manifestly lower stage of cultural evolution.

General George Crook was in a good position to speak of the red men's virtues, for as a fighting man he resembled them. In the field he dispensed with the army uniform and seemed only at ease when he was free of all cumbersome marks of civilization. Crook left one post, he tells us, "with one change of underclothes, toothbrush, etc., and went to investigate matters, intending to be gone a week. But I got interested after the Indians and did not return there again for over two years."

In the harsh campaigns in the Southwest, Crook taught his men to move over the land like Apaches, and when white men failed him, he was adept in recruiting Indians for army service. Frederic Remington observed Crook's methods and saw they made officers less "Indian fighters" than "Indian thinkers." "He's more of an Indian than I am," marveled one Apache. Crook repaid such compliments; back at West Point to deliver a graduation address, he may have shocked many with this observation:

> With all his faults, and he has many, the American Indian is not half so black as he has been painted. He is cruel in war, treacherous at times, and not over cleanly. But so were our forefathers. His nature, however, is responsive to treatment which assures him that it is based upon justice, truth, honesty, and common sense. . . .

Crook hesitated to condemn even the most ferocious Apaches, because he respected their spirit and believed that "we are too culpable as a nation, for the existing condition of affairs."

In the view of many officers the weaknesses of their own culture were more glaring than the faults of their enemy. "Barbarism torments the body; civilization torments the soul," one colonel concluded. "The savage remorselessly takes your scalp, your civilized friend as remorselessly swindles you out of your property." Indeed, many of the officers who led the fight for civilization seemed to accept Indian culture on its own terms. Colonel Henry B. Carrington—one of the field officers who supplied Sheridan with maddening accounts of Indian outrages—was an interesting case study. Carrington's official report of the eighty fallen soldiers under his command in the Fetterman fight in Wyoming in 1866 provided grisly reading:

> Eyes torn out and laid on the rocks; teeth chopped out; joints of fingers cut off; brains taken out and placed on rocks, with members of the body; entrails taken out and exposed; hands and feet cut off; arms taken out from sockets; eyes, ears, mouth, and arms penetrated with spearheads, sticks, and arrows; punctures upon every sensitive part of the body, even to the soles of the feet and the palms of the hand.

Yet Carrington's own response to this carnage was not vengeful but reflective, even scholarly. A year later Margaret Carrington, the colonel's wife, published *Ab-sa-ra-ka*, a study of the region the Army had fought to control. In her book she treated this Indian act of warfare with impressive open-mindedness, never directly condemning it. She did note that "the noblest traits of the soldiers were touchingly developed as they carefully handled the mutilated fragments" from the battlefield—but she also praised the Indian: "In ambush and decoy, *splendid.*" Close observers, she wrote, overcame anger to become reconciled, even sympathetic, to "the bold warrior in his great struggle."

As he took charge of enlarged sections of *Ab-sa-ra-ka* in the 1870's Colonel Carrington expanded on this theme of noble resistance. To him the barbarities of the *whites*, in their "irresponsible speculative emigration," overshadowed the red "massacre" of Fetterman's men. Carrington confessed, like Custer, "if I had been a red man as I was a white man, I should have fought as bitterly, if not as brutally, as the Indian fought." And standing before the American Association for the Advancement of Science in 1880 to read his official report of the Fetterman mutilations again, Carrington explained to the scientists that the Indian's disposition of enemies was intended to disable his foe in the afterlife, and so was quite understandable. Nor did he disparage the red man's values, but rather closed his address by suggesting some inadequacies on the other—his own—side: "From 1865 until the present time, there has not been a border campaign which did not have its impulse in the aggressions of a white man."

Few men in the West raised more unusual questions about both cultures than Captain John Bourke. He entered the campaigns, he wrote later, "with the sincere conviction that the only good Indian was a dead Indian, and that the only use to make of him was that of a fertilizer." But the notebooks of this odd, inquiring soul reveal a man haunted by the details of the enemy's life. Mastering several Indian languages, Bourke produced an impressive series of monographs on native religious ceremonies, and in 1895 he became president of the American Folklore Society. Learning proved corrosive to his early cultural pride, and at the end of his army service he was willing to admit that "the American aborigine is not indebted to his pale-faced brother, no matter what nation or race he may be, for lessons in tenderness and humanity."

Admittedly, Captain Bourke's appreciation of native culture was more complex than the respect paid by other Indian fighters. Acknowledging the red man's fighting prowess and noble character, Bourke was more deeply interested in Indian snake ceremonies and scatological rites—mysteries thoroughly repulsive to most white sensibilities. Indeed, his interest in these ceremonies was as intense and sustained as were his protestations of "horror" during each "filthy" and "disgusting" rite. He put all this scholarship and his rather prurient curiosity to work in *Scatologic Rites of All Nations*, where he observed such "orgies" throughout the development of Western civilization, even surviving in nations of what he called "high enlightenment." Here was no sentimental accommodation with Indian culture but a panoramic reminder to the white race of its own barbaric past. Thus the Indians' vices, no less than their virtues, set up a mirror before the advancing Christian whites.

It did not, of course, deter the whites. However noble their image of the savage may have been, it is important to recognize in all of these Indian fighters a fundamental conviction that the price of civilization was not too high. Aware as they were of the ambiguities of their mission, their sympathies and remorse never swayed them from their duty, and no officer of tender conscience was provoked to resign his commission.

How were such mixed emotions sustained? In point of fact, the military's apologia for the red man answered certain professional and psychological needs of the workaday Army. The Army, for both noble and ignoble reasons, wanted to assume control of the administration of Indian affairs that had been held by civilians—a few good words for the long-suffering red man smoothed the way to this goal. Further, by praising the Plains Indians as relentless and efficient warriors the military justified its own ruthless strategy—and setbacks. Nor was frontier ethnology exactly disinterested; close study of the Indians often yielded military advantage for white men. And while empathy for the enemy clearly made the assignment to ''redeem'' the Indian more painful, there were some emotional satisfactions to be derived from even the most generous attitudes toward the Indians' way of life.

In some instances an officer's respect for the primitive's unfettered aggressiveness happily loosened his own. Thus General George Schofield, commander of the Department of the Missouri, could confess that ''civilized man . . . never feels so happy as when he throws off a large part of his civilization and reverts to the life of a semi-savage.'' When Schofield acted on his own advice on a long hunting trip, he returned invigorated, recording that ''I wanted no other occupation in life than to ward off the savage and kill off his food until there should no longer be an Indian frontier in our beautiful country.'' One of Sherman's aides reached a similar ominous conclusion after saluting the red man's way of life. This officer was deeply impressed by his colleagues' glowing reports of the nobility of Indian religion, and, he mused,

> There is no doubt the Indians have, at times, been shamefully treated. . . . And there is no doubt a man of spirit would rebel. . . . However, it is useless to moralize about the Indians. Their fate is fixed, and we are so near their end, it is easy to see what that fate is to be. That the Indian might be collected, and put out of misery by being shot deliberately, (as it would be done to a disabled animal), would seem shocking, but something could be said in favor of such procedure.

This puzzling mixture of aggression and regret is less surprising if we take into account the ways, according to contemporary psychologists, that anger and frustration can give rise to these contrasting

Sioux chiefs at Pine Ridge, South Dakota, in 1891.
This followed the Battle of Wounded Knee.

emotions. The officer corps was enraged by much of what it saw happening to America. The Indians' tactics seemed horrible yet ingenious. Their culture was repellent, but also alluring for its integrity. At the same time, evident in the reports and memoirs of these officers is a disturbing sense of having been abandoned by their own unworthy civilization. Army training and experience prevented these men from acting out their anger, and some anger was instead internalized and expressed in the mourning and guilt they exhibited so frequently. Their appreciation of the native Americans for what they had been was combined with a determination to punish a society for what it refused to become. Their fight for civilized settlement as it should be was troubled by their anger that some virtues, retained by the Indians, were slipping away from the white man.

If we appreciate the military's doubts—of its mandate, of its justice, of its ability, as well as of its commitments to civilization, duty, and progress—the tragedy of the West does not go away. It deepens. Was there an escape from the emotional trap in which the Army found itself? To refuse to win the West would have required a conversion to primitivism hard to imagine inside the ranks of army life and scarcely imaginable in ordinary men living ordinary lives outside of the Army. But the career of one lieutenant in the Nez Perce war illustrates that such a transformation was possible.

Charles Erskine Scott Wood (1852–1944) served on General O. O. Howard's staff, and it was he who took down the very moving speech of the defeated Chief Joseph. Wood's reflections on the Nez Perce campaign, published in the early 1880's, struck the conventional balance between remorse and pride. Surveying the shameful record of white treaty violations, he warned his army colleagues that retribution might follow. Yet there seemed to be no other possible outcome—"forces" were "silently at work, beyond all human control," against the red man's survival. Wood, a gifted literary man, proceeded to join the somewhat crowded celebration of the culture he had worked to destroy, hymning the vividness and nobility of the Indian, qualities that seemed poignant by their passing. But in all this he declined to attack directly the civilization that had corrupted and supplanted the Indians', and his fashionable sympathy sounded much like General Custer's.

But Wood was, in time, to change greatly. He quit the Army, entered the Columbia Law School, and began to cause trouble. Not satisfied with the state of letters or the law in his time, Wood allied himself with the radical Industrial Workers of the World and searched for a literary form to express his increasingly anarchistic temperament. The fruit of this veteran's singular rehabilitation was a long experimental poem, *The Poet in the Desert*, an affecting personal renunciation of "civilization" and a call for the revolt of the masses against privilege. Wood, with booming voice and flowing white beard, was in the twentieth century rather like Father Time—reminding Americans of sins against the Indians. He knew:

> *I have lain out with the brown men*
> *And know they are favored.*
> *Nature whispered to them her secrets,*
> *But passed me by.*
>
> *I sprawled flat in the bunch-grass, a target*
> *For the just bullets of my brown brothers betrayed.*
> *I was a soldier, and, at command,*
> *Had gone out to kill and be killed.*
>
> *We swept like fire over the smoke-browned tee-pees;*
> *Their conical tops peering above the willows.*
> *We frightened the air with crackle of rifles,*
> *Women's shrieks, children's screams,*
> *Shrill yells of savages;*
> *Curses of Christians.*
> *The rifles chuckled continually.*
> *A poor people who asked nothing but freedom,*
> *Butchered in the dark.*

Wood's polemic is more straightforward than many that are asserted today on behalf of the native Americans. He learned—and his colleagues in the Army demonstrated—that respect and compassion for another culture are very unsure checks on violence. And Wood's life points out one of the costs of war that Americans have generally been spared: in a prolonged campaign the victor can emerge attracted to his enemy's faith. Our frontier officers had put a civil war behind them and were not ready to turn against their society to save the red man. But their thoughtfully expressed ambivalence toward their task of winning the West throws a revealing light on a history that is still too often falsified with glib stereotypes.

Part Two
Impact of Industrialism

Robert L. Heilbroner

ANDREW CARNEGIE: CAPTAIN OF INDUSTRY

The driving force behind late nineteenth-century economic
growth, social change, and the thousand new developments that
heralded the birth of modern America was the rapid expansion of
industry. Industrialization made the United States the richest
nation in the world and placed some of its citizens among the
world's richest men. At one and the same time it fostered the belief
that individuals could rise from rags to riches in a generation and
the fear that great extremes between the wealthy and the poor
would destroy opportunity, even democracy. It lent credence to
the idea that Americans were gross materialists, but it also
produced a philanthropic outpouring of unprecedented
dimensions.

The career of Andrew Carnegie reflects all these tendencies.
Carnegie came to America as a poor immigrant boy and became
the master of the American steel industry. He was a "robber
baron" in the eyes of his critics, an "industrial statesman" in his
own eyes and in those of many of his contemporaries. He
accumulated material goods on an immense scale but dispensed
hundreds of millions of dollars to a variety of worthy causes. He
was even an intellectual of sorts, writing books and articles about
the character of American society, the industrial system, and the
duties and obligations of rich men like himself.

Professor Robert L. Heilbroner, an economist at the New School
for Social Research, the author of this essay on Carnegie, has
written extensively in the field of economic history and thought.
In works such as *The Worldly Philosophers, The Great Ascent,* and
The Limits of American Capitalism he has repeatedly demonstrated
that it is possible to write history that is at once popular and
scholarly even when dealing with highly technical material.

Toward the end of his long life, at the close of World War I, Andrew Carnegie was already something of a national legend. His meteoric rise, the scandals and successes of his industrial generalship—all this was blurred into nostalgic memory. What was left was a small, rather feeble man with a white beard and pale, penetrating eyes, who could occasionally be seen puttering around his mansion on upper Fifth Avenue, a benevolent old gentleman who still rated an annual birthday interview but was even then a venerable relic of a fast-disappearing era. Carnegie himself looked back on his career with a certain savored incredulity. "How much did you say I had given away, Poynton?" he would inquire of his private secretary; "$324,657,399" was the answer. "Good Heaven!" Carnegie would exclaim. "Where did I ever get all that money?"

Where he *had* got all that money was indeed a legendary story, for even in an age known for its acquisitive triumphs, Carnegie's touch had been an extraordinary one. He had begun, in true Horatio Alger fashion, at the bottom; he had ended, in a manner that put the wildest of Alger's novels to shame, at the very pinnacle of success. At the close of his great deal with J. P. Morgan in 1901, when the Carnegie steel empire was sold to form the core of the new United States Steel Company, the banker had extended his hand and delivered the ultimate encomium of the times: "Mr. Carnegie," he said, "I want to congratulate you on being the richest man in the world."

It was certainly as "the richest man in the world" that Carnegie attracted the attention of his contemporaries. Yet this is hardly why we look back on him with interest today. As an enormous moneymaker Carnegie was a flashy, but hardly a profound, hero of the times; and the attitudes of Earnestness and Self-Assurance, so engaging in the young immigrant, become irritating when they are congealed in the millionaire. But what lifts Carnegie's life above the rut of a one-dimensional success story is an aspect of which his contemporaries were relatively unaware.

Going through his papers after his death, Carnegie's executors came across a memorandum that he had written to himself fifty years before, carefully preserved in a little yellow box of keepsakes and mementos. It brings us back to December, 1868, when Carnegie, a young man flushed with the first taste of great success, retired to his suite in the opulent Hotel St. Nicholas in New York, to tot up his profits for the year. It had been a tremendous year and the calculation must have been extremely pleasurable. Yet this is what he wrote as he reflected on the figures:

> Thirty-three and an income of $50,000 per annum! By this time two years I can so arrange all my business as to secure at least $50,000 per annum. Beyond this never earn—make no effort to increase fortune, but spend the surplus each year for benevolent purposes. Cast aside business forever, except for others.
>
> Settle in Oxford and get a thorough education, making the

acquaintance of literary men—this will take three years of active work—pay especial attention to speaking in public. Settle then in London and purchase a controlling interest in some newspaper or live review and give the general management of it attention, taking part in public matters, especially those connected with education and improvement of the poorer classes.

Man must have an idol—the amassing of wealth is one of the worst species of idolatry—no idol more debasing than the worship of money. Whatever I engage in I must push inordinately; therefore should I be careful to choose that life which will be the most elevating in its character. To continue much longer overwhelmed by business cares and with most of my thoughts wholly upon the way to make more money in the shortest time, must degrade me beyond hope of permanent recovery. I will resign business at thirty-five, but during the ensuing two years I wish to spend the afternoons in receiving instruction and in reading systematically.

It is a document which in more ways than one is Carnegie to the very life: brash, incredibly self-confident, chockablock with self-conscious virtue—and more than a little hypocritical. For the program so nobly outlined went largely unrealized. Instead of retiring in two years, Carnegie went on for thirty-three more; even then it was with considerable difficulty that he was persuaded to quit. Far from shunning further money-making, he proceeded to roll up his fortune with an uninhibited drive that led one unfriendly biographer to characterize him as "the greediest little gentleman ever created." Certainly he was one of the most aggressive profit seekers of his time. Typically, when an associate jubilantly cabled: "No. 8 furnace broke all records today," Carnegie coldly replied, "What were the other furnaces doing?"

It is this contrast between his hopes and his performance that makes Carnegie interesting. For when we review his life, what we see is more than the career of another nineteenth-century acquisitor. We see the unequal struggle between a man who loved money—loved making it, having it, spending it—and a man who, at bottom, was ashamed of himself for his acquisitive desires. All during his lifetime, the money-maker seemed to win. But what lifts Carnegie's story out of the ordinary is that the other Carnegie ultimately triumphed. At his death public speculation placed the size of his estate at about five hundred million dollars. In fact it came to $22,881,575. Carnegie *had* become the richest man in the world—but something had also driven him to give away ninety per cent of his wealth.

Actually, his contemporaries knew of Carnegie's inquietude about money. In 1889, before he was world-famous, he had written an article for the *North American Review* entitled "The Gospel of Wealth"—an article that contained the startling phrase: "The man who dies

*Andrew Carnegie,
the Steelmaster.*

thus rich dies disgraced.'' It was hardly surprising, however, if the
world took these sentiments at a liberal discount: homiletic millionaires who preached the virtues of austerity were no novelty; Carnegie
himself, returning in 1879 from a trip to the miseries of India, had
been able to write with perfect sincerity, ''How very little the millionaire has beyond the peasant, and how very often his additions tend
not to happiness but to misery.''

What the world may well have underestimated, however, was a
concern more deeply rooted than these pieties revealed. For, unlike
so many of his self-made peers, who also rose from poverty, Carnegie
was the product of a *radical* environment. The village of Dunfermline,
Scotland, when he was born there in 1835, was renowned as a center
of revolutionary ferment, and Carnegie's family was itself caught
up in the radical movement of the times. His father was a regular
speaker at the Chartist rallies, which were an almost daily occurrence
in Dunfermline in the 1840's, and his uncle was an impassioned
orator for the rights of the working class to vote and strike. All this
made an indelible impression on Carnegie's childhood.

''I remember as if it were yesterday,'' he wrote seventy years later, "being awakened during the night by a tap at the back window by men who had come to inform my parents that my uncle, Bailie Morrison, had been thrown in jail because he dared to hold a meeting which had been forbidden . . . It is not to be wondered at that, nursed amid such surroundings, I developed into a violent young Republican whose motto was 'death to privilege.' "

From another uncle, George Lauder, Carnegie absorbed a second passion that was also to reveal itself in his later career. This was his love of poetry, first that of the poet Burns, with its overtones of romantic egalitarianism, and then later, of Shakespeare. Immense quantities of both were not only committed to memory, but made into an integral—indeed, sometimes an embarrassingly evident—part of his life: on first visiting the Doge's palace in Venice he thrust a companion in the ducal throne and held him pinioned there while he orated the appropriate speeches from *Othello*. Once, seeing Vanderbilt walking on Fifth Avenue, Carnegie smugly remarked, "I would not exchange his millions for my knowledge of Shakespeare."

But it was more than just a love of poetry that remained with Carnegie. Virtually alone among his fellow acquisitors, he was driven by a genuine respect for the power of thought to seek answers for questions that never even occurred to them. Later, when he "discovered" Herbert Spencer, the English sociologist, Carnegie wrote to him, addressing him as "Master," and it was as "Master" that Spencer remained, even after Carnegie's lavishness had left Spencer very much in his debt.

But Carnegie's early life was shaped by currents more material than intellectual. The grinding process of industrial change had begun slowly but ineluctably to undermine the cottage weaving that was the traditional means of employent in Dunfermline. The Industrial Revolution, in the shape of new steam mills, was forcing out the hand weavers, and one by one the looms which constituted the entire capital of the Carnegie family had to be sold. Carnegie never forgot the shock of his father returning home to tell him, in despair, "Andra, I can get nae mair work."

A family council of war was held, and it was decided that there was only one possible course—they must try their luck in America, to which two sisters of Carnegie's mother, Margaret, had already emigrated. With the aid of a few friends the money for the crossing was scraped together, and at thirteen Andrew found himself transported to the only country in which his career would have been possible.

It hardly got off to an auspicious start, however. The family made their way to Allegheny, Pennsylvania, a raw and bustling town where Carnegie's father again sought work as an independent weaver. But it was as hopeless to compete against the great mills in America as in Scotland, and soon father and son were forced to seek work in the local cotton mills. There Andrew worked from six in the morning until six at night, making $1.20 as a bobbin boy.

After a while his father quit—factory work was impossible for the traditional small enterpriser—and Andrew got a "better" job with a new firm, tending an engine deep in a dungeon cellar and dipping newly made cotton spools in a vat of oil. Even the raise to $3 a week—and desperately conjured visions of Wallace and the Bruce—could not overcome the horrors of that lonely and foul-smelling basement. It was perhaps the only time in Carnegie's life when his self-assurance deserted him: to the end of his days the merest whiff of oil could make him deathly sick.

Yet he was certain, as he wrote home at sixteen, that "anyone could get along in this Country," and the rags-to-riches saga shortly began. The telegraph had just come to Pittsburgh, and one evening over a game of checkers, the manager of the local office informed Andrew's uncle that he was looking for a messenger. Andy got the job and, in true Alger fashion, set out to excel in it. Within a few weeks he had carefully memorized the names and the locations, not only of the main streets in Pittsburgh, but of the main firms, so that he was the quickest of all the messenger boys.

He came early and stayed late, watched the telegraphers at work, and at home at night learned the Morse code. As a result he was soon the head of the growing messenger service, and a skilled telegrapher himself. One day he dazzled the office by taking a message "by ear" instead of by the commonly used tape printer, and since he was then only the third operator in the country able to turn the trick, citizens used to drop into the office to watch Andy take down the words "hot from the wire."

One such citizen who was especially impressed with young Carnegie's determination was Thomas A. Scott, in time to become one of the colorful railway magnates of the West, but then the local superintendent of the Pennsylvania Railroad. Soon thereafter Carnegie became "Scott's Andy"—telegrapher, secretary, and general factotum—at thirty-five dollars a month. In his *Autobiography* Carnegie recalls an instance which enabled him to begin the next stage of his career.

> One morning I reached the office and found that a serious accident on the Eastern Division had delayed the express passenger train westward, and that the passenger train eastward was proceeding with a flagman in advance at every curve. The freight trains in both directions were standing on the sidings. Mr. Scott was not to be found. Finally I could not resist the temptation to plunge in, take the responsibility, give "train orders" and set matters going. "Death or Westminster Abbey" flashed across my mind. I knew it was dismissal, disgrace, perhaps criminal punishment for me if I erred. On the other hand, I could bring in the wearied freight train men who had lain out all night. I knew I could. I knew just what to do, and so I began.

Signing Scott's name to the orders, Carnegie flashed out the necessary instructions to bring order out of the tangle. The trains moved; there were no mishaps. When Scott reached the office Carnegie told him what he had done. Scott said not a word but looked carefully over all that had taken place. After a little he moved away from Carnegie's desk to his own, and that was the end of it. "But I noticed," Carnegie concluded good-humoredly, "that he came in very regularly and in good time for some mornings after that."

It is hardly to be wondered at that Carnegie became Scott's favorite, his "white-haired Scotch devil." Impetuous but not rash, full of enthusiasm and good-natured charm, the small lad with his blunt, open features and his slight Scottish burr was every executive's dream of an assistant. Soon Scott repaid Andy for his services by introducing him to a new and very different kind of opportunity. He gave Carnegie the chance to subscribe to five hundred dollars' worth of Adams Express stock, a company which Scott assured Andy would prosper mightily.

Carnegie had not fifty dollars saved, much less five hundred, but it was a chance he could ill afford to miss. He reported the offer to his mother, and that pillar of the family unhesitatingly mortgaged their home to raise the necessary money. When the first dividend check came in, with its ornate Spencerian flourishes, Carnegie had something like a revelation. "I shall remember that check as long as I live," he subsequently wrote. "It gave me the first penny of revenue from capital—something that I had not worked for with the sweat of my brow. 'Eureka!' I cried, 'Here's the goose that lays the golden eggs.'" He was right; within a few years his investment in the Adams Express Company was paying annual dividends of $1,400.

It was not long thereafter that an even more propitious chance presented itself. Carnegie was riding on the Pennsylvania line one day when he was approached by a "farmer-looking" man carrying a small green bag in his hand. The other introduced himself as T. T. Woodruff and quite frankly said that he wanted a chance to talk with someone connected with the railroad. Whereupon he opened his bag and took out a small model of the first sleeping car.

Carnegie was immediately impressed with its possibilities, and he quickly arranged for Woodruff to meet Scott. When the latter agreed to give the cars a trial, Woodruff in appreciation offered Carnegie a chance to subscribe to a one-eighth interest in the new company. A local banker agreed to lend Andy the few hundred dollars needed for the initial payment—the rest being financed from dividends. Once again Andy had made a shrewd investment: within two years the Woodruff Palace Car Company was paying him a return of more than $5,000 a year.

Investments now began to play an increasingly important role in Carnegie's career. Through his railroad contacts he came to recognize the possibilities in manufacturing the heavy equipment needed by the rapidly expanding lines, and soon he was instrumental in organizing companies to meet these needs. One of them, the Keystone Bridge Company, was the first successful manufacturer of iron railway bridges. Another, the Pittsburgh Locomotive Works, made engines. And most important of all, an interest in a local iron works run by an irascible German named Andrew Kloman brought Carnegie into actual contact with the manufacture of iron itself.

None of these new ventures required any substantial outlay of cash. His interest in the Keystone Bridge Company, for instance, which was to earn him $15,000 in 1868, came to him "in return for services rendered in its promotion"—services which Carnegie, as a young railroad executive, was then in a highly strategic position to deliver. Similarly the interest in the Kloman works reflected no contribution on Carnegie's part except that of being the human catalyst and buffer between some highly excitable participants.

By 1865 his "side" activities had become so important that he decided to leave the Pennsylvania Railroad. He was by then superintendent, Scott having moved up to a vice presidency, but his salary of $2,400 was already vastly overshadowed by his income from various ventures. One purchase alone—the Storey farm in Pennsylvania oil country, which Carnegie and a few associates picked up for $40,000—was eventually to pay the group a million dollars in dividends in *one* year. About this time a friend dropped in on Carnegie and asked him how he was doing. "Oh, I'm rich, I'm rich!" he exclaimed.

He was indeed embarked on the road to riches, and determined, as he later wrote in his *Autobiography*, that "nothing could be allowed to interfere for a moment with my business career." Hence it comes as a surprise to note that it was at this very point that Carnegie retired to his suite to write his curiously introspective and troubled thoughts about the pursuit of wealth. But the momentum of events was to prove far too strong for these moralistic doubts. Moving his headquarters to New York to promote his various interests, he soon found himself swept along by a succession of irresistible opportunities for money-making.

One of these took place quite by chance. Carnegie was trying to sell the Woodruff sleeping car at the same time that a formidable rival named George Pullman was also seeking to land contracts for his sleeping car, and the railroads were naturally taking advantage of the competitive situation. One summer evening in 1869 Carnegie found himself mounting the resplendent marble stairway of the St. Nicholas Hotel side by side with his competitor.

"Good evening, Mr. Pullman," said Carnegie in his ebullient manner. Pullman was barely cordial.

"How strange we should meet here," Carnegie went on, to which the other replied nothing at all.

"Mr. Pullman," said Carnegie, after an embarrassing pause, "don't you think we are making nice fools of ourselves?" At this Pullman evinced a glimmer of interest: "What do you mean?" he inquired. Carnegie quickly pointed out that competition between the two companies was helping no one but the railroads. "Well," said Pullman, "what do you suggest we do?"

"Unite!" said Carnegie. "Let's make a joint proposition to the

Union Pacific, your company and mine. Why not organize a new company to do it?'' ''What would you call it?'' asked Pullman suspiciously. ''The Pullman Palace Car Company,'' said Carnegie and with this shrewd psychological stroke won his point. A new company was formed, and in time Carnegie became its largest stockholder.

Meanwhile, events pushed Carnegie into yet another lucrative field. To finance the proliferating railway systems of America, British capital was badly needed, and with his Scottish ancestry, his verve, and his excellent railroad connections Carnegie was the natural choice for a go-between. His brief case stuffed with bonds and prospectuses, Carnegie became a transatlantic commuter, soon developing intimate relations both with great bankers like Junius Morgan (the father of J. P. Morgan), and with the heads of most of the great American roads. These trips earned him not only large commissions—exceeding on occasion $100,000 for a single turn—but even more important, established connections that were later to be of immense value. He himself later testified candidly on their benefits before a group of respectfully awed senators:

> For instance, I want a great contract for rails. Sidney Dillon of the Union Pacific was a personal friend of mine. Huntington was a friend. Dear Butler Duncan, that called on me the other day, was a friend. Those and other men were presidents of railroads . . . Take Huntington; you know C. P. Huntington. He was hard up very often. He was a great man, but he had a great deal of paper out. I knew his things were good. When he wanted credit I gave it to him. If you help a man that way, what chance has any paid agent going to these men? It was absurd.

But his trips to England brought Carnegie something still more valuable. They gave him steel. It is fair to say that as late as 1872 Carnegie did not see the future that awaited him as the Steel King of the world. The still modest conglomeration of foundries and mills he was gradually assembling in the Allegheny and Monongahela valleys was but one of many business interests, and not one for which he envisioned any extraordinary future. Indeed, to repeated pleas that he lead the way in developing a steel industry for America by substituting steel for iron rails, his reply was succinct: ''Pioneering don't pay.''

What made him change his mind? The story goes that he was awe-struck by the volcanic, spectacular eruption of a Bessemer converter, which he saw for the first time during a visit to a British mill. It was precisely the sort of display that would have appealed to Carnegie's mind—a wild, demonic, physical process miraculously contained and controlled by the dwarfed figures of the steel men themselves. At any rate, overnight Carnegie became the perfervid prophet of steel. Jumping on the first available steamer, he rushed home with the cry, ''The day of iron has passed!'' To the conster-

*The drama of the Bessemer Process is depicted
in Aaron Bohrod's 1948 painting,* The Big Blow.

nation of his colleagues, the hitherto reluctant pioneer became an
advocate of the most daring technological and business expansion;
he joined them enthusiastically in forming Carnegie, McCandless &
Company, which was the nucleus of the empire that the next thirty
years would bring forth.

The actual process of growth involved every aspect of successful
business enterprise of the times: acquisition and merger, pools and
commercial piracy, and even, on one occasion, an outright fraud
in selling the United States government overpriced and underdone
steel armor plate. But it would be as foolish to maintain that the
Carnegie empire grew by trickery as to deny that sharp practice
had its place. Essentially what lay behind the spectacular expansion
were three facts.

The first of these was the sheer economic expansion of the industry
in the first days of burgeoning steel use. Everywhere steel replaced
iron or found new uses—and not only in railroads but in ships, buildings, bridges, machinery of all sorts. As Henry Frick himself once
remarked, if the Carnegie group had not filled the need for steel
another would have. But it must be admitted that Carnegie's company did its job superlatively well. In 1885 Great Britain led the
world in the production of steel. Fourteen years later her total output
was 695,000 tons less than the output of the Carnegie Steel Company
alone.

Second was the brilliant assemblage of personal talent with which

Carnegie surrounded himself. Among them, three in particular stood out. One was Captain William Jones, a Homeric figure who lumbered through the glowing fires and clanging machinery of the works like a kind of Paul Bunyan of steel, skilled at handling men, inventive in handling equipment, and enough of a natural artist to produce papers for the British Iron and Steel Institute that earned him a literary as well as a technical reputation. Then there was Henry Frick, himself a self-made millionaire, whose coke empire naturally complemented Carnegie's steelworks. When the two were amalgamated, Frick took over the active management of the whole, and under his forceful hand the annual output of the Carnegie works rose tenfold. Yet another was Charles Schwab, who came out of the tiny monastic town of Loretto, Pennsylvania, to take a job as a stake driver. Six months later he had been promoted by Jones into the assistant managership of the Braddock plant.

These men, and a score like them, constituted the vital energy of the Carnegie works. As Carnegie himself said, "Take away all our money, our great works, ore mines and coke ovens, but leave our organization, and in four years I shall have re-established myself."

But the third factor in the growth of the empire was Carnegie himself. A master salesman and a skilled diplomat of business at its highest levels, Carnegie was also a ruthless driver of his men. He pitted his associates and subordinates in competition with one another until a feverish atmosphere pervaded the whole organization. "You cannot imagine the abounding sense of freedom and relief I experience as soon as I get on board a steamer and sail past Sandy Hook," he once said to Captain Jones. "My God!" replied Jones. "Think of the relief to us!"

But Carnegie could win loyalties as well. All his promising young men were given gratis ownership participations—minuscule fractions of one per cent, which were enough, however, to make them millionaires in their own right. Deeply grateful to Jones, Carnegie once offered him a similar participation. Jones hemmed and hawed and finally refused; he would be unable to work effectively with the men, he said, once he was a partner. Carnegie insisted that his contribution be recognized and asked Jones what he wanted. "Well," said the latter, "you might pay me a hell of a big salary." "We'll do it!" said Carnegie. "From this time forth you shall receive the same salary as the President of the United States." "Ah, Andy, that's the kind of talk," said Captain Bill.

Within three decades, on the flood tide of economic expansion, propelled by brilliant executive work and relentless pressure from Carnegie, the company made immense strides. "Such a magnificent aggregation of industrial power has never before been under the domination of a single man," reported a biographer in 1902, describing the Gargantuan structure of steel and coke and ore and transport. Had the writer known of the profits earned by this aggregation he might have been even more impressed: three and a half million dollars in 1889, seven million in 1897, twenty-one million in 1899, and an immense forty million in 1900. "Where is there such a business!" Carnegie had exulted, and no wonder—the majority share of all these earnings, without hindrance of income tax, went directly into his pockets.

Nevertheless, with enormous success came problems. One of these was the restiveness of certain partners, under the "Iron-Clad" agreement, which prevented any of them from selling their shares to anyone but the company itself—an arrangement which meant, of course, that the far higher valuation of an outside purchaser could not be realized. Particularly chagrined was Frick, when, as the culmination of other disagreements between them, Carnegie sought to buy him out "at the value appearing on the books." Another problem was a looming competitive struggle in the steel industry itself that presaged a period of bitter industrial warfare ahead. And last was Carnegie's own growing desire to "get out."

Already he was spending half of each year abroad, first traveling, and then, after his late marriage, in residence in the great Skibo Castle he built for his wife on Dornoch Firth, Scotland. There he ran his business enterprises with one hand while he courted the literary and creative world with the other, entertaining Kipling and Matthew Arnold, Paderewski and Lloyd George, Woodrow Wilson and Theodore Roosevelt, Gladstone, and of course, Herbert Spencer, the Master. But even his career as "Laird" of Skibo could not remove him from the worries—and triumphs—of his business: a steady flow of cables and correspondence intruded on the "serious" side of life.

It was Schwab who cut the knot. Having risen to the very summit of the Carnegie concern he was invited in December, 1900, to give a speech on the future of the steel industry at the University Club in New York. There, before eighty of the nation's top business leaders he painted a glowing picture of what could be done if a super-company of steel were formed, integrated from top to bottom, self-sufficient with regard to its raw materials, balanced in its array of final products. One of the guests was the imperious J. P. Morgan, and as the speech progressed it was noticed that his concentration grew more and more intense. After dinner Morgan rose and took the young steel man by the elbow and engaged him in private conversation for half an hour while he plied him with rapid and penetrating questions; then a few weeks later he invited him to a private meeting in the great library of his home. They talked from nine o'clock in the evening until dawn. As the sun began to stream in through the library windows, the banker finally rose. "Well," he said to Schwab, "if Andy wants to sell, I'll buy. Go and find his price."

Carnegie at first did not wish to sell. Faced with the actual prospect of a withdrawal from the business he had built into the mightiest single industrial empire in the world, he was frightened and dismayed. He sat silent before Schwab's report, brooding, loath to inquire into details. But soon his enthusiasm returned. No such opportunity was likely to present itself again. In short order a figure of $492,000,000 was agreed on for the entire enterprise, of which Carnegie himself was to receive $300,000,000 in five per cent gold bonds and preferred stock. Carnegie jotted down the terms of the transaction on a slip of paper and told Schwab to bring it to Morgan. The banker glanced only briefly at the paper. "I accept," he said.

After the formalities were in due course completed, Carnegie was in a euphoric mood. "Now, Pierpont, I am the happiest man in the world," he said. Morgan was by no means unhappy himself: his own banking company had made a direct profit of $12,500,000 in the underwriting transaction, and this was but a prelude to a stream of lucrative financings under Morgan's aegis, by which the total capitalization was rapidly raised to $1,400,000,000. A few years later, Morgan and Carnegie found themselves aboard the same steamer en route to Europe. They fell into talk and Carnegie confessed, "I made one mistake, Pierpont, when I sold out to you."

"What was that?" asked the banker.

"I should have asked you for $100,000,000 more than I did."

Morgan grinned. "Well," he said, "you would have got it if you had."

Thus was written *finis* to one stage of Carnegie's career. Now it would be seen to what extent his "radical pronouncements" were serious. For in the *Gospel of Wealth*—the famous article combined with others in book form—Carnegie had proclaimed the duty of the millionaire to administer and distribute his wealth *during his lifetime*. Though he might have "proved" his worth by his fortune, his heirs had shown no such evidence of their fitness. Carnegie bluntly concluded: "By taxing estates heavily at his death, the State marks its condemnation of the selfish millionaire's unworthy life."

Coming from the leading millionaire of the day, these had been startling sentiments. So also were his views on the "labor question" which, if patronizing, were nonetheless humane and advanced for their day. The trouble was, of course, that the sentiments were somewhat difficult to credit. As one commentator of the day remarked, "His vision of what might be done with wealth had beauty and breadth and thus serenely overlooked the means by which wealth had been acquired."

For example, the novelist Hamlin Garland visited the steel towns from which the Carnegie millions came and bore away a description of work that was ugly, brutal, and exhausting: he contrasted the lavish care expended on the plants with the callous disregard of the pigsty homes: "the streets were horrible; the buildings poor; the sidewalks sunken and full of holes . . . Everywhere the yellow mud of the streets lay kneaded into sticky masses through which groups of pale, lean men slouched in faded garments . . ." When the famous Homestead strike erupted in 1892, with its private army of Pinkerton detectives virtually at war with the workers, the Carnegie benevolence seemed revealed as shabby fakery. At Skibo Carnegie stood firmly behind the company's iron determination to break the strike. As a result, public sentiment swung sharply and suddenly against him; the St. Louis *Post-Dispatch* wrote: "Three months ago Andrew Carnegie

The Homestead Strike as it was pictured in a drawing from Harper's Weekly.

was a man to be envied. Today he is an object of mingled pity and contempt. In the estimation of nine-tenths of the thinking people on both sides of the ocean he has . . . confessed himself a moral coward.''

In an important sense the newspaper was right. For though Carnegie continued to fight against ''privilege,'' he saw privilege only in its fading aristocratic vestments and not in the new hierarchies of wealth and power to which he himself belonged. In Skibo Castle he now played the role of the benign autocrat, awakening to the skirling of his private bagpiper and proceeding to breakfast to the sonorous accompaniment of the castle organ.

Meanwhile there had also come fame and honors in which Carnegie wallowed unashamedly. He counted the ''freedoms'' bestowed on him by grateful or hopeful cities and crowed. ''I have fifty-two and Gladstone has only seventeen.'' He entertained the King of England and told him that democracy was better than monarchy, and met the German Kaiser: ''Oh, yes, yes,'' said the latter worthy on being introduced. ''I have read your books. You do not like kings.'' But Mark Twain, on hearing of this, was not fooled. ''He says he is a scorner of kings and emperors and dukes,'' he wrote, ''whereas he is like the rest of the human race: a slight attention from one of these

A New York World *cartoonist labeled Carnegie "The Modern Baron with the Old Methods."*

can make him drunk for a week . . ."

And yet it is not enough to conclude that Carnegie was in fact a smaller man than he conceived himself. For this judgment overlooks one immense and irrefutable fact. He did, in the end, abide by his self-imposed duty. He did give nearly all of his gigantic fortune away.

As one would suspect, the quality of the philanthropy reflected the man himself. There was, for example, a huge and sentimentally administered private pension fund to which access was to be had on the most trivial as well as the most worthy grounds: if it included a number of writers, statesmen, scientists, it also made room for two maiden ladies with whom Carnegie had once danced as a young man, a boyhood acquaintance who had once held Carnegie's books while he ran a race, a merchant to whom he had once delivered a telegram and who had subsequently fallen on hard times. And then, as one would expect, there was a benevolent autocracy in the administration of the larger philanthropies as well. "Now everybody vote Aye," was the way Carnegie typically determined the policies of the philanthropic "foundations" he established.

Yet if these flaws bore the stamp of one side of Carnegie's personality, there was also the other side—the side that, however crudely, asked important questions and however piously, concerned itself with great ideals. Of this the range and purpose of the main philanthropies gave unimpeachable testimony. There were the famous libraries— three thousand of them costing nearly sixty million dollars; there

A contrasting view, captioned "The Macmillion," from London's Punch.

were the Carnegie institutes in Pittsburgh and Washington, Carnegie Hall in New York, the Hague Peace Palace, the Carnegie Endowment for International Peace, and the precedent-making Carnegie Corporation of New York, with its original enormous endowment of $125,-000,000. In his instructions to the trustees of this first great modern foundation, couched in the simplified spelling of which he was an ardent advocate, we see Carnegie at his very best:

> Conditions on erth [*sic*] inevitably change; hence, no wise man will bind Trustees forever to certain paths, causes, or institutions. I disclaim any intention of doing so . . . My chief happiness, as I write these lines lies in the thot [*sic*] that, even after I pass away, the welth [*sic*] that came to me to administer as a sacred trust for the good of my fellow men is to continue to benefit humanity . . .

If these sentiments move us—if Carnegie himself in retrospect moves us at last to grudging respect—it is not because his was the triumph of a saint or a philosopher. It is because it was the much more difficult triumph of a very human and fallible man struggling to retain his convictions in an age, and in the face of a career, which subjected them to impossible temptations. Carnegie is something of America writ large; his is the story of the Horatio Alger hero *after* he has made his million dollars. In the failures of Andrew Carnegie we see many of the failures of America itself. In his curious triumph, we see what we hope is our own steadfast core of integrity.

David Boroff

THE DIASPORA IN AMERICA: A STUDY OF JEWISH IMMIGRATION

Because except for Indians all Americans are themselves at least the descendants of immigrants, it is perhaps not surprising that "native born" citizens have often displayed a kind of love-hate attitude toward newcomers. They recognize in these newcomers their own successes and failures, their pride in what they have forgotten or rejected in their heritage. This ambivalence has been exacerbated by the very real conflicts that immigration has caused. On the one hand, the immigrant has always been a national asset—his labor and intelligence add to the productivity and wealth of society; his culture enriches and diversifies American civilization. On the other hand, the immigrant has represented competition, strangeness, unsettling change. Most immigrants have been poor, many upon arrival have been ill-adjusted to American values and habits. Social and economic problems have frequently resulted, especially when large numbers have flooded into the country in relatively short periods of time. This last point explains why the late nineteenth and early twentieth centuries produced the movement to restrict immigration, for the influx was greater then than at any other time.

In this essay the late David Boroff of New York University discusses the impact of Jewish immigrants on the United States and the impact of the nation on these immigrants. He focuses chiefly on the period after 1880, when Jewish immigration was heaviest. His account provides a vivid picture of the life of these people, and helps explain both why they, as well as other immigrants, were sometimes disliked and why they were themselves at times ambivalent in their reactions to America.

It started with a tiny trickle and ended in a roaring flood. The first to come were just twenty-three Jews from Brazil who landed in New Amsterdam in 1654, in flight from a country no longer hospitable to them. They were, in origin, Spanish and Portuguese Jews (many with grandiloquent Iberian names) whose families had been wandering for a century and a half. New Amsterdam provided a chilly reception. Governor Peter Stuyvesant at first asked them to leave, but kinder hearts in the Dutch West India Company granted them the right to stay, "provided the poor among them . . . be supported by their own nation." By the end of the century, there were perhaps one hundred Jews; by the middle of the eighteenth century, there were about three hundred in New York, and smaller communities in Newport, Philadelphia, and Charleston.

Because of their literacy, zeal, and overseas connections, colonial Jews prospered as merchants, though there were artisans and laborers among them. The Jewish community was tightly knit, but there was a serious shortage of trained religious functionaries. There wasn't a single American rabbi, for example, until the nineteenth century. Jews were well regarded, particularly in New England. Puritan culture leaned heavily on the Old Testament, and Harvard students learned Hebrew; indeed, during the American Revolution, the suggestion was advanced that Hebrew replace English as the official language of the new country. The absence of an established national religion made it possible for Judaism to be regarded as merely another religion in a pluralistic society. The early days of the new republic were thus a happy time for Jews. Prosperous and productive, they were admitted to American communal life with few restrictions. It is little wonder that a Jewish spokesman asked rhetorically in 1820: "On what spot in this habitable Globe does an Israelite enjoy more blessings, more privileges?"

The second wave of immigration during the nineteenth century is often described as German, but that is misleading. Actually, there were many East European Jews among the immigrants who came in the half century before 1870. However, the German influence was strong, and there was a powerful undercurrent of Western enlightenment at work. These Jews came because economic depression and the Industrial Revolution had made their lot as artisans and small merchants intolerable. For some there was also the threatening backwash of the failure of the Revolution of 1848. Moreover, in Germany at this time Jews were largely disfranchised and discriminated against. During this period, between 200,000 and 400,000 Jews emigrated to this country, and the Jewish population had risen to about half a million by 1870.

This was the colorful era of the peddler and his pack. Peddling was an easy way to get started—it required little capital—and it often rewarded enterprise and daring. Jewish peddlers fanned out through the young country into farmland and mining camp, frontier and Indian territory. The more successful peddlers ultimately settled in one place as storekeepers. (Some proud businesses—including that of Senator Goldwater's family—made their start this way.) Feeling somewhat alienated from the older, settled Jews, who had a reputation for declining piety, the new immigrants organized their own synagogues and community facilities, such as cemeteries and hospitals. In general, these immigrants were amiably received by native Americans, who, unsophisticated about differences that were crucial to the immigrants themselves, regarded all Central Europeans as "Germans."

Essentially, the emigration route was the same between 1820 and 1870 as it would be in the post-1880 exodus. The travellers stayed in emigration inns while awaiting their ship, and since they had all their resources with them, they were in danger of being robbed. The journey itself was hazardous and, in the days of the sailing vessels when a good wind was indispensable, almost interminable. Nor were the appointments very comfortable even for the relatively well to do. A German Jew who made the journey in 1856 reported that his cabin, little more than six feet by six feet, housed six passengers in tripledecker bunks. When a storm raged, the passengers had to retire to their cabins lest they be washed off the deck by waves. "Deprived of air," he wrote, "it soon became unbearable in the cabins in which six sea-sick persons breathed." On this particular journey, sea water began to trickle into the cabins, and the planks had to be retarred.

Still, the emigration experience was a good deal easier than it would be later. For one thing, the immigrants were better educated and better acquainted with modern political and social attitudes than the oppressed and bewildered East European multitudes who came after 1880. Fewer in number, they were treated courteously by ships' captains. (On a journey in 1839, described by David Mayer, the ship's captain turned over his own cabin to the Jewish passengers for their prayers and regularly visited those Jews who were ill.) Moreover, there was still the bloom of adventure about the overseas voyage. Ships left Europe amid the booming of cannon, while on shore ladies enthusiastically waved their handkerchiefs. On the way over, there was a holiday atmosphere despite the hazards, and there was great jubilation when land was sighted.

There were, however, rude shocks when the voyagers arrived in this country. The anguish of Castle Garden and Ellis Island was well in the future when immigration first began to swell. But New York seemed inhospitable, its pace frantic, the outlook not entirely hopeful. Isaac M. Wise, a distinguished rabbi who made the journey in 1846, was appalled. "The whole city appeared to me like a large shop," he wrote, "where everyone buys or sells, cheats or is cheated. I had never before seen a city so bare of all art and of every trace of good taste; likewise I had never witnessed anywhere such rushing, hurrying, chasing, running . . . Everything seemed so pitifully small and paltry; and I had had so exalted an idea of the land of freedom." Moreover, he no sooner landed in New York than he was abused by a German drayman whose services he had declined. "Aha! thought I," he later wrote, "you have left home and kindred in order to get away from the disgusting Judaeophobia and here the first German greeting that sounds in your ears is hep! hep!'' (The expletive was a Central European equivalent of "Kike.") Another German Jew who worked as a clothing salesman was affronted by the way customers were to be "lured" into buying ("I did not think this occupation corresponded in any way to my views of a merchant's dignity").

After 1880, Jewish immigration into the United States was in flood tide. And the source was principally East Europe, where by 1880 three quarters of the world's 7.7 million Jews were living. In all, over two million Jews came to these shores in little more than three decades—about one third of Europe's Jewry. Some of them came, as their predecessors had come, because of shrinking economic opportunities. In Russia and in the Austro-Hungarian empire, the growth of large-scale agriculture squeezed out Jewish middlemen as it destroyed the independent peasantry, while in the cities the development of manufacturing reduced the need for Jewish artisans. Vast numbers of Jews became petty tradesmen or even *luftmenschen* (men without visible means of support who drifted from one thing to another). In Galicia, around 1900, there was a Jewish trader for

Her decks jammed with hopeful immigrants, the S.S. Patricia *arrives at Ellis Island in 1906.*

every ten peasants, and the average value of his stock came to only twenty dollars.

Savage discrimination and pogroms also incited Jews to emigrate. The Barefoot Brigades—bands of marauding Russian peasants— brought devastation and bloodshed to Jewish towns and cities. On a higher social level, there was the ''cold pogrom,'' a government policy calculated to destroy Jewish life. The official hope was that one third of Russia's Jews would die out, one third would emigrate, and one third would be converted to the Orthodox Church. Crushing restrictions were imposed. Jews were required to live within the Pale of Settlement in western Russia, they could not Russify their names, and they were subjected to rigorous quotas for schooling and professional training. Nor could general studies be included in the curriculum of Jewish religious schools. It was a life of poverty and fear.

Nevertheless, the *shtetl*, the typical small Jewish town, was a triumph of endurance and spiritual integrity. It was a place where degradation and squalor could not wipe out dignity, where learning flourished in the face of hopelessness, and where a tough, sardonic humor provided catharsis for the tribulations of an existence that was barely endurable. The abrasions and humiliations of everyday life were healed by a rich heritage of custom and ceremony. And there was always Sabbath—''The Bride of the Sabbath,'' as the Jews called the day of rest—to bring repose and exaltation to a life always sorely tried.

To be sure, even this world showed signs of disintegration. Secular learning, long resisted by East European Jews and officially denied to them, began to make inroads. Piety gave way to revolutionary fervor, and Jews began to play a heroic role in Czarist Russia's bloody history of insurrection and suppression.

This was the bleak, airless milieu from which the emigrants came. A typical expression of the Jewish attitude toward emigration from Russia—both its hopefulness and the absence of remorse—was provided by Dr. George Price, who had come to this country in one of the waves of East European emigration:

> Should this Jewish emigrant regret his leave-taking of his native land which fails to appreciate him? No! A thousand times no! He must not regret fleeing the clutches of the blood-thirsty crocodile. Sympathy for this country? How ironical it sounds! Am I not despised? Am I not urged to leave? Do I not hear the word *Zhid* constantly? . . . Be thou cursed forever my wicked homeland, because you remind me of the Inquisition . . . May you rue the day when you exiled the people who worked for your welfare.

After 1880, going to America—no other country really lured— became the great drama of redemption for the masses of East European Jews. (For some, of course, Palestine had that role even in the late nineteenth century, but these were an undaunted Zionist cadre prepared to endure the severest hardships.) The assassination of Czar

Alexander II in 1881, and the subsequent pogrom, marked the beginning of the new influx. By the end of the century, 700,000 Jews had arrived, about one quarter of them totally illiterate, almost all of them impoverished. Throughout East Europe, Jews talked longingly about America as the "goldene medinah" (the golden province), and biblical imagery—"the land of milk and honey"—came easily to their lips. Those who could write were kept busy composing letters to distant kin—or even to husbands—in America. (Much of the time, the husband went first, and by abstemious living saved enough to fetch wife and children from the old country.) Children played at "emigrating games," and for the entire *shtetl* it was an exciting moment when the mail-carrier announced how many letters had arrived from America.

German steamship companies assiduously advertised the glories of the new land and provided a one-price rate from *shtetl* to New York. Emigration inns were established in Brody (in the Ukraine) and in the port cities of Bremen and Hamburg, where emigrants would gather for the trip. There were rumors that groups of prosperous German Jews would underwrite their migration to America; and in fact such people often did help their co-religionists when they were stranded without funds in the port cities of Germany. Within Russia itself, the government after 1880 more or less acquiesced in the emigration of Jews, and connived in the vast business of "stealing the border" (smuggling emigrants across). After 1892, emigration was legal—except for those of draft age—but large numbers left with forged papers, because that proved to be far easier than getting tangled in the red tape of the Czarist bureaucracy. Forged documents, to be sure, were expensive—they cost twenty-five rubles, for many Jews the equivalent of five weeks' wages. Nor was the departure from home entirely a happy event. There were the uncertainties of the new life, the fear that in America "one became a gentile." Given the Jewish aptitude for lugubriousness, a family's departure was often like a funeral, lachrymose and anguished, with the neighbors carting off the furniture that would no longer be needed.

For people who had rarely ventured beyond the boundaries of their own village, going to America was an epic adventure. They travelled with pitifully little money; the average immigrant arrived in New York with only about twenty dollars. With their domestic impedimenta—bedding, brass candlesticks, samovars—they would proceed to the port cities by rail, cart, and even on foot. At the emigration inns, they had to wait their turn. Thousands milled around, entreating officials for departure cards. There were scenes of near chaos—mothers shrieking, children crying; battered wicker trunks, bedding, utensils in wild disarray. At Hamburg, arriving emigrants were put in the "unclean" section of the *Auswandererhallen* until examined by physicians who decided whether their clothing and baggage had to be disinfected. After examination, Jews could not leave the center; other emigrants could.

The ocean voyage provided little respite. (Some elected to sail by way of Liverpool at a reduction of nine dollars from the usual rate of thirty-four dollars.) Immigrants long remembered the "smell of ship," a distillation of many putrescences. Those who went in steerage slept on mattresses filled with straw and kept their clothes on to keep warm. The berth itself was generally six feet long, two feet wide, and two and a half feet high, and it had to accommodate the passenger's luggage. Food was another problem. Many Orthodox Jews subsisted on herring, black bread, and tea which they brought because they did not trust the dietary purity of the ship's food. Some ships actually maintained a separate galley for kosher food, which was coveted by non-Jewish passengers because it was allegedly better.

Unsophisticated about travel and faced by genuine dangers, Jewish emigrants found the overseas trip a long and terrifying experience. But when land was finally sighted, the passengers often began to cheer and shout. "I looked up at the sky," an immigrant wrote years later. "It seemed much bluer and the sun much brighter than in the old country. It reminded me on [sic] the Garden of Eden."

Unhappily, the friendly reception that most immigrants envisioned in the new land rarely materialized. Castle Garden in the Battery, at the foot of Manhattan—and later Ellis Island in New York Harbor—proved to be almost as traumatic as the journey itself. "Castle Garden," an immigrant wrote, "is a large building, a Gehenna, through which all Jewish arrivals must pass to be cleansed before they are considered worthy of breathing freely the air of the land of the almighty dollar. . . . If in Brody, thousands crowded about, here tens of thousands thronged about; if there they were starving, here they were dying; if there they were crushed, here they were simply beaten."

One must make allowances for the impassioned hyperbole of the suffering immigrant, but there is little doubt that the immigration officials were harassed, overworked, and often unsympathetic. Authorized to pass on the admissibility of the newcomers, immigration officers struck terror into their hearts by asking questions designed to reveal their literacy and social attitudes. "How much is six times six?" an inspector asked a woman in the grip of nervousness, then casually asked the next man, "Have you ever been in jail?"

There were, of course, representatives of Jewish defense groups present, especially from the Hebrew Immigrant Aid Society. But by this time, the immigrants, out of patience and exhausted, tended to view them balefully. The Jewish officials tended to be highhanded, and the temporary barracks which they administered on Ward's Island for those not yet settled became notorious. Discontent culminated in a riot over food; one day the director—called The Father—had to swim ashore for his life, and the police were hastily summoned.

Most immigrants went directly from Castle Garden or Ellis Island to the teeming streets of Manhattan, where they sought relatives or landsleit (fellow townsmen) who had gone before them. Easy marks for hucksters and swindlers, they were overcharged by draymen for carrying their paltry possessions, engaged as strikebreakers, or hired at shamelessly low wages.

*Immigrant women and children at Ellis Island
eating their first American meal (1906).*

"Greenhorn" or "greener" was their common name. A term of vilification, the source of a thousand cruel jokes, it was their shame and their destiny. On top of everything else, the immigrants had to abide the contempt of their co-religionists who had preceded them to America by forty or fifty years. By the time the heavy East European immigration set in, German Jews had achieved high mercantile status and an uneasy integration into American society. They did not want to be reminded of their kinship with these uncouth and impoverished Jews who were regarded vaguely as a kind of Oriental influx. There was a good deal of sentiment against "aiding such paupers to emigrate to these shores." One charitable organization declared: "Organized immigration from Russia, Roumania, and other semi-barbarous countries is a mistake and has proved to be a failure. It is no relief to the Jews of Russia, Poland, etc., and it jeopardizes the well-being of the American Jews."

A genuine uptown-downtown split soon developed, with condescension on one side and resentment on the other. The German Jews objected as bitterly to the rigid, old-world Orthodoxy of the immigrants as they did to their new involvement in trade unions. They were fearful, too, of the competition they would offer in the needle trades. (Indeed, the East Europeans ultimately forced the uptown Jews out of the industry.) On the other side of the barricades, Russian Jews complained that at the hands of their uptown brethren, "every man is questioned like a criminal, is looked down upon . . . just as if he were standing before a Russian official." Nevertheless, many German Jews responded to the call of conscience by providing funds for needy immigrants and setting up preparatory schools for immigrant children for whom no room was yet available in the hopelessly overcrowded public schools.

Many comfortably settled German Jews saw dispersion as the answer to the problem. Efforts were made to divert immigrants to small towns in other parts of the country, but these were largely ineffective. There were also some gallant adventures with farming in such remote places as South Dakota, Oregon, and Louisiana. Though the Jewish pioneers were brave and idealistic, drought, disease, and ineptitude conspired against them. (In Oregon, for example, they tried to raise corn in cattle country, while in Louisiana they found themselves in malarial terrain.) Only chicken farming in New Jersey proved to be successful to any great degree. Farm jobs for Jews were available, but as one immigrant said: "I have no desire to be a farm hand to an ignorant Yankee at the end of the world. I would rather work here at half the price in a factory; for then I would at least be able to spend my free evenings with my friends."

It was in New York, then, that the bulk of the immigrants settled —in the swarming, tumultuous Lower East Side—with smaller concentrations in Boston, Philadelphia, and Chicago. Far less adaptable than the German Jews who were now lording it over them, disoriented and frightened, the East European immigrants constituted a vast and exploited proletariat. According to a survey in 1890, sixty per cent of all immigrant Jews worked in the needle trades. This industry had gone through a process of decentralization in which contractors carried out the bulk of production, receiving merely the cut goods from the manufacturer. Contracting establishments were everywhere in the Lower East Side, including the contractors' homes, where pressers warmed their irons on the very stove on which the boss's wife was preparing supper. The contractors also gave out "section" work to families and *landsleit* who would struggle to meet the quotas at home. The bondage of the sewing machine was therefore extended into the tenements, with entire families enslaved by the machine's voracious demands. The Hester Street "pig market," where one could buy anything, became the labor exchange; there tailors, operators, finishers, basters, and pressers would congregate on Saturday in the hope of being hired by contractors.

Life in the sweatshops of the Lower East Side was hard, but it made immigrants employable from the start, and a weekly wage of five dollars—the equivalent of ten rubles—looked good in immigrant eyes. Moreover, they were among their own kin and kind, and the sweatshops, noisome as they were, were still the scene of lively political and even literary discussions. (In some cigar-making shops, in fact, the bosses hired "readers" to keep the minds of the workers occupied with classic and Yiddish literature as they performed their repetitive chores.) East European Jews, near the end of the century, made up a large part of the skilled labor force in New York, ranking first in twenty-six out of forty-seven trades, and serving, for example, as

The immigrants' new home: a crowded, noisy, but friendly street on New York's Lower East Side.

bakers, building-trade workers, painters, furriers, jewellers, and tinsmiths.

Almost one quarter of all the immigrants tried their hands as tradesmen—largely as peddlers or as pushcart vendors in the madhouse bazaar of the Lower East Side. For some it was an apprenticeship in low-toned commerce that would lead to more elegant careers. For others it was merely a martyrdom that enabled them to subsist. It was a modest enough investment—five dollars for a license, one dollar for a basket, and four dollars for wares. They stocked up on pins and needles, shoe laces, polish, and handkerchiefs, learned some basic expressions ("You wanna buy somethin'?"), and were on their hapless way.

It was the professions, of course, that exerted the keenest attraction to Jews, with their reverence for learning. For most of them it was too late; they had to reconcile themselves to more humble callings. But it was not too late for their children, and between 1897 and 1907, the number of Jewish physicians in Manhattan rose from 450 to 1,000. Of all the professions it was medicine that excited the greatest veneration. (Some of this veneration spilled over into pharmacy, and "druggists'' were highly respected figures who were called upon to prescribe for minor—and even major—ills, and to serve as scribes for the letters that the immigrants were unable to read and write themselves.) There were Jewish lawyers on the Lower East Side and by 1901 over 140 Jewish policemen, recruited in part by Theodore Roosevelt, who, as police commissioner, had issued a call for ''the Maccabee or fighting Jewish type.''

The Lower East Side was the American counterpart of the ghetto for Jewish immigrants, as well as their glittering capital. At its peak, around 1910, it packed over 350,000 people into a comparatively small area—roughly from Canal Street to Fourteenth Street—with as many as 523 people per acre, so that Arnold Bennett was moved to remark that ''the architecture seemed to sweat humanity at every window and door.'' The most densely populated part of the city, it held one sixth of Manhattan's population and most of New York's office buildings and factories. ''Uptowners'' used to delight in visiting it (as a later generation would visit Harlem) to taste its exotic flavor. But the great mass of Jews lived there because the living was cheap, and there was a vital Jewish community that gave solace to the lonely and comfort to the pious.

A single man could find lodgings of a sort, including coffee morning and night, for three dollars a month. For a family, rent was about ten dollars a month, milk was four cents a quart, kosher meat twelve cents a pound, bread two cents a pound, herring a penny or two. A kitchen table could be bought for a dollar, chairs at thirty-five cents each. One managed, but the life was oppressive. Most families lived in the notorious ''dumbbell'' flats of old-law tenements (built prior to 1901). Congested, often dirty and unsanitary, these tenements were six or seven stories high and had four apartments on each floor. Only one room in each three or four room apartment received direct air and sunlight, and the families on each floor shared a toilet in the hall.

Many families not only used their flats as workshops but also took in boarders to make ends meet. Jacob Riis tells of a two-room apartment on Allen Street which housed parents, six children, and six boarders. ''Two daughters sewed clothes at home. The elevator railway passed by the window. The cantor rehearses, a train passes, the shoemaker bangs, ten brats run around like goats, the wife putters. . . . At night we all try to get some sleep in the stifling, roach-infested two rooms.'' In the summer, the tenants spilled out into fire escapes and rooftops, which were converted into bedrooms.

Nevertheless, life on the Lower East Side had surprising vitality. Despite the highest population density in the city, the Tenth Ward had one of the lowest death rates. In part, this was because of the strenuous personal cleanliness of Jews, dictated by their religion. Though only eight per cent of the East European Jews had baths, bathhouses and steam rooms on the Lower East Side did a booming business. There was, of course, a heavy incidence of tuberculosis—''the white plague.'' Those who were afflicted could be heard crying out, ''*Luft! Gib mir luft!*'' (''Air! Give me air!''). It was, in fact, this

terror of "consumption" that impelled some East Side Jews to become farmers in the Catskills at the turn of the century, thus fore-
running the gaudy career of the Catskill Borscht Belt resort hotels.
The same fear impelled Jews on the Lower East Side to move to
Washington Heights and the Bronx, where the altitude was higher, the
air presumably purer.

Alcoholism, a prime affliction of most immigrant groups, was almost unknown among Jews. They drank ritualistically on holidays but
almost never to excess. They were, instead, addicted to seltzer or soda
water—Harry Golden's "2¢ plain"—which they viewed as "the
worker's champagne." The suicide rate was relatively low, though
higher than in the *shtetl,* and there was always a shudder of sympathy
when the Yiddish press announced that someone had *genumen di ges*
(taken gas).

The Lower East Side was from the start the scene of considerable
crime. But its inhabitants became concerned when the crime rate
among the young people seemed to rise steeply around 1910. There
was a good deal of prostitution. The dancing academies, which achieved
popularity early in this century, became recruiting centers for prostitutes. In 1908–9, of 581 foreign women arrested for prostitution,
225 were Jewish. There was the notorious Max Hochstim Association,
which actively recruited girls, while the New York Independent
Benevolent Association—an organization of pimps—provided sick
benefits, burial privileges, bail, and protection money for prostitutes.

A New York sweatshop,
photographed about 1910.

The membership was even summoned to funerals with a two-dollar fine imposed on those who did not attend. Prostitution was so taken for granted that Canal Street had stores on one side featuring sacerdotal articles, while brothels were housed on the other.

Family life on the Lower East Side was cohesive and warm, though there was an edge of shrillness and hysteria to it. Marriages were not always happy, but if wives were viewed as an affliction, children were regarded as a blessing. The kitchen was the center of the household, and food was almost always being served to either family or visitors. No matter how poor they were, Jewish families ate well—even to excess—and mothers considered their children woefully underweight unless they were well cushioned with fat.

It was a life with few conventional graces. Handkerchiefs were barely known, and the Yiddish newspapers had to propagandize for their use. Old men smelled of snuff, and in spite of bathing, children often had lice in their hair and were sent home from school by the visiting nurse for a kerosene bath. Bedbugs were considered an inevitability, and pajamas were viewed as an upper-class affectation. Parents quarrelled bitterly—with passionate and resourceful invective —in the presence of their children. Telephones were virtually unknown, and a telegram surely meant disaster from afar.

The zeal of the immigrants on behalf of their children was no less than awe-inspiring. Parents yearned for lofty careers for their offspring, with medicine at the pinnacle. In better-off homes, there was always a piano ("solid mahogany"), and parents often spent their precious reserves to arrange a "concert" for their precocious youngsters, followed by a ball in one of the Lower East Side's many halls.

To be sure, the children inspired a full measure of anxiety in their parents. "Amerikane kinder" was the rueful plaint of the elders, who could not fathom the baffling new ways of the young. Parents were nervous about their daughters' chastity, and younger brothers—often six or seven years old—would be dispatched as chaperones when the girls met their boy friends. There was uneasiness about Jewish street gangs and the growing problem of delinquency. The old folks were vexed by the new tides of secularism and political radicalism that were weaning their children from traditional pieties. But most of all, they feared that their sons would not achieve the success that would redeem their own efforts, humiliations, and failures in the harsh new land. Pressure on their children was relentless. But on the whole the children did well, astonishingly well. "The ease and rapidity with which they learn," Jacob Riis wrote, "is equalled only by their good behavior and close attention while in school. There is no whispering and no rioting at these desks." Samuel Chotzinoff, the music critic, tells a story which reveals the attitude of the Jewish schoolboy. When an altercation threatened between Chotzinoff and a classmate, his antagonist's reaction was to challenge him to spell "combustible."

The Lower East Side was a striking demonstration that financial want does not necessarily mean cultural poverty. The immigrant Jews were nearly always poor and often illiterate, but they were not culturally deprived. In fact, between 1890 and World War I, the Jewish community provides a remarkable chapter in American cultural history. Liberated from the constrictions of European captivity, immigrant Jews experienced a great surge of intellectual vitality. Yiddish, the Hebrew-German dialect which some people had casually dismissed as a barbarous "jargon," became the vehicle of this cultural renascence. Between 1885 and 1914, over 150 publications of all kinds made their appearance. But the new Yiddish journalism reached its apogee with the *Jewish Daily Forward* under the long editorial reign of Abraham Cahan. The *Forword* was humanitarian, pro-labor, and socialistic. But it was also an instrument for acclimatizing immigrants in the new environment. It provided practical hints on how to deal with the new world, letters from the troubled (*Bintel Brief*), and even, at one time, a primer on baseball ("explained to non-sports"). The *Forward* also published and fostered an enormous amount of literature in Yiddish—both original works by writers of considerable talent, and translations of classic writers.

In this cultural ferment, immigrants studied English in dozens of night schools and ransacked the resources of the Aguilar Free Library on East Broadway. "When I had [a] book in my hand," an immigrant wrote, "I pressed it to my heart and wanted to kiss it." The Educational Alliance, also on East Broadway, had a rich program designed to make immigrant Jews more American and their sons more Jewish. And there were scores of settlement houses, debating clubs, ethical societies, and literary circles which attracted the young. In fact, courtships were carried on in a rarefied atmosphere full of lofty talk about art, politics, and philosophy. And though there was much venturesome palaver about sexual freedom, actual behavior tended to be quite strait-laced.

But the most popular cultural institution was the café or coffee house, which served as the Jewish saloon. There were about 250 of them, each with its own following. Here the litterateurs sat for hours over steaming glasses of tea; revolutionaries and Bohemians gathered to make their pronouncements or raise money for causes; actors and playwrights came to hold court. For immigrant Jews, talk was the breath of life itself. The passion for music and theatre knew no bounds. When Beethoven's Ninth Symphony was performed one summer night in 1915, mounted police had to be summoned to keep order outside Lewisohn Stadium, so heavy was the press of crowds eager for the twenty-five-cent stone seats. Theatre (in Yiddish) was to the Jewish immigrants what Shakespeare and Marlowe had been to the groundlings in Elizabethan England. Tickets were cheap—twenty-five cents to one dollar—and theatregoing was universal. It was a raucous, robust, and communal experience. Mothers brought their babies (except in some of the "swellest" theatres, which forbade it), and peddlers hawked their wares between the acts. There were theatre parties for trade unions and *landsmanschaften* (societies of fellow townsmen), and the audience milled around and renewed old friendships or argued the merits of the play. The stage curtain had bold advertisements of stores or blown-up portraits of stars.

There was an intense cult of personality in the Yiddish theatre and a system of claques not unlike that which exists in grand opera today. The undisputed monarch was Boris Thomashefsky, and a theatre program of his day offered this panegyric:

> Thomashefsky! Artist great!
> No praise is good enough for you!
> Of all the stars you remain the king
> You seek no tricks, no false quibbles;
> One sees truth itself playing.
> Your appearance is godly to us
> Every movement is full of grace
> Pleasing is your every gesture
> Sugar sweet your every turn
> You remain the king of the stage
> Everything falls to your feet.

Many of the plays were sentimental trash—heroic "operas" on historical themes, "greenhorn" melodramas full of cruel abandonments and tearful reunions, romantic musicals, and even topical dramas dealing with such immediate events as the Homestead Strike, the Johnstown Flood, and the Kishinev Pogrom of 1903. Adaptability and a talent for facile plagiarism were the essence of the playwright's art in those days, and "Professor" Moses Horwitz wrote 167 plays, most of them adaptations of old operas and melodramas. The plays were so predictable that an actor once admitted he didn't even have to learn his lines; he merely had to have a sense of the general situation and then adapt lines from other plays.

There was, of course, a serious Yiddish drama, introduced principally by Jacob Gordin, who adapted classical and modernist drama to the Yiddish stage. Jewish intellectuals were jubilant at this development. But the process of acculturation had its amusing and grotesque aspects. Shakespeare was a great favorite but *"verbessert and vergrossert"* (improved and enlarged). There was the Jewish *King Lear* in which Cordelia becomes Goldele. (The theme of filial ingratitude was a "natural" on the Lower East Side, where parents constantly made heroic sacrifices.) *Hamlet* was also given a Jewish coloration, the prince becoming a rabbinical student who returns from the seminary to discover treachery at home. And *A Doll's House* by Ibsen was transformed into *Minna,* in which a sensitive and intelligent young woman, married to an ignorant laborer, falls in love with her boarder and ultimately commits suicide.

Related to the Jewish love of theatre was the immigrant's adoration of the cantor, a profession which evoked as much flamboyance and egotistical preening as acting did. (In fact, actors would sometimes grow beards before the high holydays and find jobs as cantors.) Synagogues vied with each other for celebrated cantors, sometimes as a way of getting out of debt, since tickets were sold for the high-holyday services.

The Lower East Side was a vibrant community, full of color and gusto, in which the Jewish immigrant felt marvelously at home, safe from the terrors of the alien city. But it was a setting too for fierce conflict and enervating strain. There were three major influences at work, each pulling in a separate direction: Jewish Orthodoxy, assimilationism, and the new socialist gospel. The immigrants were Orthodox, but their children tended to break away. *Cheders* (Hebrew schools) were everywhere, in basements and stores and tenements, and the old custom of giving a child a taste of honey when he was beginning to learn to read—as symbolic of the sweetness of study— persisted. But the young, eager to be accepted into American society, despised the old ways and their "greenhorn" teachers. Fathers began to view their sons as "freethinkers," a term that was anathema to them. Observance of the Law declined, and the Saturday Sabbath was ignored by many Jews. A virulent antireligious tendency developed among many "enlightened" Jews, who would hold profane balls on the most sacred evening of the year—Yom Kippur—at which they would dance and eat nonkosher food. (Yom Kippur is a fast day.) And the trade-union movement also generated uneasiness among the pious elders of the Lower East Side. "Do you want us to bow down to your archaic God?" a radical newspaper asked. "Each era has its new Torah. Ours is one of freedom and justice."

But for many immigrants the basic discontent was with their American experience itself. The golden province turned out to be a place of tenements and sweatshops. A familiar cry was *"a klug af Columbus!"* ("a curse on Columbus") or, "Who ever asked him, Columbus, to discover America?" Ellis Island was called *Trernindzl* (Island of Tears), and Abraham Cahan, in his initial reaction to the horrors of immigration, thundered: "Be cursed, immigration! Cursed by those conditions which have brought you into being. How many souls have you broken, how many courageous and mighty souls have you shattered." The fact remains that most Jewish immigrants, in the long run, made a happy adjustment to their new land.

After 1910, the Lower East Side went into a decline. Its strange glory was over. New areas of Jewish settlement opened up in Brooklyn, the Bronx, and in upper Manhattan. By the mid-twenties, less than ten per cent of New York's Jews lived on the Lower East Side, although it still remained the heartland to which one returned to shop, to see Yiddish theatre, and to renew old ties. By 1924 Jewish immigration into the United States was severely reduced by new immigration laws, and the saga of mass immigration was done. But the intensities of the Jewish immigrant experience had already made an indelible mark on American culture and history that would endure for many years.

Bernard A. Weisberger

THE IMMIGRANT: WHITE AND BLACK

Coexistent with the flood of "new" immigrants that poured into
American cities from eastern and southern Europe beginning
in the 1880's was a similar migration of American blacks from
the South. Like so many of the Europeans, they were from rural
backgrounds and essentially peasants. These black "immigrants"
had the advantage of being American citizens and of speaking
English from the start, but besides lacking in experience in city
ways, they labored under the handicap of racial prejudice, less
rigid than in the South but nevertheless stultifying in its effects.
Thus, as Bernard Weisberger shows in this discussion of their
fate before the Great Depression of the 1930's, they endured all
the burdens of their European fellows and then some, although,
again like the Europeans, they also profited from the opportunities
that city life provided.

As any really thoughtful statesman knows, it is one of the ironies of history that great decisions often have entirely unexpected consequences. Until men are given the gift of prophecy, "Forgive them; for they know not what they do" is an appropriate motto for those who judge political performances. But in some cases, "Congratulate them; for they know not what they do" might be as apt.

It is hard to say which version applies to the congressmen who passed the Johnson-Reed immigration restriction act of 1924. In that year they heeded a warning sounded by a New England poet some twenty years earlier. "Wide open and unguarded stand our gates," Thomas Bailey Aldrich intoned, and through them, he warned, poured a "motley throng" of immigrants. If not checked, they would soon tear the clustered stars from Liberty's brow and trample them in the dust.

By passing an immigration act that sharply limited the number of admissible newcomers, particularly those of Southern and Eastern European origin, the lawmakers appeared to answer the cry of Aldrich and others like him. They shut the gate on further "unassimilable" additions to the American "melting pot." Yet at the very time of this action another wave of immigration into the great cities was gathering momentum. No restrictive laws could bar it, for it was made up of freeborn American citizens. They were black men and women, moving from a poverty-stricken South to the urban frontier.

That was the first paradox. And there was a second. The children of the "motley throng," who presumably could not be Americanized, became, in the forty years after the gates were slammed shut, largely absorbed into the major currents of American life. But, for complex reasons, the children of the "immigrant within," the northward-moving black, still remained unmelted.

To understand these ironies is to learn much about the meaning of success and its connection with race and nationality in the United States.

The reaction against unlimited immigration arose in part from the sheer volume of the influx after 1900. Where some fourteen million newcomers had arrived in the forty years between 1860 and 1900, thirteen million more poured in during the fifteen years that followed. Such a torrent of immigrants was bound to disturb even a relatively tolerant society, with plenty of land and jobs for all. Americans of the pre-World War I era watched the frontier's free land disappear and wondered anxiously if the bull market for labor might not, in due course, dry up as well. Nor were they quite as tolerant as their grandfathers had been. Doubts about the economics of immigration were supplemented by unhappiness with its changing sources after 1900. Post-1900 immigrants were no longer mainly from Germany, England, Ireland, or Scandinavia. They came instead from Italy and from the undigested religious and national minorities within the sprawling Hohenzollern, Ottoman, Hapsburg, and Ro-

manov empires. They were Jews, Catholics, and followers of Eastern
Orthodox rites.

The palpable ''differentness'' of the newcomers disturbed a
basically Protestant population of Northern European origin. This
disturbance resulted in a series of charges against them. They undermined American standards of living by working for a pittance. They
were milking the United States of dollars to send home but returning
nothing to their communities. They voted docilely at the summons of
the ward leaders for a dollar or two a head. They were radical agi-
tators. They crammed the jails and charity hospitals. They helplessly,
hopelessly, lacked the Anglo-Saxon genius for self-improvement and
self-rule.

It was under the sway of such arguments that Congress passed
not one, but a series of restrictive acts, beginning in 1917 and climax-
ing in 1924. But hardly was the ink dry on the lawbooks before the
children of the fearfully regarded ''new'' immigrants began to make
the grade in America, despite all the gloomy predictions. Except in
the Depression era they found plenty of jobs. In the needle trades,
in construction gangs, in steel mills and railroads, the Italians, Poles,
Bohemians, Hungarians, Greeks, and other ''ethnics'' furnished
muscle for growing industries. Others set up grocery stores, bars,
barbershops, drugstores, laundries, or restaurants to serve the urban
neighborhoods into which they moved. Still others made their way to
farms, which provided food for the multiplying mouths of urban
regions.

Economic success fuelled physical mobility. There were still unsettled areas around the cities that beckoned to those who disliked
the crowded streets of the Promised Land. Around New York an
Italian family could easily find, in Queens or Staten Island, a reasonably priced house with land enough for gardening. Or a Jewish store-
keeper could escape the Lower East Side, if he had a good year or
two, and find ocean breezes in Brooklyn.

Jobs and housing were two rungs of the ladder that led up from
steerage. Then there were the schools. Urban classrooms were crowded,
but not to the breaking point. In them, thousands of immigrant
children learned the rules of civic behavior by which all Americans
supposedly lived. More significantly, they acquired the skills that
spelled job advancement. High-school training in basic English and
mathematics equipped young new Americans for sales and secretarial
work or minor civil-service posts. It was more than adequate for a
skilled or semiskilled worker—a painter, plumber, or electrician. And
with a little post-high-school training, say two years of night college,
doors were opened to nursing, pharmacy, accounting, and even law
and medicine.

Finally, the traditionally hospitable political machine embraced
the immigrants and their children, especially as the latter reached
voting age. At first given only minor slots on the tickets, Italians,

Recently there has been a renewed interest in the paintings of the black artist Jacob Lawrence. In the late 1930's he painted a series of sixty panels as a record of the black exodus from the South. Shown here are two powerful visual statements of some of the reasons for the mass migration: (above) a lynching and (below) the white planter who often gave short weight or otherwise managed to cheat his sharecropping tenants.

Poles, and Jews gradually turned up as mayors, governors, senators, and Cabinet members. . . .

Meanwhile, what of the blacks? As European immigrants moved upward, the wave of Negro arrivals from the South flowed into the jobs and neighborhoods, at the bottom levels of desirability, that had just been vacated. From the start, as always, the blacks marched a hard road to a different drum. The journey of black families to a Promised Land under the North Star was, in one sense, part of a universal movement. They were rural people, and everywhere in developing nations rural people pricked up their ears at the sound of the factory whistle. And the nearly nine million American Negroes who lived in the South in 1910 (and made up 90 per cent of the nation's total black population) were predominantly a peasantry, living on farms, confronting permanent tenantry, poverty, ignorance, and disease. A government commission studying farm labor crisply summarized their plight that year: "There is absolutely nothing before them on the farm . . . no prospect . . . but to continue until they die." From this desperation they began to flee, in a movement that still continues in the 1970's. By 1970 about half of black America lived outside what might well be called their "old country."

They came to the cities by train in the early days, pouring onto the platforms with their bundles and their boxes, looking around, filling their eyes with the sights of Mecca. They came in response to letters and messages from relatives—or sometimes in response to nothing more than ads clipped from the Pittsburgh *Courier*, the *Amsterdam News*, the Baltimore *Afro-American*, or the Chicago *Defender* that said things like "3000 laborers to work on railroad. Factory hires all race help. More positions open than men for them." It was very encouraging. True, the unions would not easily accept black men, so the factory jobs turned out many times to be the hardest, the dirtiest, the ones offering the smallest promise of advancement. Or else they were jobs for strikebreakers, which was a dangerous way to earn a living. Even a scab's work was not always available, so black men (and women) had to do the traditional chores of their people in America: cooking, cleaning, fetching, and grooming for white men.

Still, it was the North. Schools were better than those open to Negroes in the South. The coarser humiliations of legalized segregation were somewhat muted. Voting was possible, and there might be a future for the young. There was an air of promise. Many black men in the city, members of Booker T. Washington's National Negro Business League, were making money as owners of their own barbershops, funeral parlors, and livery stables. Washington's well-known antagonist, W. E. B. DuBois, was talking about a "talented tenth" of the Negro race, which would save its future. In 1909 DuBois and other Negro leaders had helped to found the National Association for the Advancement of Colored People, then a "radical" force fighting courtroom battles for black rights. At their side were sympathetic and brilliant whites like Mary White Ovington, Joel Spingarn, Oswald Garrison Villard, and Moorefield Storey. In 1910 the National Urban League was founded to set about opening job opportunities for blacks. A new day did seem on the way.

There were drawbacks, of course. Living quarters were scarce. Northern whites would seldom accept black neighbors except perhaps along the alleys behind their houses; so old Negro districts, cramped for expansion, grew desperately crowded. The poet Langston Hughes, born in 1902, lived with his family in Cleveland in 1916 and remembered that they always seemed to inhabit attics or basements and to pay a lot for them. When white people did finally rent to Negroes, they would cut up their houses into five or six apartments and charge goldrush prices for each—and for garages and sheds, too.

But a northern city offered a little acceptance to Negroes when they were still definitely a minority. Hughes went to Central High School. Once it had taught the children of proper Clevelanders; by 1916 it was full of the children of the foreign-born, divided mainly between mutually suspicious Jews and Catholics. When elections were held for class officers, Hughes often won as the "compromise candidate," having apparently the advantage of being considered neither Jew nor Gentile. On a summer vacation he visited Chicago, which was also exciting. South State Street was "in its glory" in 1918, "a teeming Negro street with crowded theaters, restaurants, and cabarets. And excitement from noon to noon. Midnight was like day. The street was full of workers and gamblers, prostitutes and pimps, church folks and sinners. The tenements on either side were very congested. For neither love nor money could you find a decent place to live."

Even more attractive than Chicago for many a bright young Negro was a place that had once been a quiet Manhattan suburb, "the rural retreat of the aristocratic New Yorker"—a place called Harlem. After 1900, Negro real-estate operators began to buy buildings there, hoping to open the ownership of tidy homes to worthy blacks. They undoubtedly had profits in mind, but they also hoped to avoid the creation in New York of a "Niggertown," a "Buzzard's Alley," a "Bronzeville," as Negro slums were already called in other cities. And though New York's Negro population began to increase markedly after 1910, they seemed for a while to be succeeding. White residents, unsurprisingly, fled before the migrants, who were described by one newspaper as "black hordes . . . eating through the very heart of Harlem." But they left behind a Harlem that suddenly became a magnet for black artists and intellectuals, who made it their cultural capital.

While young whites revelled in Mencken, Hemingway, Eliot, Pound, Stravinsky, cubism, and Dada, black poets and writers like James Weldon Johnson and Claude McKay and Countee Cullen, black scholars like Carter G. Woodson, Alain Locke, and E. Franklin Frazier, and black musicians like Bessie Smith and Duke Ellington

Harlem in 1927.

sang their various lyrics of emancipation. Not all of them lived in Harlem, but for most it was at least their spiritual home. Langston Hughes spoke for a whole black generation when he described how it was to come up from the subway under Harlem after a long absence. ''I stood there, dropped my bags, took a deep breath and felt happy again.''

And yet there was another side to Harlem in the 1920's. It might float the mirage of a ''new Negro'' before the eyes of intellectuals, but they quickly perceived that New York was a place where good jobs for blacks were scarce and pay was skimpy. And when, between 1920 and 1930, the city's black population rose by another 115 per cent, good will and hope collapsed. Black and white slumlords found that milking decayed buildings for a few years was more profitable than long-time investments in repairs, and so black Harlemites endured falling plaster, exposed wiring, malfunctioning plumbing and heating systems, and rats and roaches. Disease flourished in Harlem; Negro death rates climbed.

From this squalor Negroes sought everywhere for escape. A few turned to political radicalism; more to red-hot religion—Christianity melted in the crucible of memory and pain. Sometimes they pursued the anodyne of hope by gambling on a ''hit'' in the numbers game.

Sometimes they clutched the transient solace of liquor or drugs. Each night the squeals and swoops of jazz mingled with the exhortations of preachers in storefront churches, while the pushers and whores and gamblers—black themselves—separated other blacks from what cash the grocer and landlord had left them.

And, slowly, many of the children whose parents had moved north to give them a second chance died spiritually. Small dark wraiths wandered the streets with keys on strings around their necks, while fathers who had given up the fight drifted, somewhere, and mothers scrubbed kitchens in white people's homes. Those black youngsters who made it to school were bowed by psychological burdens that few white teachers understood. Not only were they recent "immigrants," but they also suffered from the peculiar inadequacy of their southern background.

Despite the glamour of the "Harlem Renaissance," the nation's best-known black community had become by 1930 what it would remain for forty years at least—a place of enmity between policeman and community, where many local businessmen were outsiders and enemies. It was a pit of dilapidation and of fury often turned inward by blacks to become self-destruction, a center of narcotics traffic and crime. . . .

William V. Shannon

THE AGE OF THE BOSSES

The rapid industrialization of the United States after the Civil War, which produced great tycoons like Andrew Carnegie and encouraged millions of work-hungry Europeans to migrate, changed the shape of society in a variety of ways. One of the most obvious and important of these was industrialization's effect on where and how people lived. Huge industrial concerns brought together masses of workers in one place; commercial and service enterprises sprang up alongside the factories; in short, great cities rapidly developed and America was on its way to becoming an urban nation.

The advantages of urbanization were great—new wealth, better educational opportunities, a wide range of amusements; soon a more refined and complex culture emerged. But great problems also appeared—crowded, unhealthy living conditions, crime and vice, and countless others. Not the least of these was the problem of how to govern these gigantic agglomerations. *More* government was essential to run a city, yet the nation had lived for the better part of a century by the motto: "that government is best which governs least." New *kinds* of government were necessary—building and sanitary codes, social services, a system of representation suited to a mass but atomized society—for which no precedents existed.

It was this situation, as William V. Shannon explains below, that produced the big-city political machines and the bosses who ran them. Shannon shows that the bosses served a function; they filled a gap in the political system created by the changes resulting from swift industrialization and urban growth. Eventually better machinery than the "machine" was devised to perform that function, although the proper government of cities still eludes us today. As an editor of the *New York Times,* Mr. Shannon brings to this subject a thorough knowledge of modern urban politics and, as the author of *The American Irish,* an equally solid understanding of the old boss system.

The big cities and the political bosses grew up together in America. Bossism, with all its color and corruption and human drama, was a natural, perhaps even a necessary accompaniment to the rapid development of cities. The new urban communities did not grow slowly and according to plan; on the contrary, huge conglomerations of people from all over the world and from widely varying backgrounds came together suddenly, and in an unplanned, unorganized fashion fumbled their way toward communal relationships and a common identity. The political bosses emerged to cope with this chaotic change and growth. Acting out of greed, a ruthless will for mastery, and an imperfect understanding of what they were about, the bosses imposed upon these conglomerations called cities a certain feudal order and direction.

By 1890 virtually every sizable city had a political boss or was in the process of developing one. By 1950, sixty years later, almost every urban political machine was in an advanced state of obsolescence and its boss in trouble. The reason is not hard to find. Some of the cities kept growing and all of them kept changing, but the bosses, natural products of a specific era, could not grow or change beyond a certain point. The cities became essentially different, and as they did, the old-style organizations, like all organisms which cannot adapt, began to die. The dates vary from city to city. The system began earlier and died sooner in New York. Here or there, an old-timer made one last comeback. In Chicago, the organization and its boss still survive. But exceptions aside, the late nineteenth century saw the beginning, and the middle twentieth, the end, of the Age of the Bosses. What follows is a brief history of how it began, flourished, and passed away.

Soft-spoken Irish farmers from County Mayo and bearded Jews from Poland, country boys from Ohio and sturdy peasants from Calabria, gangling Swedes from near the Arctic Circle and Chinese from Canton, laconic Yankees from Vermont villages and Negro freedmen putting distance between themselves and the old plantation—all these and many other varieties of human beings from every national and religious and cultural tradition poured into America's cities in the decades after the Civil War.

Rome and Alexandria in the ancient world had probably been as polyglot, but in modern times the diversity of American cities was unique. Everywhere in the Western world, cities were growing rapidly in the late nineteenth century; but the Germans from the countryside who migrated to Hamburg and Berlin, the English who moved to Birmingham and London, and the French who flocked to Paris stayed among fellow nationals. They might be mocked as country bumpkins and their clothes might be unfashionable, but everyone they met spoke the same language as themselves, observed the same religious and secular holidays, ate the same kind of food, voted—if they had the franchise at all—in the same elections, and shared the same sentiments and expectations. To move from farm or village to a big

Two of the most memorable and politically long-lived of the bosses were Jersey City's Frank Hague (left) and Boston's James M. Curley (right).

European city was an adventure, but one still remained within the reassuring circle of the known and the familiar.

In American cities, however, the newcomers had nothing in common with one another except their poverty and their hopes. They were truly "the up-rooted." The foreign-born, unless they came from the British Isles, could not speak the language of their new homeland. The food, the customs, the holidays, the politics, were alien. Native Americans migrating to the cities from the countryside experienced their own kind of cultural shock: they found themselves competing not with other Americans but with recently arrived foreigners, so that despite their native birth they, too, felt displaced, strangers in their own country.

It was natural for members of each group to come together to try to find human warmth and protection in Little Italy or Cork Hill or Chinatown or Harlem. These feelings of clannish solidarity were one basis of strength for the political bosses. A man will more readily give his vote to a candidate because he is a neighbor from the old country or has some easily identifiable relationship, if only a similar name or the same religion, than because of agreement on some impersonal issue. Voters can take vicarious satisfaction from his success: "One of our boys' is making good."

With so many different races and nationalities living together, however, mutual antagonisms were present, and the opportunity for hostility to flare into open violence was never far away. Ambitious, unscrupulous politicians could have exploited these antagonisms for their own political advantage, but the bosses and the political organizations which they developed did not function that way. If a man could vote and would "vote right," he was accepted, and that was the end of the matter. What lasting profit was there in attacking his religion or deriding his background?

Tammany early set the pattern of cultivating every bloc and faction and making an appeal as broad-based as possible. Of one precinct captain on the Lower East Side it was said: "He eats corned beef and kosher meat with equal nonchalance, and it's all the same to him whether he takes off his hat in the church or pulls it down over his ears in the synagogue."

Bosses elsewhere instinctively followed the same practice. George B. Cox, the turn-of-the-century Republican boss of Cincinnati, pasted together a coalition of Germans, Negroes, and old families like the Tafts and the Longworths. James M. Curley, who was mayor of Boston on and off for thirty-six years and was its closest approximation to a political boss, ran as well in the Lithuanian neighborhood of South Boston and the Italian section of East Boston as he did in the working-class Irish wards. In his last term in City Hall, he conferred minor patronage on the growing Negro community and joined the N.A.A.C.P.

The bosses organized neighborhoods, smoothed out antagonisms, arranged ethnically balanced tickets, and distributed patronage in accordance with voting strength as part of their effort to win and hold power. They blurred divisive issues and buried racial and religious hostility with blarney and buncombe. They were not aware that they were actually performing a mediating, pacifying function. They did not realize that by trying to please as many people as possible they were helping to hold raw new cities together, providing for inexperienced citizens a common meeting ground in politics and an experience in working together that would not have been available if the cities had been governed by apolitical bureaucracies. Bossism was usually corrupt and was decidedly inefficient, but in the 1960's, when antipoverty planners try to stimulate "community action organizations" to break through the apathy and disorganization of the slums, we can appreciate that the old-style machines had their usefulness.

When William Marcy Tweed, the first and most famous of the big-city bosses, died in jail in 1878, several hundred workingmen showed up for his funeral. The *Nation* wrote the following week:

> Let us remember that he fell without loss of reputation among the bulk of his supporters. The bulk of the poorer voters of this city today revere his memory, and look on him as the victim of rich men's malice; as, in short, a friend of the needy who applied the public funds, with as little waste as was possible under the circumstances, to the purposes to which they ought to be applied—and that is to the making of work for the working man. The odium heaped on him in the pulpits last Sunday does not exist in the lower stratum of New York society.

This split in attitude toward political bosses between the impoverished many and the prosperous middle classes lingers today and still colors historical writing. To respectable people, the boss was an exotic, even grotesque figure. They found it hard to understand why anyone would vote for him or what the sources of his popularity were. To the urban poor, those sources were self-evident. The boss ran a kind of ramshackle welfare state. He helped the unemployed find jobs, interceded in court for boys in trouble, wrote letters home to the old country for the illiterate; he provided free coal and baskets of food to tide a widow over an emergency, and organized parades, excursions to the beach, and other forms of free entertainment. Some bosses, such as Frank Hague in Jersey City and Curley in Boston, were energetic patrons of their respective city hospitals, spending public funds lavishly on new construction, providing maternity and children's clinics, and arranging medical care for the indigent. In an era when social security, Blue Cross, unemployment compensation, and other public and private arrangements to cushion life's shocks did not exist, these benefactions from a political boss were important.

In every city, the boss had his base in the poorer, older, shabbier section of town. Historians have dubbed this section the "walking city" because it developed in the eighteenth and early nineteenth centuries, when houses and businesses were jumbled together, usually near the waterfront, and businessmen and laborers alike had to live within walking distance of their work. As transportation improved, people were able to live farther and farther from their place of work. Population dispersed in rough concentric circles: the financially most successful lived in the outer ring, where land was plentiful and the air was clean; the middle classes lived in intermediate neighborhoods;

and the poorest and the latest arrivals from Europe crowded into the now-rundown neighborhoods in the center, where rents were lowest. Politics in most cities reflected a struggle between the old, boss-run wards downtown and the more prosperous neighborhoods farther out, which did not need a boss's services and which championed reform. The more skilled workingmen and the white-collar workers who lived in the intermediate neighborhoods generally held the balance of power between the machine and the reformers. A skillful boss could hold enough of these swing voters on the basis of ethnic loyalty or shared support of a particular issue. At times, he might work out alliances with business leaders who found that an understanding with a boss was literally more businesslike than dependence upon the vagaries of reform.

But always it was the poorest and most insecure who provided the boss with the base of his political power. Their only strength, as Professor Richard C. Wade of the University of Chicago has observed, was in their numbers.

> These numbers were in most cases a curse; housing never caught up with demand, the job market was always flooded, the bread-winner had too many mouths to feed. Yet in politics such a liability could be turned into an asset. If the residents could be mobilized, their combined strength would be able to do what none could do alone. Soon the "boss" and the "machine" arose to organize this potential. The boss system was simply the political expression of inner city life.

At a time when many newcomers to the city were seeking unskilled work, and when many families had a precarious economic footing, the ability to dispense jobs was crucial to the bosses. First, there were jobs to be filled on the city payroll. Just as vital, and far more numerous, were jobs on municipal construction projects. When the machine controlled a city, public funds were always being spent for more schools, hospitals, libraries, courthouses, and orphanages. The growing cities had to have more sewer lines, gas lines, and waterworks, more paved streets and trolley tracks. Even if these utilities were privately owned, the managers needed the goodwill of city hall and were responsive to suggestions about whom to hire.

The payrolls of these public works projects were often padded, but to those seeking a job, it was better to be on a padded payroll than on no payroll. By contrast, the municipal reformers usually cut back on public spending, stopped projects to investigate for graft, and pruned payrolls. Middle- and upper-income taxpayers welcomed these reforms, but they were distinctly unpopular in working-class wards.

Another issue that strengthened the bosses was the regulation of the sale of liquor. Most women in the nineteenth century did not drink, and with their backing, the movement to ban entirely the manufacture and sale of liquor grew steadily stronger. It had its greatest support among Protestants with a rural or small-town background.

To them the cities, with their saloons, dance halls, cheap theatres, and red-light districts, were becoming latter-day versions of Sodom and Gomorrah.

Many of the European immigrants in the cities, however, had entirely different values. Quite respectable Germans took their wives to beer gardens on Sundays. In the eyes of the Irish, keeping a "public house" was an honorable occupation. Some Irish women drank beer and saw no harm in going to the saloon or sending an older child for a bucketful—"rushing the growler," they called it. Poles, Czechs, Italians, and others also failed to share the rage of the Prohibitionists against saloons. Unable to entertain in their cramped tenements, they liked to congregate in neighborhood bars.

The machine also appealed successfully on the liquor issue to many middle-class ethnic voters who had no need of the machine's economic assistance. Thus, in New York in 1897, Tammany scored a sweeping victory over an incumbent reform administration that had tried to enforce a state law permitting only hotels to sell liquor on Sundays. As one of the city's three police commissioners, Theodore Roosevelt became famous prowling the tougher neighborhoods on the hunt for saloon violations, but on the vaudeville stage the singers were giving forth with the hit song, "I Want What I Want When I Want It!" As a character in Alfred Henry Lewis' novel *The Boss* explained it, the reformers had made a serious mistake: "They got between the people and its beer!"

In 1902, Lincoln Steffens, the muckraker who made a name for himself writing about political bossism, visited St. Louis to interview Joseph W. Folk, a crusading district attorney. "It is good businessmen that are corrupting our bad politicians," Folk told him. "It is good business that causes bad government in St. Louis." Thirty-five years later, Boss Tom Pendergast was running the entire state of Missouri on that same reciprocal relationship.

Although many factory owners could be indifferent to politics, other businessmen were dependent upon the goodwill and the efficiency of the municipal government. The railroads that wanted to build their freight terminals and extend their lines into the cities, the contractors who erected the office buildings, the banks that held mortgages on the land and loaned money for the construction, the utility and transit companies, and the department stores were all in need of licenses, franchises, rights of way, or favorable rulings from city inspectors and agencies. These were the businesses that made the big pay-offs to political bosses in cash, blocks of stock, or tips on land about to be developed.

In another sense, profound, impersonal, and not corrupt, the business community needed the boss. Because the Industrial Revolution hit this country when it was still thinly populated and most of its cities were overgrown towns, American cities expanded with astonishing speed. For example, in the single decade from 1880 to 1890, Chicago's population more than doubled, from a half million to over a million. Minneapolis and St. Paul tripled in size. New York City increased from a million to a million and a half; Detroit, Milwaukee, Columbus, and Cleveland grew by sixty to eighty per cent.

Municipal governments, however, were unprepared for this astonishing growth. Planning and budgeting were unknown arts. City charters had restrictive provisions envisaged for much smaller, simpler communities. The mayor and the important commissioners were usually amateurs serving a term or two as a civic duty. Authority was dispersed among numerous boards and special agencies. A typical city would have a board of police commissioners, a board of health, a board of tax assessors, a water board, and many others. The ostensible governing body was a city council or board of aldermen which might have thirty, fifty, or even a hundred members. Under these circumstances, it was difficult to get a prompt decision, harder still to coordinate decisions taken by different bodies acting on different premises, and easy for delays and anomalies to develop.

In theory, the cities could have met their need for increased services by municipal socialism, but the conventional wisdom condemned that as too radical, although here and there a city did experiment with publicly owned utilities. In theory also, the cities could have financed public buildings and huge projects such as water and sewer systems by frankly raising taxes or floating bonds. But both taxes and debt were no more popular then than they are now. Moreover, the laissez-faire doctrine which holds that "that government is best which governs least" was enshrined orthodoxy in America from the 1870's down to the 1930's.

As men clung to such orthodox philosophies, the structures of government became obsolete; they strained to meet unexpected demands as a swelling number of citizens in every class clamored for more services. In this climate the bosses emerged. They had no scruples about taking shortcuts through old procedures or manipulating independent boards and agencies in ways that the original city fathers had never intended. They had no inhibiting commitment to any theory of limited government. They were willing to spend, tax, and build— and to take the opprobrium along with the graft. Sometimes, like Hague in Jersey City, Curley in Boston, and Big Bill Thompson in Chicago, they got themselves elected mayor and openly assumed responsibility. More often, like Pendergast in Kansas City, Cox in Cincinnati, the leaders of Tammany, and the successive Republican bosses of Philadelphia, they held minor offices or none, stayed out of the limelight, and ran city government through their iron control of the party organization. In ruling Memphis for forty years, Ed Crump followed one pattern and then the other. Impeached on a technicality after being elected three times as mayor, Crump retreated to the back rooms and became even more powerful as the city's political boss.

What manner of men became political bosses? They were men of little education and no social background, often of immigrant parentage. A college-educated boss like Edward Flynn of The Bronx was a rarity. Bosses often began as saloonkeepers, because the saloon was a natural meeting place in poorer neighborhoods in the days before

Prohibition. They were physically strong and no strangers to violence. Seventy-five years ago, most men made their living with brawn rather than brain, and a man who expected to be a leader of men had to be tough as well as shrewd. Open violence used to be common at polling places on Election Day, and gangs of repeaters roamed from one precinct to another. Although the typical boss made his way up through that roughneck system, the logic of his career led him to suppress violence. Bloody heads make bad publicity, and it is hard for any political organization to maintain a monopoly on violence. Bosses grew to prefer quieter, more lawful, less dangerous methods of control. Ballot-box stuffing and overt intimidation never disappeared entirely, but gradually they receded to weapons of last resort.

Political bosses varied in their idiosyncrasies and styles. A few, like Curley, became polished orators; others, like the legendary Charles Murphy of Tammany Hall, never made speeches. They were temperate, businesslike types; among them a drunk was as rare as a Phi Beta Kappa. If they had a generic failing it was for horses and gambling. Essentially they were hardheaded men of executive temper and genuine organizing talents; many, in other circumstances and with more education, might have become successful businessmen.

They have disappeared now, most of them. Education has produced a more sophisticated electorate; it has also encouraged potential bosses to turn away from politics toward more secure, prestigious, and profitable careers. A young man who had the energy, persistence, and skill in 1899 to become a successful political boss would in 1969 go to college and end up in an executive suite.

The urban population has also changed. The great flood of bewildered foreigners has dwindled to a trickle. In place of the European immigrants of the past, today's cities receive an influx of Negroes from the rural South, Puerto Ricans, Mexicans, and the white poor from Appalachia. As they overcome the language barrier and widen their experience, the Puerto Ricans are making themselves felt in urban politics. New York City, where they are most heavily concentrated, may have a Puerto Rican mayor in the not too distant future.

But the other groups are too isolated from the rest of the community to put together a winning political coalition of have-nots. The Mexicans and the ex-hillbillies from Appalachia are isolated by their unique cultural backgrounds, the Negroes by the giant fact of their race. Inasmuch as they make up a quarter to a third of the population in many cities, are a cohesive group, and still have a high proportion of poor who have to look to government for direct help, the Negroes might have produced several bosses and functioning political machines had they been of white European ancestry. But until Negroes attain a clear numerical majority, they find it difficult to take political power in any city because various white factions are reluctant to coalesce with them.

Regardless of the race or background of the voters, however, there are factors which work against the old-style machines. Civil service

In this contemporary cartoon Michael Ramus has pictured Mayor Daley of Chicago as "The Last Leaf" on the blasted tree of old-style urban bossism.

regulations make it harder to create a job or pad a payroll. Federal income taxes and federal accounting requirements make it more difficult to hide the rewards of graft. Television, public relations, and polling have created a whole new set of political techniques and undermined the personal ties and neighborhood loyalties on which the old organizations depended.

The new political style has brought an increase in municipal government efficiency and probably some decline in political corruption and misrule. But the politics of the television age puts a premium on hypocrisy. Candor has gone out the window with the spoils system. There is still a lot of self-seeking in politics and always will be. But gone are the days of Tammany's Boss Richard Croker, who when asked by an investigating committee if he was "working for his own pocket," shot back: "All the time—same as you." Today's politicians are so busy tending their images that they have become incapable of even a mildly derogatory remark such as Jim Curley's: "The term 'codfish aristocracy' is a reflection on the fish."

Curley entitled his memoirs *I'd Do It Again*. But the rough-and-tumble days when two-fisted, rough-tongued politicians came roaring out of the slums to take charge of America's young cities are not to come again.

Robert L. Beisner

TWO EARLY CRITICS
OF INDUSTRIAL AMERICA

Critics, as creators have always been quick to point out, are
seldom truly objective in their judgments; they tend to impose
their own prejudices on the work they presume to evaluate. This
has been as true of social critics as of persons who review books
or theatrical productions. Robert L. Beisner's essay on E. L.
Godkin and Charles Eliot Norton, two sharp critics of post-Civil
War American society, proves beyond question that these men
were fundamentally subjective in their attitudes. They disliked the
changes that industrialization was bringing to America and,
viewing their world with jaundiced eyes, exaggerated and
distorted the evils they complained about. Furthermore, they
sought to reverse irreversible trends, to turn back the clock of
history. Since we know—actually they knew it too—that this was
impossible, we tend either to scorn or laugh at critics like
Godkin and Norton, to dismiss them as crabbed, selfish
reactionaries. Yet their criticism was not necessarily inaccurate
because it was self-serving. And, as Beisner shows, it had a
constructive as well as a destructive side; dislike of what was
happening to American society did not destroy their commitment
to that society.

Professor Beisner, who is professor of history at The American
University, is a specialist in late nineteenth-century social and
intellectual history. His book *Twelve Against Empire: The
Anti-Imperialists, 1898–1900* won the Allan Nevins prize of the
Society of American Historians.

It used to be said in Cambridge, Massachusetts, that all of the dogs in the town wailed mournfully whenever E. L. Godkin and Charles Eliot Norton got together to swap their pessimistic views on the state of the nation. In the summer of 1897 Norton wrote Godkin that he had recently been forced to put his paper aside one evening "because with each note or article the gloom deepened till it grew darker than it used to be even in my study when after an evening of talk you declared that it was enough to make Rome howl." For more than thirty years Godkin and Norton sustained and fed each other's pessimism, sorely disappointed as they both were with developments in post-Civil War America. They believed that American morality had declined precipitately since the early days of the republic. They lamented the lack of good men in politics and the domination of the public service by men of coarse and corrupt nature. They watched with jaundiced eyes as millions of immigrants poured into their country. They took in the "General Grant" architecture, read the new literature, deplored the new wealth, saw successful businessmen gain entrance to their private clubs, faced America's plunge into imperialism and the glaring headlines of the yellow press—and declared it an age of vulgarity and a nation of "chromo-civilization."

There have always been such men, convinced in the core of their being that what had been in their youth a world of gold had lately turned to dross. In the era of industrialism and mass democracy these Jeremiahs have more often than not come from the ranks of the old landed, learned, or professional elites most in danger of being superseded or ignored by a democratic and acquisitive society. The quicker the rate of change and the fresher the memory of better times, the greater the likelihood that these gentle Brahmins would deplore the life around them. The rapidly changing America which emerged from the Civil War provoked just such an outcry of genteel despair—a dismay eloquently expressed by E. L. Godkin and Charles Eliot Norton. Both men placed the blame for their unhappiness on precisely those features of American civilization which were most highly valued by the majority of their countrymen: material prosperity and democratic government.

Edwin Lawrence Godkin was born in Moyne, County Wicklow, Ireland, on October 2, 1831. His father was a Presbyterian clergyman who became a political journalist after being ejected from the pulpit for his advocacy of home rule for Ireland. Young Edwin, too, went into journalism after making an indifferent record at Queen's College, Belfast. Already the youthful author of a history of Hungary, Godkin left for the Crimea in 1853 as a war correspondent for the London *Daily News*. Upon his return two years later he resolved to emigrate to the United States. In November of 1856 he reached America, where for nearly a decade (except for a short period spent in Ireland and Europe) he occupied himself with law studies and writing letters on American affairs for the London *Daily News*. His early friends included a number of important eastern Republicans, and in 1865, when they decided to found a journal that would reflect their political and

The critics: Editor Edwin Lawrence Godkin (left) and Professor Charles Eliot Norton (right).

economic views, they established the weekly *Nation* and selected to edit it the thirty-four-year-old Godkin. One of the prime backers of the enterprise and a close friend of the new editor was Charles Eliot Norton.

Godkin's sharp and authoritative editorials quickly made the *Nation* a habit for thousands of readers (one would be hard put to recognize it in the *Nation* that is published today); later on, his work performed the same service for the daily New York *Evening Post* (equally unrecognizable in the modern *Post*), whose editor he became in 1881 while retaining his position on the *Nation*. The critical tone of the *Nation* made it seem to some a "weekly judgment day," and neither it nor the *Evening Post* attracted a large circulation. Both, however, exercised wide influence. College students adopted Godkin's opinions for their own the way later generations of students would parrot H. L. Mencken and Walter Lippmann. And other newspapermen paid close attention to Godkin's editorials. Once when New York's Democratic Governor David B. Hill was under attack by the *Evening Post* he remarked: "I don't care anything about the handful of Mugwumps who read it in New York [City]. The trouble with the damned sheet is that every editor in New York State reads it."

Yet Godkin had formidable critics. The most vehement among them was Theodore Roosevelt, who called Godkin almost every disagreeable epithet that came to his fertile mind. To him Godkin was an unpatriotic man, "a malignant and dishonest liar" who suffered from "a species of moral myopia, complicated with intellectual strabismus." Lincoln Steffens, who worked for a short time with Godkin, thought that his editorials were "clever, forceful, [and] ripping" but also "personal and not very thoughtful." The Boston banker and philanthropist Henry L. Higginson believed that as Godkin's career unfolded, his words became "so twisted and stained by great conceit, arrogance, evil temper, that they lost their fairness, their perspicacity, their virtue and therefore their value."

Charles Eliot Norton had those qualities of gentleness and contemplativeness that his friend Godkin lacked. He too was the son of a clergyman, Andrews Norton, a prominent Unitarian divine. Born in Cambridge, Massachusetts, in 1827, Norton spent his youth in the scholarly surroundings of a home frequented by such distinguished visitors as Francis Parkman, George Bancroft, George Ticknor, and Henry Wadsworth Longfellow. While still a youth he developed a great passion for rare books and art objects, thus demonstrating an early and serious interest in the field to which he was unable to devote his full attention until he was nearly fifty. He made Phi Beta Kappa at Harvard, and after his graduation in 1846 spent a decade in business. The next twenty years were passed in studying, living in Europe, writing and editing books, supervising Union propaganda activities during the Civil War, and working both as editor and contributor for the cream of American journals—the *Atlantic Monthly, North American Review*, and the *Nation*. Finally, in 1875, he was appointed Harvard's first professor of fine arts, a post which he retained until he retired in 1897.

As a scholar, Norton was an acknowledged master of medieval studies and a respected translator of Dante. He wrote an important volume entitled *Historical Studies of Church-Building in the Middle Ages* as well as studies of Dante, Donne, Ruskin, Gray, Michelangelo, Holbein, and Turner. In addition, he edited the letters of James Russell Lowell, the Thomas Carlyle-Ralph Waldo Emerson correspondence, the Carlyle-Goethe correspondence, and the letters he had received from John Ruskin. As a teacher, Norton's aim was to advance aesthetic values and inculcate high standards of taste. Art was not to be studied merely for its own sake. Norton believed that man had reached his greatest moral and intellectual heights in ancient Greece and medieval Italy, and he thought that this superiority could be seen in the artistic achievements of those epochs. It was his habit in class to illustrate this relationship between art and morality with frequent deprecating references to the barrenness of American art and the moral and intellectual inferiority of American life.

The story is told that Norton once began a lecture on the idea of the "gentleman" by remarking airily: "None of you, probably, has ever seen a gentleman." It was inevitable that a teacher with such a rarefied taste for the antique would become the subject of parodies and the source of much campus amusement. One story has it, for instance, that an undergraduate emerged after three meetings of Norton's Fine Arts 3 course with his total notes reading:

          (1) Greece.

          (2) Bully for Greece.

          (3) There are no flies on Greece.

Norton's general aesthetic sensibilities and his displeasure with the design of many new buildings at Harvard were parodied in a tale to the effect that he had died and was about to enter heaven when he suddenly drew back, shaded his eyes and exclaimed: "Oh! Oh! Oh! So overdone! So garish! So Renaissance!" Despite the numerous campus jokes made at his expense, Norton's encouragement of the fine arts and his efforts to direct public attention to the advancing deterioration of America's landscape and cities made him an important figure in post-Civil War America—a friend of art museums, conservation projects, parks, and schools. In the opinion of Van Wyck Brooks, "no one aroused the country more to a sense of its general ugliness and a will to create a beautiful civilization."

In politics Godkin and Norton were mugwumps—independents who refused to commit themselves to the fortunes of any particular party. Both feared that American politics had rejected the country's "good men," and hoped for a breakup of the old party organizations. As early as 1859 Godkin had complained that the "nominating conventions toss men like Clay and Webster aside, and fish out from amongst the obscurities Pierces and Buchanans as likely to prove more pliable instruments in factious hands." The political machines, he charged, put up such bad men to run for office that good men were

A Harvard student drew this caricature of Professor of Fine Arts Norton in 1901.

no longer tempted to enter public affairs.

For Godkin and Norton the decline in political morality was but one aspect of a more serious decline in the quality of American life. Each felt that the United States had once enjoyed a Golden Age of reason, simplicity, and high morality. But the push toward an industrial way of life was transforming the social and physical landscape of their once-Arcadian America, and wherever they looked they now saw deterioration and decadence. Godkin deplored the ''moral anarchy'' of modern business methods and despised those who employed them. He fought the admission of businessmen to the Century Club of New York, complaining that most of them ''rarely open a book'' and ''know no more, read no more, and have no more to say than the bricklayer and the plumber.'' For his part, Norton was particularly concerned with the aesthetic changes and the unfortunate transformation in the tone of society. The country he had known had vanished under a wave of vulgarity. The ''barren'' art and literature of the late nineteenth century depressed him:

> Nowhere in the civilized world are the practical concerns of life more engrossing; nowhere are the conditions of life more prosaic; nowhere is the poetic spirit less evident, and the love of beauty less diffused. The concern for beauty, as the highest end of work, and as the noblest expression of life, hardly exists among us, and forms no part of our character as a nation.

Norton told a friend in 1873 that America had lost its original bright promise and was ''not a pleasing child.'' Only Harvard, Yale, the *Nation,* and the *North American Review* stood firm as ''solid

barriers against the invasion of modern barbarism & vulgarity.'' The
other landmarks and manners of an earlier and better day were dis-
appearing before his very eyes. Even Cambridge was slipping away;
Norton felt himself a stranger in his birthplace. The few houses that
remained from his childhood were occupied by ''new people.'' Norton
could find only ''half a dozen men or women'' who could converse
on those general subjects once familiar to all people of education—
''My fair neighbor asks, 'What are Pericles?' '' Thus Norton, condemned to live in an age of industrialization and specialization, sighed
under his burden of nostalgia. One of his students—young Josephine
Peabody, who heard him lecture at Radcliffe in 1895, wrote:

> Professor Norton lectured in Italian 4 this afternoon. The dear
> old man looks so mildy happy and benignant while he regrets
> everything in the age and the country—so contented, while he
> gently tells us it were better for us had we never been born in
> this degenerate and unlovely age.

What had brought America to its present condition? Godkin
found in the very heart of the American Experiment—in its commitment to political democracy and social equality—the cause of what
he deemed to be its failure. These noble ideals simply did not work in
practice. The triumph of popular rule had come to mean only that
politicians catered to the lowest level of understanding. The ideal of
equality, which in theory referred to an ''equality of burdens,'' had
in actuality degenerated into a contempt for the excellent and superior,
a ''disregard for special fitness.'' Could anything but disaster be
expected from the masses whom this egalitarian democracy had thrown
to the top? Godkin wrote in 1870:

> Their rush into the forum and into the temples and palaces and
> libraries is not an agreeable sight to witness, and it would be
> foolish to expect that under their ruthless touch many gifts and
> graces will not be obscured, many arts will not be lost, many a
> great ideal, at whose shrine the best men and women of three
> generations have found courage and inspiration, will not vanish
> from the earth . . .

Along with equality and democracy both Godkin and Norton
believed that the third agent of destruction was prosperity. Norton
had long maintained that there was a causal connection between
great wealth and the dissolution of national character. The decline of
Greece had been set off by the ''increase of private luxury [and]
selfishness'' and the rise of ''unrestrained individuality.'' Surely it
was vanity to believe that America could be spared the disastrous
effects of excessive material wealth. As early as 1853 Norton had
warned that the long and uninterrupted history of prosperity enjoyed
by the United States was beginning to take its toll in a declining
national character. After the Civil War the blight grew worse and
spread beyond the frontiers and across the ocean. Money-getting was
proving the ruin of literature and was blunting the intelligence of

the people; even in Europe materialism was leaving its imprint. A foolish optimism was in the air. From Florence in 1869 Norton wrote:

> Italy in losing tyrants, in becoming constitutional, in taking to trade, is doing what she can to spoil her charm. The railroad whistle just behind the church of Santa Maria Novella, or just beyond the Campo Santo at Pisa, sounds precisely as it sounds on the Back Bay or at the Fitchburg Station,—and it and the common school are Americanizing the land to a surprising degree. Happy country! Fortunate people! Before long they may hope for their Greeleys, their Beechers, and their Fisks.

Norton did not deny that democracy could "work," but as he said following the election of 1884, it appeared to work "ignobly, ignorantly, brutally." Or it could work as it had begun to in Europe, bringing about "the destruction of old shrines, the disregard of beauty, the decline in personal distinction, the falling off in manners." What was clear was that democracy did not work as Norton had hoped it would. In his view democracy was supposed to mean that everyone in society would be public-spirited. But it had turned out in practice to mean that everyone was involved in the selfish pursuit of private interests. Rather than heightening the individual's awareness of his civic responsibilities, universal suffrage had furnished "a distinct source of moral corruption." Rather than increasing the wisdom of all citizens, democracy had diminished the regard for intelligent counsel and produced a general "rejection of authority." The sense of license and the smug complacency that had been created by democracy and prosperity had made "extravagant self-confidence" and willful conduct the hallmarks of the American people. Writing in 1896, Norton declared: "It seems to me not unlikely that for a considerable time to come there will be an increase of lawlessness and of public folly."

Godkin was savage in his dislike for the many immigrants who were so rapidly being incorporated into the American political system. Their votes gave power to the corrupt urban bosses who exploited them. One could see on every hand, Godkin exclaimed, the "ignorant" foreign voter "eating away the political structure, like a white ant, with a group of natives standing over him and encouraging him." In 1891 he proposed that all immigrants be shut out unless they could read and write the English language. This would mean, he admitted, that all but a few immigrants would perforce come from the British Isles, "but why not, if the restriction be really undertaken in the interest of American civilization? We are under no obligation to see that all races and nations enjoy an equal chance of getting here." Godkin called it natural law "that the more intelligent and thoughtful of the race shall inherit the earth and have the best time, and that all others shall find life on the whole dull and unprofitable."

Godkin did not pretend to have answers to the problems of the age that he and Norton castigated. The structure of American life seemed too corrupt to save, too rotten to shore up with marginal improvements, and he eventually determined to return to England rather than witness its expected collapse. Norton had no answers either, but his pessimism was relieved by a limited belief in the worth of ameliorative action, and his distrust of acquisitiveness and democracy was mitigated by his interest in the unprecedented material and educational achievements of America's lower classes.

As an active participant in the social and political processes, Norton established a night school for the poor in 1846; he promoted better housing for the underprivileged; he was in the forefront of the campaign for female suffrage and education (with the hope that women would raise the ideals and tone of American society); and, in the interest of preserving at least the landscape of America, he fought hard and effectively to save both the Adirondacks and Niagara Falls from exploitation and desecration. In an effort to exert direct influence upon public opinion, Norton founded the Ashfield "academy dinners," held each summer from 1879 to 1903 in Ashfield, Massachusetts. On these occasions civil-service reform, tariff reduction, Negro education, and anti-imperialism, as well as many other mugwump interests, were discussed by William Dean Howells, George Washington Cable, William James, James Russell Lowell, Booker T. Washington, and many others, including Norton himself.

Norton was consoled and reassured by the knowledge that, in his country, the economic and educational level of the lower classes had been elevated to the highest point in history. When William Dean Howells inquired of him, "Well, after all, if you could change, would you rather have been an Englishman than an American?" Norton unhesitatingly replied: "No, if I could choose I would rather have been American."

But, at best, progress came at a maddeningly slow pace, and Norton succeeded only intermittently in maintaining his optimism. In 1871 he bitterly predicted that the creation of a really sound republic would take as long as the evolution from monkey to man. In 1884 he described himself as an "absolute" pessimist—a man who had learned not to hope for any good in the world and who thus lived a life free of expectations and complaints:

> Your out-and-out pessimist is cheerful, even though nature herself plays false, and uses loaded dice against him in the game. Darwinism has helped us a good deal. You expect less of men when you look at them not as a little lower than the angels, but as a little higher than the anthropoid apes.

By the mid-1890's E. L. Godkin and Charles Eliot Norton had lived for a third of a century believing that their country was in a steady decline, that its onetime promise had been largely submerged by a rising tide of corruption, immorality, tastelessness, and stupidity. Thus it was more than coincidental that, at this time, the thoughts of each man turned to the fall of Rome. In 1895 Godkin wrote Norton:

> You see I am not sanguine about the future of democracy. I think we shall have a long period of decline like that which

followed the fall of the Roman Empire, and then a recrudescence under some other form of society.

A year later Norton wrote an English friend:

It is hard to have the whole background of life grow darker as one grows old. I can understand the feeling of a Roman as he saw the Empire breaking down, and civilization dying out. It will take much longer than we once hoped, for the world to reorganize itself upon a democratic basis, and for a new and desirable social order to come into existence.

But—with the faith that never completely left him—he added: "If we set our hope far enough forward we need not lose it."

By 1895 Godkin and Norton had come to sound increasingly like men who were close to abandoning all hope for their country. From the *Nation* and from Harvard they watched the ailing American Experiment falter and fail. It was the Spanish-American War and the expansionism that accompanied it that administered the *coup de grâce*. Godkin and Norton were angry and saddened but not surprised, for they had expected all along that something of the sort would happen. The times had long been out of joint, and imperialism was but another blow—albeit the heaviest—against the America they had known. Only one question remained for them: was the blow fatal?

For thirty years Godkin had been an opponent of expansionism, hammering away against every annexation scheme that dared to raise its head. Three months before the outbreak of the Spanish-American War, when the Senate was considering the annexation of Hawaii, Godkin had summarized his objections to a policy of territorial annexation in a *Nation* editorial:

The sudden departure from our traditions; the absence from our system of any machinery for governing dependencies; the admission of alien, inferior, and mongrel races to our nationality; the opening of fresh fields to carpetbaggers, speculators, and corruptionists; the un-Americanism of governing a large body of people against their will, and by persons not responsible to them; the entrance on a policy of conquest and annexation while our own continent was still unreclaimed, our population unassimilated, and many of our most serious political problems still unsolved; and finally the danger of the endorsement of a gross fraud for the first time by a Christian nation.

At the close of the war in August, 1898, Godkin remained firmly opposed to all annexation schemes, and throughout the rest of that year and all of the next he repeatedly emphasized the difficulties the United States would face if it became an imperialist power. He believed that the establishment of a colonial administration would necessitate a drastic overhaul of the American government, "a complete change in our destiny, political, military, and naval." If the United States annexed the Philippines and had to defend them from the covetousness of other powers, it would be necessary to arm to the teeth with naval and military forces capable of being "instantly" mobilized and dispatched to any danger spot on the globe. And we would need a "permanent" colonial service:

> It will not do to vote money and build ships, simply, and drill armies and sailors. If we are going to annex and rule over countries the population of which differs from us in race, religion, language, in history and every variety of antecedent, and who will probably hate us and treat our rule as a "yoke," we shall have to get administrators ready, as well as guns and ships. We shall have to do what the other conquering and colonizing nations do, what England does, what Russia and Germany do.

In his anger Godkin railed at the expansionists for their betrayal of American principles. In the Philippines, he charged, McKinley, "drunk with glory and flattery," had substituted "keen effective slaughter for Spanish old-fashioned, clumsy slaughter." When eager missionaries began planning new translations of the Bible in the various tongues of the Filipinos, the *Nation* derisively commented that they should read: "Mow down the natives like grass and say unto them, the Syndicate has arrived." But there was no longer much heart in Godkin's protest, for he had concluded that the fight was virtually lost. In late 1898 and early 1899 he gave way to utter despair, publicly declaring that "the old American republic is in a bad way." In private letters he poured out his full sorrow:

> I am, heart and soul, an American of the *vielle roche*. American ideals were the intellectual food of my youth, and to see America converted into a senseless, Old World conqueror, embitters my age. [May, 1899]

> I came here fifty years ago with high and fond ideals about America. . . . They are now all shattered, and I have apparently to look elsewhere to keep even moderate hopes about the human race alive. [Late 1899]

> I have suffered from seeing the America of my youthful dreams vanish from my sight, and the commencement on this continent of the old story. . . . [November 13, 1899]

Godkin suffered a stroke in February of 1900. Fifteen months later he left his adopted country and returned to England. Occasionally the bitter humor of former days would return to him, as when he wrote James Bryce: "Do come over soon, and we'll lie under a tree at Dublin while you abuse Great Britain and I abuse the United States." He died in Devon on May 21, 1902, and was buried in the Hazelbeach churchyard, Northampton, to rest forever in England. In America, the country he had abandoned, the *Nation* published a fitting epitaph:

He grew old in an age he condemned
Felt the dissolving throes
Of a Social order he loved,
And, like Theban seer,
  Died in his enemies' day.

Charles Eliot Norton, like Godkin, interpreted the Spanish-American War and its aftermath as final proof that his early hopes for a special American destiny had been in vain. Amid the popular enthusiasm aroused by early American victories in Cuba and at Manila Bay, he advised students not to enlist (familiar note!) and declared before an audience in Cambridge that the United States had rashly:

hurried into war, and . . . she who more than any other land was pledged to peace and goodwill on earth, unsheathes her sword, compels a weak and unwilling nation to a fight, rejecting without due consideration her earnest and repeated offers to meet every legitimate demand of the United States. It is a bitter disappointment to the lover of his country; it is a turning-back from the path of civilization to that of barbarism.

Godkin and Norton were among those nineteenth-century idealists who had hoped, like the Puritans of the seventeenth century, that America would be a city set on a hill—a state and civilization that would attract the admiration of and serve as an example to the world. Despite disappointments, these two remarkable men, schooled in the genteel tradition, were never able to resist the lingering hope that America might yet be saved, and they flattered themselves that men such as they might yet create in the distant future a superior civilization in America. In 1902—with Americans in control of Cuba, Puerto Rico, and the Philippines—Norton counselled his friends not to give up:

While all the congregation of the children of Israel are wandering in the wilderness of Sin . . . we, the little remnant of the house of Judah that has escaped, must comfort one another as best we may. . . . we are defeated for the time; but the war is not ended, and we are enlisted for the war.

Richard Hofstadter

THE MYTH OF THE HAPPY YEOMAN

The following essay, like Oliver La Farge's essay on the American Indian in Volume One, is a study in the differences between reality and people's view of reality. Usually the historian seeks only for the reality and discards the myths that surround it in the records of the past. But in some contexts the myths themselves are vitally important and thus the proper subject of historical analysis.

The concept of the yeoman farmer had, as the late Professor Richard Hofstadter of Columbia University demonstrates, a solid basis in fact in early America. Farming was for many a way of life, not primarily a way of making a living. But national growth and development changed this steadily, and after the rapid expansion of industrialization the true yeoman practically disappeared. Why the myth persisted is the subject of Hofstadter's inquiry. The tale is part of the larger story of the impact of the Industrial Revolution on American thought, a subject which Hofstadter developed at greater length in his Pulitzer Prize history, *The Age of Reform.*

The United States was born in the country and has moved to the city. From the beginning its political values as well as ideas were of necessity shaped by country life. The early American politician, the country editor, who wished to address himself to the common man, had to draw upon a rhetoric that would touch the tillers of the soil; and even the spokesman of city people knew that his audience had been in very large part reared upon the farm.

But what the articulate people who talked and wrote about farmers and farming—the preachers, poets, philosophers, writers, and statesmen—liked about American farming was not, in every respect, what the typical working farmer liked. For the articulate people were drawn irresistibly to the noncommercial, non-pecuniary, self-sufficient aspect of American farm life. To them it was an ideal.

Writers like Thomas Jefferson and Hector St. John de Crèvecœur admired the yeoman farmer not for his capacity to exploit opportunities and make money but for his honest industry, his independence, his frank spirit of equality, his ability to produce and enjoy a simple abundance. The farmer himself, in most cases, was in fact inspired to make money, and such self-sufficiency as he actually had was usually forced upon him by a lack of transportation or markets, or by the necessity to save cash to expand his operations.

For while early American society was an agrarian society, it was fast becoming more commercial, and commercial goals made their way among its agricultural classes almost as rapidly as elsewhere. The more commercial this society became, however, the more reason it found to cling in imagination to the noncommercial agrarian values. The more farming as a self-sufficient way of life was abandoned for farming as a business, the more merit men found in what was being left behind. And the more rapidly the farmers' sons moved into the towns, the more nostalgic the whole culture became about its rural past. Throughout the nineteenth and even in the twentieth century, the American was taught that rural life and farming as a vocation were something sacred.

This sentimental attachment to the rural way of life is a kind of homage that Americans have paid to the fancied innocence of their origins. To call it a "myth" is not to imply that the idea is simply false. Rather the "myth" so effectively embodies men's values that it profoundly influences their way of perceiving reality and hence their behavior.

Like any complex of ideas, the agrarian myth cannot be defined in a phrase, but its component themes form a clear pattern. Its hero was the yeoman farmer, its central conception the notion that he is the ideal man and the ideal citizen. Unstinted praise of the special virtues of the farmer and the special values of rural life was coupled with the assertion that agriculture, as a calling uniquely productive and uniquely important to society, had a special right to the concern and protection of government. The yeoman, who owned a small farm and worked it with the aid of his family, was the incarnation of the simple, honest, independent, healthy, happy human being. Because he lived in close communion with beneficent nature, his life was believed to have a wholesomeness and integrity impossible for the depraved populations of cities.

His well-being was not merely physical, it was moral: it was not merely personal, it was the central source of civic virtue; it was not merely secular but religious, for God had made the land and called man to cultivate it. Since the yeoman was believed to be both happy and honest, and since he had a secure propertied stake in society in the form of his own land, he was held to be the best and most reliable sort of citizen. To this conviction Jefferson appealed when he wrote: "The small land holders are the most precious part of a state."

In origin the agrarian myth was not a popular but a literary idea, a preoccupation of the upper classes, of those who enjoyed a classical education, read pastoral poetry, experimented with breeding stock, and owned plantations or country estates. It was clearly formulated and almost universally accepted in America during the last half of the eighteenth century. As it took shape both in Europe and America, its promulgators drew heavily upon the authority and the rhetoric of classical writers—Hesiod, Xenophon, Cato, Cicero, Virgil, Horace, and others—whose works were the staples of a good education. A learned agricultural gentry, coming into conflict with the industrial classes, welcomed the moral strength that a rich classical ancestry brought to the praise of husbandry.

Chiefly through English experience, and from English and classical writers, the agrarian myth came to America, where, like so many other cultural importations, it eventually took on altogether new dimensions in its new setting. So appealing were the symbols of the myth that even an arch-opponent of the agrarian interest like Alexander Hamilton found it politic to concede in his *Report on Manufactures* that "the cultivation of the earth, as the primary and most certain source of national supply . . . has intrinsically a strong claim to pre-eminence over every other kind of industry." And Benjamin Franklin, urban cosmopolite though he was, once said that agriculture was "the only *honest way*" for a nation to acquire wealth, "wherein man receives a real increase of the seed thrown into the ground, a kind of continuous miracle, wrought by the hand of God in his favour, as a reward for his innocent life and virtuous industry."

Among the intellectual classes in the eighteenth century the agrarian myth had virtually universal appeal. Some writers used it to give simple, direct, and emotional expression to their feelings about life and nature; others linked agrarianism with a formal philosophy of natural rights. The application of the natural rights philosophy to land tenure became especially popular in America. Since the time of Locke it had been a standard argument that the land is the common stock of society to which every man has a right—what Jefferson called "the fundamental right to labour the earth"; that since the occupancy and use of land are the true criteria of valid ownership, labor expended in cultivating the earth confers title to it; that since govern-

According to this 1869 engraving from The Prairie Farmer, *each occupation has its uses, but the farmer alone foots all the bills.*

ment was created to protect property, the property of working land-holders has a special claim to be fostered and protected by the state.

At first the agrarian myth was a notion of the educated classes, but by the early nineteenth century it had become a mass creed, a part of the country's political folklore and its nationalist ideology. The roots of this change may be found as far back as the American

Revolution, which, appearing to many Americans as the victory of a band of embattled farmers over an empire, seemed to confirm the moral and civic superiority of the yeoman, made the farmer a symbol of the new nation, and wove the agrarian myth into his patriotic sentiments and idealism.

Still more important, the myth played a role in the first party battles under the Constitution. The Jeffersonians appealed again and again to the moral primacy of the yeoman farmer in their attacks on the Federalists. The family farm and American democracy became indissolubly connected in Jeffersonian thought, and by 1840 even the more conservative party, the Whigs, took over the rhetorical appeal to the common man, and elected a President in good part on the strength of the fiction that he lived in a log cabin.

The Jeffersonians, moreover, made the agrarian myth the basis of a strategy of continental development. Many of them expected that the great empty inland regions would guarantee the preponderance of the yeoman—and therefore the dominance of Jeffersonianism and the health of the state—for an unlimited future. The opening of the trans-Allegheny region, its protection from slavery, and the purchase of the Louisiana Territory were the first great steps in a continental strategy designed to establish an internal empire of small farms. Much later the Homestead Act was meant to carry to its completion the process of continental settlement by small homeowners. The failure of the Homestead Act "to enact by statute the fee-simple empire" was one of the original sources of Populist grievances, and one of the central points at which the agrarian myth was overrun by the commercial realities.

Above all, however, the myth was powerful because the United States in the first half of the nineteenth century consisted predominantly of literate and politically enfranchised farmers. Offering what seemed harmless flattery to this numerically dominant class, the myth suggested a standard vocabulary to rural editors and politicians. Although farmers may not have been much impressed by what was said about the merits of a noncommercial way of life, they could only enjoy learning about their special virtues and their unique services to the nation. Moreover, the editors and politicians who so flattered them need not in most cases have been insincere. More often than not they too were likely to have begun life in little villages or on farms, and what they had to say stirred in their own breasts, as it did in the breasts of a great many townspeople, nostalgia for their early years and perhaps relieved some residual feelings of guilt at having deserted parental homes and childhood attachments. They also had the satisfaction in the early days of knowing that in so far as it was based upon the life of the largely self-sufficient yeoman the agrarian myth was a depiction of reality as well as the assertion of an ideal.

Oddly enough, the agrarian myth came to be believed more widely and tenaciously as it became more fictional. At first it was propagated with a kind of genial candor, and only later did it acquire overtones of insincerity. There survives from the Jackson era a painting that shows Governor Joseph Ritner of Pennsylvania standing by a primitive plow at the end of a furrow. There is no pretense that the Governor has actually been plowing—he wears broadcloth pants and a silk vest, and his tall black beaver hat has been carefully laid in the grass beside him—but the picture is meant as a reminder of both his rustic origin and his present high station in life. By contrast, Calvin Coolidge posed almost a century later for a series of photographs that represented him as haying in Vermont. In one of them the President sits on the edge of a hay rig in a white shirt, collar detached, wearing highly polished black shoes and a fresh pair of overalls; in the background stands his Pierce Arrow, a secret service man on the running board, plainly waiting to hurry the President away from his bogus rural labors. That the second picture is so much more pretentious and disingenuous than the first is a measure of the increasing hollowness of the myth as it became more and more remote from the realities of agriculture.

Throughout the nineteenth century hundreds upon hundreds of thousands of farm-born youths sought their careers in the towns and cities. Particularly after 1840, which marked the beginning of a long cycle of heavy country-to-city migration, farm children repudiated their parents' way of life and took off for the cities where, in agrarian theory if not in fact, they were sure to succumb to vice and poverty.

When a correspondent of the *Prairie Farmer* in 1849 made the mistake of praising the luxuries, the "polished society," and the economic opportunities of the city, he was rebuked for overlooking the fact that city life "*crushes, enslaves,* and *ruins so many thousands of our young men* who are insensibly made the victims of *dissipation,* of *reckless speculation,* and of *ultimate crime.*" Such warnings, of course, were futile. "Thousands of young men," wrote the New York agriculturist Jesse Buel, "who annually forsake the plough, and the honest profession of their fathers, if not to win the fair, at least form an opinion, too often confirmed by mistaken parents, that agriculture is not the road to wealth, to honor, nor to happiness. And such will continue to be the case, until our agriculturists become qualified to assume that rank in society to which the importance of their calling, and their numbers, entitle them, and which intelligence and self-respect can alone give them."

Rank in society! That was close to the heart of the matter, for the farmer was beginning to realize acutely not merely that the best of the world's goods were to be had in the cities and that the urban middle and upper classes had much more of them than he did but also that he was losing in status and respect as compared with them. He became aware that the official respect paid to the farmer masked a certain disdain felt by many city people. "There has . . . a certain class of individuals grown up in our land," complained a farm writer in 1835, "who treat the cultivators of the soil as an inferior caste . . . whose utmost abilities are confined to the merit of being able to discuss a boiled potato and a rasher of bacon." The city was symbolized as the home of loan sharks, dandies, fops, and aristocrats with European ideas who despised farmers as hayseeds.

The growth of the urban market intensified this antagonism. In areas like colonial New England, where an intimate connection had existed between the small town and the adjacent countryside, where a community of interests and even of occupations cut across the town line, the rural-urban hostility had not developed so sharply as in the newer areas where the township plan was never instituted and where isolated farmsteads were more common. As settlement moved west, as urban markets grew, as self-sufficient farmers became rarer, as farmers pushed into commercial production for the cities they feared and distrusted, they quite correctly thought of themselves as a vocational and economic group rather than as members of a neighborhood. In the Populist era the city was totally alien territory to many farmers, and the primacy of agriculture as a source of wealth was reasserted with much bitterness. "The great cities rest upon our broad and fertile prairies," declared Bryan in his "Cross of Gold" speech. "Burn down your cities and leave our farms, and your cities will spring up again as if by magic; but destroy our farms, and the grass will grow in the streets of every city in the country." Out of the beliefs nourished by the agrarian myth there had arisen the notion that the city was a parasitical growth on the country. Bryan spoke for a people raised for generations on the idea that the farmer was a very special creature, blessed by God, and that in a country consisting largely of farmers the voice of the farmer was the voice of democracy and of virtue itself.

The agrarian myth encouraged farmers to believe that they were not themselves an organic part of the whole order of business enterprise and speculation that flourished in the city, partaking of its character and sharing in its risks, but rather the innocent pastoral victims of a conspiracy hatched in the distance. The notion of an innocent and victimized populace colors the whole history of agrarian controversy.

For the farmer it was bewildering, and irritating too, to think of the great contrast between the verbal deference paid him by almost everyone and the real economic position in which he found himself. Improving his economic position was always possible, though this was often done too little and too late; but it was not within anyone's power to stem the decline in the rural values and pieties, the gradual rejection of the moral commitments that had been expressed in the early exaltations of agrarianism.

It was the fate of the farmer himself to contribute to this decline. Like almost all good Americans he had innocently sought progress from the very beginning, and thus hastened the decline of many of his own values. Elsewhere the rural classes had usually looked to the past, had been bearers of tradition and upholders of stability. The American farmer looked to the future alone, and the story of the American land became a study in futures.

In the very hours of its birth as a nation Crèvecœur had congratulated America for having, in effect, no feudal past and no industrial present, for having no royal, aristocratic, ecclesiastical, or monarchial power, and no manufacturing class, and had rapturously concluded: "We are the most perfect society now existing in the world." Here was the irony from which the farmer suffered above all others: the United States was the only country in the world that began with perfection and aspired to progress.

To what extent was the agrarian myth actually false? During the colonial period, and even well down into the nineteenth century, there were in fact large numbers of farmers who were very much like the yeomen idealized in the myth. They were independent and self-sufficient, and they bequeathed to their children a strong love of craftsmanlike improvisation and a firm tradition of household industry. These yeomen were all too often yeomen by force of circumstance. They could not become commercial farmers because they were too far from the rivers or the towns, because the roads were too poor for bulky traffic, because the domestic market for agricultural produce was too small and the overseas markets were out of reach. At the beginning of the nineteenth century, when the American population was still living largely in the forests and most of it was east of the Appalachians, the yeoman farmer did exist in large numbers, living much as the theorists of the agrarian myth portrayed him.

But when the yeoman practiced the self-sufficient economy that was expected of him, he usually did so not because he wanted to stay out of the market but because he wanted to get into it. "My farm," said a farmer of Jefferson's time, "gave me and my family a good living on the produce of it; and left me, one year with another, one hundred and fifty dollars, for I have never spent more than ten dollars a year, which was for salt, nails, and the like. Nothing to wear, eat, or drink was purchased, as my farm provided all. With this saving, I put money to interest, bought cattle, fatted and sold them, and made great profit." Great profit! Here was the significance of self-sufficiency for the characteristic family farmer. Commercialism had already begun to enter the American Arcadia.

For, whatever the spokesman of the agrarian myth might have told him, the farmer almost anywhere in early America knew that all around him there were examples of commercial success in agriculture—the tobacco, rice, and indigo, and later the cotton planters of the South, the grain, meat, and cattle exporters of the middle states.

The farmer knew that without cash he could never rise above the hardships and squalor of pioneering and log-cabin life. So the savings from his self-sufficiency went into improvements—into the purchase of more land, of herds and flocks, of better tools; they went into the building of barns and silos and better dwellings. Self-sufficiency, in short, was adopted for a time in order that it would eventually be unnecessary.

Between 1815 and 1860 the character of American agriculture was transformed. The rise of native industry created a home market for agriculture, while demands arose abroad for American cotton and foodstuffs, and a great network of turnpikes, canals, and railroads helped link the planter and the advancing western farmer to the new markets. As the farmer moved out of the forests onto the flat, rich prairies, he found possibilities for machinery that did not exist in the forest. Before long he was cultivating the prairies with horse-drawn mechanical reapers, steel plows, wheat and corn drills, and threshers.

The farmer was still a hardworking man, and he still owned his own land in the old tradition. But no longer did he grow or manufacture almost everything he needed. He concentrated on the cash crop, bought more and more of his supplies from the country store. To take full advantage of the possibilities of mechanization, he engrossed as much land as he could and borrowed money for his land and machinery. The shift from self-sufficient to commercial farming varied in time throughout the West and cannot be dated with precision, but it was complete in Ohio by about 1830 and twenty years later in Indiana, Illinois, and Michigan. All through the great Northwest, farmers whose fathers might have lived in isolation and self-sufficiency were surrounded by jobbers, banks, stores, middlemen, horses, and machinery.

This transformation affected not only what the farmer did but how he felt. The ideals of the agrarian myth were competing in his breast, and gradually losing ground, to another, even stronger ideal, the notion of opportunity, of career, of the self-made man. Agrarian sentiment sanctified labor in the soil and the simple life; but the prevailing Calvinist atmosphere of rural life implied that virtue was rewarded with success and material goods. Even farm boys were taught to strive for achievement in one form or another, and when this did not take them away from the farms altogether, it impelled them to follow farming not as a way of life but as a *career*—that is, as a way of achieving substantial success.

The sheer abundance of the land—that very internal empire that had been expected to insure the predominance of the yeoman in American life for centuries—gave the *coup de grâce* to the yeomanlike way of life. For it made of the farmer a speculator. Cheap land invited extensive and careless cultivation. Rising land values in areas of new settlement tempted early liquidation and frequent moves. Frequent and sensational rises in land values bred a boom psychology in the American farmer and caused him to rely for his margin of profit more on the appreciation in the value of his land than on the sale of crops. It took a strong man to resist the temptation to ride skyward on lands that might easily triple or quadruple their value in one decade and then double in the next.

What developed in America, then, was an agricultural society whose real attachment was not, like the yeoman's, to the land but to land values. The characteristic product of American rural society, as it developed on the prairies and the plains, was not a yeoman or a villager, but a harassed little country businessman who worked very hard, moved all too often, gambled with his land, and made his way alone.

While the farmer had long since ceased to act like a yeoman, he

was somewhat slower in ceasing to think like one. He became a businessman in fact long before he began to regard himself in this light. As the
nineteenth century drew to a close, however, various things were
changing him. He was becoming increasingly an employer of labor,
and though he still worked with his hands, he began to look with suspicion upon the working classes of the cities, especially those organized in trade unions, as he had once done upon the urban fops and
aristocrats. Moreover, when good times returned after the Populist
revolt of the 1890's, businessmen and bankers and the agricultural
colleges began to woo the farmer, to make efforts to persuade him
to take the businesslike view of himself that was warranted by the
nature of his farm operations. "The object of farming," declared a
writer in the *Cornell Countryman* in 1904, "is not primarily to make
a living, but it is to make money. To this end it is to be conducted on
the same business basis as any other producing industry."

The final change, which came only with a succession of changes in
the twentieth century, wiped out the last traces of the yeoman of old,
as the coming first of good roads and rural free delivery, and mail
order catalogues, then the telephone, the automobile, and the tractor,
and at length radio, movies, and television largely eliminated the
difference between urban and rural experience in so many important
areas of life. The city luxuries, once so derided by farmers, are now
what they aspire to give to their wives and daughters.

In 1860 a farm journal satirized the imagined refinements and
affectations of a city girl in the following picture:

> Slowly she rises from her couch. . . . Languidly she gains
> her feet, and oh! what vision of human perfection appears
> before us: Skinny, bony, sickly, hipless, thighless, formless,
> hairless, teethless. What a radiant belle! . . . The ceremony of
> enrobing commences. In goes the dentist's naturalization efforts;
> next the witching curls are fashioned to her "classically molded
> head." Then the womanly proportions are properly adjusted;
> hoops, bustles, and so forth, follow in succession, then a pro-
> fuse quantity of whitewash, together with a "permanent rose
> tint" is applied to a sallow complexion; and lastly the "killing"
> wrapper is arranged on her systematical and matchless form.

But compare this with these beauty hints for farmers' wives from
the *Idaho Farmer*, April, 1935:

> Hands should be soft enough to flatter the most delicate
> of the new fabrics. They must be carefully manicured, with
> none of the hot, brilliant shades of nail polish. The lighter
> and more delicate tones are in keeping with the spirit of fresh-
> ness. Keep the tint of your fingertips friendly to the red of your
> lips, and check both your powder and your rouge to see that they
> best suit the tone of your skin in the bold light of summer.

Nothing can tell us with greater finality of the passing of the
yeoman ideal than these light and delicate tones of nail polish.

Unemployed white and black workers parade in New York City in 1909 to protest discriminatory hiring practices.

Part Three
Age of Reform

Thurman Arnold

ECONOMIC REFORM AND THE SHERMAN ANTITRUST ACT

The growth of industry in the United States produced not only more manufactured goods but bigger manufacturing establishments, and these large organizations tended to combine with one another into huge complexes called trusts. This development roused profound anxieties in the minds of many persons. The fear of monopoly, which these trusts created, was only the surface manifestation of these anxieties; more basic was the fear that these enormous enterprises presaged the appearance of sharp cleavages between rich and poor and the development of a rigid social structure. Thus, it was thought that the trusts might undermine democracy itself. The Sherman Antitrust Act of 1890 was one result of the public distaste for these large organizations.

The Sherman act did not check the trend toward large-scale manufacturing, but over a period of time bigness itself proved less dangerous than late nineteenth-century citizens had feared. Democracy has survived despite U.S. Steel and General Motors, although there have been (and still are) those who see such giants as a threat to American institutions. Nevertheless, the Sherman act has remained on the statute books, and it has served a useful if changing function as the character of American industry has evolved. The author of this essay, Thurman Arnold, headed the federal government's antitrust division from 1938 to 1943. His books include *The Folklore of Capitalism* and *Democracy and Free Enterprise*.

E ver since the Civil War ended there has been a continuous conflict between two opposing ideals in American economic thinking. The first of them states that business management, if relieved from the rigors of cutthroat competition, will be fair and benevolent. The age of competition is over, the theory continues, and great corporations with the power to dominate prices benefit the economy. In the field of big business, this philosophy justifies giant mergers. In the field of small business, it leads to the passage of fair trade laws and similar forms of legalized price fixing.

J. P. Morgan is the traditional hero of this philosophy. He organized United States Steel, our first billion-dollar enterprise, to make investments secure, and to eliminate cutthroat competition in steel. Andrew Carnegie, who was doing pretty well as an aggressive competitor, was paid twice what he thought his business was worth to go along. Morgan made the steel business safer for the investor but tough on the consumer, and it has been so ever since.

The opposing economic ideal says that industrial progress can best be obtained in a free market, where prices are fixed by competition and where success depends on efficiency rather than market control. Under this theory it becomes the government's function not to control or regulate but only to maintain freedom in the market place by prosecuting combinations whenever they become large enough to fix prices. Henry Ford represents this ideal. By producing cars at cut prices on a nationwide scale, he helped wreck many of the existing automobile companies. But he also revolutionized the industry.

This second ideal is also represented by a remarkable piece of legislation called the Sherman Antitrust Act, passed by Congress on July 2, 1890, which states that "Every contract, combination in the form of trust or otherwise, or conspiracy, in restraint of trade or commerce among the several States, or with foreign nations, is hereby declared to be illegal." The act goes on to authorize the federal government to proceed against trusts which violate the act, and empowers federal circuit courts with jurisdiction over such violations.

If I may be permitted to say so, as one who has had some experience with enforcing it, this law is historically unique. Prior to the Second World War, no other nation had any legislation like it. It is different from any other criminal statute because it makes it a crime to violate a vaguely stated economic policy—and a policy, what is more, on which public attitudes often change. The average American citizen—and, indeed, the average court which administers the Sherman act—would like to believe simultaneously in both of the conflicting economic ideals described above. For that reason, the Supreme Court swings back and forth in Sherman act cases, in more important ones splitting five to four. The history of the Sherman act is the history of the conflicts and compromises between these two economic ideals.

But the dominant ideal in our American economic thinking has been the ideal of the Sherman act. The business pressures against its actual enforcement are great, but support of the *principle* of the act is so unanimous that no one ever suggests its repeal. Big business, labor, farmers—each economic group wants the Sherman act strictly enforced, against everyone but itself.

In meeting these pressures the Sherman act has shown extraordinary elasticity. It may bend at times, but it always bounces back. Thus it is like a constitutional provision rather than an ordinary statute, and its history tells much about our national attempt to create an economy that will be at the same time both disciplined and free.

How was this ideal born in the first place? The most improbable feature of the Sherman act is that this apparently anti-big business measure was introduced by a senator who was a high-tariff advocate and an extreme conservative, and was passed with only one dissenting vote by a big-business Republican Congress.

The initial pressure for it came from agriculture, which since the Civil War had been reduced to a fairly steady depression. Railroad monopolies were charging farmers all the traffic would bear, and sometimes a little more. Rates were rigged to favor big railroad customers and ruin small ones. As farm income fell, prices that farmers had to pay rose steadily. Monopolies kept them high. If the pressure from the agricultural states was strong, so was the rebellion against other aspects of the dog-eat-dog business ethics of the times. The necessity of some restraint on such practices came at last to be recognized even by business itself.

Big business during the latter half of the nineteenth century had come to regard competition as an unmitigated evil which could be alleviated only by combination. At first the combinations took the form of "pools" or agreements—regional rather than national—to restrain trade, to control prices, to restrict output and divide markets. But businessmen soon learned that agreements between members of an industry were too weak. Only the surrender of business independence by the units could make domination of the market certain.

Pools gave way to trusts, the first of which, established by Standard Oil in 1879, became a model for subsequent business combinations. Each party to the trust surrendered his stock-voting power to trustees, receiving trust certificates in return. Thus the nine trustees of the Standard Oil Trust, without the investment of a dollar, obtained absolute power over the nation's oil industry. The pattern set by Standard Oil was so widely followed that the name "trust" became a byword for any large industrial combination even after the trust device had been abandoned.

Prior to the Sherman act the federal government had no power to prevent predatory business activities. Therefore, the states themselves began an ineffective attack on the trusts in state courts. In 1887 Louisiana prosecuted the Cotton Oil Trust. In 1889 California prosecuted the Sugar Trust; in 1890 Nebraska prosecuted the Whiskey Trust. The attorney general of Ohio sought to repeal the charter of the Standard Oil Company of Ohio.

In 1892 the supreme court of Ohio ordered the local oil company to sever its connections with the Standard Oil Trust. The order was never effectively enforced. But these state attacks on it made the device

In 1888 Senator John Sherman introduced the resolution that two years later became the Sherman Antitrust Act.

so risky that corporate organizations looked for some other form of combination that could not be prosecuted under state law. New Jersey provided the model, by amending its incorporation statute to permit one corporation to own the stock of another. From then on it was easy.

Corporations A, B, and C would give 51 per cent of their stock to holding company X. Holding company X would in turn give 51 per cent of its stock to holding company Y. Thus holding company Y, with only about 25 per cent interest in the operating companies, controlled them completely. Y would transfer enough stock to Z, at which point Z needed only 12½ per cent to control the industry. And so on until fantastic pyramids were built up. No state could attack these pyramids because they were legal in the state of incorporation. Only Congress could interfere with this process.

In July, 1888, John Sherman, senator from Ohio, introduced the resolution that led to the passage of the Sherman act. He had been Secretary of the Treasury under President Hayes and was known as an expert in finance and taxation. He was big business-minded and an ardent advocate of high tariffs. In this important respect, he was opposed to the very interests that were demanding antimonopoly legislation. In the farm belt the tariff was called the mother of monopoly. Sherman could have no part in such radical doctrine. His resolution reconciled that contradiction very neatly. It asked the Finance Committee to report on a bill that would

> tend to preserve freedom of trade and production, the natural competition of increasing production, the lowering of prices by such competition, and the full benefit designed by and hitherto conferred by the policy of the government to protect and encourage American industries by levying duties on imported goods.

In other words, Sherman contended that the increased production by local industry protected by tariffs would more than offset the increased prices due to the tariffs, if domestic competition was free and unrestrained.

The Sherman act as it reads today was passed in the Senate 52 yeas to 1 nay, and signed by President Harrison on July 2, 1890. No votes were cast against it in the House.

The act is unexampled in economic legislation. In effect it says: "We want competition in the United States and we will leave it to the federal judiciary to determine, case by case, just what action constitutes a restraint on competition." That this law could be passed by a conservative Republican Congress whose most influential leaders were closely associated with big business is remarkable in the extreme. Many writers have argued that the act was a hypocritical piece of legislation, designed as a political sop to the farm belt, and that no one expected it to be of any consequence. For example, Senator Nelson W. Aldrich, who was known as J. P. Morgan's floor broker in the Senate, voted for it.

Such facts are sometimes cited to support the view that the original passage of the bill was only an attempt to placate western senators in exchange for votes on higher tariffs. But this interpretation has been completely refuted by Hans B. Thorelli in his recent book, *The Federal Antitrust Policy*, the most complete and objective analysis of the history of American monopoly policy. Thorelli concludes that a majority of congressmen were sincere and that the Sherman act represented for men of both parties the symbol and the image of what they sincerely desired the American economy to become.

By that I do not mean that the Republican supporters of the act would have welcomed the breakup of great American combinations into smaller units. At the same time, they would have instinctively rejected the system of domestic and international cartels that had been growing up in Germany and spreading to France from 1870 on, which would surely have become the American pattern if the Sherman act had not been passed.

The Sherman act fitted in with the American economic and legal philosophy that was religiously held in 1890 and which is still our dominant philosophy today. In 1890 Americans distrusted any form of governmental regulation. It was the tradition of the American common law that the relation between business and government should be based on some broad common-law principle which would acquire definite meaning only through a series of court decisions. The Sherman act followed that tradition. Our faith in the common law was such that Congress believed that the courts could give a better and more practical meaning to the principles of the act than Congress could possibly do by further definition or regulation.

The Sherman act was definitely on the shelf during the administrations of Presidents Harrison, Cleveland, and McKinley. Cleveland's attorney general not only instituted no proceedings but dropped the prosecution of the notorious Cash Register Trust, even though he had won a victory in the lower court. Under Cleveland the principal impact of the Sherman act was against labor in breaking the Pullman strike. McKinley was equally indifferent to the Sherman act. During his four and one half years only three suits were brought.

The first Sherman act decision by the Supreme Court was in the case of United States *v.* E. C. Knight & Co. It amounted to a virtual repeal of the act. The Supreme Court held that the Sugar Trust, in acquiring a monopoly over sugar manufacturing, affected interstate commerce only indirectly and, therefore, did not violate the act. As Justice John Marshall Harlan pointed out in his dissent: "While the opinion of the Court in this case does not declare the Act of 1890 to be unconstitutional, it defeats the main object for which it was passed." The Knight case thus emasculated the Sherman act. As a result of that decision the government became powerless to prevent the formation of a monopoly through the device of a holding company.

Yet within the short space of eight years, through the daring and ingenuity of Theodore Roosevelt, the Sherman act was transformed again from a meaningless and ineffective formula into a sharp weapon. Theodore Roosevelt was one of the few politicians of his time who had seriously studied the antitrust problem. He had his first experience with monopoly power as a New York State assemblyman during the investigation of Jay Gould. He campaigned for re-election on the antimonopoly issue in 1882. In 1899, as governor, he wrote: "I have been in a great quandary over trusts. I do not know what attitude to take. I do not intend to play a demagogue. On the other hand, I do intend, so far as in me lies, to see that the rich man is held to the same accountability as the poor man, and when the rich man is rich enough *to buy unscrupulous advice from very able lawyers, this is not always easy.*" (Italics added.)

It was the empire-building ambition of J. P. Morgan that gave Theodore Roosevelt his chance. During the last year of the McKinley Administration the Northern Securities Company had been formed as a compromise between E. H. Harriman and Morgan in their fight to control the Northern Pacific Railroad. The holding company device was used to combine under one management two of the nation's largest competing railroads, the Northern Pacific and the Great Northern. Had the scheme succeeded, it could have led to the domination of all American railroads by this group. It could have created a pattern for the cartelization of all American industry.

Roosevelt, as one of the first acts of his Administration, determined to attack this respected citadel of corporate power. This enterprise was very different from that of using the act to attack mere dishonesty in business, and Roosevelt must have realized that the legal odds were very much against him. A careful lawyer would have advised him that the Knight case exempted J. P. Morgan's ambitious plans. The decision in the Knight case stood for the principle that the acquisition of monopoly control was immune from attack because, though it affected prices "indirectly," it was not a conspiracy to fix them "directly."

The issue as Roosevelt saw it went far beyond the merger of the two railroads involved in Northern Securities. The issue was nothing less than effective national sovereignty. The federal government had been relegated to such minor roles as distributing the mail and collecting tariff duties. Big business was the real sovereign in infinitely

Joseph Keppler, the founder of Puck, *captioned this 1904 cartoon of Teddy Roosevelt fighting the merger- and monopoly-minded titans of American business, "Jack and the Wall Street Giants."*

more important areas. In the Northern Securities case, Theodore Roosevelt was to obtain for the federal government a magna carta limiting the power of the business princes.

Roosevelt gambled that the Supreme Court, with new faces in it since the Knight case, would repudiate or at least alter that decision. He directed Attorney General Philander C. Knox to draw up a case against the Northern Securities Company. It was to be a head-on attack on the philosophy of the Knight case decision. Fully aware of the tremendous pressures that would be exerted against him, he directed Knox to prepare the prosecution in complete secrecy. Not even his close friend and adviser, Elihu Root, the Secretary of War, was told.

When Knox finally released to the press his intention to prosecute Northern Securities, there was consternation and panic in the financial world. Root, a Wall Street lawyer, was dismayed and resentful. Morgan and his like-minded friend, Senator Chauncey Depew of New York, descended upon the White House like the emissaries of some independent sovereignty whose rights were being invaded. But by that time the prosecution was a *fait accompli*.

On this case all of Roosevelt's antitrust program depended. It came before the Supreme Court in March, 1904. By that time, Roosevelt had appointed Oliver Wendell Holmes to the Court, believing that Holmes's reputation as a liberal was an indication that he would vote against the tremendous extension of monopoly power. In this hope he was to be bitterly disappointed. Had Holmes been able to win over to his side Justice David Brewer, as he thought he had, the legitimacy of monopoly would have been established, perhaps for all time, in this country as it was in Europe.

The Court was bitterly divided, five to four. The majority held that the Sherman act was intended to prevent giant combinations formed under any device and that such exercise of congressional power over industry was not unconstitutional.

Holmes, who wrote one of the two principal dissents, made the statement, believed by many at that time, that the Sherman act was not intended to prevent combinations in restraint of trade. He said: "It was the ferocious extreme of competition with others, not the cessation of competition among the partners, that was the evil feared."

Justice Holmes had faith in the benevolence and efficiency of the rich. He believed that the Constitution should protect them in their efforts to create industrial empires. But the ideal of a dynamic competitive economy and government-maintained freedom of industrial opportunity, I believe, was beyond him. He would have approved of the system of domestic and international cartels that dominated industry and caused it to stagnate in Europe before World War II.

Roosevelt, though a rich man himself, was one of the few men of his time to realize the destiny of America as a land of economic freedom. He had the ability to infuse the public with his point of view. Senator Sherman initiated the antitrust act, but it was Teddy Roosevelt who gave it vigor and meaning, made the policy of the Sherman act an economic religion and its violation an economic sin, and, finally, made it emotionally impossible for American business to co-operate in the European cartel system.

To appraise the effect of the Sherman act on American business institutions correctly we must view it apart from particular prosecutions, or particular periods of enforcement or nonenforcement. Theodore Roosevelt's achievement was to enshrine the ideal of the act as part of our national folklore. And its influence has continued in a far more potent way than perhaps any other statute on the books. The image of the Sherman act has not prevented tremendous concentrations of economic power, but it has prevented such concentrations from obtaining legitimate status.

Only once since its passage has the principle of the act been repudiated. That was in production codes of the National Recovery Administration during Franklin D. Roosevelt's New Deal. They were designed to raise prices and restrict production, after the European model. The theory was that this would protect investments and rescue business from insolvency.

But the competitive tradition represented by the Sherman act was too strong for the NRA. The Sherman act over the years, even when it was unenforced, had built up an abiding faith that the elimination of competition in business was morally and economically wrong. Then the Supreme Court threw out the NRA, and Franklin Roosevelt turned back to the antitrust laws as a major instrument of economic policy, and placed me in charge of their enforcement.

When I took office, years of disuse of the Sherman act, culminating in its repudiation by NRA, had made violation of the antitrust laws common, almost respectable. I will never forget the amazement of the Wisconsin Alumni Research Foundation, an organization whose profits were used to support the University of Wisconsin, when the Justice Department charged it with using a vitamin patent to raise prices and restrict manufacture of important food products. It never occurred to the high-minded management of this foundation that it was doing anything wrong. The indictment was considered an attack on education itself.

Thurman Arnold, former head of the Antitrust Division of the Justice Department, testifying before the Senate Banking Committee in 1949.

I believed that my principal function was to convince American businessmen that the Sherman act represented something more than a pious platitude; second, that its enforcement was an important economic policy. But there was very little support among economists for the latter notion.

As indictments of respectable people began to pour out from the Justice Department in unprecedented numbers, cries of outrage could be heard from coast to coast. I will never forget the pain and astonishment caused when criminal charges were brought against the American Medical Association, which had established a pretty effective boycott on all forms of group health plans. I was pictured as a wild man whose sanity was in considerable doubt. One major newspaper referred to me as ''an idiot in a powder mill.'' Letters of protest poured into the White House. Adverse publicity reached its peak when the Associated Press was charged with violation of the Sherman act for refusing to sell its news service to any new newspaper that would be competing with one of its member publications. Editorials appeared from coast to coast accusing the department of destroying freedom of the press.

Yet the enforcement program of the Antitrust Division on a nationwide scale between 1938 and the outbreak of World War II survived all such attacks. This was because American businessmen did not want to repudiate the principle of the Sherman act, however much they disliked particular prosecutions. It showed that the Henry Ford tradition was still dominant.

It is difficult now to appraise the economic effect of the revival of the Sherman act at that time. Opinions differ, and my own is, of course, biased. But this at least can be said: American business learned that the Sherman act was something more than a false front to our business structure. The public gained an idea of the purpose of the act, the act itself gained renewed vitality, and American business approved this revival.

There are two principal evils of concentrated economic power in a democracy. The first is the power of concentrated industry to charge administered prices rather than prices based on competitive demand. A second is the tendency of such empires to swallow up local businesses and drain away local capital. Prior to the Depression this condition had advanced so far that our concentrated industrial groups had helped destroy their own markets by siphoning off the dollars that could have been a source of local purchasing power.

It is idle to say that periodic enforcement of the antitrust laws has solved these problems, but the laws themselves have given us an image of what our economy should be. In a cartel economy no one could question the legitimacy of the recent rises in steel—or any other—prices. In an antitrust-minded economy it seems a legitimate and natural thing for a congressional committee to call the companies to account. . . .

John A. Garraty

WAS BRYAN A REFORMER?

The leading figures of the Progressive Era have suffered
considerably at the hands of historians in recent years. Their
insensitivity to the fate of black citizens becomes ever more
apparent as scholars study their attitudes toward racial
minorities. Their middle-class orientation stands in stark contrast
to their radical rhetoric. Their inconsistent record on such
questions as immigration and labor legislation, as well as their
wide-spread support of imperialistic ventures, appears less than
liberal from a contemporary point of view. Indeed, one historian,
Gabriel Kolko, has titled his study of the Progressive Era *The
Triumph of Conservatism.*

The following essay criticizes one leading Progressive from a
different perspective and is in part an attempt to cast certain
doubts on the character of most American reform movements and
their leaders. The subject examined here—William Jennings
Bryan—was certainly a prominent Progressive. He, most of his
contemporaries, and most historians have considered him a
reformer. Yet as I have tried to show, his personal inadequacies
raise serious questions about his liberalism, as well as about his
judgment.

The President of the United States may be an ass," wrote H. L. Mencken during the reign of Calvin Coolidge, "but he at least doesn't believe that the earth is square, and that witches should be put to death, and that Jonah swallowed the whale." The man to whom the vitriolic Mencken was comparing President Coolidge was William Jennings Bryan of Nebraska, one of the dominant figures in the Progressive movement. According to Mencken, Bryan was a "peasant," a "zany without sense or dignity," a "poor clod," and, in addition, an utter fraud. "If the fellow was sincere, then so was P. T. Barnum," he sneered.

It was certainly easy enough, and tempting, for sophisticates to come to the conclusion that Bryan was a buffoon and a fake. His undignified association in his declining years with the promotion of Florida real estate and his naïve and bigoted religious views, so pitilessly exposed by Clarence Darrow during the famous "Monkey Trial" in Dayton, Tennessee, lent substance to the Mencken view of his character. So did Bryan's smug refusal, while Secretary of State under Woodrow Wilson, to serve alcoholic beverages at Department receptions and dinners because of his personal disapproval of drinking, and his objection to the appointment of ex-President Charles W. Eliot of Harvard as Ambassador to China on the ground that Eliot was a Unitarian, and therefore not a real Christian. "The new Chinese civilization," said Bryan, "was founded upon the Christian movement." Eliot's appointment might undermine the work of generations of pious missionaries, he implied. Bryan's unabashed partisanship—he talked frankly after Wilson's election of filling government positions with "deserving Democrats"—did not seem to jibe with his pretensions as a reformer. And his oratorical style, magnificent but generally more emotional than logical, was disappointing to thinking people. John Hay called him a "Baby Demosthenes" and David Houston, one of his colleagues in Wilson's Cabinet, stated that "one could drive a prairie schooner through any part of his argument and never scrape against a fact." Being largely a creature of impulse, Bryan was, Houston added, "constantly on the alert to get something which has been represented to him as a fact to support or sustain his impulses."

But these flaws and blind spots were not fundamental weaknesses; they should never be allowed to overshadow Bryan's long years of devoted service to the cause of reform. If there were large areas about which he knew almost nothing, there were others where he was alert, sensible, and well-informed; certainly he was not a stupid man, nor was he easily duped or misled. Although a professional politician, as his remark about "deserving Democrats" makes clear, he was utterly honest personally and devoted to the cause of the people, as he understood it.

He was perfectly attuned to the needs and aspirations of rural America. In the early nineties he was in the forefront of the fight against high tariffs on manufactured goods. Later in the decade he battled for currency reform. At the turn of the century he was leading the assault against imperialism. During Theodore Roosevelt's primacy he was often far ahead of the intrepid Teddy, advocating a federal income tax, the eight-hour day, the control of monopoly and the strict regulation of public utilities, woman suffrage, and a large number of other startling innovations. Under Wilson he played a major part in marshaling support in Congress for the Federal Reserve Act and other New Freedom measures. Whatever his limitations, his faults, or his motives, few public men of his era left records as consistently "progressive" as Bryan's.

For years he led the Democratic party without the advantage of holding office. Three times he was a presidential candidate; although never elected, he commanded the unswerving loyalty of millions of his fellow citizens for nearly thirty years. He depended more on his intuition than on careful analysis in forming his opinions, but his intuition was usually sound; he was more a man of heart than of brain, but his heart was great.

Bryan was known as the Great Commoner, and the title was apt. He was a man of the people in origin and by instinct. He was typical of his age in rendering great respect to public opinion, whether it was informed or not. To Bryan the voice of the people was truly the voice of God. "I don't know anything about free silver," he announced while running for Congress early in the nineties. "The people of Nebraska are for free silver and I am for free silver. I will look up the arguments later." (It should be added that he did indeed "look up the arguments later." Less than a year after making this promise he arose in the House to deliver without notes a brilliant three-hour speech on the money question, a speech of great emotional power, but also fact-laden, sensible, and full of shrewd political arguments. When he sat down, the cheers rang out from both sides of the aisle.)

Bryan was born in Salem, Illinois, in 1860, a child of the great Middle West. Growing up in the heart of the valley of democracy, he absorbed its spirit and its sense of protest from his earliest years. After being graduated from Illinois College in 1881, he studied law in Chicago and for a time practiced his profession in Jacksonville, Illinois. But in 1887, stimulated by a talk with a law-school classmate from that city, he moved west to Lincoln, Nebraska. He quickly made his way in this new locale. Within a year he was active in the local Democratic organization, and in 1890, a month before his thirtieth birthday, he won his party's nomination for congressman.

Nebraska was traditionally a Republican state, its loyalty to the party of Lincoln forged in the heat of the Civil War. But by 1890 tradition was rapidly losing its hold on voters all over the Middle West. For the farmers of the American heartland were in deep trouble, and the Republican party seemed unwilling to do much to help them.

Tumultuous social and economic changes shaped the nation in the years after Appomattox. Within a single generation the United States was transformed from what was essentially a land of farmers into a modern industrial society, and in the process the Middle West was caught in a relentless economic vise. During the flush times of the sixties, when the Union Army was buying enormous amounts of food and fodder, and foreign demand was unusually high, the farmers of the region had gone into debt in order to buy more land and machinery. In the seventies and eighties, however, agricultural prices, especially those of such major staple crops as wheat and cotton, fell steeply. Wheat, which had sold as high as $2.50 a bushel in wartime, was down to fifty cents by the early nineties.

The impact of this economic decline was intensified by the changing social status of the farmer. Agriculture was losing its predominant place in American life. In the days of the Founding Fathers, about ninety per cent of the population was engaged in working the soil, and the farmer was everywhere portrayed as the symbol of American self-reliance and civic virtue. ''Those who labor in the earth,'' Jefferson said, ''are the chosen people of God.'' But as the factory began to outstrip the farm, the farmer lost much of his standing. While the old symbol remained—it was especially in evidence around election time—a new and disturbing image of the farmer as a hick, a rube, a hayseed—a comic mixture of cocky ignorance, shrewd self-interest, and monumental provincialism—began to challenge it.

Naturally the farmers resented their loss of both income and prestige, but there was little they could do about either. Price declines were largely a response to worldwide overproduction, resulting from improvements in transportation and the opening up of new farmlands in Australia, Argentina, Canada, Russia, and elsewhere. Nor did the farmers, who desired manufactured goods as much as everyone else, really want to reverse the trend that was making them a minority group in a great industrial nation. But as they cast about for some way out of their plight, they were profoundly disturbed by certain results of the new development which did seem amenable to reform.

Industrial growth meant the mushrooming of great cities. These gave birth to noxious slums where every kind of vice flourished, where corrupt political organizations like the venal Tweed Ring in New York were forged, and where radical political concepts like socialism and anarchism sought to undermine ''the American way of life.'' In the words of Jefferson, the farmers' hero, cities were ''ulcers on the body politic.''

Giant industries also attracted hordes of immigrants; these seemed to threaten the Middle West both by their mere numbers and by their ''un-American'' customs and points of view. Could the American melting pot absorb such strange ingredients without losing much of its own character?

Furthermore, to the citizens of Nebraska and other agricultural states, the new industrial barons appeared bent on making vassals of every farmer in America. The evidence seemed overwhelming: Huge impersonal corporations had neither souls nor consciences; profit was their god, materialism their only creed. The ''interests,'' a tiny group of powerful tycoons in great eastern centers like Boston, New York, and Philadelphia, were out to enslave the rest of the country. Farmers worked and sweated only to see the "interests" make off with most of the fruit of their toil. Too many useless middlemen grew fat off the mere "handling" of wheat and cotton. Monopolistic railroads overcharged for carrying crops to market, unscrupulous operators of grain elevators falsely downgraded prime crops and charged exorbitant fees. Cynical speculators drove the price of staples up and down, sometimes making and losing millions in a matter of minutes, without the slightest regard for the effect of their operations on the producers whose sweat made their deadly game possible.

Conspiring with bankers and mortgage holders, all these groups combined to dictate the federal government's money policy. Population and production were surging forward; more money was needed simply to keep up with economic growth. Yet the government was deliberately cutting down on the amount of money in circulation by retiring Civil War greenbacks. On debt-ridden farmers plagued by overproduction, the effect of this deflation was catastrophic. Or so it seemed from the perspective of rural America.

While undoubtedly exaggerated, this indictment of the "interests" was taken as gospel throughout large sectors of the South and West. As a result, demands for "reform" quickly arose. The leading reformers were for the most part sincere, but few of them were entirely altruistic and many were decidedly eccentric. Participating in the movement for a variety of motives but without coming to grips with the main problem of American agriculture—overproduction—were coarse demagogues like Senator "Pitchfork Ben" Tillman of South Carolina, and unwashed characters like the wise-cracking congressman from Kansas, "Sockless Jerry" Simpson. There were professional orators like the angry Mary Ellen Lease (her detractors called her "Mary Yellin' "), and homespun economic theorists like "Coin" Harvey and "General" Jacob Coxey, who believed so strongly in paper money that he named his son Legal Tender. The excesses of such people frightened off many Americans who might otherwise have lent a sympathetic ear to the farmers' complaints; others who might have been friendly observed the antics of the reformers with contempt and wrote off the whole movement as a joke.

Since neither of the major parties espoused the farmers' cause wholeheartedly, much of the protest found its way into various third-party organizations. At first, discontented elements concentrated on opposing the government's policy of retiring the paper money put in circulation during the Civil War. To save these greenbacks from extinction a Greenback (later Greenback-Labor) party sprang up. In 1878 its candidates polled a million votes, but decline followed as currency reformers turned to other methods of inflation.

Meanwhile the Patrons of Husbandry, better known as the Grange, originally a social organization for farm families, had begun to agitate in local politics against the middlemen who were draining off such a large percentage of the farmers' profits. In the seventies the Grangers became a power in the Middle West; in state after state they obtained the passage of laws setting maximum rates for railroads and prohibiting various forms of discrimination. The operations of grain elevators were also subjected to state regulation by ''Granger Laws'' in states such as Illinois, Iowa, Wisconsin, and Minnesota. The Grange abandoned political activity in the eighties, but other farm organizations quickly took its place. These coalesced first into the Northern Alliance and the Southern Alliance, and around 1890 the two Alliances joined with one another to become the Populist party.

Although William Jennings Bryan was a Democrat, he had grown up amid the agitations of the Granger movement. His father had even run for Congress in the seventies with Greenback party support. The aspirations and the general point of view of the midwestern farmers were young Bryan's own. Public men, he admitted late in life to the journalist Mark Sullivan, are ''the creatures of their age. . . . I lived in the very center of the country out of which the reforms grew, and was quite naturally drawn to the people's side.''

And they to his, one must add. Discontented farmers in his district were on the lookout for men who understood them and their problems. In 1888 the Republicans had carried the seat by 3,000 votes; now, in 1890, Bryan swept in with a lead of 6,713.

*A wood engraving from a newspaper
in 1873 showing a gathering of Grangers.*

Bryan made an excellent record in his first Congress. He was a hard-working member, studying the technicalities of the tariff question for months before making his first important speech. But he saw that the tariff was rapidly being replaced by the money question as the crucial issue of the day. When he yielded the floor after completing his tariff speech, he collared a young Texas congressman named Joseph W. Bailey, who posed as a financial expert. Sitting on a sofa in the rear of the House chamber, he quizzed Bailey about the problem of falling prices. Bailey told him the tariff had little or no effect on the plight of the farmer; the whole difficulty arose from "an appreciation in value of gold." Interested, Bryan demanded a list of books on the subject and was soon deep in a study of the money question.

To a man like Bryan, studying the money question meant searching for some means of checking the deflationary trend that was so injurious to his farmer constituents. He quickly discovered that most farm-belt financial authorities felt this could best be done by providing for the free coinage of silver. In 1873 the United States had gone on the gold standard, which meant that only gold was accepted for coinage at the mint. By going back to bimetallism, the amount of bullion being coined would be increased, and if the favorable ratio of sixteen to one between silver and gold were established, the production of silver for coinage would be greatly stimulated.

To press for the free coinage of silver at a ratio of sixteen to one with gold seemed less radical or dangerous than to demand direct inflation of the currency through the printing of greenbacks. Silver, after all, was a precious metal; coining it could not possibly lead to the sort of "runaway" inflation that had helped ruin the South during the Civil War. Debtors and other friends of inflation could also count on the powerful support of silver-mine interests. The free-coinage issue thus had a powerful political appeal. Despite the opposition of most conservative businessmen, the silverites were able, in 1878 and again in 1890, to obtain legislation providing for the coinage of *some* silver, although not enough to check the downward trend of prices.

Within a month after his tariff speech Bryan was calling for free coinage, and he stressed the issue in his successful campaign for re-election in 1892. But the new President, Democrat Grover Cleveland, was an ardent gold-standard man, and when a severe depression struck the country early in 1893, he demanded that the Silver Purchase Act of 1890, which had raised the specter of inflation in the minds of many businessmen, be repealed by Congress at once. In this way he committed his party to the resumption of the single gold standard.

Bryan refused to go along with this policy. Threatening to "serve my country and my God under some other name" than "Democrat" unless the Administration changed its mind, he resisted the repeal of the silver act in a brilliant extemporaneous speech. Cleveland carried the day for repeal, but Bryan emerged as a potential leader of the silver wing of the Democrats.

In 1894 he sought a wider influence by running for the United States Senate. In those days senators were still chosen by the state legislatures; to be elected Bryan would need the support of Nebraska's Populists as well as of his own party. He worked hard for fusion, but Populist support was not forthcoming. Though the Democrats backed Populist candidate Silas A. Holcomb for the governorship, the Populists refused to reciprocate and ran their own man for the Senate seat. The Republican candidate therefore won easily.

At this stage the Populists were trying hard to become a truly national party. Their program, besides demanding the free coinage of silver and various land reforms desired by farmers, called for government ownership of railroads, a graduated income tax, the direct election of U.S. senators, the eight-hour day, and a number of additional reforms designed to appeal to eastern workingmen and other dissatisfied groups. As early as 1892 their presidential candidate, James B. Weaver, had polled over a million votes; in 1894 the party won six seats in the Senate and seven in the House of Representatives. At least in Nebraska, the Populists were not yet ready to merge with the "conservative" Democratic organization.

Defeat for the Senate did not harm Bryan politically. He was still in his early thirties; to one so young, merely having run for the Senate brought considerable prestige. Also, he had conducted an intelligent and forceful campaign. Even so it was a defeat, certainly not calculated to lead him to the remarkable decision that he made after the Nebraska legislature had turned him down. This decision was to seek nomination for the Presidency of the United States itself!

The young man's "superlative self-assurance" (one might call it effrontery but for the fact that his daring plan succeeded) staggers the imagination. Many men within his party were far better known than he, and his state, Nebraska, was without major influence in Democratic affairs. With Cleveland and the national organization dead-set against free coinage and other inflationary schemes, Bryan's chances of capturing the nomination seemed infinitesimal. But if bold, his action was by no means foolish. Democratic voters were becoming more and more restive under Cleveland's conservative leadership. At least in Bryan's part of the nation, many thoughtful members of the party were beginning to feel that they must look in new directions and find new leaders if they were not to be replaced by the Populists as the country's second major party. Recognizing this situation before most politicians did, Bryan proceeded to act upon his insight with determination and dispatch.

First of all, he set out to make himself known beyond his own locality. Accepting the editorship of the Omaha *World-Herald* at a tiny salary in order to obtain a forum, he turned out a stream of editorials on the silver question, which he sent to influential politicians all over the country. He toured the South and West with his message, speaking everywhere and under all sorts of conditions: to close-packed, cheering throngs and to tiny groups of quiet listeners. His argument was simple but forceful, his oratory magnetic and compelling. Always he made sure to meet local leaders and to subject them to his genial smile, his youthful vigor, his charm, his sincerity. He did not push himself forward; indeed, he claimed to be ready to support any honest man whose program was sound. But he lost no chance to point out to all concerned his own availability. "I don't suppose your delegation is committed to any candidate," he wrote to a prominent Colorado Democrat in April of 1896. "Our delegation may present my name." When the Democratic convention finally met in Chicago, Bryan believed that he was known personally to more of the delegates than any other candidate.

Few delegates took his campaign seriously, however. At the convention, one senator asked Bryan who he thought would win out. Bryan replied characteristically that he believed he himself "had as good a chance to be nominated as anyone," and proceeded to tick off the sources of his strength: Nebraska, "half of the Indian Territory, . . ." but before Bryan could mention his other backers the senator lost interest and walked off with some of his cronies. The candidate, amiable and serene, took no offense. A majority of the delegates favored his position on silver. No one had a clear lead in the race. All he needed was a chance to plead his case.

The opportunity—Bryan called it an "unexpected stroke of luck," although he planned for it brilliantly—came when he was asked to close the debate on the platform's silver plank. When he came forward to address the jam-packed mob in the Chicago auditorium he was tense, but there was a smile on his face, and to observers he seemed the picture of calm self-confidence. He began quietly, but his voice resounded in the farthest corners of the great hall and commanded the attention of every delegate. He was conscious of his own humble position, he told the throng, but he was "clad in the armor of a righteous cause" and this entitled him to speak. As he went on, his tension evaporated and his voice rose. When he recounted the recent history of the struggle between the forces of gold and silver, the audience responded eagerly. "At the close of a sentence," he wrote later, "it would rise and shout, and when I began upon another sentence, the room was still as a church."

He spoke for silver as against gold, for the West over the East, for "the hardy pioneers who have braved all the dangers of the wilderness" as against "the few financial magnates who, in a back room, corner the money of the world."

> We have petitioned, and our petitions have been scorned; we have entreated, and our entreaties have been disregarded; we have begged, and they have mocked when our calamity came. We beg no longer; we entreat no more; we petition no more. *We defy them!*

The crowd thundered its agreement. Bryan proceeded. One after another he met the arguments of the party's Cleveland wing head on. Free silver would disturb the business interests? "Gold bugs" were defining the term too narrowly. Remember that wage earners, crossroads merchants, and farmers were also businessmen. The cities favored the gold standard? Their prosperity really depended upon the

*This 1896 cartoon entitled "The Sacrilegious Candidate" implies
that Bryan used religious metaphors for opportunistic purposes.*

prosperity of the great agricultural regions of the land, which
favored bimetallism. "Burn down your cities and leave our farms,"
he said, "and your cities will spring up again as if by magic; but
destroy our farms and the grass will grow in the streets of every city
in the country."

Now Bryan was absolute master of the delegates. "I thought of a
choir," he recalled afterward, "as I noted how instantaneously and in
unison they responded to each point made." The crowd cheered because he was reflecting its sentiments, but also because it recognized,
suddenly, its leader—handsome, confident, righteously indignant, yet
also calm, restrained, and ready for responsibility. His mission accomplished, it was time to close, and Bryan had saved a marvelous figure
of speech, tested in many an earlier oration, for his climax. "You
shall not press down upon the brow of labor this crown of thorns," he
warned, bringing his hands down suggestively to his temples; "you
shall not crucify mankind upon a cross of gold." Dramatically he
extended his arms to the side, the very figure of the crucified Christ.

Amid the hysterical demonstration that followed, it was clear that Bryan had accomplished his miracle. The next day, July 9, he was nominated for the Presidency on the fifth ballot.

The issue was clear-cut, for the Republicans had already declared for the gold standard and nominated the handsome, genial, and thoroughly conservative William McKinley. As a result, the Populists were under great pressure to go along with Bryan. While the Democrats had not adopted all the radical Populist demands, their platform contained a number of liberal planks in addition to that on free silver, including one calling for a federal income tax and another for stiffer controls of the railroad network. For the Populists to insist on nominating a third candidate would simply insure the election of the "gold bug" McKinley. Not every important Populist favored fusion; some were ready to concede defeat in 1896 and build their party for the future on broadly radical lines. "The Democratic idea of fusion," said Tom Watson of Georgia angrily, is "that we play Jonah while they play whale." But the rich scent of victory in the air was too much for the majority to resist. "I care not for party names," said "Sockless Jerry" Simpson bluntly; "it is the substance we are after, and we have it in William J. Bryan." Indeed, Bryan's friendly association with the Populists in earlier campaigns and his essentially Populistic views on most questions made it difficult for the party to oppose him. "We put him to school," one anti-Bryan Populist later remarked, "and he wound up by stealing the school-books." In any case, the Populist convention endorsed him; thus the silver forces united to do battle with the Republicans.

Both Bryan and McKinley men realized at once that this was to be a close and crucial contest. Seldom have the two great parties divided so clearly on fundamental issues; a showdown was inevitable; a major turning point in American history had been reached. Silver against gold was but the surface manifestation of the struggle. City against countryside, industry against agriculture, East against South and West, the nineteenth century against the twentieth—these were the real contestants in 1896.

After Bryan's nomination McKinley's manager, Mark Hanna, abandoned plans for a vacation cruise in New England waters and plunged into the work of the campaign. The situation was "alarming," he told McKinley. A "communistic spirit" was abroad, business was "all going to pieces." A mighty effort was called for. Hanna raised huge sums by "assessing" the great bankers, oil refiners, insurance men, and meat packers, using the threat of impending business chaos and wild inflation to loosen the purse strings of the tycoons. While McKinley, "the advance agent of prosperity," conducted a dignified and carefully organized campaign from his front porch in Canton, Ohio, 1,400 paid speakers beat the bushes for votes in every doubtful district. The Republican campaign committee distributed more than 120,000,000 pieces of literature printed in ten languages to carry its

*Bryan's presidential campaign opponent
in 1896, William McKinley, making his
nomination acceptance speech in
the manner in which he conducted his
campaign: on the front porch of
his house in Canton, Ohio.*

message to the voters. Boiler-plate editorials and other releases were
sent free to hundreds of small-town newspapers. Hanna, Theodore
Roosevelt said, "has advertised McKinley as if he were a patent medicine!" The Republican organization reached a peak of efficiency and
thoroughness never before approached in a political contest; the campaign marked a methodological revolution that has profoundly affected
every presidential contest since.

Bryan had little money, and no organizational genius like Hanna
to direct his drive. But he too effected a revolution that has left its
mark on modern campaigning. McKinley's front porch technique was
novel only in the huge number of visiting delegations that Hanna
paraded across his man's lawn and the exaggerated care that the candidate took to avoid saying anything impolitic. It had always been
considered undignified for a presidential nominee to go out and hunt
for votes on his own. Bryan cast off this essentially hypocritical tradition at the very start. He realized that the concerted power of business
and the press were aligned against him, and that his own greatest assets
were his magnificent ability as a political orator and his personal
sincerity and charm. His opponent could afford to sit tight; *he* must
seek out the people everywhere if they were to receive his message.
Between summer and November he traveled a precedent-shattering
18,000 miles, making more than 600 speeches and addressing directly
an estimated 5,000,000 Americans. His secretary estimated that he
uttered between 60,000 and 100,000 words every day during the
campaign.

On the stump he was superb. Without straining his voice he could
make himself heard to a restless open-air throng numbered in the tens
of thousands. He was equally effective at the whistle stops, outlining
his case from the rear platform of his train while a handful of country
people gazed earnestly upward from the roadbed. He was unfailingly
pleasant and unpretentious. At one stop, while he was shaving in his
compartment, a small group outside the train began clamoring for a
glimpse of him. Flinging open the window and beaming through the
lather, he cheerfully shook hands with each of these admirers. Neither
he nor they, according to the recorder of this incident, saw anything
unusual or undignified in the performance. Thousands of well-wishers
sent him good luck charms and messages of encouragement. "If the
people who have given me rabbits' feet in this campaign will vote for
me, there is no possible doubt of my election," he said in one speech.
It was because of this simple friendliness that he became known as
"the Great Commoner."

Bryan was also unfailingly interesting. Even his most unsympathetic
biographer admits that he spoke so well that at every stop the baggage-
men from the campaign train would run back to listen to his talk—
and this despite a schedule that called for as many as thirty speeches
a day.

Such a campaign is an effective means of projecting an image of
a candidate and his general point of view. It is not well suited for the

An 1896 Bryan campaign poster bearing the full text of his "Cross of Gold" speech.

making of complicated arguments and finely drawn distinctions; for that the McKinley approach was far superior. Wisely, for it was clearly the issue uppermost in the minds of most voters, Bryan hammered repeatedly at the currency question. He did not avoid talking about other matters: he attacked the railroads and the great business monopolists and the "tyranny" of the eastern bankers. He deplored the use of militia in labor disputes and of the injunction as a means of breaking strikes. He spoke in favor of income taxes, higher wages, and relief for hard-pressed mortgagees. But the silver issue was symbolic, and the Democratic position sound. There *was* a currency shortage; deflation *was* injuring millions of debtors and pouring a rich unearned increment into the pockets of bondholders. To say, as Henry Demarest Lloyd did at the time and as many liberal historians have since, that Bryan made free silver the "cowbird" of the reform movement, pushing out all other issues from the reform nest and thus destroying them, is an exaggeration and a distortion. All effective politicians stick to a small number of simple issues while on the stump; otherwise, in the hectic conflict of a hot campaign, they project no message at all. There is no reason to suspect that, if elected, Bryan would have forgotten about other reform measures and concentrated only on the currency.

For a time Bryan's gallant, singlehanded battle seemed to be having an effect on public opinion, and Republican leaders became thoroughly frightened. In addition to money, threats and imprecations now became weapons in the campaign. A rumor was circulated that Bryan was insane. The *New York Times* devoted columns to the possibility, and printed a letter from a supposed psychologist charging that he was suffering from "paranoia querulenta," "graphomania," and "oratorical monomania." "Men," one manufacturer told his workers, "vote as you please, but if Bryan is elected . . . the whistle will not blow Wednesday morning." According to the *Nation*, which was supporting McKinley, many companies placed orders with their suppliers "to be executed in case Mr. Bryan is defeated, and not otherwise." A Chicago company that held thousands of farm mortgages politely asked all its "customers" to indicate their presidential preferences—a not very subtle form of coercion but probably an effective one. In some cases men were actually fired because of their political opinions.

By the time election day arrived the McKinley managers were so confident of victory that Hanna began returning new contributions as no longer necessary. Nevertheless, a final monumental effort was made to get out the vote. Free transportation was provided to carry citizens to and from the polls, men were paid for time lost in voting, and in doubtful districts floaters and other disreputables were rounded up and paraded to the ballot boxes. Everywhere in the crucial North Central states the Hanna machine expended enormous efforts, and in these states the decision was made. McKinley carried them all and with them the nation. In the electoral college McKinley won by 271 to 176, but the popular vote was close—7,036,000 to 6,468,000. The change of a relative handful of votes in half a dozen key states would have swung the election to Bryan.

The victory, however, was McKinley's, and conservatives all over America—and the world—echoed the sentiment of Hanna's happy telegram to the President-elect: GOD'S IN HIS HEAVEN, ALL'S RIGHT WITH THE WORLD! A watershed in the economic and social history of the United States had been crossed. The rural America of the nineteenth century was making way for the industrial America of the twentieth. Soon business conditions began to improve, agricultural prices inched upward, new discoveries of gold relieved the pressure on the money supply. While McKinley and Hanna (now senator from Ohio) ruled in Washington, the era of complacent materialism and easy political virtue that had entered American politics on the coattails of General Grant seemed destined to continue indefinitely. Reform, it appeared, was dead.

That these appearances were deceiving was due in considerable measure to William Jennings Bryan. Unchastened by defeat and always cheerful ("It is better to have run and lost than never to have run at all," he said), he maintained the leadership of his party. Consistently he took the liberal position on important issues. Despite his strong pacifism he approved of fighting Spain in 1898 in order to free Cuba. "Humanity demands that we should act," he said simply. He enlisted in the Army and rose to be a colonel, although he saw no action during the brief conflict. The sincerity of his motives was proved when the war ended, for he then fought against the plan to annex former Spanish colonies. Running for President a second time in 1900, he made resistance to imperialism an issue in the campaign along with free silver. It both of these were poorly calculated to win votes in 1900, they were nonetheless solidly in the liberal tradition. Bryan lost to McKinley again, this time by 861,459 votes, and leadership of the reform movement passed, after McKinley's assassination, to Theodore Roosevelt. But Bryan continued the fight. In 1904, battling almost alone against conservatives in his own party, he forced the adoption of a fairly liberal platform (including strong antitrust, pro-labor, and antitariff planks), and when the conservative Judge Alton B. Parker was nonetheless nominated for President, Bryan kept up his outspoken criticism. While remaining loyal to the Democratic party he announced boldly: "The fight on economic questions . . . is not abandoned. As soon as the election is over I shall . . . organize for the campaign of 1908."

In that campaign Bryan, once more the Democratic nominee, was once more defeated in his personal quest of the Presidency, this time by Roosevelt's handpicked successor, William Howard Taft. Immediately he announced that he would not seek the office again, thus throwing the field open to other liberals.

Although he thus abandoned formal leadership of the Democrats, Bryan continued to advocate reform. Throughout the Taft administration he campaigned up and down the country to bolster the liberal wing of his party. When the 1912 nominating convention met in Baltimore, he introduced and won approval of a highly controversial resolution denouncing Wall Street influence, and he stated repeatedly that he would not support any candidate who was under the slightest obligation to Tammany Hall. The platform, as one historian says, "was a progressive document, in the best Bryan tradition." In the end Bryan threw his support to Woodrow Wilson. While this alone did not account for Wilson's nomination, it was very important in his election, for it assured him the enthusiastic backing of millions of loyal Bryanites.

Nothing reveals Bryan's fine personal qualities better than his support of Wilson, for the former Princeton professor had opposed the Great Commoner since 1896, when he had called the Cross of Gold speech "ridiculous." In 1904 he had publicly demanded that the Bryan wing be "utterly and once and for all driven from Democratic counsels." As late as 1908 he had refused to appear on the same platform with Bryan. Mr. Bryan, he said, "is the most charming and lovable of men personally, but foolish and dangerous in his theoretical beliefs." During the campaign of that year he refused to allow Bryan to deliver a campaign speech on the Princeton campus.

By 1912 Wilson had become far more liberal and no longer opposed most of Bryan's policies; even so, had Bryan been a lesser man he would not have forgiven these repeated criticisms. But he was more concerned with Wilson's 1912 liberalism than with personal matters, despite the publication of an old letter in which Wilson had expressed the wish to "knock Mr. Bryan once and for all into a cocked hat!" He shrugged off the "cocked hat" letter, and when Wilson paid him a handsome public tribute they became good friends. Furthermore, during the 1912 campaign, Bryan campaigned vigorously for Wilson, making well over four hundred speeches within a period of seven weeks. When Wilson won an easy victory in November, Bryan reacted without a trace of envy or bitterness. "It is a great triumph," he declared, "Let every Democratic heart rejoice." A few months later he said in a speech in Chicago:

> Sometimes I have had over-sanguine friends express regret that I did not reach the presidency. . . . But I have an answer ready for them. I have told them that they need not weep for me. . . . I have been so much more interested in the securing of the things for which we have been fighting than I have been in the name of the man who held the office, that I am happy in the thought that this government, through these reforms, will be made so good that a citizen will not miss a little thing like the presidency.

Wilson made Bryan Secretary of State. He was needed in the administration to help manage his many friends in Congress. The strategy worked well, for Bryan used his influence effectively. His role was particularly crucial in the hard fight over the Federal Reserve bill, but his loyal aid was also important in passing income tax legislation and a new antitrust law and in other matters as well.

In managing foreign affairs Bryan was less successful, for in this field he was ill-prepared. Because of his frank belief in the spoils system, he dismissed dozens of key professional diplomats, replacing them with untrained political hacks. Naturally the Foreign Service was badly injured. His policy of not serving alcoholic beverages at official functions because of his personal convictions caused much criticism at home and abroad. "W. J. Bryan not only suffers for his principles and mortifies his flesh, as he has every right to do," the London *Daily Express* complained, "but he insists that others should suffer and be mortified." The Secretary's continuing Chautauqua lectures, at which he sometimes appeared on the same platform with vaudeville entertainers and freaks, were attacked by many as undignified for one who occupied such a high official position.

Bryan had answers to all these criticisms: the State Department had been overly snobbish and undemocratic; Wilson had agreed to his "grape juice" policy before appointing him; no one should be ashamed of speaking to the American people. He could also point to his "cooling-off treaties" with some twenty nations, which provided machinery for avoiding blow-ups over minor diplomatic imbroglios.

Unfortunately Bryan had but a dim understanding of Latin American problems and unwittingly fostered American imperialism on many occasions. His narrow-minded belief that he knew better than local leaders what was "good" for these small countries showed that he had no comprehension of cultural and nationalistic elements in other lands. Although well intended, his policies produced much bad feeling in South and Central America. Bryan did suggest lending Latin American nations money "for education, sanitation and internal development," a policy that anticipated our modern Point Four approach to underdeveloped areas. Wilson, however, dismissed the idea because he thought it "would strike the whole country . . . as a novel and radical proposal."

When the World War broke out in 1914, Bryan, like his chief, adopted a policy of strict neutrality. America, he said, should attempt to mediate between the belligerents by suggesting "a more rational basis of peace." Bryan believed in real neutrality far more deeply than Wilson, who was not ready to face the possibility of a German victory. "We cannot have in mind the wishes of one side more than the wishes of the other side," Bryan warned the President after the latter had prepared a stiff note of protest against German submarine warfare. And when, after the sinking of the *Lusitania*, Wilson sent a series of threatening messages to Germany, Bryan resigned as Secretary of State. He never again held public office.

It would have been better for Bryan's reputation if he had died in 1915; instead he lived on for another decade, as amiable and well-intentioned as ever but increasingly out of touch with the rapidly changing times. He made no effort to keep up with the abrupt intel-

lectual developments of the twentieth century, yet he was accustomed
to speak his mind on current issues and continued to do so. There had
always been those who had considered his uncomplicated faith in
time-tested moral principles and in popular rule rather naïve; in the
cynical, scientific, and amoral twenties only a relative handful of
rural oldtimers saw much virtue in his homilies on the people's unfailing instinct to do always what was "right" and "good." In the
world of Calvin Coolidge the old Populist fires no longer burned very
brightly, and Bryan's anti-business bias seemed terribly old-fashioned.
Many had considered him an anachronism even in Wilson's day; by
Harding's he had simply ceased to count in politics. More and more he
confined himself to religious questions. His ardent piety was heart-
warming, but he was a smug and intolerant Fundamentalist whose
ignorance of modern science and ethics did not prevent him from
expounding his "views" on these subjects at length. The honest
opinions of "the people," he believed, could "settle" scientific and
philosophical questions as easily as political ones.

*Bryan (right) at the end of his career
with Clarence Darrow during the Scopes trial.*

Advancing age, as well as increasing preoccupation with revealed religion, was making Bryan less tolerant. Never one to give much thought to reasoned counterarguments, he became, in the twenties, an outspoken foe of many aspects of human freedom. He defended prohibition, refused to condemn the Ku Klux Klan, and participated eagerly in the notorious Scopes anti-evolution trial in Dayton, Tennessee, with all its overtones of censorship and self-satisfied ignorance. The final great drama of Bryan's life occurred when Clarence Darrow mercilessly exposed his simple prejudices on the witness stand. Bryan complacently maintained, among other things, that Eve was actually made from Adam's rib and that Jonah had really been swallowed by the whale. The rural audience cheered, but educated men all over the world were appalled.

Throughout his lifetime, Bryan was subject to harsh and almost continual criticism, and at least superficially he failed in nearly everything he attempted. But he was too secure in his faith to be injured by criticism, and he knew that for over two decades his influence was greater than any of his contemporaries save Theodore Roosevelt and Wilson. His life was useful and happy, for he rightly believed that he had made a lasting contribution to his country's development. Nor is it fair to condemn him for his limited intelligence and superficial understanding of his times. Other political leaders of at best ordinary intellect have done great deeds, sometimes without appreciating the meaning of events they have helped to shape. Still, there was tragedy in Bryan's career—he was unable to grow.

In 1896 he was indeed the peerless leader, vital, energetic, dedicated, and, in a measure, imaginative. He saw the problems of Nebraska farmers, realized their wider implications, and outlined a reasonable program designed to deal with them. He was almost elected President as a result, despite his youth and inexperience. Suddenly he was a celebrity; thereafter he moved into a wider world and lived there at his ease. He did not abandon his principles, and he helped achieve many important reforms, for which we must always honor him, but he soon ceased to feed upon new ideas. In a sense, despite the defeats, life's rewards came to him too easily. His magnetic voice, his charm, his patent sincerity, the memory of the heroic fight of '96—these things secured his place and relieved him of the need to grapple with new concepts.

Although he was a man of courage, strength, and endurance, Bryan was essentially lax and complacent. He preferred baggy clothes, a full stomach, the easy, undemanding companionship of small minds. For years the momentum of 1896 carried him on, but eventually the speeding world left him far behind. Fortunately for his inner well-being, he never realized what had happened. A few days after Darrow had exposed his shallowness before the world, he died peacefully in his sleep, as serene and unruffled by events as ever.

Anne Firor Scott

JANE ADDAMS: URBAN CRUSADER

As the reputations of Progressive political leaders have declined, those of some of the social reformers of the era have risen. This is particularly true of social workers like Jane Addams and other founders of the settlement-house movement, who in modern eyes seem to have had a more profound grasp of the true character of the problems of their age and to have worked more effectively and with greater dedication in trying to solve those problems than did any of the politicians.

These social workers were quite different from those of today—they were more personally involved and far less professionally oriented. Many were also, it is true, somewhat patronizing in their approach to those they sought to help and took a rather romantic and thus unrealistic view of the potentialities both of the poor and of their own capacity to help the poor. This essay by Professor Anne Firor Scott of Duke University makes clear, however, that Jane Addams of Chicago's Hull-House was neither patronizing nor a romantic. Professor Scott is the author of *The Southern Lady: From Pedestal to Politics* and *The American Woman: Who Was She?*

If Alderman Johnny Powers of Chicago's teeming nineteenth ward had only been prescient, he might have foreseen trouble when two young ladies not very long out of a female seminary in Rockford, Illinois, moved into a dilapidated old house on Halsted Street in September, 1889, and announced themselves "at home" to the neighbors. The ladies, however, were not very noisy about it, and it is doubtful if Powers was aware of their existence. The nineteenth ward was well supplied with people already—growing numbers of Italians, Poles, Russians, Irish, and other immigrants—and two more would hardly be noticed.

Johnny Powers was the prototype of the ward boss who was coming to be an increasingly decisive figure on the American political scene. In the first place, he was Irish. In the second, he was, in the parlance of the time, a "boodler": his vote and influence in the Chicago Common Council were far from being beyond price. As chairman of the council's finance committee and boss of the Cook County Democratic party he occupied a strategic position. Those who understood the inner workings of Chicago politics thought that Powers had some hand in nearly every corrupt ordinance passed by the council during his years in office. In a single year, 1895, he was to help to sell six important city franchises. When the mayor vetoed Powers' measures, a silent but significant two-thirds vote appeared to override the veto.

Ray Stannard Baker, who chanced to observe Powers in the late nineties, recorded that he was shrewd and silent, letting other men make the speeches and bring upon their heads the abuse of the public. Powers was a short, stocky man, Baker said, "with a flaring gray pompadour, a smooth-shaven face [sic], rather heavy features, and a restless eye." One observer remarked that "the shadow of sympathetic gloom is always about him. He never jokes; he has forgotton how to smile . . ." Starting life as a grocery clerk, Powers had run for the city council in 1888 and joined the boodle ring headed by Alderman Billy Whalen. When Whalen died in an accident two years later, Powers moved swiftly to establish himself as successor. A few weeks before his death Whalen had collected some thirty thousand dollars— derived from the sale of a city franchise—to be divided among the party faithful. Powers alone knew that the money was in a safe in Whalen's saloon, so he promptly offered a high price for the furnishings of the saloon, retrieved the money, and divided it among the gang—at one stroke establishing himself as a shrewd operator and as one who would play the racket fairly.

From this point on he was the acknowledged head of the gang. Charles Yerkes, the Chicago traction tycoon, found in Powers an ideal tool for the purchase of city franchises. On his aldermanic salary of three dollars a week, Powers managed to acquire two large saloons of his own, a gambling establishment, a fine house, and a conspicuous collection of diamonds. When he was indicted along with two other corrupt aldermen for running a slot machine and keeping a "common gambling house," Powers was unperturbed. The three appeared before a police judge, paid each other's bonds, and that was the end of that.

Proof of their guilt was positive, but convictions were never obtained.

On the same day the Municipal Voters League published a report for the voters on the records of the members of the city council. John Powers was described as "recognized leader of the worst element in the council . . . [who] has voted uniformly for bad ordinances." The League report went on to say that he had always opposed securing any return to the city for valuable franchises, and proceeded to document the charge in detail.

To his constituents in the nineteenth ward, most of whom were getting their first initiation into American politics, Powers turned a different face. To them, he was first and last a friend. When there were celebrations, he always showed up: if the celebration happened to be a bazaar, he bought freely, murmuring piously that it would all go to the poor. In times of tragedy he was literally Johnny on the spot. If the family was too poor to provide the necessary carriage for a respectable funeral, it appeared at the doorstep—courtesy of Johnny Powers and charged to his standing account with the local undertaker. If the need was not so drastic, Powers made his presence felt with an imposing bouquet or wreath. "He has," said the Chicago *Times-Herald,* "bowed with aldermanic grief at thousands of biers."

Christmas meant literally tons of turkeys, geese, and ducks—each one handed out personally by a member of the Powers family, with good wishes and no questions asked. Johnny provided more fundamental aid, too, when a breadwinner was out of work. At one time he is said to have boasted that 2,600 men from his ward (about one third of

The antagonists: Jane Addams (left) in London in 1888 just prior to taking on Johnny Powers, Democratic ward boss, seen here (right) in a photograph taken about 1910.

the registered voters) were working in one way or another for the city of Chicago. This did not take into account those for whom the grateful holders of traction franchises had found a place. When election day rolled around, the returns reflected the appreciation of job-holders and their relatives.

The two young ladies on Halsted Street, Jane Addams and Ellen Starr, were prototypes too, but of a very different kind of figure: they were the pioneers of the social settlement, the original "social workers." They opposed everything Johnny Powers stood for.

Jane Addams' own background could hardly have been more different from that of John Powers. The treasured daughter of a well-to-do small-town businessman from Illinois, she had been raised in an atmosphere of sturdy Christian principles.

From an early age she had been an introspective child concerned with justifying her existence. Once in a childhood nightmare she had dreamed of being the only remaining person in a world desolated by some disaster, facing the responsibility for rediscovering the principle of the wheel! At Rockford she shared with some of her classmates a determination to live to "high purpose," and decided that she would become a doctor in order to "help the poor."

After graduation she went to the Woman's Medical College of Philadelphia, but her health failed and she embarked on the grand tour of Europe customary among the wealthy. During a subsequent trip to Europe in 1888, in the unlikely setting of a Spanish bull ring, an idea that had long been growing in her mind suddenly crystallized: she would rent a house "in a part of the city where many primitive and actual needs are found, in which young women who had been given over too exclusively to study, might restore a balance of activity along traditional lines and learn something of life from life itself . . ." So the American settlement-house idea was born. She and Ellen Starr, a former classmate at the Rockford seminary who had been with her in Europe, went back to Chicago to find a house among the victims of the nineteenth century's fast-growing industrial society.

The young women—Jane was twenty-nine and Ellen thirty in 1889 —had no blueprint to guide them when they decided to take up residence in Mr. Hull's decayed mansion and begin helping "the neighbors" to help themselves. No school of social work had trained them for this enterprise: Latin and Greek, art, music, and "moral philosophy" at the seminary constituted their academic preparation. Toynbee Hall in England—the world's first settlement house, founded in 1884 by Samuel A. Barnett—had inspired them. Having found the Hull house at the corner of Polk and Halsted—in what was by common consent one of Chicago's worst wards—they leased it, moved in, and began doing what came naturally.

Miss Starr, who had taught in an exclusive girls' preparatory school, inaugurated a reading party for young Italian women with George Eliot's *Romola* as the first book. Miss Addams, becoming aware of the desperate problem of working mothers, began at once to organize a kindergarten. They tried Russian parties for the Russian neighbors, organized boys' clubs for the gangs on the street, and offered to bathe all babies. The neighbors were baffled, but impressed. Very soon children and grownups of all sorts and conditions were finding their way to Hull-House—to read Shakespeare or to ask for a volunteer midwife; to learn sewing or discuss socialism; to study art or to fill an empty stomach. There were few formalities and no red tape, and the young ladies found themselves every day called upon to deal with some of the multitude of personal tragedies against which the conditions of life in the nineteenth ward offered so thin a cushion.

Before long, other young people feeling twinges of social conscience and seeking a tangible way to make their convictions count in the world of the 1890's came to live at Hull-House. These "residents," as they were called, became increasingly interested in the personal histories of the endless stream of neighbors who came to the House each week. They began to find out about the little children sewing all day long in the "sweated" garment trade, and about others who worked long hours in a candy factory. They began to ask why there were three thousand more children in the ward than there were seats in its schoolrooms, and why the death rate was higher there than in almost any other part of Chicago. They worried about youngsters whose only playground was a garbage-spattered alley that threatened the whole population with disease. (Once they traced a typhoid epidemic to its source and found the sewer line merging with the water line.) In the early days Hull-House offered bathtubs and showers, which proved so popular a form of hospitality that the residents became relentless

Chicago's old Hull mansion, refurbished and renamed Hull-House, about 1910.

lobbyists for municipal baths.

Hull-House was not the only American settlement house—indeed, Jane Addams liked to emphasize the validity of the idea by pointing out that it had developed simultaneously in several different places. But Hull-House set the pace, and in an astonishingly short time its founder began to acquire a national reputation. As early as 1893 Jane Addams wrote to a friend: "I find I am considered the grandmother of social settlements." She was being asked to speak to gatherings of learned gentlemen, sociologists and philosophers, on such subjects as "The Subjective Necessity for Social Settlements." When the Columbian Exposition attracted thousands of visitors to Chicago in 1893, Hull-House became—along with the lake front and the stockyards— one of the things a guest was advised not to miss. By the mid-nineties, distinguished Europeans were turning up regularly to visit the House and examine its workings. W. T. Stead, editor of the English *Review of Reviews,* spent much time there while he gathered material for his sensational book, *If Christ Came to Chicago.* By that time two thousand people a week were coming to Hull-House to participate in some of its multifarious activities, which ranged from philosophy classes to the Nineteenth Ward Improvement Association.

Neither her growing reputation nor the increasing demand for speeches and articles, however, distracted Jane Addams from what was to be for forty years the main focus of a many-sided life: Hull-House and the nineteenth ward. Much of her early writing was an attempt to portray the real inner lives of America's proliferating immigrants, and much of her early activity, an effort to give them a voice to speak out against injustice.

The Hull-House residents were becoming pioneers in many ways, not least in the techniques of social research. In the *Hull-House Maps and Papers*, published in 1895, they prepared some of the first careful studies of life in an urban slum, examining the details of the "home-work" system of garment making and describing tumble-down houses, overtaxed schools, rising crime rates, and other sociological problems. The book remains today an indispensable source for the social historian of Chicago in the nineties.

Jane Addams' own interest in these matters was far from academic. Her concern for the uncollected garbage led her to apply for—and receive—an appointment as garbage inspector. She rose at six every morning and in a horse-drawn buggy followed the infuriated garbage contractor on his appointed rounds, making sure that every receptacle was emptied. Such badgering incensed Alderman Powers, in whose hierarchy of values cleanliness, though next to godliness, was a good bit below patronage—and he looked upon garbage inspection as a job for one of his henchmen. By now John Powers was becoming aware of his new neighbors; they were increasingly inquisitive about things close to Johnny Powers' source of power. By implication they were raising a troublesome question: Was Johnny Powers really "taking care of the poor"?

For a while, as one resident noted, the inhabitants of the House were "passive though interested observers of their representative, declining his offers of help and co-operation, refusing politely to distribute his Christmas turkeys, but feeling too keenly the smallness of their numbers to work against him." They were learning, though, and the time for passivity would end.

In company with many other American cities, Chicago after 1895 was taking a critical look at its political life and at the close connections that had grown up between politics and big business during the explosive era of industrial expansion following the Civil War. "The sovereign people may govern Chicago in theory," Stead wrote; "as a matter of fact King Boodle is monarch of all he surveys. His domination is practically undisputed."

The Municipal Voters League, a reform organization that included many of Jane Addams' close friends, was founded in 1896 in an effort to clean up the Common Council, of whose sixty-eight aldermen fifty-eight were estimated to be corrupt. The League aimed to replace as many of the fifty-eight as possible with honest men. But it was not easy: in 1896, as part of this campaign, a member of the Hull-House Men's Club ran for the second aldermanic position in the ward and against all expectations was elected. Too late, his idealistic backers found that their hero had his price: Johnny Powers promptly bought him out.

Jane Addams was chagrined but undiscouraged. By the time Powers came up for re-election in 1898, she had had time to observe him more closely and plan her attack. Her opening gun was a speech—delivered,

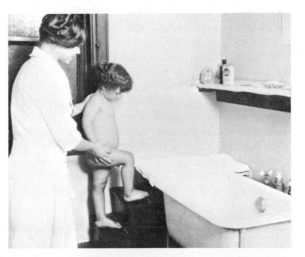

Children were Hull-House's first concern. Infants were bathed (right) and moppets put into nursery school (below).

Older boys (right) took shop lessons to prepare them to become successful artisans.

improbably enough, to the Society for Ethical Culture—with the ponderous and apparently harmless title, ''Some Ethical Survivals in Municipal Corruption.'' But appearances were deceptive: once under way, she took the hide off Powers and was scarcely easier on his opponents among the so-called ''better elements.''

She began by pointing out that for the immigrants, who were getting their first initiation in self-government, ethics was largely a matter of example: the officeholder was apt to set the standard and exercise a permanent influence upon their views. An engaging politician whose standards were low and ''impressed by the cynical stamp of the corporations'' could debauch the political ideals of ignorant men and women, with consequences that might, she felt, take years to erase.

Ethical issues were further complicated, she said, by habits of thought brought to the New World from the Old. Many Italians and Germans had left their respective fatherlands to escape military service; the Polish and Russian Jews, to escape government persecution. In all these cases, the government had been cast in the role of oppressor. The Irish, in particular, had been conditioned by years of resentment over English rule to regard any successful effort to feed at the public crib as entirely legitimate, because it represented getting the better of their bitterest enemies.

On the other hand, Miss Addams continued, there was nothing the immigrants admired more than simple goodness. They were accustomed to helping each other out in times of trouble, sharing from their own meager store with neighbors who were even more destitute. When Alderman Powers performed on a large scale the same good deeds which they themselves were able to do only on a small scale, was it any wonder that they admired him?

Given this admiration, and their Old World resentments toward government, the immigrants' developing standards of political morality suffered when Powers made it clear that he could ''fix'' courts or find jobs for his friends on the city payroll. It cheapened their image of American politics when they began to suspect that the source of their benefactor's largess might be a corrupt bargain with a traction tycoon, or with others who wanted something from the city of Chicago and were willing to pay for it.

Hull-House residents, Miss Addams said, very early found evidence of the influence of the boss's standards. When the news spread around the neighborhood that the House was a source of help in time of trouble, more and more neighbors came to appeal for aid when a boy was sent to jail or reform school, and it was impossible to explain to them why Hull-House, so ready to help in other ways, was not willing to get around the law as the Alderman did.

Removing Alderman Powers from office, Jane Addams told the sober gentlemen of the Society for Ethical Culture, would be no simple task. It would require a fundamental change in the ethical standards of the community, as well as the development of a deeper insight on the part of the reformers. These latter, she pointed out, with all their zeal for well-ordered, honest politics, were not eager to undertake the responsibilities of self-government 365 days a year. They were quite willing to come into the nineteenth ward at election time to exhort the citizenry, but were they willing to make a real effort to achieve personal relationships of the kind that stood Johnny Powers in such good stead?

On this last point, Hull-House itself had some experience. As Florence Kelley—a Hull-House resident who was to become a pioneer in the Illinois social reform movement—subsequently wrote:

> The question is often asked whether all that the House undertakes could not be accomplished without the wear and tear of living on the spot. The answer, that it could not, grows more assured as time goes on. You must suffer from the dirty streets, the universal ugliness, the lack of oxygen in the air you daily breathe, the endless struggle with soot and dust and insufficient water supply, the hanging from a strap of the overcrowded street car at the end of your day's work; you must send your children to the nearest wretchedly crowded school, and see them suffer the consequences, if you are to speak as one having authority and not as the scribes . . .

By 1898, after nine years of working with their neighbors, the Hull-House residents were ready to pit their influence against that of Powers. Jane Addams' philosophical address to the Ethical Culture society was followed by others in which she explained more concretely the relationships between Yerkes, Chicago's traction czar, and the city council, relationships in which Johnny Powers played a key role. With several important deals in the making, 1898 would be a bad year for Yerkes to lose his key man in the seats of power.

The election was scheduled for April. The reformers—led by Hull-House and supported by independent Democrats, the Cook County Republicans, and the Municipal Voters League—put up a candidate of their own, Simeon Armstrong, to oppose Powers, and undertook to organize and underwrite Armstrong's campaign. By the end of January, the usually imperturbable Powers suddenly began paying attention to his political fences. The newspapers noted with some surprise that it was the first time he had felt it necessary to lift a finger more than two weeks in advance of election day.

His first move was an attack on Amanda Johnson, a Hull-House resident who had succeeded Miss Addams as garbage inspector. A graduate of the University of Wisconsin and described by the papers as blond, blue-eyed, and beautiful, she had taken the civil service examination and duly qualified for the position. Alderman Powers announced to the world that Miss Johnson, shielded by her civil service status, was telling his constituents not to vote for him. The Chicago *Record* dropped a crocodile tear at the sad picture of the martyred alderman:

General sympathy should go out to Mr. Powers in this, his

latest affliction. Heretofore he has been persecuted often by people opposed to bad franchise ordinances. He has been hounded by the upholders of civil service reform. He has suffered the shafts of criticism directed at his career by disinterested citizens. A grand jury has been cruel to him. Invidious comments have been made in his hearing as to the ethical impropriety of gambling institutions. . . . It is even believed that Miss Johnson in her relentless cruelty may go so far as to insinuate that Mr. Powers' electioneering methods are no better than those attributed to her—that, indeed, when he has votes to win, the distinctions of the civil service law do not deter him from going after those votes in many ways.

Powers' next move was to attempt a redistricting that would cut off the eastern, or Italian, end of his ward, which he took to be most seriously under Hull-House influence. It was reported that he also felt this area had been a "large source of expense to him through the necessity of assisting the poor that are crowded into that district." "These people," the Chicago *Record* reported, "formerly tied to him by his charities are said to be turning toward Hull-House and will vote solidly against him next spring."

Neither of Powers' first efforts was notably successful. A few days after his attack on Miss Johnson the *Tribune* reported:

Trouble sizzled and boiled for Alderman John Powers in his own bailiwick last night. The Nineteenth Ward Independent club raked over the Alderman's sins . . . and . . . much indignation was occasioned by Alderman Powers' opposition to Miss Amanda Johnson. One Irish speaker says Johnny is a disgrace to the Irish race now that he has descended to fighting "poor working girls."

Meantime, Powers' colleagues on the council redistricting committee had no intention of saving his skin at the expense of their own, and stood solidly against his gerrymandering effort. Now the shaken boss began to show signs of losing his temper. He told reporters that if Miss Addams didn't like the ninteenth ward she should move out. Later, still more infuriated, he announced that Hull-House should be driven out. "A year from now there will be no such institution," he said flatly, adding that the women at Hull-House were obviously jealous of his charities. The *Record* published a cartoon showing Powers pushing vainly against the wall of a very substantial house.

The news of the campaign soon spread beyond the bounds of Chicago. The New York *Tribune* commented that Powers

wouldn't mind Miss Addams saying all those things about him if he didn't begin to fear that she may succeed in making some of his well-meaning but misled constituents believe them. She is a very practical person, and has behind her a large volunteer staff of other practical persons who do not confine their efforts to "gassin' in the parlors," but are going about to prove to the plain people of the nineteenth ward that a corrupt and dishonest man does not necessarily become a saint by giving a moiety of his ill-gotten gains to the poor.

By March the campaign was waxing warm, and Powers resorted to an attempt to stir up the Catholic clergy against Miss Addams and the reform candidate. One of the Hull-House residents, a deputy factory inspector and a Catholic herself, went directly to the priests to find out why they were supporting Powers. When she reported, Jane Addams wrote to a friend:

> As nearly as I can make out, the opposition comes from the Jesuits, headed by Father Lambert, and the parish priests are not in it, and do not like it. Mary talked for a long time to Father Lambert and is sure it is jealousy of Hull-House and money obligations to Powers, that he does not believe the charges himself. She cried when she came back.

In another letter written about the same time, Miss Addams said that Powers had given a thousand dollars to the Jesuit "temperance cadets," who had returned the favor with a fine procession supporting Powers' candidacy. "There was a picture of your humble servant on a transparency and others such as 'No petticoat government for us . . .' We all went out on the corner to see it, Mr. Hinsdale carefully shielding me from the public view."

By now the battle between Hull-House and Johnny Powers was sharing headlines in Chicago newspapers with the blowing up of the *Maine* in Havana's harbor and the approach of the war with Spain. "Throughout the nineteenth ward," said the *Tribune,* "the one absorbing topic of conversation wherever men are gathered is the fight being made against Alderman Powers." It was rumored that Powers had offered a year's free rent to one of the opposition leaders if he would move out of the ward before election day, and the Hull-House group let it be known that the Alderman was spending money freely in the ward, giving his lieutenants far more cash to spread around than was his custom. "Where does the money come from?" Jane Addams asked, and answered her own question: "From Mr. Yerkes." Powers was stung, and challenged her to prove that he had ever received one dollar from any corporation.

"Driven to desperation," said the *Tribune,* "Ald. Powers has at last called to his aid the wives and daughters of his political allies." Determined to fight fire with fire, he dropped his opposition to "petticoat politicians" and gave his blessing to a Ladies Auxiliary which was instructed to counteract the work of the women of Hull-House. An enterprising reporter discovered that few of the ladies had ever seen Miss Addams or been to Hull-House, but all were obediently repeating the charge that she had "blackened and maligned the whole ward" by saying that its people were ignorant, criminal, and poor.

As the campaign became more intense, Jane Addams received numbers of violent letters, nearly all of them anonymous, from Powers' partisans, as well as various communications from lodginghouse keepers quoting prices for votes they were ready to deliver! When the Hull-House residents discovered evidence of ties between banking, ecclesiastical, and journalistic interests, with Powers at the center, they proceeded to publicize all they knew. This brought upon their heads a violent attack by the Chicago *Chronicle,* the organ of the Democratic ring.

Suddenly a number of nineteenth-ward businessmen who had signed petitions for the reform candidate came out for Powers. They were poor and in debt; Powers gave the word to a landlord here, a coal dealer there, and they were beaten. The small peddlers and fruit dealers were subjected to similar pressure, for each needed a license to ply his trade, and the mere hint of a revocation was enough to create another Powers man.

When Alderman John M. Harlan, one of the stalwarts of the Municipal Voters League, came into the ward to speak, Powers supplied a few toughs to stir up a riot. Fortunately Harlan was a sturdy character, and offered so forcefully to take on all comers in fisticuffs that no volunteers appeared. Allowed to proceed, he posed some embarrassing questions: Why did nineteenth-ward residents have to pay ten-cent trolley fares when most of the city paid five? Why, when Powers was head of the city council's free-spending committee on street paving, were the streets of the ward in execrable condition? Why were the public schools so crowded, and why had Powers suppressed a petition, circulated by Hull-House, to build more of them?

Freely admitting Powers' reputation for charity, Harlan made the interesting suggestion that the councilman's motives be put to the test: Would he be so generous as a private citizen? "Let us retire him to private life and see."

Powers was pictured by the papers as being nearly apoplectic at this attack from Miss Addams' friend. He announced that he would not be responsible for Harlan's safety if he returned to the nineteenth ward. (Since no one had asked him to assume any such responsibility, this was presumed to be an open threat.) Harlan returned at once, telling a crowd well-laced with Powers supporters that he would "rather die in my tracks than acknowledge the right of John Powers to say who should and who should not talk in this ward." Summoning up the memory of Garibaldi, he urged the Italians to live up to their tradition of freedom and not allow their votes to be "delivered."

In a quieter vein, Miss Addams too spoke at a public meeting of Italians, where, it was reported, she received profound and respectful attention. "Show that you do not intend to be governed by a boss," she told them. "It is important not only for yourselves but for your children. These things must be made plain to them."

As the campaign progressed, the reformers began to feel they had a real chance of defeating Powers. Jane Addams was persuaded to go in search of funds with which to carry out the grand finale. "I sallied forth today and got $100," she wrote, and "will have to keep it up all week; charming prospect, isn't it?" But on about the twentieth of

March she began to have serious hopes, too, and redoubled her efforts.

As election day, April 6, approached, the Chicago *Tribune* and the Chicago *Record* covered the campaign daily, freely predicting a victory for the reformers. Alas for all predictions. When election day came, Powers' assets, which Jane Addams had so cogently analyzed in that faraway speech to the Society for Ethical Culture, paid off handsomely. It was a rough day in the nineteenth ward, with ten saloons open, one man arrested for drawing a gun, and everything, as Miss Addams wrote despondently when the count began to come in, "as bad as bad can be." Too many election judges were under Powers' thumb. The reform candidate was roundly defeated. Hull-House went to court to challenge the conduct of the election, but in the halls of justice Powers also had friends. It was no use.

Even in victory, however, Powers was a bit shaken. Hull-House had forced him, for the first time, to put out a great effort for re-election. It was obviously *not* going to move out of the nineteenth ward; indeed, if the past was any portent, its influence with his constituents would increase.

Powers decided to follow an ancient maxim, "If you can't lick 'em, join 'em." Early in the 1900 aldermanic campaign, several Chicago papers carried a straight news story to the effect that Hull-House and Johnny Powers had signed a truce, and quoted various paternally benevolent statements on the Alderman's part. In the *Chronicle,* for example, he was reported to have said: "I am not an Indian when it comes to hate . . . let bygones be bygones." A day or two later another rash of stories detailed a number of favors the Alderman was supposed to have done for Hull-House.

Jane Addams was furious, and after considerable deliberation she decided to reply. It was one of the few times in her long public career when she bothered to answer anything the newspapers said about her. She knew that with his eye on the campaign, the master politician was trying to give the appearance of having taken his most vigorous enemy into camp. She had been observing him too long not to realize what he was up to, and she could not possibly let him get away with it.

On February 20, 1900, a vigorous letter from Miss Addams appeared in nearly all the Chicago papers, reaffirming the attitude of Hull-House toward Mr. Powers. "It is needless to state," she concluded, "that the protest of Hull-House against a man who continually disregards the most fundamental rights of his constituents must be permanent."

Permanent protest, yes, but as a practical matter there was no use waging another opposition campaign. Powers held too many of the cards. When all was said and done, he had proved too tough a nut to crack, though Hull-House could—and did—continue to harass him. An observer of the Municipal Voters League, celebrating its success in the *Outlook* in June, 1902, described the vast improvement in the Common Council, but was forced to admit that a few wards were "well-nigh hopeless." He cited three: those of "Blind Billy" Kent, "Bathhouse John" Coughlin, and Johnny Powers.

From a larger standpoint, however, the battle between "Saint Jane" (as the neighbors called Jane Addams when she was not around) and the Ward Boss was not without significance. It was one of numerous similar battles that would characterize the progressive era the country over, and many of them the reformers would win. Because of her firsthand experience, because she lived *with* the immigrants instead of coming into their neighborhood occasionally to tell them what to do, Jane Addams was perhaps the first of the urban reformers to grasp the real pattern of bossism, its logic, the functions it performed, and the reason it was so hard to dislodge. Years later political scientists, beginning to analyze the pattern, would add almost nothing to her speech of 1898. If copies of *The Last Hurrah* have reached the Elysian fields, Jane Addams has spent an amused evening seeing her ideas developed so well in fictional form.

The campaign of 1898 throws considerable light on Jane Addams' intensely practical approach to politics, and upon a little-known aspect of the settlement-house movement. If anyone had told her and Ellen Starr in 1889 that the logic of what they were trying to do would inevitably force them into politics, they would have hooted. But in due time politics, in many forms, became central to Hull-House activity. For Jane Addams herself, the campaign against Powers was the first in a long series of political forays, all essentially based on the same desire—to see that government met the needs of the "other half."

The regulation of child labor, for example, was one political issue in which Hull-House residents became involved because of their knowledge of the lives of the neighbors. The first juvenile court in Chicago was set up as a result of their efforts; it was a direct response to the anxious mothers who could not understand why Hull-House would not help get their boys out of jail. The first factory inspection law in Illinois was also credited to Hull-House, and Florence Kelley became the first inspector. Another Hull-House resident—Dr. Alice Hamilton—pioneered in the field of industrial medicine. Because of their intimate acquaintance with the human cost of industrialization, settlement workers became vigorous advocates of promoting social justice through law.

It was a long jump but not an illogical one from the campaign against Powers to the stage of the Chicago Coliseum in August, 1912, when Jane Addams arose to second the nomination of Teddy Roosevelt by the Progressive party on a platform of social welfare. More remarkable than the ovation—larger than that given to any other seconder—was the fact that the huge audience seemed to listen carefully to what she had to say.

Some newspapers grandly estimated her value to T.R. at a million votes. "Like the report of Mark Twain's death," she commented, "the report is greatly exaggerated." But she campaigned vigorously, in the face of criticism that this was not a proper role for a woman, and when the Bull Moose cause failed, she did not believe it had been a waste of time. It had brought about, she wrote Roosevelt, more discussion of social reform than she had dared to hope for in her lifetime.

Alderman Powers was still in office—as were many like him—but the sources of his power were being attacked at the roots.

When the 1916 campaign came around, Democrats and Republicans alike made bids for Jane Addams' support. The outbreak of war in Europe had turned her attention, however, in a different direction. As early as 1907, in a book called *Newer Ideals of Peace,* she had begun to elaborate William James's notion of a "moral equivalent of war," and had suggested that the experience of polyglot immigrant populations in learning to live together might be laying the foundations for a true international order. Like her ideals of social justice, those that she conceived on international peace had their beginning in the nineteenth ward.

To her, as to so many idealistic progressives, world war came as a profound shock. Her response was a vigorous effort to bring together American women and women from all the European countries to urge upon their governments a negotiated peace. In Europe, where she went in 1915 for a meeting of the Women's International Peace Conference, she visited prime ministers; at the end of that year she planned to sail on Henry Ford's peace ship, but illness forced her to withdraw at the last moment. At home she appealed to President Wilson. Unshaken in her pacifism, she stood firmly against the war, even after the United States entered it.

Her popularity seemed to melt overnight. Many women's clubs and social workers, who owed so much to her vision, deserted her. An Illinois judge who thought it dangerous for her to speak in wartime was widely supported in the press. For most of 1917 and 1918 she was isolated as never before or again. But she did not waver.

When the war ended she began at once to work for means to prevent another. Through the twenties she was constantly active in searching for ways in which women could cut across national lines in their work for peace. In 1931, in her seventy-first year, she received the Nobel Peace Prize—the second American to be so recognized. She died, full of honors, in 1935.

As for Johnny Powers, he had lived to a ripe old age and died in 1930, remaining alderman almost to the end, still fighting reform mayors, still protesting that he and Miss Addams were really friends, after all. From whichever department of the hereafter he ended up in, he must have looked down—or up—in amazement at the final achievements of his old enemy, who had been so little troubled by his insistence that there should be "no petticoats in politics."

Gerald H. Carson

CONSUMER PROTECTION: THE PURE FOOD AND DRUGS ACT

If early twentieth-century reform is seen as the attempt to solve problems resulting from industrialization and urbanization, then the relative paucity of significant federal legislation that the Progressive Era produced becomes easy to explain: most of the problems appeared to the people of those days to require local, or at most, state action. Except for regulating railroads and large corporations engaged in interstate commerce, there seemed to be little that the national government could do about contemporary evils. The career of Jane Addams, for example, illustrates this point. In her political battles with Boss Powers and her broader concerns with the needs of Chicago slum dwellers, it was to the state and the city (and to local voters) that she turned for assistance or support.

One national reform that was accomplished during this period, however, was the passage of the Pure Food and Drugs Act of 1906. The story of this reform and of its leading advocate and technician, Dr. Harvey W. Wiley, is told here by Gerald Carson, a former advertising executive who has won a richly deserved reputation as a social historian. Mr. Carson's books include *The Old Country Store,* which won the Dunning Prize of the American Historical Association, *The Social History of Bourbon,* and *The Golden Egg: The Personal Income Tax.*

On a hot humid July morning in 1902, a burly 200-pound scientist and connoisseur of good food and drink sat hunched over his desk in a red brick building in Washington, D.C., and he planned deliberately to feed twelve healthy young men a diet containing borax. Dr. Harvey W. Wiley, chief chemist of the Department of Agriculture, had in mind a double objective: first, to determine the effects upon human beings of certain chemicals then commonly used to preserve processed foods; and, more broadly, to educate the public in the need for a federal "pure food" law. Food preparation was becoming industrialized and subject to more complicated processing; products were traveling longer distances, passing through many hands. Manufacturers, facing a novel situation, turned to dubious additives to make their products appear more appetizing or to preserve them. Borax compounds, the first object of Dr. Wiley's investigations, were used to make old butter seem like new.

Volunteers for the experiment were recruited from the Department of Agriculture. They pledged themselves to obey the rules. A small kitchen and dining room were fitted out in the basement of the Bureau of Chemistry offices with the assistant surgeon-general in attendance to see to it that the subjects of the experiment did not get too much borax, and Dr. Wiley to see that they got enough. A bright reporter, George Rothwell Brown, of the Washington *Post,* gave the volunteers an enduring handle, "the poison squad"; and before long the public began referring to Wiley, affectionately or otherwise according to the point of view, as "Old Borax."

Six of Dr. Wiley's co-operators at the hygienic table got a normal ration plus measured doses of tasteless, odorless, invisible boracic acid. The other six also enjoyed a wholesome diet, with equally tasteless, odorless, invisible borate of soda added to their menu. The resulting chemical and physiological data was quite technical. But the meaning was clear. The effects of borax included nausea and loss of appetite, symptoms resembling those of influenza and overburdened kidneys. The feeding experiments continued over a five-year period. After the borax initiation, which made a popular sensation, the squad subsequently breakfasted, lunched, and dined on dishes containing salicylates sulfurous acid and sulfites, benzoates, formaldehyde, sulfate of copper, and saltpeter. Seldom has a scientific experiment stirred the public imagination as did Dr. Wiley's novel procedures in, as he said, "trying it on the dog."

"My poison squad laboratory," said Dr. Wiley, "became the most highly advertised boarding-house in the world."

A popular versifier wrote a poem about it, the "Song of the Pizen Squad." Lew Dockstader introduced a topical song into his minstrel show. The chorus closed with the prediction:

> *Next week he'll give them mothballs à la Newburgh or else*
> > *plain:*
> *O they may get over it but they'll never look the same!*

The New York *Sun* sourly handed Wiley the title of "chief janitor

Dr. Harvey W. Wiley (center rear) and his youthful "poison squad" in 1903.

and policeman of the people's insides,'' an expression of one line of attack which the opposition was to take—invasion of personal liberty.

The movement to protect the health and pocketbook of the consumer was directed no less at ''the patent medicine evil'' than it was at the chaotic situation in the food manufacturing field. The ''cures'' for cancer, tuberculosis, ''female weakness,'' the dangerous fat reducers and ''Indian'' cough remedies were a bonanza for their proprietors, and many an advertising wizard who knew little enough of drugs or materia medica came to live in a jigsaw mansion and drive a spanking pair of bays because he was a skillful manipulator of hypochondria and mass psychology. Slashing exposés in the popular magazines told of babies' soothing syrups containing morphine and opium, of people who became narcotic addicts, of the use of tonics that depended upon alcohol to make the patient feel frisky.

''Gullible America,'' said Samuel Hopkins Adams in an angry but thoroughly documented series of articles, ''will spend this year [1905] some seventy-five millions of dollars'' in order to ''swallow huge quantities of alcohol . . . narcotics . . . dangerous heart depressants . . . insidious liver stimulants.''

The nostrum vendors at first looked upon the Food and Drugs Act as a joke. In time the manufacturers of Pink Pills for Pale People learned the hard way that they were living dangerously when they ignored the precept, ''Thou shalt not lie on the label.''

As public interest rose in ''the food question,'' powerful groups took their places in the line of battle to contest the pure food and drug bills which appeared, and died, in Congress with monotonous regularity. On the one side were aligned consumer groups—the General

Federation of Women's Clubs, the National Consumers' League, the Patrons of Husbandry, and the labor unions. With them stood food chemists who had had experience in state control work, the American Medical Association, important periodicals (*Collier's Weekly,* Bok's *Ladies' Home Journal, World's Work, The Independent, Cosmopolitan),* President Theodore Roosevelt, and Dr. Wiley.

In opposition were the food manufacturers and manufacturers of articles used in the adulteration of foods and drugs such as cottonseed oil, the proprietary medicine industry, the distillers, canners, *Leslie's Weekly* (to which Dr. Wiley was anathema), newspaper publishers opposed for business reasons, Chicago meat packers, and powerful lobbyists holed up at the Willard and the Raleigh Hotel; also an obdurate Senate, responsive to pressures from big business. Wiley, as the leading personality in the fight for a food bill, achieved the uncommon distinction of acquiring almost as many enemies as did President Roosevelt himself.

When the average member of Congress, newspaper publisher, or pickle manufacturer smelled socialism and deplored the effects of the proposed legislation upon business, he was only responding normally to two powerful stimuli: self-interest and the nostalgic memory of his lost youth. Most mature Americans of the 1880–1900 period were born on farms or in rural areas and knew the conditions of life of a scattered population. The close-knit farm family was the dominant economic unit. It raised, processed, cured, and stored what it ate, and there is abundant evidence that it ate more and better food than the common man of Europe had ever dreamed of tasting. There was no problem of inspection or of deceptive labels. No "Short-weight Jim" invaded the home kitchen or smokehouse. If the preparation was unsanitary, it was no one else's business. What wasn't raised locally was obtained by barter. There were adequate forces of control over that simple transaction—face-to-face bargaining, community of interest, fear of what the neighbors would say.

As to drugs and medicines, grandma could consult the "family doctor" book and compound her home remedies from roots, herbs, and barks gathered along the edge of forest, meadow, and stream: catnip for colic, mullein leaf for asthma, the dandelion for dyspepsia, and so on through the list of simples, essences, flowers, tinctures, and infusions, whose chief merit was that they did not interfere with the tendency of the living cell to recover.

When Americans were called to the cities by the factory whistle, a dramatic change took place in their food supply. No longer was there personal contact between the producer and consumer, nor could the buyer be wary even if he would. For how could a city man candle every egg, test the milk, inquire into the handling of his meat supply, analyze the canned foods which he consumed in increasing quantities?

Since foodstuffs had to stand up in their long transit from the plant to the home, it is not surprising that unhealthy practices developed. During the "embalmed beef" scandal, for example, there was a debate as to whether a little boric acid in fresh beef was after

all only an excusable extension of the ancient and accepted use
of saltpeter in corning beef. Analytical chemistry was called upon
increasingly to make cheap foods into expensive ones, to disguise
and simulate, to arrest the processes of nature. The food manufacturers raided the pharmacopœia. But the salicylic acid that was approved
in the treatment of gout or rheumatism was received with mounting
indignation on the dining room table where it proved to be a
depressant of the processes of metabolism. It was objectionable on
another ground too—that it led to carelessness in the selection,
cleansing, and processing of foodstuffs.

It is difficult to picture today the vast extent of adulteration at
the beginning of this century. More than half the food samples
studied in the Indiana state laboratory were sophisticated. Whole
grain flour was ''cut'' with bran and corn meal. The food commissioner of North Dakota declared that his state alone consumed ten
times as much ''Vermont maple syrup'' as Vermont produced. The
Grocer's Companion and Merchant's Hand-Book (Boston, 1883),
warned the food retailer, in his own interest, of the various tricks
used to alter coffee and tea, bread and flour, butter and lard, mustard,
spices, pepper, pickles, preserved fruits, sauces, potted meats, cocoa,
vinegar, and candies. A New York sugar firm was proud to make the
point in its advertising of the 1880's that its sugar contained ''neither
glucose, muriate of tin, muriatic acid, nor any other foreign, deleterious
or fraudulent substance whatever.'' The canned peas looked garden-
fresh after treatment with $CuSO_4$ by methods known as ''copper-
greening.'' The pork and beans contained formaldehyde, the catsup
benzoic acid. As a capstone of inspired fakery, one manufacturer
of flavored glucose (sold as pure honey) carefully placed a dead bee in
every bottle to give verisimilitude.

The little man of 1900 found himself in a big, big world, filled
with butterine and mapleine.

This is not to suggest that the pioneer food manufacturer was
as rascally as his contemporaries, the swamp doctor and the lightning
rod peddler. What was occurring was less a collapse of human
probity than an unexpected testing of human nature in a new
context. Someone has said that all morality is based upon the
assumption that somebody might be watching. In the milieu of late
nineteenth-century business, nobody seemed to be watching. Thus
the food crusade became necessary as a means of redressing the
balance in the market which had turned so cruelly against the
ordinary American and, indeed, against the honest manufacturer.

The ensuing controversy was symptomatic of the passing—painful, nostalgic to many, including no doubt many a big business
senator—of the old, simple life of village and farm which was
doomed by the expanding national life. It was, one feels, not solely in
defense of the hake (sold as genuine codfish with boric acid as a
preservative) that Senator George Frisbie Hoar of Massachusetts
rose in the Senate to exalt ''the exquisite flavor of the codfish, salted,
made into balls, and eaten on a Sunday morning by a person whose

ATHLOPHOROS.

FOR RHEUMATISM AND NEURALGIA

NO MORE RHEUMATISM FOR ME

The Pure Food and Drugs Act, which demanded accurate labeling, meant the end of flamboyant, misleading advertising for such products as "Athlophoros" and other nostrums.

theology is sound, and who believes in the five points of Calvinism.''

The friends of food reform needed all the courage and public discussion they could muster. Since 1879, when the first federal bill was proposed, 190 measures to protect the consumer had been introduced in Congress, of which 49 had some kind of a subsequent history, and 141 were never heard of again. Meanwhile the states did what they could. About half of them had passed pure food laws by 1895. But there was no uniformity in their regulations. Foods legal in one state might be banned in another. Some of the laws were so loosely drawn that it was quite conceivable that Beechnut Bacon might be seized by the inspectors because no beechnuts were involved in its curing. Was Grape-Nuts misbranded because the great Battle Creek ''brain food'' had only a fanciful connection with either grapes or nuts? One bill actually proposed a numerical count of the contents of a package—the grains of salt, the cherries in a jar of preserves. What if Mr. Kellogg had to count every corn flake which went into his millions of packages?

Conflicts and foolish regulations could be ironed out over a period of time. The fatal flaw was that individual states had no power to get at the real problem: interstate traffic in the ''patented'' bitters, cancer cures, and strawberry jellies made out of dyed glucose, citric acid, and timothy seed.

The act which Wiley drew up was first introduced in 1902. It was successfully sidetracked in one legislative branch or the other for four years. The provisions were simple. In essence, it was a labeling act.

''Tell the truth on the label,'' Dr. Wiley said, ''and let the consumer judge for himself.''

Some of the legislators who opposed the act were states' rights Democrats, concerned about constitutional interpretation, who in the end fortunately saw the wisdom of sacrificing principle for expediency. Others were Old Guard Republicans who were special custodians of the *status quo* and highly sensitive to the sentiments of the business community: men like Senators Aldrich of Rhode Island (wholesale groceries), Kean of New Jersey (preserving and canning), Platt of Connecticut (home of the great Kickapoo Indian remedies), Hale and Frye of Maine, along whose rock-bound coast the familiar Maine herring became ''imported French sardines,'' packaged in boxes with French labels.

The tactic in the Senate was one of unobtrusive obstruction and lip service to the idea of regulation. Open opposition was never much of a factor. ''The 'right' to use deceptive labels,'' observed *The Nation*, ''is not one for which impassioned oratory can be readily invoked.'' When a serious try was made to pass a general pure food law in 1902-3, Senator Lodge was able to direct the attention of the Senate to legislation more urgently needed, such as a Philippine tariff bill. In the last session of the 59th Congress (1904-5) the food bill was considered less pressing than a proposal to award naval commissions to a couple of young men who had been expelled from the Academy for hazing but still wanted very much to become officers in the United States Navy.

President Roosevelt finally decided to push the issue. ''Mr. Dooley'' offered a version of how it happened. ''Tiddy,'' he said, was reading Upton Sinclair's novel, *The Jungle*, a grisly sociological tract on ''Packingtown.'' ''Tiddy was toying with a light breakfast an' idly turnin' over th' pages iv th' new book with both hands. Suddenly he rose fr'm th' table, an' cryin': 'I'm pizened,' begun throwin' sausages out iv th' window. Th' ninth wan struck Sinitor Biv'ridge on th' head an' made him a blond. It bounced off, exploded, an' blew a leg off a secret-service agent, an' th' scatthred fragmints desthroyed a handsome row iv ol' oak-trees. Sinitor Biv'ridge rushed in, thinkin' that th' Prisidint was bein' assassynated be his devoted followers in th' Sinit, an' discovered Tiddy engaged in a hand-to-hand conflict with a potted ham. Th' Sinitor fr'm Injyanny, with a few well-directed wurruds, put out th' fuse an' rendered th' missile harmless. Since thin th' Prisidint, like th' rest iv us, has become a viggytaryan. . . .'' At any rate, in his annual message to Congress, December 5, 1905, Roosevelt recommended in the interest of the consumer and the legitimate manufacturer ''that a law be enacted to regulate interstate commerce in misbranded and adulterated foods, drinks and drugs,'' and the bill was re-introduced in the Senate by Senator Weldon B. Heyburn of Idaho. Pressure from the American Medical Association, the graphic exposé of revolting conditions in the Chicago packing houses, and Roosevelt's skillful use of the report of an official commission which investigated the stockyards, finally forced a favorable vote in the Senate and then the House on the Pure Food and Drugs Bill. The meat inspection problem was, actually, a different matter. But an angry public was in no mood to make fine distinctions. Meat, processed foods, and fake medicines all tapped the family pocketbook, all went into the human stomach, and all smelled to high heaven in the spring of 1906. Roosevelt signed the bill into law on June 30, 1906.

The enforcement of the law was placed in the hands of Dr. Wiley. According to the Doctor, it was after the bill became law that the real fight began. Most food and drug manufacturers and dealers adjusted their operations to the new law, and found themselves in a better position because of it, with curtailment of the activities of fly-by-night competition and re-establishment of the consumers' confidence in goods of known quality. But there were die-hards like the sugar and molasses refiners, the fruit driers, whisky rectifiers, and purveyors of wahoo bitters, Peruna and Indian Doctor wonder drugs.

The administration of the Food and Drugs Act involved the Bureau of Chemistry in thousands of court proceedings, *United States* v. *Two Barrels of Desiccated Eggs, United States* v. *One Hundred Barrels of Vinegar*; and one merciful judge noted that Section 6 extended the protection of the act to our four-footed friends. Pure food inspectors had seized 620 cases of spoiled canned cat food. When the case of the smelly tuna fish turned up in the western district court of the state of Washington, the judge cited man's experience with cats throughout recorded time: "Who will not feed cats must feed mice and rats." He confirmed the seizure and directed an order of condemnation.

The law was subsequently strengthened both by legal interpretations and by legislative action, as experience developed needs not met by the original act. Government technicians worked with private industry in the solution of specific problems such as refrigeration and the handling of food. When Dr. Wiley retired from public service in 1912, a revolution had occurred in food processing in only six years' time. Yet the food industry had hardly begun to grow.

"The conditions created by the passage of the act," said Clarence Francis, former president and chairman of the board of General Foods Corporation, "invited responsible business men to put real money into the food business."

The next 25 years saw the decline of the barrel as a food container and its replacement by the consumer unit package; the setting of official standards for the composition of basic food products; and the banning of quack therapeutic mechanical devices such as the electric belt, whose galvanic properties were once presented so vividly to the "Lost Manhood" market. We still have with us in some measure the "horse beef" butcher and the "butterlegger." Tap water remains a tempting means of "extending" many foods. But there is no question about the general integrity of our food supply, the contribution to the national well-being of the original food law, as amended, and the readiness of today's food industry leaders to accept what is now called the Food, Drug, and Cosmetic Act as a proper blueprint of their obligation to the nation's consumers.

Robert S. Gallagher

THE FIGHT FOR WOMEN'S SUFFRAGE: AN INTERVIEW WITH ALICE PAUL

An increasingly popular technique being used by students of recent history, a kind of technological advance made possible by the tape recorder, is the personal interview. "Oral history," a term coined by Allan Nevins, who founded the great oral history archive at Columbia University, provides a method of preserving the recollections of participants in historical events. Superficially it resembles autobiography, an ancient literary form, but it has the great advantage of drawing out the speaker, prodding his memory, forcing him to confront contradictions and respond to criticism. The interviewer is able to direct the subject's thoughts toward the most significant and important aspects of the topic, matters which an autobiographer might ignore out of modesty or embarrassment. This type of research requires that the interviewer be thoroughly familiar with the interviewee's career and with the events surrounding it, and also that the interviewer be able to establish a rapport with the subject.

The following interview with Alice Paul, a leader in the early twentieth-century women's suffrage movement, is a fine example of the value of the interview technique. Ms. Paul is both frank and unprepossessing; she does not hesitate to speak her mind, yet she is perfectly capable of admitting sometimes that she no longer remembers all the details of her career. The interviewer, Robert S. Gallagher, a contributing editor of *American Heritage,* had done his "homework" well and, as the reader will quickly recognize, had gained Ms. Paul's confidence. Her responses tell us a great deal about the fight for women's suffrage and also about the mood and spirit of the suffragists.

A merican women won the right to vote in 1920 largely
through the controversial efforts of a young Quaker named
Alice Paul. She was born in Moorestown, New Jersey, on
January 11, 1885, seven years after the woman-suffrage amendment
was first introduced in Congress. Over the years the so-called Susan
B. Anthony amendment had received sporadic attention from the
national legislators, but from 1896 until Miss Paul's dramatic arrival
in Washington in 1912 the amendment had never been reported out
of committee and was considered moribund. As the Congressional
Committee chairman of the National American Woman Suffrage
Association, Miss Paul greeted incoming President Woodrow Wilson
with a spectacular parade down Pennsylvania Avenue. Congress soon
began debating the suffrage amendment again. For the next seven
years—a tumultuous period of demonstrations, picketing, politicking,
street violence, beatings, jailings, and hunger strikes—Miss Paul led
a determined band of suffragists in the confrontation tactics she had
learned from the militant British feminist Mrs. Emmeline Pankhurst.
This unrelenting pressure on the Wilson administration finally paid
off in 1918, when an embattled President Wilson reversed his position
and declared that woman suffrage was an urgently needed "war
measure."

The woman who, despite her modest disclaimers, is accorded major
credit for adding the Nineteenth Amendment to the Constitution is a
1905 graduate of Swarthmore College. She received her master's
degree (1907) and her Ph.D. (1912) from the University of Pennsylvania. Miss Paul combined her graduate studies in 1908 and 1909 at
the London School of Economics with volunteer work for the British
suffrage movement. Together with another American activist, Lucy
Burns, she was jailed several times in England and Scotland and returned to this country in 1910 with a reputation as an energetic and
resourceful worker for women's rights. She promptly enlisted in the
American suffrage movement, and opponents and friends alike soon
were—and still are—impressed by her unflinching fearlessness. "Alice
Paul is tiny and her hair has turned gray," a sympathetic feminist
writer recently observed, "but she is not a sweet little gray-haired
lady."

Miss Paul's single-minded devotion to The Cause is, of course,
legendary in the women's movement. . . .

How did you first become interested in woman suffrage?

It wasn't something I had to think about. When the Quakers were
founded in England in the 1600's, one of their principles was and is
equality of the sexes. So I never had any other idea. And long before
my time the Yearly Meeting in Philadelphia, which I still belong to,
formed a committee to work for votes for women. The principle was
always there.

Then you had your family's encouragement in your work?

My father—he was president of the Burlington County [New Jersey] Trust Company—died when I was quite young, but he and Mother were both active in the Quaker movement. Mother was the clerk of the Friend's Meeting in our hometown. I would say that my parents supported all the ideals that I had.

In 1912 wasn't it a bit unusual for a woman to receive a Ph.D. degree?

Oh, no. There were no women admitted, of course, to the under-graduate school at the University of Pennsylvania, but there were a number of women graduate students.

When did you actually become involved in suffrage work?

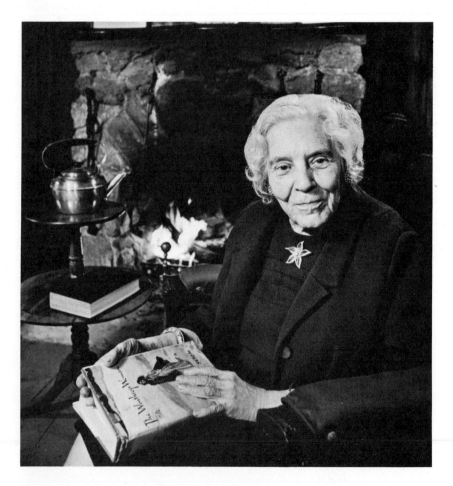

This striking portrait of Alice Paul was taken at the same time as the interview reported in this article. She was 87.

Well, after I got my master's in 1907, my doctoral studies took me to the School of Economics in London. The English women were struggling hard to get the vote, and everyone was urged to ,come in and help. So I did. That's all there was to it. It was the same with Lucy Burns.

You met Miss Burns in London?

Yes, we met in a police station after we were both arrested. I had been asked to go on a little deputation that was being led by Mrs. [Emmeline] Pankhurst to interview the Prime Minister. I said I'd be delighted to go, but I had no idea that we'd be arrested. I don't know what the charge was. I suppose they hadn't made all the preparations for the interview with the Prime Minister or something. At any rate, I noticed that Miss Burns had a little American flag pin on her coat, so I went up to her, and we became great friends and allies and comrades. Well, we got out of that, and, of course, afterwards we were immediately asked to do something else. And that way you sort of get into the ranks.

What sort of things were you asked to do?

The next thing I was asked to do was to go up to Norwich and "rouse the town," as they say. Winston Churchill was in the British cabinet and was going to make a speech there. Well, the English suffragists knew that the government was completely opposed to suffrage, and they conceived this plan to publicly ask all the cabinet members what they were going to do about votes for women. For that moment at least, the whole audience would turn to the subject of suffrage. We considered it an inexpensive way of advertising our cause. I thought it was a very successful method.

What happened at Norwich?

I went to Norwich with one other young woman, who was as inexperienced as I was, and we had street meetings in the marketplace, where everyone assembled for several nights before Mr. Churchill's speech. I don't know whether we exactly "roused the town," but by the time he arrived, I think Norwich was pretty well aware of what we were trying to do. The night he spoke, we had another meeting outside the hall. We were immediately arrested. You didn't have to be a good speaker, because the minute you began, you were arrested.

Were you a good speaker?

Not particularly. Some people enjoyed getting up in public like that, but I didn't. I did it, though. On the other hand, Lucy Burns was a very good speaker—she had what you call that gift of the Irish—and she was extremely courageous, a thousand times more courageous than I was. I was the timid type, and she was just naturally valiant. Lucy became one of the pillars of our movement. We never, never, never could have had such a campaign in this country without her.

In her book about the suffrage movement Inez Haynes Irwin tells about your hiding overnight on the roof of St. Andrew's Hall in Glasgow, Scotland, in order to break up a political rally the next day.

Did Mrs. Irwin say that? Oh, no. I never hid on any roof in my life. In Glasgow I was arrested, but it was at a street meeting we organized there. Maybe Mrs. Irwin was referring to the Lord Mayor's banquet in London. I think it was in December of 1909, and Miss Burns and I were asked to interrupt the Lord Mayor. I went into the hall, not the night before but early in the morning when the charwomen went to work, and I waited up in the gallery all day. That night Lucy went in down below with the banquet guests. I don't remember whether she got up and interrupted the mayor. I only remember that I did.

What happened?

I was arrested, of course.

Was this the time you were imprisoned for thirty days and forcibly fed to break your hunger strike?

I can't remember how long I was in jail that time. I was arrested a number of times. As for forcible feeding, I'm certainly not going to describe that.

The whole concept of forcible feeding sounds shocking.

Well, to me it was shocking that a government of men could look with such extreme contempt on a movement that was asking nothing except such a simple little thing as the right to vote. Seems almost unthinkable now, doesn't it? With all these millions and millions of women going out happily to work today, and nobody, as far as I can see, thinking there's anything unusual about it. But, of course, in some countries woman suffrage is still something that has to be won.

Do you credit Mrs. Pankhurst with having trained you in the militant tactics you subsequently introduced into the American campaign?

That wasn't the way the movement was, you know. Nobody was being trained. We were just going in and doing the simplest little things that we were asked to do. You see, the movement was very small in England, and small in this country, and small everywhere, I suppose. So I got to know Mrs. Pankhurst and her daughter, Christabel, quite well. I had, of course, a great veneration and admiration for Mrs. Pankhurst, but I wouldn't say that I was very much trained by her. What happened was that when Lucy Burns and I came back, having both been imprisoned in England, we were invited to take part in the campaign over here; otherwise nobody would have ever paid any attention to us.

That was in 1913?

I came back in 1910. It was in 1912 that I was appointed by the National American Woman Suffrage Association to the chairmanship of their Congressional Committee in Washington, which was to work for the passage of the amendment that Susan B. Anthony had helped draw up. And Lucy Burns was asked to go with me. Miss Jane Addams, who was on the national board, made the motion for our appointments. They didn't take the work at all seriously, or else they wouldn't have entrusted it to us, two young girls. They did make one condition, and that was that we should never send them any bills, for as much as one dollar. Everything we did, we must raise the money ourselves. My predecessor, Mrs. William Kent, the wife of the congressman from California, told me that she had been given ten dollars the previous year by the national association, and at the end of her term she gave back some change.

Weren't you discouraged by the national association's attitude?

Well, when we came along, we tried to do the work on a scale which we thought, in our great ignorance, might bring some success. I had an idea that it might be a one year's campaign. We would explain it to every congressman, and the amendment would go through. It was so clear. But it took us seven years. When you're young, when you've never done anything very much on your own, you imagine that it won't be so hard. We probably wouldn't have undertaken it if we had known the difficulties.

How did you begin?

I went down to Washington on the seventh of December, 1912. All I had at the start was a list of people who had supported the movement, but when I tried to see them, I found that almost all of them had died or moved, and nobody knew much about them. So we were left with a tiny handful of people.

With all these obstacles how did you manage to organize the tremendous parade that greeted President-elect Wilson three months later?

Well, it wasn't such a tremendous parade. We called it a procession. I don't know whether there were five thousand or ten thousand marchers, maybe, but it wasn't a very big one. The idea for such a parade had been discussed at the 1912 suffrage convention, although some of the delegates thought it was too big an undertaking. It was unusual. There had never been a procession of women for any cause under the sun, so people did want to go and see it.

The press estimated the crowd at a half million. Whose idea was it to have the parade the day before Wilson's inaugural?

That was the only day you could have it if you were trying to impress the new President. The marchers came from all over the country at their own expense. We just sent letters everywhere, to every name we could find. And then we had a hospitality committee headed by Mrs. Harvey Wiley, the wife of the man who put through the first pure-food law in America. Mrs. Wiley canvassed all her friends in Washington and came up with a tremendous list of people who were willing to entertain the visiting marchers for a day or two. I mention these names to show what a wonderful group of people we had on our little committee. . . .

Didn't the parade start a riot?

The press reports said that the crowd was very hostile, but it wasn't hostile at all. The spectators were practically all tourists who had come for Wilson's inauguration. We knew there would be a large turnout for our procession, because the company that put up the grandstands was selling tickets and giving us a small percentage. The money we got—it was a gift from heaven—helped us pay for the procession. I suppose the police thought we were only going to have a couple of hundred people, so they made no preparations. We were worried about this, so another member of our committee, Mrs. John Rogers, went the night before to see her brother-in-law, Secretary of War [Henry L.] Stimson, and he promised to send over the cavalry from Fort Myer if there was any trouble.

Did you need his help?

Yes, but not because the crowd was hostile. There were just so many people that they poured into the street, and we were not able to walk very far. So we called Secretary Stimson, and he sent over the troops, and they cleared the way for us. I think it took us six hours to go from the Capitol to Constitution Hall. Of course, we did hear a lot of shouted insults, which we always expected. You know, the usual things about why aren't you home in the kitchen where you belong. But it wasn't anything violent. Later on, when we were actually picketing the White House, the people did become almost violent. They would tear our banners out of our hands and that sort of thing.

Were you in the front ranks of the 1913 parade?

No. The national board members were at the head of it. I walked in the college section. We all felt very proud of ourselves, walking along in our caps and gowns. One of the largest and loveliest sections was made up of uniformed nurses. It was very impressive. Then we had a foreign section, and a men's section, and a Negro women's section from the National Association of Colored Women, led by Mary Church Terrell. She was the first colored woman to graduate from Oberlin, and her husband was a judge in Washington. Well, Mrs. Terrell got together a wonderful group to march, and then, suddenly, our members from the South said they wouldn't march. Oh, the newspapers just thought this was a wonderful story and developed it to the utmost. I remember that that was when the men's section came to the rescue. The leader, a Quaker I knew, suggested that the men march between the southern delgations and the colored women's section, and that finally satisfied the southern women. That was the greatest hurdle we had.

If the parade didn't cause any real trouble, why was there a subsequent congressional investigation that resulted in the ouster of the district police chief?

The principal investigation was launched at the request of our women delegates from Washington, which was a suffrage state. These women were so indignant about the remarks from the crowd. And I remember that Congressman Kent was very aroused at the things that were shouted at his daughter, Elizabeth, who was riding on the California float, and he was among the first in Congress to demand an investigation into why the police hadn't been better prepared. As I said, the police just didn't take our little procession seriously. I don't think it was anything intentional. We didn't testify against the police, because we felt it was just a miscalculation on their part.

What was your next move after the parade?

A few weeks after Mr. Wilson became President, four of us went to see him. And the President, of course, was polite and as much of a gentleman as he always was. He told of his own support, when he had been governor of New Jersey, of a state referendum on suffrage, which had failed. He said that he thought this was the way suffrage should come, through state referendums, not through Congress. That's all we accomplished. We said we were going to try and get it through Congress, that we would like to have his help and needed his support very much. And then we sent him another delegation and another and another and another and another and another and another— every type of women's group we could get. We did this until 1917, when the war started and the President said he couldn't see any more delegations.

So you began picketing the White House?

We said we would have a perpetual delegation right in front of the White House, so he wouldn't forget. Then they called it picketing. We didn't know enough to know what picketing was, I guess.

How did you finance all this work?

Well, as I mentioned, we were instructed not to submit any bills to the National American. Anything we did, we had to raise the money for it ourselves. So to avoid any conflict with them we decided to form a group that would work exclusively on the Susan B. Anthony amendment. We called it the Congressional Union for Woman's Suffrage. You see, the Congressional Committee was a tiny group, so the Congressional Union was set up to help with the lobbying, to help with the speechmaking, and especially to help in raising money.

The first year we raised $27,000. It just came from anybody who wanted to help. Mostly small contributions. John McLean, the owner of the Washington *Post*, I think, gave us a thousand dollars. That was the first big gift we ever got.

The records indicate that you raised more than $750,000 over the first eight years. Did your amazing fund-raising efforts cause you any difficulties with the National American?

I know that at the end of our first year, at the annual convention of the National American, the treasurer got up—and I suppose this would be the same with any society in the world—she got up and made a speech, saying, "Well, this group of women has raised a tremendous sum of money, and none of it has come to my treasury," and she was very displeased with this. Then I remember that Jane Addams stood up and reminded the convention that we had been instructed to pay our own debts, and so that was all there was to it. Incidentally, the Congressional Union paid *all* the bills of that national convention, which was held in Washington that year. I remember we paid a thousand dollars for the rent of the hall. If you spend a hard time raising the money, you remember about it.

Were you upset about not being reappointed chairman of the Congressional Committee?

No, because they asked me to continue. But they said if I were the committee chairman, I would have to drop the Congressional Union. I couldn't be chairman of both. Some of the members on the National American board felt that all the work being put into the federal amendment wasn't a good thing for the entire suffrage campaign. I told them I had formed this Congressional Union and that I wanted to keep on with it.

Was it true, as some historians of the movement maintain, that the National American's president, Dr. Anna Shaw, was "suspicious" of unusual activity in the ranks?

No, I don't think she was. She came down to Washington frequently and spoke at our meetings, and she walked at the head of our 1913 procession. But I think we did make the mistake perhaps of spending too much time and energy just on the campaign. We didn't take enough time, probably, to go and explain to all the leaders why we thought [the federal amendment] was something that could be accomplished. You see, the National American took the position—not Miss Anthony, but the later people—that suffrage was something that didn't exist anywhere in the world, and therefore we would have to go more slowly and have endless state referendums to indoctrinate the men of the country.

Obviously you didn't agree with this. Was this what caused the Congressional Union to break with the National American?

We didn't break with the National American. In a sense we were expelled. At the 1913 convention they made lots and lots of changes in the association's constitution. I don't recall what they were, and I didn't concern myself with the changes at the time. At any rate, the Congressional Union was affiliated with the National American under one classification, and they wrote to us and said if we would resign from that classification and apply for another classification, there would be a reduction in our dues. So we did what they told us, and then when we applied for the new classification, they refused to accept us, and we were out.

Why did the National American do this to your group?

The real division was over the Shafroth-Palmer amendment that the National American decided to substitute for the Anthony amendment in the spring of 1914. Under this proposal each state would hold a referendum on woman suffrage *if* more than 8 per cent of the legal voters in the last preceding election—males, of course—signed a petition for it. This tactic had been tried without much success before, and with all the time and money such campaigns involve, I don't think many women would have ever become voters. Our little group wanted to continue with the original amendment, which we called the Susan B. Anthony because the women of the country, if they knew anything about the movement, had heard the name Susan B. Anthony. Now the great part of the American women were very loyal to this amendment, and when the National American suddenly switched to Shafroth-Palmer, we thought that the whole movement was going off on a sidetrack. And that is the reason we later formed the National Woman's Party, because if we hadn't continued, there would have been nobody in Washington speaking up for the original amendment.

You didn't have much faith in state referendums?

The first thing I ever did—after I graduated from Swarthmore, I did some social work in New York City—one of the suffragists there asked me to go with her to get signatures for a suffrage referendum in New York State. So I went with her, and she was a great deal older and much more experienced than I was. I remember going into a little tenement room with her, and a man there spoke almost no English, but he could vote. Well, we went in and tried to talk to this man and ask him to vote for equality for women. And almost invariably these men said, "No, we don't think that it is the right thing. We don't do that in Italy, women don't vote in Italy." You can hardly go through one of those referendum campaigns and not think what a waste of the strength of women to try and convert a majority of men in the state. From that day on I was convinced that the way to do it was through Congress, where there was a smaller group of people to work with.

Then the National Woman's Party was formed to continue the work on the federal amendment?

We changed our name from the Congressional Union to the National Woman's Party in 1916, when we began to get so many new members and branches. Mainly people who disagreed with the National American's support of the Shafroth-Palmer. And the person who got us to change our name was Mrs. [Alva E.] Belmont.

Would you tell me about Mrs. Belmont?

She was, of course, a great supporter of the suffrage movement financially, and we didn't even know her the first year we were in Washington. People said to me that she was a wonderfully equipped person who was very fond of publicity, and they suggested that I invite her to come down and sit on one of the parade floats. Well, I didn't know who she was at all, but I wrote her an invitation, and I remember thinking what a queer person she must be to want to sit on a float. She turned out to be anything but the type she was described, and, of course, she didn't sit on any float. Anyway, a year later, after we had been expelled from the National American and couldn't have been more alone and more unpopular and more unimportant, one of our members, Crystal Eastman [Benedict], contacted Mrs. Belmont. And Mrs. Belmont invited me to come have dinner and spend the night at her home in New York City. Well, I like to go to bed early, but Mrs. Belmont was the type that liked to talk all night. So all night we talked about how we could probably get suffrage. A little later Mrs. Belmont withdrew entirely from the old National American and threw her whole strength into our movement. The first thing she did was give us five thousand dollars. We had never had such a gift before.

Why do you think Mrs. Belmont crossed over to your group?

She was entirely in favor of our approach to the problem. She wanted to be immediately put on our national board, so she could have some direction. And then, after suffrage was won, she became the president of the Woman's Party, and at that time she gave us most of the money to buy the house in Washington that is still the party's headquarters. Over the years Mrs. Belmont did an enormous amount for the cause of women's equality. She was just one of those people who were born with the feeling of independence for herself and for women.

Did Mrs. Belmont have something to do with the decision to campaign against the Democrats in the November, 1914, elections?

Yes. You see, here we had an extremely powerful and wonderful man —I thought Woodrow Wilson was a very wonderful man—the leader of his party, in complete control of Congress. But when the Democrats in Congress caucused, they voted against suffrage. You just naturally felt that the Democratic Party was responsible. Of course, in England they were up against the same thing. They couldn't get this measure through Parliament without getting the support of the party that was in complete control.

Didn't this new policy of holding the party in power responsible represent a drastic change in the strategy of the suffrage movement?

Up to this point the suffrage movement in the United States had regarded each congressman, each senator, as a friend or a foe. It hadn't linked them together. And maybe these men were individual friends or foes in the past. But we deliberately asked the Democrats to bring it up in their caucus, and they did caucus against us. So you couldn't regard them as your allies anymore. I reported all this to the National American convention in 1913, and I said that it seemed to us that we must begin to hold this party responsible. And nobody objected to my report. But when we began to put it into operation, there was tremendous opposition, because people said that this or that man has been our great friend, and here you are campaigning against him.

Would you have taken the same position against the Republicans if that party had been in power in 1914?

Of course. You see, we tried very hard in 1916—wasn't it [Charles Evans] Hughes running against Wilson that year?—to get the Republicans to put federal suffrage in their platform, and we failed. We also failed with the Democrats. Then we tried to get the support of Mr. Hughes himself. Our New York State committee worked very hard on Mr. Hughes, and they couldn't budge him. So we went to see former President [Theodore] Roosevelt at his home at Oyster Bay to see if *he* could influence Mr. Hughes. And I remember so vividly what Mr. Roosevelt said. He said, "You know, in political life you must always remember that you not only must be on the right side of a measure, but you must be on the right side at the right time." He told us that that was the great trouble with Mr. Hughes, that Mr. Hughes is certainly for suffrage, but he can't seem to know that he must do it in time. So Mr. Hughes started on his campaign around the country, and when he came to Wyoming, where women were already voting, he couldn't say he was for the suffrage amendment. And he went on and on, all around the country. Finally, when he came to make his final speech of the campaign in New York, he had made up his mind, and he came out strongly for the federal suffrage amendment. So it was true what Mr. Roosevelt had said about him. . . .

In the 1914 elections women voted for forty-five members of Congress, and the Democrats won only nineteen of these races, often by drastically reduced pluralities. Weren't you at all concerned about defeating some of your strongest Democratic supporters in Congress?

Not really. Whoever was elected from a suffrage state was going to be prosuffrage in Congress anyway, whether he was Republican or Democrat. But how else were we going to demonstrate that women could be influential, independent voters? One of the men we campaigned against was Representative—later Senator—Carl Hayden of Arizona, and he finally became a very good friend of the movement, I thought. But it is true that most of them really did resent it very much. . . .

You were once quoted to the effect that in picking volunteers you pre-ferred enthusiasm to experience.

Yes. Well, wouldn't you? I think everybody would. I think every re-form movement needs people who are full of enthusiasm. It's the first thing you need. I was full of enthusiasm, and I didn't want any luke-warm person around. I still am, of course.

One of your most enthusiastic volunteers was Inez Milholland Boisse-vain, wasn't she?

Inez Milholland actually gave her life for the women's movement. I think Inez was our most beautiful member. We always had her on horseback at the head of our processions. You've probably read about this, but when Inez was a student at Vassar, she tried to get up a suffrage meeting, and the college president refused to let her hold the meeting. So she organized a little group, and they jumped over a wall at the edge of the college and held the first suffrage meeting at Vassar in a cemetery. Imagine such a thing happening at a women's college so short a time ago. You can hardly believe such things oc-curred. But they did.

How did Miss Milholland give her life for the movement?

After college Inez wanted to study law, but every prominant law school refused to admit a girl. She finally went to New York Univer-sity, which wasn't considered much of a university then, and got her law degree. Then she threw her whole soul into the suffrage move-ment and really did nothing else but that. Well, in 1916, when we were trying to prevent the re-election of Woodrow Wilson, we sent speakers to all the suffrage states, asking people not to vote for Wil-son, because he was opposing the suffrage which they already had. Inez and her sister, Vita, who was a beautiful singer, toured the suffrage states as a team. Vita would sing songs about the women's movement, and then Inez would speak. Their father, John Milholland, paid all the expenses for their tour, which began in Wyoming. Well, when they got to Los Angeles, Inez had just started to make her speech when she suddenly collapsed and fell to the floor, just from complete exhaustion. Her last words were "Mr. President, how long must women wait for liberty?" We used her words on picket banners outside the White House. I think she was about twenty-eight or twen-ty-nine. . . . She was brought back and buried near her family home in New York State. We decided to have a memorial service for her in Statuary Hall in the Capitol on Christmas Day. . . .

Did you invite President Wilson and his family?

Oh, no. We did send a delegation to him from the meeting, but he wouldn't receive them. Finally on January 9, 1917, he agreed to meet

Inez Milholland in a demonstration parade. She was driving her own automobile, a most unusual thing for a woman at that time.

with women from all over the country who brought Milholland resolutions. The women asked him once more to lend the weight and influence of his great office to the federal amendment, but the President rejected the appeal and continued to insist that he was the follower, not the leader, of his party. The women were quite disappointed when they returned to Cameron House, where we had established our headquarters across Lafayette Square from the White House. That afternoon we made the decision to have a perpetual delegation, six days a week, from ten in the morning until half past five in the evening, around the White House. We began the next day.

And this perpetual delegation, or picketing, continued until the President changed his position?

Yes. Since the President had made it clear that he wouldn't see any more delegations in his office, we felt that pickets outside the White House would be the best way to remind him of our cause. Every day when he went out for his daily ride, as he drove through our picket line he always took off his hat and bowed to us. We respected him very much. I always thought he was a great President. Years later, when I was in Geneva [Switzerland] working with the World Woman's Party, I was always so moved when I would walk down to the League of Nations and see the little tribute to Woodrow Wilson. . . .

Do you want to talk about the violence that occurred on the White House picket line?

Not particularly. It is true that after the United States entered the war [April 6, 1917], there was some hostility, and some of the pickets were attacked and had their banners ripped out of their hands. The feeling was—and some of our own members shared this and left the movement—that the cause of suffrage should be abandoned during wartime, that we should work instead for peace. But this was the same argument used during the Civil War, after which they wrote the word "male" into the Constitution. Did you know that "male" appears three times in the Fourteenth Amendment? Well, it does. So we agreed that suffrage came *before* war. Indeed, if we had universal suffrage throughout the world, we might not even have wars. So we continued picketing the White House, even though we were called traitors and pro-German and all that. . . .

It is true, isn't it, that you were arrested outside the White House on October 20, 1917, and sentenced to seven months in the District of Columbia jail?

Yes.

And that when you were taken to the cell-block where the other suffragists were being held, you were so appalled by the stale air that you broke a window with a volume of Robert Browning's poetry you had brought along to read?

No. I think Florence Boeckel, our publicity girl, invented that business about the volume of Browning's poetry. What I actually broke the window with was a bowl I found in my cell.

Was this the reason you were transferred to solitary confinement in the jail's psychopathic ward?

I think the government's strategy was to discredit me. That the other leaders of the Women's Party would say, well, we had better sort of disown this crazy person. But they didn't.

During the next three or four weeks you maintained your hunger strike. Was this the second or third time you underwent forcible feeding?

Probably, but I'm not sure how many times.

Is this done with liquids through a tube put down through your mouth?

I think it was done through the nose, if I remember right. And they didn't use the soft tubing that is available today.

While you were held in solitary confinement your own lawyer, Dudley Field Malone, could not get in to see you. And yet one day David Lawrence, the journalist, came in to interview you. How do you explain this?

I think he was a reporter at that time, but anyway he was a very great supporter of and, I guess, a personal friend of President Wilson's. I didn't know then what he was, except that he came in and said he had come to have an interview with me. Of course, a great many people thought that Lawrence, because of his close connection with the White House, had been encouraged to go look into what the women were doing and why they were making all this trouble and so on.

You and all the other suffragist prisoners were released on November 27 and 28, just a few days after Lawrence's visit. Could this action have been based on his report to the President?

I wouldn't know about that. Of course, the only way we could be released would be by act of the President.

And on January 9, 1918, President Wilson formally declared for federal suffrage. The next day the House passed the amendment 274–136, and the really critical phase of the legislative struggle began.

Yes. Well, when we began, Maud Younger, our congressional chairman, got up this card catalogue, which is now on loan to the Library of Congress. We had little leaflets printed, and each person who interviewed a congressman would write a little report on where this or that man stood. We knew we had the task of winning them over, man by man, and it was important to know what our actual strength was in Congress at all times. These records showed how, with each Congress, we were getting stronger and stronger, until we finally thought we were at the point of putting the Anthony amendment to a vote. And of course this information was very helpful to our supporters in Congress.

Yet when the Senate finally voted on October 1, 1918, the amendment failed by two votes of the necessary two thirds. What happened?

We realized that we were going to lose a few days before the vote. We sat there in the Senate gallery, and they talked on and on and on, and finally Maud Younger and I went down to see what was going on, why they wouldn't vote. People from all over the country had come. The galleries were filled with suffragists. We went to see Senator Curtis, the Republican whip, and the Republican leader, Senator Gallinger. It was then a Republican Senate. And there they stood, each with a tally list in their hands. So we said, why don't you call the roll. And they said, well, Senator Borah has deserted us, he has decided to oppose the amendment, and there is no way on earth we can change his mind. . . .

Was it about this time that your members began burning the President's statements in public?

I'm not sure when it started. We had a sort of perpetual flame going in an urn outside our headquarters in Lafayette Square. I think we used rags soaked in kerosene. It was really very dramatic, because when President Wilson went to Paris for the peace conference, he was always issuing some wonderful, idealistic statement that was impossible to reconcile with what he was doing at home. And we had an enormous bell—I don't recall how we ever got such an enormous bell—and every time Wilson would make one of these speeches, we would toll this great bell, and then somebody would go outside with the President's speech and, with great dignity, burn it in our little caldron. I remember that Senator Medill McCormick lived just down the street from us, and we were constantly getting phone calls from him saying they couldn't sleep or conduct social affairs because our bell was always tolling away.

You had better results from the next Congress, the Sixty-sixth, didn't you?

Yes. President Wilson made a magnificent speech calling for the amendment as a war measure back in October, 1918, and on May 20, 1919, the House passed the amendment. Then on June 4 the Senate finally passed it.

Did you go to hear the President?

I don't believe we were there, because when the President spoke, everybody wanted tickets, and the Woman's Party has never asked for tickets, because we still don't want to be in any way under any obligation. I know we were in the gallery when the Senate actually voted, because nobody wanted tickets then. Our main concern was that the Senate might try to reinstate the seven-year clause that had been defeated in the House.

The seven-year clause?

This clause required the amendment to be ratified by the states within seven years or else the amendment would be defeated. We got the clause eliminated on the suffrage amendment, but we were unable to stop Congress from attaching it to the present equal rights amendment.

Were you relieved when the Anthony amendment finally passed?

Yes, for many reasons. But we still had to get it ratified. We went to work on that right away and worked continuously for the fourteen months it took. But that last state . . . we thought we never would get that last state. And, you know, President Wilson really got it for us. What happened was that Wilson went to the governor of Tennessee, who was a Democrat. The President asked him to call a special session of the state legislature so the amendment could be ratified in time for women to vote in the 1920 Presidential election.

That was on August 18, 1920, and there is a well-known photograph of you, on the balcony of your headquarters, unfurling the suffrage flag with thirty-six stars. What were your feelings that day?

You know, you are always so engrossed in the details that you probably don't have all the big and lofty thoughts you should be having. I think we had this anxiety about how we would pay all our bills at the end. So the first thing we did was to just do nothing. We closed our headquarters, stopped all our expenses, stopped publishing our weekly magazine, *The Suffragist,* stopped everything and started paying off the bills we had incurred. Maud Younger and I got the tiniest apartment we could get, and she took over the housekeeping, and we got a maid who came in, and we just devoted ourselves to raising this money. . . .

Then the following year, on February 15, 1921, we had our final convention to decide what to do. Whether to disband or whether to continue and take up the whole equality program—equality for women in all fields of life—that had been spelled out at the Seneca Falls convention in 1848. We decided to go on, and we elected a whole new national board, with Elsie Hill as our new chairman. We thought we ought to get another amendment to the Constitution, so we went to many lawyers—I remember we paid one lawyer quite a large sum, for us, at least—and asked them to draw up an amendment for equal rights. We had another meeting up in Seneca Falls on the seventy-fifth anniversary of the original meeting, and there we adopted the program we have followed ever since on the equal-rights amendment. That was 1923. So that is when we started.

Was that the year the first equal-rights amendment was introduced?

We hadn't been able to get any lawyer to draft an amendment that satisfied us, so I drafted one in simple ordinary English, not knowing anything about law, and we got it introduced in Congress. But at the first hearing our little group was the only one that supported it. All these other organizations of women that hadn't worked to get the vote, these professional groups and so on, opposed the amendment on the grounds that it would deprive them of alimony and force them to work in the mines, and they would lose these special labor laws that protect women. So it was obvious to us—and to the Congress— that we were going to have to change the thinking of American women first. So we began going to convention after convention of women, trying to get them to endorse E.R.A. It took many years. The American Association of University Women just endorsed it in 1972. Imagine, all the years and years and years that women have been going to universities. But the new generation of college women were so hopeless on this subject.

It was like forty years in the wilderness, wasn't it?

Yes, more or less. But during that time we opened—and by "we" I mean the whole women's movement—we opened a great many doors to women with the power of the vote, things like getting women into the diplomatic service. And don't forget we were successful in getting equality for women written into the charter of the United Nations in 1945.

Do you think the progress of the equal-rights amendment has been helped by the women's liberation movement?

I feel very strongly that if you are going to do anything, you have to take one thing and do it. You can't try lots and lots of reforms and get them all mixed up together. Now, I think the liberation movement has been a good thing, because it has aroused lots of women from their self-interest, and it has made everyone more aware of the inequalities that exist. But the ratification of the equal-rights amendment has been made a bit harder by these people who run around advocating, for instance, abortion. As far as I can see, E.R.A. has nothing whatsoever to do with abortion.

How did abortion become involved with equal rights?

At the 1968 Republican convention our representative went before the platform committee to present our request for a plank on equal rights, and as soon as she finished, up came one of the liberation ladies, a well-known feminist, who made a great speech on abortion. So then all the women on the platform committee said, well, we're not going to have the Republican Party campaigning for abortion. So they voted not to put *anything* in the party platform about women's rights. That was the first time since 1940 that we didn't get an equal-rights plank in the Republican platform. And then that feminist showed up at the Democratic convention, and the same thing happened with their platform. It was almost the same story at the 1972 conventions, but this time we managed to get equal rights back into the platforms.

It's really the principle of equal rights that you're concerned with, isn't it, not the specific applications?

I have never doubted that equal rights was the right direction. Most reforms, most problems are complicated. But to me there is nothing complicated about ordinary equality. Which is a nice thing about our campaign. It really is true, at least to my mind, that only good will come to everybody with equality. If we get to the point where everyone has equality of opportunity—and I don't expect to see it, we have such a long, long way ahead of us—then it seems to me it is not our problem how women use their equality or how men use their equality.

Miss Paul, how would you describe your contribution to the struggle for women's rights?

I always feel . . . the movement is a sort of mosaic. Each of us puts in one little stone, and then you get a great mosaic at the end.

*Battleships of the Great White
Fleet en route to Japan lie
at anchor in San Francisco
harbor in this 1908 photograph.*

Part Four
America in World Affairs

William E. Leuchtenburg

THE NEEDLESS WAR
WITH SPAIN

Seldom have events so pregnant with future significance occurred
in an atmosphere so devoid of an understanding of their
significance as in 1898 when the United States went to war with
Spain. It is perhaps not quite accurate to say that the United
States emerged from that war as a world power. In retrospect the
nation was a world power well before the war began. But the war
made Americans aware that the United States was a world power,
and from that awareness flowed American imperialism, American
participation in World War I, and much that followed.

As William E. Leuchtenburg explains in this essay, there was
no shortage of "aggressive, expansionist, jingoistic" feeling in
America during the early 1890's. But the conflict with Spain
derived chiefly from the desire of Americans to help the
beleaguered Cubans with their independence from Spain.
Americans wanted the war (which could well have been avoided)
but they had little understanding of what the results of that war
would be.

Mr. Leuchtenburg, professor of history at Columbia University,
is the author of *Franklin D. Roosevelt and the New Deal,*
1932–1940, which won a Francis Parkman Prize, awarded each
year to the book in American history that best combines sound
scholarship and literary distinction. This essay also combines
these two qualities.

The United States in the 1890's became more aggressive, expansionistic, and jingoistic than it had been since the 1850's. In less than five years, we came to the brink of war with Italy, Chile, and Great Britain over three minor incidents in which no American national interest of major importance was involved. In each of these incidents, our secretary of state was highly aggressive, and the American people applauded. During these years, we completely overhauled our decrepit Navy, building fine new warships like the *Maine*. The martial virtues of Napoleon, the imperial doctrines of Rudyard Kipling, and the naval theories of Captain Alfred T. Mahan all enjoyed a considerable vogue.

There was an apparently insatiable hunger for foreign conquest. Senator Shelby M. Cullom declared in 1895: "It is time that some one woke up and realized the necessity of annexing some property. We want all this northern hemisphere, and when we begin to reach out to secure these advantages we will begin to have a nation and our lawmakers will rise above the grade of politicians and become true statesmen." When, in 1895, the United States almost became involved in a war with Great Britain over the Venezuelan boundary, Theodore Roosevelt noted: "The antics of the bankers, brokers and anglo-maniacs generally are humiliating to a degree. . . . Personally I rather hope the fight will come soon. The clamor of the peace faction has convinced me that this country needs a war." The Washington *Post* concluded: "The taste of Empire is in the mouth of the people. . . ."

In the early nineteenth century, under the leadership of men like Simon Bolivar, Spain's colonies in the New World had launched a series of successful revolutions; of the great Spanish empire that Cortes and Pizarro had built, the island of Cuba, "the Ever Faithful Isle," was the only important Spanish possession to stay loyal to the Crown. Spain exploited the economy of the island mercilessly, forcing Cubans to buy Spanish goods at prices far above the world market, and Madrid sent to Cuba as colonial officials younger sons who had no interest in the island other than making a quick killing and returning to Spain. High taxes to support Spanish officialdom crippled the island; arbitrary arrests and arbitrary trials made a mockery of justice; and every attempt at public education was stifled.

The island of Cuba had been in a state of political turbulence for years when in 1894 the American Wilson-Gorman Tariff placed duties on Cuban sugar which, coupled with a world-wide depression, brought ruin to the economy of the island. The terrible hardship of the winter was the signal for revolution; on February 24, 1895, under the leadership of a junta in New York City headed by José Martí, rebels once more took the field against Spain. At first, the American people were too absorbed with the Venezuelan crisis to pay much attention to another revolt in Cuba. Then, in September, 1895, came the event which changed the course of the Cuban rebellion: William Randolph Hearst, a young man of 32 who had been operating the San Francisco *Examiner* in a sensational fashion, purchased the New York *Morning Journal*, and immediately locked horns with Joseph Pulitzer and the

World in a circulation war that was to make newspaper history.

Hearst capitalized on the fact that the American people had only the most romantic notions of the nature of the Cuban conflict. The rebels under General Máximo Gómez, a tough Santo Domingan guerrilla fighter, embarked on a program of burning the cane fields in the hope not only of depriving the government of revenue but also of so disrupting the life of the island that the government would be forced to submit. Although there were some noble spirits in the group, much of the rebellion had an unsavory odor; one of the main financial supports for the uprising came from American property owners who feared that their sugar fields would be burned unless protection money was paid.

While Gómez was putting Cuba to the torch, American newsmen were filing reports describing the war in terms of nonexistent pitched battles between the liberty-loving Cubans and the cruel Spaniards. The war was presented, in short, as a Byronic conflict between the forces of freedom and the forces of tyranny, and the American people ate it up. When Hearst bought the *Journal* in late 1895, it had a circulation of 30,000; by 1897 it had bounded to over 400,000 daily, and during the Spanish-American War it was to go well over a million.

The sensational newspapers had influence, yet they represented no more than a minority of the press of the country; and in the South and the Middle West, where anti-Spanish feeling became most intense, the representative newspaper was much more conservative. Certainly the yellow press played a tremendous part in whipping up sentiment for intervention in Cuba, but these feelings could not be carried into action unless American political leaders of both parties were willing to assume the terrible responsibility of war.

By the beginning of 1896 the rebels had achieved such success in their guerrilla tactics that Madrid decided on firmer steps and sent General Don Valeriano Weyler y Nicolau to Cuba. When Weyler arrived in February, he found the sugar industry severely disrupted and the military at a loss to meet the rebel tactic of setting fire to the cane fields. Weyler declared martial law and announced that men guilty of incendiarism would be dealt with summarily; he was promptly dubbed ''The Butcher'' by American newspapermen.

By late 1896 Weyler still had not succeeded in crushing the insurrection, and his measures became more severe. On October 21 he issued his famous *reconcentrado* order, directing the ''reconcentration'' of the people of Pinar del Río in the garrison towns, and forbidding the export of supplies from the towns to the countryside. Reasoning that he could never suppress the rebellion so long as the rebels could draw secret assistance from people in the fields, Weyler moved the people from the estates into the towns and stripped the countryside of supplies to starve out the rebellion. Since many of the people had already fled to the towns, the *reconcentrado* policy was not as drastic as it appeared; yet the suffering produced by the policy was undeniable. Lacking proper hygienic care, thousands of Cubans, especially women and children, died like flies.

This pro-McKinley cartoon, from Puck's *April 13, 1898, issue, applauded the President's efforts to restrain war hysteria; but two days earlier McKinley had reversed his pacifistic policy.*

When William McKinley entered the White House in 1897, he had no intention of joining the War Hawks. "If I can only go out of office . . . with the knowledge that I have done what lay in my power to avert this terrible calamity," McKinley told Grover Cleveland on the eve of his inauguration, "I shall be the happiest man in the world." McKinley came to power as the "advance agent of prosperity," and business interests were almost unanimous in opposing any agitation of the Cuban question that might lead to war. Contrary to the assumptions of Leninist historians, it was Wall Street which, first and last, resisted a war which was to bring America its overseas empire.

The country had been gripped since 1893 by the deepest industrial depression in its history, a depression that was to persist until the beginning of 1897. Each time it appeared recovery might be on its way, a national crisis had cut it off: first the Venezuelan boundary war scare of December, 1895, then the bitter free silver campaign of 1896. What business groups feared more than anything else was a new crisis. As Julius Pratt writes: "To this fair prospect of a great business revival the threat of war was like a specter at the feast."

McKinley was not a strong President, and he had no intention of being one. Of all the political figures of his day, he was the man most responsive to the popular will. It was his great virtue and, his critics declared, his great weakness. Uncle Joe Cannon once remarked: "McKinley keeps his ear to the ground so close that he gets it full of grasshoppers much of the time." If McKinley was not one of our greatest Presidents, he was certainly the most representative and the most responsive. Anyone who knew the man knew that, although he was strongly opposed to war, he would not hold out against war if the popular demand for war became unmistakable. "Let the voice of the people rule"—this was McKinley's credo, and he meant it.

The threat to peace came from a new quarter, from the South and West, the strongholds of Democracy and free silver. Many Bryanite leaders were convinced that a war would create such a strain on the currency system that the opposition to free silver would collapse. Moreover, with the opposition to war strongest in Wall Street, they found it easy to believe that Administration policy was the product of a conspiracy of bankers who would deny silver to the American people, who would deny liberty to the people of Cuba, who were concerned only with the morality of the countinghouse. Moreover, Bryan was the spokesman for rural Protestantism, which was already speaking in terms of a righteous war against Spain to free the Cubans from bondage. These were forces too powerful for McKinley to ignore. McKinley desired peace, but he was above all, a Republican partisan, and he had no intention of handing the Democrats in 1900 the campaign cry of Free Cuba and Free Silver.

While McKinley attempted to search out a policy that would preserve peace without bringing disaster to the Republican party, the yellow press made his job all the more difficult by whipping up popular anger against Spain. On February 12 the *Journal* published a dispatch from Richard Harding Davis, reporting that as the American steamship *Olivette* was about to leave Havana Harbor for the United States, it was boarded by Spanish police officers who searched three young Cuban women, one of whom was suspected of carrying messages from the rebels. The *Journal* ran the story under the headline, "Does Our Flag Protect Women?" with a vivid drawing by Frederic Remington across one half a page showing Spanish plainclothes men searching a wholly nude woman. War, declared the *Journal*, "is a dreadful thing, but there are things more dreadful than even war, and one of them is dishonor." It shocked the country, and Congressman Amos Cummings immediately resolved to launch a congressional inquiry into the *Olivette* outrage. Before any steps could be taken, the true story was revealed. The *World* produced one of the young women who indignantly protested the *Journal*'s version of the incident. Pressured by the *World*, the *Journal* was forced to print a letter from Davis explaining that his article had not said that male policemen had searched the women and that, in fact, the search had been conducted quite properly by a police matron with no men present.

The *Olivette* incident was manufactured by Hearst, but by the spring of 1897 the American press had a new horror to report which was all too true. Famine was stalking the island. Cuba had been in a serious economic state when the rebellion broke out in 1895; two years of war would, under any circumstances, have been disastrous, but the deliberate policies pursued both by the insurgents and by the government forces made the situation desperate. It was a simple matter for Hearst and Pulitzer reporters to pin the full responsibility on Weyler.

By the middle of July, McKinley had formulated a policy which he set down in a letter of instructions to our new American minister

Frederic Remington's rendition of the Olivette *incident was actually the work of Hearst, who had Remington exaggerate the supposed impropriety.*

to Spain, General Stewart L. Woodford. The letter emphasized the need of bringing the Cuban war to an end and said that this could be done to the mutual advantage of both Spain and the Cubans by granting some kind of autonomy to Cuba. If Spain did not make an offer to the rebels and if the "measures of unparalleled severity" were not ended, the United States threatened to intervene.

On August 8 an Italian anarchist assassinated the Spanish premier; and when Woodford reached Madrid in September, a new government was about to take over headed by Señor Sagasta and the Liberals, who had repeatedly denounced the "barbarity" of the previous government's policy in Cuba. Sagasta immediately removed General Weyler, and the prospects for an agreement between the United States and Spain took a decided turn for the better.

While Woodford was carrying on skillful diplomatic negotiations for peace in Madrid, the Hearst press was creating a new sensation in this country with the Cisneros affair. Evangelina Cisneros was a young Cuban woman who had been arrested and imprisoned in the Rocojidas in Havana, guilty, according to the American press, of no other crime than protecting her virtue from an unscrupulous Spanish colonel, an aide to Butcher Weyler. The Rocojidas, Hearst's reporter told American readers, was a cage where the innocent beauty was herded with women criminals of every type, subject to the taunts and vile invitations of men who gathered outside.

When it was reported that Señorita Cisneros, whose father was a rebel leader, was to be sent for a long term to a Spanish penal colony in Africa or in the Canaries, the *Journal* launched one of the most fabulous campaigns in newspaper history. "Enlist the women of America!" was the Hearst war cry, and the women of America proved willing recruits. Mrs. Julia Ward Howe signed an appeal to Pope Leo XIII, and Mrs. Jefferson Davis, the widow of the president of the Confederacy, appealed to the queen regent of Spain to "give Evangelina Cisneros to the women of America to save her from a fate worse than death." When the *Journal* prepared a petition on be-

half of Señorita Cisneros, it obtained the names of Mrs. Nancy Mc-
Kinley, the mother of the President, and Mrs. John Sherman, the wife
of the secretary of state, as well as such other prominent ladies as
Julia Dent Grant and Mrs. Mark Hanna.

It was a startling coup for Mr. Hearst, but he had not yet even begun to display his ingenuity. On October 10, 1897, the *Journal* erupted
across its front page with the banner headline: "An American Newspaper Accomplishes at a Single Stroke What the Best Efforts of
Diplomacy Failed Utterly to Bring About in Many Months." Hearst
had sent Karl Decker, one of his most reliable correspondents, to
Havana in late August with orders to rescue the Cuban Girl Martyr
"at any hazard"; and Decker had climbed to the roof of a house near
the prison, broken the bar of a window of the jail, lifted Evangelina
out, and, after hiding her for a few days in Havana, smuggled her onto
an American steamer. Decker, signing his dispatch to the *Journal*
"Charles Duval," wrote: "I have broken the bars of Rocojidas and
have set free the beautiful captive of monster Weyler. Weyler could
blind the Queen to the real character of Evangelina, but he could not
build a jail that would hold against *Journal* enterprise when properly
set to work." The Cuban Girl Martyr was met at the pier by a great
throng, led up Broadway in a triumphal procession, taken to a reception at Delmonico's where 120,000 people milled about the streets
surrounding the restaurant, and hailed at a monster reception in
Madison Square Garden. The Bishop of London cabled his congratula-
tions to the *Journal,* while Governor Stephens of Missouri proposed
that the *Journal* send down 500 of its reporters to free the entire
island.

On October 23 Sagasta announced a "total change of immense
scope" in Spanish policy in Cuba. He promised to grant local autonomy
to the Cubans immediately, reserving justice, the armed forces, and
foreign relations to Spain. On November 13 Weyler's successor,
Captain-General Blanco, issued a decree modifying considerably the
reconcentrado policy, and on November 25 the queen regent signed
the edicts creating an autonomous government for the island. In essence, Madrid had acceded to the American demands.

While Woodford was conducting negotiations with a conciliatory
Liberal government in Madrid and while there was still hope for
peace, the fatal incident occurred which made war virtually inevitable.
On January 12, 1898, a riot broke out in Havana, and Spanish officers
attacked newspaper offices. The nature of the riot is still not clear; it
was over in an hour, and it had no anti-American aspects. If the
United States now sent a naval vessel to Havana, it might be buying
trouble with Spain. Yet if a riot did break out and Americans were
killed, the Administration would be stoned for not having a ship there
to protect them. For several days McKinley wavered; then he ordered
the *Maine* to Havana, but with the explanation that this was a courtesy
visit demonstrating that so nonsensical were the rumors of danger to
American citizens that our ships could again resume their visits to the
island.

As the *Maine* lay at anchor in Havana Harbor, the rebels, with a perfect sense of timing, released a new propaganda bombshell. In December, 1897, in a private letter, Señor Enrique Dupuy de Lôme, the Spanish minister at Washington, had set down his opinions of President McKinley's annual message to Congress: "Besides the ingrained and inevitable bluntness (*grosería*) with which it repeated all that the press and public opinion in Spain have said about Weyler," De Lôme wrote, "it once more shows what McKinley is, weak and a bidder for the admiration of the crowd, besides being a would-be politician (*politicastro*) who tries to leave a door open behind himself while keeping on good terms with the jingoes of his party." De Lôme added: "It would be very advantageous to take up, even if only for effect, the question of commercial relations, and to have a man of some prominence sent here in order that I may make use of him to carry on a propaganda among the Senators and others in opposition to the junta."

De Lôme had, to be sure, written all this in a private letter (which was stolen by an insurgent spy in the Havana post office), not in his official capacity, and his characterization of McKinley was not wholly without merit, but it was a blunder of the highest magnitude. Not only had De Lôme attacked the President, but he had gone on to suggest that the negotiations then going on over a commercial treaty were not being conducted in good faith. Throughout the letter ran precisely the tone which Hearst had been arguing expressed the Spanish temper —a cold, arrogant contempt for democratic institutions. The State Department immediately cabled Woodford to demand the recall of the Spanish minister, but Madrid had the good fortune of being able to tell Woodford that De Lôme, informed of the disaster the night before, had already resigned.

A week after the publication of the De Lôme indiscretion, at 9:40 on the night of February 15, 1898, came the terrible blow which ended all real hope for peace. In the harbor of Havana, the *Maine* was blown up by an explosion of unknown origin. In an instant, the ship was filled with the sounds of shrieking men and rushing water. The blast occurred in the forward part of the ship where, a half hour before, most of the men had turned in for the night; they were killed in their hammocks. Of the 350 officers and men on board, 260 were killed. By morning the proud *Maine* had sunk into the mud of Havana Harbor.

"Public opinion should be suspended until further report," Captain Sigsbee cabled to Washington, but even Sigsbee could not down his suspicions. The *Maine* had gone to a Spanish possession on a courtesy call, and the *Maine* now lay at the bottom of Havana Harbor. What could it mean but war? "I would give anything if President McKinley would order the fleet to Havana tomorrow," wrote Theodore Roosevelt. "The *Maine* was sunk by an act of dirty treachery on the part of the Spaniards." Volunteers lined up for war service, even though there was no one to enlist them; in New York 500 sharpshooting Westchester businessmen volunteered as a unit for the colors. The *Journal* reported: "The Whole Country Thrills With War Fever."

On February 15, 1898, the battleship Maine
exploded; with it went any chance for peace.

The cause of the explosion of the *Maine* has never been finally
established. That Spain deliberately decided to blow up the *Maine* is
inconceivable, although it is possible that it might have been the work
of unauthorized Spanish extremists. The one group which had everything to gain from such an episode was the rebels; yet it seems unlikely
that either they or Spanish hotheads could have carried out such an
act and remained undetected. The most likely explanation is that it
was caused by an explosion of internal origin; yet the evidence for this
is not conclusive. In any event, this was the explanation that the Navy
in 1898 was least willing to consider since it would reflect seriously
on the care with which the Navy was operating the *Maine*.

The move toward war seemed relentless. On March 9 Congress
unanimously voted $50,000,000 for war preparations. Yet the days
went by and there was no war, in part because important sectors of
American opinion viewed Hearst's stories of the atrocious conditions
on the island with profound skepticism. Senator Redfield Proctor of
Vermont decided to launch his own investigation into conditions on the
island. On March 17, after a tour of Cuba, Proctor made one of the
most influential speeches in the history of the United States Senate.

Proctor, who Roosevelt reported was "very ardent for the war,"
had not generally been regarded as a jingo, and no man in the Senate
commanded greater respect for personal integrity. Proctor declared

that he had gone to Cuba skeptical of reports of suffering there, and he had come back convinced. "Torn from their homes, with foul earth, foul air, foul water, and foul food or none, what wonder that one-half have died and that one-quarter of the living are so diseased that they can not be saved?" Proctor asked. "Little children are still walking about with arms and chest terribly emaciated, eyes swollen, and abdomen bloated to three times the natural size. . . . I was told by one of our consuls that they have been found dead about the markets in the morning, where they had crawled, hoping to get some stray bits of food from the early hucksters."

The question of peace or war now lay with McKinley. The Spaniards, Woodford had conceded, had gone about as far as they could go; but with the *Maine* in the mud of Havana Harbor, with the country, following Proctor's speech, crying for war, how much longer could McKinley hold out? The jingoes were treating his attempt to preserve peace with outright contempt; McKinley, Roosevelt told his friends, "has no more backbone than a chocolate éclair."

"We will have this war for the freedom of Cuba," Roosevelt shouted at a Gridiron Dinner on March 26, shaking his fist at Senator Hanna, "in spite of the timidity of the commercial interests." Nor was McKinley permitted to forget the political consequences. The Chicago *Times-Herald* warned: "Intervention in Cuba, peacefully if we can, forcibly if we must, is immediately inevitable. Our own internal political conditions will not permit its postponement. . . . Let President McKinley hesitate to rise to the just expectations of the American people, and who can doubt that 'war for Cuban liberty' will be the crown of thorns the free silver Democrats and Populists will adopt at the elections this fall?"

On March 28 the President released the report of the naval court of inquiry on the *Maine* disaster. "In the opinion of the court the *Maine* was destroyed by the explosion of a submarine mine, which caused the partial explosion of two or more of the forward magazines," the report concluded. Although no one was singled out for blame, the conclusion was inescapable that if Spain had not willfully done it, Spain had failed to provide proper protection to a friendly vessel on a courtesy visit in its waters. Overnight a slogan with the ring of a child's street chant caught the fancy of the country:

Remember the Maine!
To hell with Spain!

"I have no more doubt than that I am now standing in the Senate of the United States," declared Henry Cabot Lodge, "that that ship was blown up by a government mine, fired by, or with the connivance of, Spanish officials."

Desiring peace yet afraid of its consequences, McKinley embarked on a policy of attempting to gain the fruits of war without fighting. On March 29 Woodford demanded that Spain agree to an immediate armistice, revoke the reconcentration order, and co-operate with the United States to provide relief; Spain was given 48 hours to reply.

On March 31 Spain replied that it had finally revoked the reconcentration orders in the western provinces; that it had made available a credit of three million pesetas to resettle the natives; that it was willing to submit the *Maine* controversy to arbitration; and that it would grant a truce if the insurgents would ask for it. In short, Spain would yield everything we demanded, except that it would not concede defeat; the appeal for a truce would have to come from the rebels. Since the rebels would not make such an appeal, since they were confident of ultimate American intervention, the situation was hopeless; yet Spain had come a long way. Woodford cabled to Washington: "The ministry have gone as far as they dare go to-day. . . . No Spanish ministry would have dared to do one month ago what this ministry has proposed to-day."

For a week the Spaniards attempted to cling to their last shreds of dignity. On Saturday, April 9, Madrid surrendered. Driven to the wall by the American demands, the Spanish foreign minister informed Woodford that the government had decided to grant an armistice in Cuba immediately. Gratified at achieving the final concession, Woodford cabled McKinley: "I hope that nothing will now be done to humiliate Spain, as I am satisfied that the present Government is going, and is loyally ready to go, as fast and as far as it can."

It was too late. McKinley had decided on war. Spain had conceded everything, but Spain had waited too long. Up until the very last moment, Spanish officials had feared that if they yielded to American demands in Cuba, it might mean the overturn of the dynasty, and they preferred even a disastrous war to that. Proud but helpless in the face of American might, many Spanish officials appeared to prefer the dignity of being driven from the island in a heroic defensive war to meek surrender to an American ultimatum. In the end they surrendered and promised reforms. But they had promised reforms before— after the Ten Years' War which ended in 1878—and they had not kept these promises. Throughout the nineteenth century, constitutions had been made and remade, but nothing had changed. Even in the last hours of negotiations with the American minister, they had told Woodford that the President had asked the Pope to intervene, when the President had done nothing of the sort. Even if their intentions were of the best, could they carry them out? Spain had had three full years to end the war in Cuba and, with vastly superior numbers of troops, had not been able to do it. And the insurgents would accept nothing from Madrid, not even peace.

On Monday, April 11, McKinley sent his message to Congress, declaring that "the forcible intervention of the United States as a neutral to stop the war, according to the large dictates of humanity and following many historical precedents" was "justifiable on rational grounds." The fact that Spain had met everything we had asked was buried in two paragraphs of a long plea for war. It took Congress a full week to act. On Monday night, April 18, while the resolution shuttled back and forth between the two chambers and the conference room, congressmen sang "The Battle Hymn of the Republic" and

"Dixie" and shook the chamber with the refrain of "Hang General Weyler to a Sour Apple Tree." At three o'clock the next morning the two houses reached an agreement—the United States recognized the independence of Cuba, asserted that we would not acquire Cuba for ourselves, and issued an ultimatum to Spain to withdraw within three days. On April 20 President McKinley signed the resolution. War had come at last. But not quite. Although hostilities had begun, not until four days later did Congress declare war. When it did declare war, it dated it from McKinley's action in establishing a blockade four days before. To the very end, we protested our peaceful intentions as we stumbled headlong into war.

We entered a war in which no vital American interest was involved, and without any concept of its consequences. Although McKinley declared that to enter such a war for high purposes, and then annex territory, would be "criminal aggression," we acquired as a result of the war the Philippines and other parts of an overseas empire we had not intended to get and had no idea how to defend. Although we roundly attacked Spain for not recognizing the rebel government, we, in our turn, refused to recognize the rebels. Although we were shocked by Weyler's policies in Cuba, we were soon in the unhappy position of using savage methods to put down a rebel uprising in the Philippines, employing violence in a measure that easily matched what Weyler had done.

It would be easy to condemn McKinley for not holding out against war, but McKinley showed considerable courage in bucking the tide. McKinley's personal sympathy for the Cubans was sincere; only after his death was it revealed that he had contributed $5,000 anonymously for Cuban relief. It would be even easier to blame it all on Hearst; yet no newspaper can arouse a people that is not willing to be aroused. At root lay the American gullibility about foreign affairs, with the penchant for viewing politics in terms of a simple morality play; equally important were the contempt of the American people for Spain as a cruel but weak Latin nation and the desire for war and expansion which permeated the decade. The American people were not led into war; they got the war they wanted. "I think," observed Senator J. C. Spooner, "possibly the President could have worked out the business without war, but the current was too strong, the demagogues too numerous, the fall elections too near."

Harold A. Larrabee

THE ENEMIES OF EMPIRE

When the war with Spain ended, the United States found itself in
control of Spain's Pacific and Caribbean colonies; what to do with
them was the first problem the new proprietor had to confront.
The controversy that developed over this issue in America was
relatively brief—by 1900 it appeared to have been settled in favor
of those who wanted to create an American empire. However, the
basic issues raised in this debate have never been settled;
the history of American foreign policy in the twentieth century is
full of the repercussions and elaborations of the arguments of
1898–1900. To what extent, if any, should questions of national
interest and honor take precedence over those of morality and the
national interests of other peoples? What is "national honor"?
Is colonialism always evil, no matter how administered or for
what end?

Professor Harold A. Larrabee of Union College and author of
Decision at the Chesapeake describes below the argument as it
first developed between imperialists and anti-imperialists after
the Spanish-American War. He takes a strong anti-imperialist
position, and few today would disagree. That he is probably too
favorable in his estimate of the anti-imperialists of that day—
many of them, for example, opposed annexing colonies because
they disliked bringing nonwhites under the American flag—
detracts little from the value of his essay as a graphic re-creation
of the mood of the times. Larrabee provides fascinating glimpses
into the minds of the anti-imperialists, the defenders of
expansionism, and those many sincere but somewhat befuddled
citizens who, like President McKinley, had great trouble
deciding between these two positions.

We know, to the hour and minute, when this country reached the point of no return on its way to becoming a world power. It was at exactly 5:39 A.M., Manila time, on Sunday, May 1, 1898, when Commodore George Dewey, U.S.N., commanding the Asiatic Squadron of four small cruisers and two gunboats, coolly turned from his position on the bridge of his flagship *Olympia,* and said to its captain in words that were to echo across distant America: "You may fire when you are ready, Gridley." The command loosed salvos of shells that swiftly crushed the decrepit fleet of the Spanish Admiral Montojo (two cruisers and seven small gunboats of an antiquated type), which had been huddling under the defenses of Manila. The battle was, in the words of the English historian Herbert W. Wilson, "a military execution rather than a real contest."

Its effects on American foreign policy, however, were incalculable, and the end is not yet. Hawaii was swiftly annexed as a territory on July 7, 1898; and by the ratification of the Treaty of Paris ending the war on February 6, 1899, we found ourselves the sovereign rulers of all the Spanish colonial possessions in the Philippines, there to remain for the next forty-seven years. The Pacific Ocean was thenceforth to be regarded as "an American lake." What we now often forget, however, is how many Americans were in those early days opposed to the idea of an American Empire. Sixty years ago imperialism, then defined as the raising of the flag by force over noncontiguous territory, and called by its friends "expansionism," was the burning issue of the day. It was bitterly contested, largely on abstract moral grounds as a gross betrayal of American principles, by a small but tenacious band of New England reformers.

The hard core of the anti-imperialist movement, both at the start and at the finish, was composed of conservative Boston lawyers and bankers, many of them lineal descendants of the Pilgrims. They soon gathered about them a remarkable nationwide galaxy of literary lights, college presidents, leaders of industry and labor, editors, and politicians, constituting what has been called "the first great national propaganda organization of the twentieth century." Their achievements were greater in the vigorous expression of their views than in practical politics. Yet they lost one of their major battles in the Senate by only one vote; for a time they threatened to endanger McKinley's re-election in 1900; and there can be no doubt that their tireless needling of the American conscience about colonialism, which continued until 1920, hastened the eventual independence of the Philippines.

Crusades being somewhat out of fashion nowadays, it may be difficult to recover the fervor of these heirs of Wendell Phillips and Charles Sumner as they denounced the extension of American rule by force in the Philippines, not because of what it might do to the Filipinos, but because of what they were convinced it was bound to do to American democratic ideals. They saw in the American seizure and retention of the Islands "the infamy of the doctrine that a people may be governed without their consent." At least some of the Filipinos, under Emilio Aguinaldo, were not "consenting" to their "pacification" by our

In Rufus Zogbaum's canvas, Commodore George Dewey directs the American victory at the Battle of Manila Bay from the bridge of the Olympia.

troops. A spineless administration in Washington, too much influenced by a group of jingoes in high places and by the yellow press, had liberated the Islanders from Spain only to try to enslave them again. This was rank apostasy from our professed principles in the Declaration of Independence and the Gettysburg Address. Could it be that Aguinaldo was fighting for *our* principles, while we had succumbed to the evil colonial policy of defeated Spain?

The expansionists' reply to this plea for democracy was the twin slogan: duty and destiny. It was, they said, the moral and religious duty of a civilized nation to accept the white man's burden, imposed upon us, in this instance, by our own idealistic crusade to free the Spanish possessions from centuries of misrule. As a moral aristocrat among nations, blessed with so many special advantages, America must, as a matter of *noblesse oblige,* undertake a self-sacrificing mission of political education in a world of backward peoples. In the words of the archexpansionist Theodore Roosevelt: "Peace cannot be had until the civilized nations have expanded in some shape over the barbarous nations." And besides, such expansion was inevitable. What John Hay called "cosmic tendency" and others invoked as Manifest Destiny (now enlarged to a global scale) was irresistibly impelling the onward march of the white men who spoke what Sir Cecil Spring-Rice called "God's language." Richard Croker, the boss of Tammany, remarked that "My idea of anti-imperialism is opposition to the fashion of shooting everybody who doesn't speak English."

What intensified and prolonged the conflict was the fact that both sides professed to want liberty for the Filipinos: the anti-imperialists believed that for us, as democrats, to deny them *immediate* liberty was to stultify our own ideals; while the expansionists maintained that the hopelessly backward Islanders were to be granted *eventual* liberty after a sufficient but indefinite period of Yankee tutelage. On both sides, then, there was an appeal to conscience by sincere but profoundly ignorant American patriots who found themselves enmeshed in the toils and tangles of historical circumstances, including domestic party politics. Since a moral issue was involved, the other side was not only wrong, but wicked, and words like "blood lust" and "murderer" were hurled at the imperialists, while the antis were denounced as "cowards" and "traitors." Nothing stirs the American people so deeply as a controversy in which both parties claim to be morally right: witness the battles over slavery, woman suffrage, and prohibition. In our day, "imperialism" has become a term battered almost beyond recognition in the cold war. But the central issue of 1898–1902—what constitutes the consent of the governed, and who is qualified to give it—has never been more alive than today, as one former colonial possession after another struggles toward a precariously independent nationhood.

"You have a wolf by the ears in the Philippines. You cannot let go of him with either dignity or safety, and he will not be easy to tame," said an anonymous American diplomat to one of our peace commissioners who was leaving for Paris in the fall of 1898. Even some of the expansionists themselves deplored our grip on the wolf in the first place, but were nevertheless extremely reluctant to let go. This was at once the strength and the weakness of the anti-imperialists' case. The imperialists had to admit, in the words of one of their leaders, Ambassador Whitelaw Reid, that "it was perfectly true that the American people did not wish for more territory, and never dreamed of distant colonies." Yet the grip on the wolf was an accomplished fact, and the practical difficulty of letting go with dignity and safety was the fatal flaw in the position into which the anti-imperialists found themselves maneuvered.

The clinching argument of the imperialists was "where once the flag goes up, it must never come down." The crucial decisions that sent Dewey to Manila in the first place, and ordered troops to his support as early as May 4, even before the news of his victory had reached Washington, were the work of a small elite group in the Republican administration who had managed to convert a pliable President. In 1897, McKinley had told Carl Schurz, "Ah, you may be sure there will be no jingo nonsense under my administration." But there was some truth in the popular conundrum: "Why is McKinley's mind like an unmade bed? Answer: Because it has to be made up for him every time he wants to use it." Theodore Roosevelt's friend Henry Adams spoke of his "alarm and horror of seeing poor weak McKinley, in gaiety . . . plunge into an inevitable war to conquer the Philippines contrary to every profession or so-called principle of our lives and history."

The ringleaders in the open conspiracy to move into the Orient via Hawaii and an isthmian canal, without ever consulting the American people, were two ardent disciples of Captain Alfred Thayer Mahan, U.S.N., the author of *The Influence of Sea Power Upon History, 1660–1783,* namely—Senator Henry Cabot Lodge of Massachusetts and the young and aggressive Assistant Secretary of the Navy, Theodore Roosevelt. It is one of the ironies of history that Captain Mahan himself was an anti-imperialist until the year 1885, and for precisely the reason most often advanced against his later followers: empire "would destroy free government." By 1890, however, a study of British sea power had converted him to the belief that the United States could take "a larger part in external affairs without risk to their institutions and with benefit to the world at large." Theodore Roosevelt, then a civil service commissioner, devoured Mahan's book, and reviewed it with enthusiasm in the *Atlantic Monthly,* later proclaiming Mahan "the only great naval expert who also possessed in international matters the mind of a statesman of the first rank."

Mahan's advice to Roosevelt in May, 1897, was: "Do nothing unrighteous; but take the [Hawaiian] islands first, and solve afterwards." The Roosevelt of 1898, described by William James as "still mentally in the *Sturm und Drang* period of early adolescence," needed little urging. He had been frustrated by President Cleveland's blocking of the annexation of Hawaii, but with the advent of a Republican administration his hopes were high. He was, however, soon indignant over the hesitancy of President McKinley, who, he said, "has no more backbone than a chocolate éclair." Behind McKinley stirred the powerful boss Mark Hanna, senator from Ohio, who flatly opposed the coming Spanish war at a Gridiron dinner on March 26, 1898, less than three weeks before it was declared. Introduced by the toastmaster at the same dinner as "At least one man connected with this administration who is not afraid to fight," Theodore Roosevelt, by that time in the Navy Department, declared: "We will have this war for the freedom of Cuba, Senator Hanna, in spite of the timidity of commercial interests." As William James put it, "Roosevelt gushes over war as the ideal condition of human society, for the manly strenuousness which it involves, and treats peace as a condition of blubberlike and swollen ignobility, fit only for huckstering weaklings, dwelling in gray twilight and heedless of the higher life. . . . One foe is as good as another, for aught he tells us."

Roosevelt's superior, Secretary John D. Long, seems to have had few inklings of what was to come, and "every time his back was turned," says David S. Barry, "Roosevelt would issue some kind of order in the line of military preparedness. . . ." On February 25, 1898, Long went home early, and as Acting Secretary of the Navy for a few hours, Roosevelt proceeded to send his momentous cable to Dewey in Hong Kong specifying "offensive operations in the Philipine [*sic*] islands." Next morning Long found that "in his precipitate way," his assistant had "come very near causing more of an explosion than happened to the *Maine* . . . He has gone at things like a bull in a china shop." Roosevelt was never again left in charge of the Navy Department for even part of a day, but his order to Dewey was not rescinded.

In this cartoon from Frank Leslie's Official History of the Spanish-American War, *captioned "Better rags with honor than patches with dishonor," Uncle Sam peers angrily over his shoulder at patches showing the* Maine *exploding and Spanish soldiers blowing off the heads of members of the Virginius' crew.*

Long seems to have thought he was dealing merely with a young subordinate who was unduly impetuous, rather than with the representative of a coterie with an elaborate imperialist philosophy and the determination to do something about it. Roosevelt was showing what a man of daring with a plan, influential associates, amenable superiors, and a little brief authority could do in the making of American foreign policy.

That the American people were unprepared for the new possessions supposedly "flung into their arms by Dewey's guns" is a gross understatement of the facts. McKinley freely confessed that, before consulting a globe, he could not have told "within two thousand miles" where the Philippines were. Incredible as it may seem to us, Dewey's staff did not include a public relations officer, and the presence of two newspapermen on board the revenue cutter *McCulloch* was a pure accident.

The public's state of bewilderment, after the first delirious celebrations of Dewey's bloodless victory had subsided, was best expressed by Finley Peter Dunne, editor of the Chicago *Journal*, whose Mr. Dooley conversed with his friend Mr. Hennessy "On the Philippines."

"I know what I'd do if I was Mack," said Mr. Hennessy, "I'd hist a flag over th' Ph'lipeens, an' I'd take in th' whole lot iv thim."

''An' yet,'' said Mr. Dooley, '' 'tis not more thin two months since ye larned whether they were islands or canned goods . . . If yer son Packy was to ask ye where th' Ph'lipeens is, cud ye give him anny good idea whether they was in Rooshia or jus' west iv th' thracks?''

''Mebbe I cudden't,'' said Mr. Hennessy, haughtily, ''but I'm f'r taking thim in, annyhow.''

Not everyone in the country, however, went along with the bulk of the press and the expansionist-led administration. One month and one day after Dewey's triumph, the first recorded protest was made against ''the insane and wicked ambition which is driving this country to ruin . . . and a slavery worse for Massachusetts, at least, than that of the Negro.'' It came in the form, classically correct for a proper Bostonian, of a letter to the editor of the *Evening Transcript* of June 2, 1898, entitled ''A Cry for Help.'' It was written by Gamaliel Bradford, father of the well-known biographer. He was a seventh-generation descendant of Governor William Bradford of Plymouth, a retired banker, a Republican mugwump (he had deserted Blaine for Cleveland in 1884), and the author of several thousand letters to the newspapers in behalf of various reforms. His offer to join with any others who would help him in securing Boston's traditional Cradle of Liberty, Faneuil Hall, resulted in the first public meeting ''to protest against the adoption of a so-called imperial policy by the United States.''

Bradford was soon joined by another Pilgrim descendant, Erving Winslow, who was to prove the most undiscourageable of all the anti-imperialists, and by the able Boston lawyer Moorfield Storey, who was to become the acknowledged long-time champion of the movement. Presiding at the June 15 meeting that he had convened, Bradford took good care to say that its purpose was not to oppose ''the vigorous prosecution of the war,'' but rather to check ''the rush of reckless and unbridled ambition for dominion'' evident in ''a certain faction in Congress,'' which might turn ''a war of liberation into a war of conquest.'' Storey laid down what was to be the most enduring plank in the anti-imperialist platform when he declared: ''When Rome began her career of conquest, the Roman Republic began to decline . . . Let us once govern any considerable body of men without their consent, and it is a question of time how soon this republic shares the fate of Rome.'' The *Evening Transcript* spoke of the meeting as ''a solemn warning against surrendering to the madness of the hour''; but Lodge depicted it to Roosevelt (en route to Cuba with his Rough Riders) as ''a very comic incident.''

The strange mixture of popular war hysteria, whipped up for their own purposes by Joseph Pulitzer of the *World* and William Randolph Hearst of the *Journal,* and the as-yet-unshaken confidence of many intellectuals in the pacific intentions of McKinley was vividly portrayed and analyzed by the philosopher William James in a letter written to his French friend François Pillon, just before James left his house in Cambridge to attend the Faneuil Hall meeting:

A curious episode of history, showing how a nation's ideals can be changed in the twinkling of an eye, by a succession of outward events partly accidental. It is quite possible that, without the explosion of the *Maine,* we should still be at peace . . . The actual declaration of war by Congress, however, was a case of *psychologie des foules,* a genuine hysteric stampede at the last moment . . . Our Executive has behaved very well. The European nations of the Continent cannot believe that our pretense of humanity, and our disclaiming of all ideas of conquest, is sincere. It has been *absolutely* sincere ! The self-conscious feeling of our people has been entirely based in a sense of philanthropic duty . . . But here comes in the psychologic factor : once the excitement of action gets loose, the taxes levied, the victories achieved, etc., the old human instincts will get into play with all their old strength, and the ambition and sense of mastery which our nation has will set up new demands. We shall never take Cuba . . . But Porto Rico, and even the Philippines, are not so sure. We had supposed ourselves (with all our crudity and barbarity in certain ways) a better nation morally than the rest, safe at home, and without the old savage ambition, destined to exert great international influence by throwing in our "moral weight," etc. Dreams ! Human Nature is everywhere the same, and at the least temptation all the old military passions rise, and sweep everything before them . . . It all shows by what short steps progress is made . . .

It soon became evident that William James had not overestimated the immense task facing the small band of anti-imperialists : no less than the complete reversal of public opinion in the face of easy victories, promised spoils, and a flag-waving press. For one thing, during the summer of 1898, history was being made at a furious pace. Whether one accepts the John Hay version, "a splendid little war," or "a jolly war," or the London *Saturday Review*'s estimate, "never a more shabby war," it was decidedly a short one. In less than four months it was all over but the disposition of "the waifs of the world deposited on our doorsteps." At a foreign policy conference at Saratoga Springs, New York, on August 18, 1898, just five days after the armistice, Carl Schurz, who had embarked upon a one-man crusade to impress Mc-Kinley, delivered a vigorous anti-imperialist address in which, ironically, he used against Senator Lodge and his fellow expansionists "the very principles which Lodge was to exalt so extravagantly twenty years later in the fight against the Covenant of the League of Nations." A delegation from the Sarotoga conference, with Samuel Gompers as one of its members, waited upon McKinley but was received only with suave hospitality.

To the public in the fall of 1898 the President offered the image of a sorely tried pacifist in doubt about the propriety of retaining the Philippines, even speculating that "if old Dewey had just sailed away after he had smashed the Spanish fleet, what a lot of trouble he would have saved us." But his every action was in line with what Lodge called "our large policy" of complete possession. McKinley packed the peace commission virtually four-to-one in favor of expansionism (three of them senators who would later have to vote on their own work), and gave them ever more sweeping instructions about what was to be demanded of the Spaniards, even though his Cabinet was divided on the issue. How he arrived at his final decision to tell the peace commission to demand "the whole archipelago or none" was told by the President himself on November 21, 1899, to a committee representing the General Missionary Committee of the Methodist Episcopal Church, then in session in Washington. Surely it is one of the most amazing descriptions of the workings of a Chief Executive's conscience in the field of foreign policy that has ever been recorded.

The delegation was about to leave the White House, when McKinley turned to them, and said earnestly:

Hold a moment longer! Not quite yet, gentlemen! Before you go I would like to say just a word about the Philippine business. I have been criticized a good deal about the Philippines, but don't deserve it. The truth is I didn't want the Philippines, and when they came to us, as a gift from the gods, I did not know what to do with them. . . . I sought counsel from all sides—Democrats as well as Republicans—but got little help. I thought first we would take only Manila; then Luzon; then other islands, perhaps, also. I walked the floor of the White House night after night until midnight; and I am not ashamed to tell you, gentlemen, that I went down on my knees and prayed Almighty God for light and guidance more than one night. And one night late it came to me this way—I don't know how it was, but it came: (1) That we could not give them back to Spain—that would be cowardly and dishonorable; (2) that we could not turn them over to France or Germany—our commercial rivals in the Orient —that would be bad business and discreditable; (3) that we could not leave them to themselves—they were unfit for self-government—and they would soon have anarchy and misrule over there worse than Spain's was; and (4) that there was nothing left for us to do but take them all, and to educate the Filipinos, and uplift and civilize and Christianize them, and by God's grace do the very best we could by them, as our fellow men for whom Christ also died. And then I went to bed, and went to sleep, and slept soundly, and the next morning I sent for the chief engineer of the War Department (our map-maker), and I told him to put the Philippines on the map of the United States [pointing to a large map on the wall of his office], and there they are, and there they will stay while I am President!

The anti-imperialists' first battle, for the mind of the President as the chief architect of the nation's foreign policy, was thus lost to higher authority before it had hardly begun. But the country might still be persuaded to reject McKinley's Philippine policy. On November 19,

1898, in the Boston office of Edward Atkinson, retired textile manufacturer—later to become notorious because of the Postmaster General's
closing of the mails to his publications—the Anti-Imperialist League
was organized. Its object was: "to oppose, by every legitimate means,
the acquisition of the Philippine Islands, or of any colonies away
from our shores, by the United States."

The only thing more remarkable than the high quality of the
League's adherents was their extreme diversity. As its perpetual secretary, Erving Winslow, remarked: "We must in our organization
stand shoulder to shoulder: Republican, Democrat, Socialist, Populist,
Gold-Man, Silver-Man, and Mugwump, for the one momentous, vital,
paramount issue, Anti-Imperialism and the preservation of the Republic." Such advice, however, was not always easy to follow, since
the anti-imperialist leader in the Senate, George F. Hoar, regular
Republican, had once called the Mugwumps "the vilest set of political
assassins that ever disgraced this or any other country."

Besides every shade in the country's political spectrum, the
League's ever-lengthening list of vice presidents, many of whom lent
only their names to the movement, included every variety of American
reformer: municipal, civil service, social welfare, single-taxer, free-
trader, pacifist, and prohibitionist. Education furnished a long list of
college presidents: Eliot, Jordan, Rogers, Alderman, Stanley Hall,
Schurman, King, and Faunce, with such distinguished teachers as
Charles Eliot Norton, George Herbert Palmer, William Graham
Sumner, Felix Adler, William James, John Dewey, and Franklin H.
Giddings. From industry and finance came the extremely active donor
Andrew Carnegie, and Richard T. Crane and George Foster Peabody.
The contribution of "interest" groups (beet sugar and tobacco),
which wanted no Philippine competition, was remarkably small.

At the peak of the League's activities in 1899, it claimed thirty
thousand members and "half a million contributors" in branches
located in a dozen large cities from Boston to Portland, Oregon. One
of its conferences, in Chicago on October 17–18, 1899, attracted ten
thousand delegates; and by 1900 the League claimed to have distributed
four hundred thousand pieces of literature. This spreading of its
work enhanced its prestige, no doubt, but it proved to be a handicap
in exerting political influence. For what leader could be found who
could win and keep the confidence of quite so many kinds of followers?

The first political battle fought by the anti-imperialists was the
one in which they came the closest to victory: the heated conflict over
the ratification of the treaty of peace with Spain in January and February, 1899. The only controversial section in the document was the
article providing for the cession of the whole Philippine archipelago
to the United States. As Peace Commissioner Whitelaw Reid put it:
he and his associates were accused of "overdoing the business, looking after the interests of the country too thoroughly . . ." Since a
two-thirds vote was required for ratification in a Senate composed of
forty-six Republicans, thirty four Democrats, and ten members of
minor parties, it was evident that a substantial number of Democratic

senators would have to be won over.

Fresh from his discharge from the Army, William Jennings Bryan announced in an interview at Savannah, Georgia, on December 13, 1898, that although he was firmly anti-imperialist, he believed that the treaty should be ratified and the issue of imperialism settled by resolution at a later date. The less politically minded anti-imperialists (Carnegie, Schurz, and Storey) regarded this as a sacrifice of principle in order to secure a campaign issue to go along with free silver (which they detested) in the election of 1900. Ten Democratic senators helped to ratify the treaty by only one vote more than the necessary two thirds, and although two or three of them may have been swayed by the outbreak of fighting, two days earlier, between Filipino and Amercian soldiers, Bryan has generally been credited with influencing the key votes. Many senators were undoubtedly influenced by Lodge's argument that failure to ratify would be a repudiation of McKinley and a continuation of the war. If there could have been a clear-cut decision regarding the retention of the Philippines, "the imperialists," says the diplomatic historian Thomas A. Bailey, "would almost certainly have failed to obtain a two-thirds majority." A few days later the Bacon amendment, pledging ultimate independence to the Filipinos, resulted in a tie vote, decided in the negative by the vote of Vice President Garret A. Hobart.

Despite this setback, the movement grew, rather than declined, as the 1900 election approached, although Bryan had created an amount of distrust in the minds of the "true" anti-imperialists, which led to talk of a third-party ticket designed to split the McKinley vote. Bryan agreed to make anti-imperialism "the paramount issue" of his campaign, and was finally endorsed by the League's Liberty Congress in Indianapolis in August, 1900. But many of the anti-imperialists refused to stomach Bryan's continued insistence upon free silver, and either voted for McKinley or held aloof from both candidates. Bryan secured fewer votes in 1900 than in 1896, and his defeat "marked the end of anti-imperialism as an important factor in American politics."

Political failure did not prevent literary success for the cause, although most of the blows struck by the pen came too late to turn the tide of public opinion. The one man whose emotional response to imperialism became enduring literature was the poet William Vaughn Moody. He risked his position as teacher of English at the University of Chicago by publishing several anti-imperialist poems in the *Atlantic Monthly*. In contrast to its noble sacrifices in the Civil War, Moody saw his country engaged in "ignoble battle," but protested:

We have not sold our loftiest heritage
The proud republic hath not stooped to cheat and scramble in the
*   market place of war . . .*
That so our hand with better ease
May wield the driver's whip and grasp the jailer's keys.

Warning the country's leaders to "tempt not our weakness, our cupidity," the poet declares that "save we let the island men go free,"

In this 1899 cartoon from Puck, E. L. Godkin, William Jennings Bryan, and other anti-imperialists are pictured defiling the favorable image which imperial adventures had won for the United States.

our soldiers will have died in vain. In a shorter poem entitled "On a Soldier Fallen in the Philippines," (*Atlantic Monthly*, February, 1901), Moody makes use of the poignant contradiction between the honor due to the fallen and the dishonor of his cause:

Toll! Let him never guess
What work we set him to . . .
Let him never dream that his bullet's scream went wide of its island
   mark,
Home to the heart of his darling land where she stumbled and sinned
   in the dark.

Moody's language was mild and temperate compared with that of his fellow Chicagoan, the novelist Henry Blake Fuller, who became convinced that McKinley's policies were not only ignorant and stupid but actually vicious. Fuller addressed the President:

   Thou sweating chattel slave to swine!
   Who dost befoul the holy shrine
   Of liberty with murder! . . .

A much saner poetic approach was that of Ernest Crosby, president of the New York branch of the movement, whose Whitmanesque lines ran:

There is only one possession worth the capturing, and that is the
hearts of men;
And these hearts can never be won by a nation of slaves.
Be free, and all mankind will flock to your standard.

Mark Twain was one literary figure who was won over from the opposition, in part by the urging of his friend William Dean Howells. "I left these shores at Vancouver [on his way to Vienna]," he wrote, "a red-hot imperialist. I wanted the American eagle to go screaming into the Pacific. It seemed tiresome and tame for it to content itself with the Rockies. Why not spread its wings over the Philippines, I asked myself? And I thought it would be a real good thing to do." But gradually Twain began to see the Philippines in a different light, for early in 1900 he wrote to Joseph Twichell: "Apparently we are not proposing to set the Filipinos free and give their islands to them . . . If these things are so, the war out there has no interest for me." From the day of Twain's triumphant return to this country in October, 1900, he joined forces with Howells in a steady barrage of articles, interviews, petitions, and pamphlets in behalf of anti-imperialism. The League made extensive use on cards of his "salutation-speech from the Nineteenth Century to the Twentieth," in which he said:

> I bring you the stately matron named Christendom, returning bedraggled, besmirched, and dishonored from pirate-raids in Kiao-Chou, Manchuria, South Africa, & the Philippines, with her soul full of meanness, her pocket full of boodle and her mouth full of pious hypocrisies. Give her soap and a towel, but hide the looking glass.

At a welcoming dinner for the young English war correspondent Winston Spencer Churchill in the Waldorf-Astoria Hotel on December 13, 1900, Mark Twain introduced the half-English, half-American speaker with these words: "I think that England sinned when she got herself into a war in South Africa which she could have avoided, just as we have sinned in getting into a similar war in the Philippines . . . yes, we are kin. And now that we are also kin in sin, there is nothing more to be desired. The harmony is complete, the blend is perfect—like Mr. Churchill himself, whom I now have the honor to present to you."

One of the most effective presentations of the case for anti-imperialism was made by the peppery Yale sociologist William Graham Sumner under the striking title, "The Conquest of the United States by Spain," but it was buried in the *Yale Law Journal* for January, 1899. Logic in terms of political theory, however, proved a poor match for the logic of events. Professor Richard Hofstadter has acutely observed that the Spanish-American War was fought because the American people wanted "not so much the freedom of Cuba as a *war for the freedom of Cuba.*" Once war was under way, in the opinion of the late Vice President Charles G. Dawes, who was a close McKinley associate, "the retention of the Philippines was inevitable. . . . No man, or no party, could have prevented it." Yet in the sober judgment of Samuel Flagg Bemis, "looking back on those years of adolescent irresponsibility, we can now see the acquisition of the Philippines, the climax of American expansion, as a great national aberration."

But it was in vain that the anti-imperialists of that era cited the words of Abraham Lincoln: "No man is good enough to govern another without that other's consent." The missing premise in the arguments of both sides was the lack of adequate knowledge of the Filipinos and their capacity for solving their immediate political problems. The anti-imperialists saw them as ready and able to govern themselves democratically; the imperialists were just as convinced that they were mostly untutored barbarians. Neither side had enough facts, and as a result both substituted passion for logic.

The anti-imperialists saw the whole problem as a simple matter of political morality, which could never be settled until settled "right." By their indefatigable agitating they administered such a shock to sensitive American consciences that the burden of guilt could not be lifted. In time it came to be assumed that the pledge of Philippine independence defeated by a single vote in 1899 had, morally speaking, been given.

What the imperialists, notably Theodore Roosevelt, could never grasp was the Filipinos' yearning for *self*-government. Both sides entertained illusions: the imperialists saw a mirage of untold wealth in trade with the Orient, which did not materialize; the anti-imperialists foresaw "tyranny at home" as the sure result of "tyranny abroad." The latter were also incorrect in their belief that their opponents would never "let go" of the archipelago, although it was not until 1935 that the Commonwealth was established, with complete independence promised in 1946. The promise was kept, and the Philippines became "the first colony ever to be surrendered voluntarily."

The annual reports of the Anti-Imperialist League, which continued until its nineteenth and last meeting in 1917, make melancholy reading as the necrology lengthened and the budgets shrank. Treasurer Greene declared doggedly: "Anti-Imperialists are not quitters"; but when Erving Winslow died in 1923, Moorfield Storey wrote: "Almost everybody who belonged to the League is dead, and the young men do not take up the work. I am still its representative, but I have no followers."

One of the striking characteristics of the League in its heyday was the lack of contact between its zealous leaders in America and the Filipinos in whose behalf they were enduring a steady rain of epithets: little Americans, seditionists, cowards, and traitors. But the Filipinos had subtle ways of showing their appreciation. Long before they were allowed the privilege of self-government, they named the square directly in front of the Malacañang Palace in Manila, the official residence of the American Governor General, *La Liga Anti-Imperialistica.*

Thomas A. Bailey

WOODROW WILSON AND THE LEAGUE OF NATIONS

Woodrow Wilson was surely one of the most paradoxical figures in American history. He was both a great idealist and a shrewd practical politician; a man capable of enormous achievements yet physically delicate; one who concealed hot emotional fires beneath an icy exterior; a brilliant public orator but a man who could seldom persuade or inspire other individuals in private confrontations.

In this essay Thomas A. Bailey, professor emeritus of history at Stanford University, analyzes the role played by Wilson's complex personality in the great tragedy that closed his brilliant career—the defeat of his plan to enroll the United States in the League of Nations. That Wilson's personal qualities had a great deal to do with the Senate's rejection of the League goes without saying. However, as Bailey makes clear, forces far larger than those exerted by any man were also involved. Thus his discussion serves as a case study of the interaction of great men with their times. It is one of Bailey's strengths as a historian that he is able to describe the difficult and tangled events of 1918–20 briefly and simply without doing violence to truth and to carry the narrative of events along swiftly and smoothly at the same time that he is focusing the attention of the reader on the personal qualities of Wilson and the other principal actors in the drama.

Among Professor Bailey's many books are *Woodrow Wilson and the Lost Peace, Woodrow Wilson and the Great Betrayal, Presidential Greatness,* and two popular textbooks, *A Diplomatic History of the American People,* and *The American Pageant.*

The story of America's rejection of the League of Nations revolves largely around the personality and character of Thomas Woodrow Wilson, the twenty-eighth President of the United States. Born in Virginia and reared in Yankee-gutted Georgia and the Carolinas, Wilson early developed a burning hatred of war and a passionate attachment to the Confederate-embraced principle of self-determination for minority peoples. From the writings of Thomas Jefferson he derived much of his democratic idealism and his invincible faith in the judgment of the masses, if properly informed. From his stiff-backed Scotch-Presbyterian forebears, he inherited a high degree of inflexibility; from his father, a dedicated Presbyterian minister, he learned a stern moral code that would tolerate no compromise with wrong, as defined by Woodrow Wilson.

As a leading academician who had first failed at law, he betrayed a contempt for ''money-grubbing'' lawyers, many of whom sat in the Senate, and an arrogance toward lesser intellects, including those of the ''pygmy-minded'' senators. As a devout Christian keenly aware of the wickedness of this world, he emerged as a fighting reformer, whether as president of Princeton, governor of New Jersey, or President of the United States.

As a war leader, Wilson was superb. Holding aloft the torch of idealism in one hand and the flaming sword of righteousness in the other, he aroused the masses to a holy crusade. We would fight a war to end wars; we would make the world safe for democracy. The phrase was not a mockery then. The American people, with an amazing display of self-sacrifice, supported the war effort unswervingly.

The noblest expression of Wilson's idealism was his Fourteen Points address to Congress in January, 1918. It compressed his war aims into punchy, placard-like paragraphs, expressly designed for propaganda purposes. It appealed tremendously to oppressed peoples everywhere by promising such goals as the end of secret treaties, freedom of the seas, the removal of economic barriers, a reduction of arms burdens,. a fair adjustment of colonial claims, and self-determination for oppressed minorities. In Poland university men would meet on the streets of Warsaw, clasp hands, and soulfully utter one word, ''Wilson.'' In remote regions of Italy peasants burned candles before poster portraits of the mighty new prophet arisen in the West.

The fourteenth and capstone point was a league of nations, designed to avert future wars. The basic idea was not original with Wilson; numerous thinkers, including Frenchmen and Britons, had been working on the concept long before he embraced it. Even Henry Cabot Lodge, the Republican senator from Massachusetts, had already spoken publicly in favor of *a* league of nations. But the more he heard about the Wilsonian League of Nations, the more critical of it he became.

A knowledge of the Wilson-Lodge feud is basic to an understanding of the tragedy that unfolded. Tall, slender, aristocratically bewhiskered, Dr. Henry Cabot Lodge (Ph.D., Harvard), had published a number of books and had been known as the scholar in politics before the appearance of Dr. Woodrow Wilson (Ph.D., Johns Hopkins). The Presbyterian professor had gone further in both scholarship and politics than the Boston Brahmin, whose mind was once described as resembling the soil of his native New England: "naturally barren but highly cultivated." Wilson and Lodge, two icy men, developed a mutual antipathy, which soon turned into freezing hatred.

The German armies, reeling under the blows of the Allies, were ready to give in by November, 1918. The formal armistice terms stipulated that Germany was to be guaranteed a peace based on the Fourteen Points, with two reservations concerning freedom of the seas and reparations.

Meanwhile the American people had keyed themselves up to the long-awaited march on Berlin; eager voices clamored to hang the Kaiser. Thus the sudden end of the shooting left inflamed patriots with a sense of frustration and letdown that boded ill for Wilson's policies. The red-faced Theodore Roosevelt, Lodge's intimate of long standing, cried that peace should be dictated by the chatter of machine guns and not the clicking of typewriters.

Wilson now towered at the dizzy pinnacle of his popularity and power. He had emerged as the moral arbiter of the world and the hope of all peoples for a better tomorrow. But regrettably his wartime sureness of touch began to desert him, and he made a series of costly fumbles. He was so preoccupied with reordering the world, someone has said, that he reminded one of the baseball player who knocks the ball into the bleachers and then forgets to touch home plate.

First came his brutally direct appeal for a Democratic Congress in October, 1918. The voters trooped to the polls the next month and, by a narrow margin, returned a Republican Congress. Wilson had not only goaded his partisan foes to fresh outbursts of fury, but he had unnecessarily staked his prestige on the outcome—and lost. When the Allied leaders met at the Paris peace table, he was the only one not entitled to be there, at least on the European basis of a parliamentary majority.

Wilson next announced that he was sailing for France, presumably to use his still enormous prestige to fashion an enduring peace. At this time no President had ever gone abroad, and Republicans condemned the decision as evidence of a dangerous Messiah complex—of a desire, as former President Taft put it, "to hog the whole show."

The naming of the remaining five men to the peace delegation caused partisans further anguish. Only one, Henry White, was a Republican, and he was a minor figure at that. The Republicans, now the majority party, complained that they had been good enough to die on the battlefield; they ought to have at least an equal voice at the peace table. Nor were any United States senators included, even though they would have a final whack at the treaty. Wilson did not have much respect for the "bungalow-minded" senators, and if he took one, the logical choice would be Henry Cabot Lodge. There were already enough feuds brewing at Paris without taking one along.

Doubtless some of the Big Business Republicans were out to "get" the President who had been responsible for the hated reformist legis-

Woodrow Wilson acknowledg-
ing a cheering crowd at the
Waldorf-Astoria in New York.

lation of 1913–14. If he managed to put over the League of Nations, his prestige would soar to new heights. He might even arrange—unspeakable thought!—to be elected again and again and again. Much of the partisan smog that finally suffocated the League would have been cleared away if Wilson had publicly declared, as he was urged to do, that in no circumstances would he run again. But he spurned such counsel, partly because he was actually receptive to the idea of a third term.

The American President, hysterically hailed by European crowds as "Voovro Veelson," came to the Paris peace table in January, 1919, to meet with Lloyd George of Britain, Clemenceau of France, and Orlando of Italy. To his dismay, he soon discovered that they were far more interested in imperialism than in idealism. When they sought to carve up the territorial booty without regard for the colonials, contrary to the Fourteen Points, the stern-jawed Presbyterian moralist interposed a ringing veto. The end result was the mandate system— a compromise between idealism and imperialism that turned out to be more imperialistic than idealistic.

Wilson's overriding concern was the League of Nations. He feared that if he did not get it completed and embedded in the treaty, the imperialistic powers might sidetrack it. Working at an incredible pace after hours, Wilson headed the commission that drafted the League Covenant in ten meetings and some thirty hours. He then persuaded the conference not only to approve the hastily constructed Covenant but to incorporate it bodily in the peace treaty. In support of his adopted brain child he spoke so movingly on one occasion that even the hard-boiled reporters forgot to take notes.

Wilson now had to return hurriedly to the United States to sign bills and take care of other pressing business. Shortly after his arrival the mounting Republican opposition in the Senate flared up angrily. On March 4, 1919, 39 senators or senators-elect—more than enough to defeat the treaty—published a round robin to the effect that they would not approve the League in its existing form. This meant that Wilson had to return to Paris, hat in hand, and there weaken his position by having to seek modifications.

Stung to the quick, he struck back at his senatorial foes in an indiscreet speech in New York just before his departure. He boasted that when he brought the treaty back from Paris, the League Covenant would not only be tied in but so thoroughly tied in that it could not be cut out without killing the entire pact. The Senate, he assumed, would not dare to kill the treaty of peace outright.

At Paris the battle was now joined in deadly earnest. Clemenceau, the French realist, had little use for Wilson, the American idealist. "God gave us the ten commandments and we broke them," he reportedly sneered. "Wilson gave us the Fourteen Points—we shall see." Clemenceau's most disruptive demand was for the German Rhineland; but Wilson, the champion of self-determination, would never consent to handing several million Germans over to the tender mercies of the French. After a furious struggle, during which Wilson was stricken with influenza, Clemenceau was finally persuaded to yield the Rhineland and other demands in return for a security treaty. Under it, Britain and America agreed to come to the aid of France in the event of another unprovoked aggression. The United States Senate shortsightedly pigeonholed the pact, and France was left with neither the Rhineland nor security.

Two other deadlocks almost broke up the conference. Italy claimed the Adriatic port of Fiume, an area inhabited chiefly by Yugoslavs. In his battle for self-determination, Wilson dramatically appealed over the head of the Italian delegation to the Italian people, whereupon the delegates went home in a huff to receive popular endorsement. The final adjustment was a hollow victory for self-determination.

The politely bowing Japanese now stepped forward to press their economic claims to China's Shantung, which they had captured from the Germans early in the war. But to submit 30,000,000 Chinese to the influence of the Japanese would be another glaring violation of self-determination. The Japanese threatened to bolt the conference, as the Italians had already done, with consequent jeopardy to the League. In the end, Wilson reluctantly consented to a compromise that left the Japanese temporarily in possession of Shantung.

The Treaty of Versailles, as finally signed in June, 1919, included only about four of the original Fourteen Points. The Germans, with considerable justification, gave vent to loud cries of betrayal. But the iron hand of circumstance had forced Wilson to compromise away many of his points in order to salvage his fourteenth point, the League of Nations, which he hoped would iron out the injustices that had crept into the treaty. He was like the mother who throws her younger children to the pursuing wolves in order to save her sturdy first-born son.

Bitter opposition to the completed treaty had already begun to form in America. Tens of thousands of homesick and disillusioned soldiers were pouring home, determined to let Europe "stew in its own juice." The wartime idealism, inevitably doomed to slump, was now plunging to alarming depths. The beloved Allies had apparently turned out to be greedy imperialists. The war to make the world safe for democracy had obviously fallen dismally short of the goal. And at the end of the war to end wars there were about twenty conflicts of varying intensity being waged all over the globe.

The critics increased their clamor. Various foreign groups, including the Irish-Americans and the Italian-Americans, were complaining that the interests of the old country had been neglected. Professional liberals, for example the editors of the *New Republic*, were denouncing the treaty as too harsh. The illiberals, far more numerous, were denouncing it as not harsh enough. The Britain-haters, like the buzz-saw Senator James Reed of Missouri and the acid-penned William R. Hearst, were proclaiming that England had emerged with undue influence. Such ultra-nationalists as the isolationist Senator William E. Borah of Idaho were insisting that the flag of no superstate should be hoisted above the glorious Stars and Stripes.

When the treaty came back from Paris, with the League firmly riveted in, Senator Lodge despaired of stopping it.

"What are you going to do? It's hopeless," he complained to Borah. "All the newspapers in my state are for it." The best that he could hope for was to add a few reservations. The Republicans had been given little opportunity to help write the treaty in Paris; they now felt that they were entitled to do a little rewriting in Washington.

Lodge deliberately adopted the technique of delay. As chairman of the powerful Senate Committee on Foreign Relations, he consumed

Henry Cabot Lodge in 1909.

A cartoon by Bronstrup in the San Francisco Chronicle captioned, "They Won't Dovetail" summed up the attitude of many opponents of the League.

two weeks by reading aloud the entire pact of 264 pages, even though it had already been printed. He then held time-consuming public hearings, during which persons with unpronounceable foreign names aired their grievances against the pact.

Lodge finally adopted the strategy of tacking reservations onto the treaty, and he was able to achieve his goal because of the peculiar composition of the Senate. There were 49 Republicans and 47 Democrats. The Republicans consisted of about twenty "strong reservationists" like Lodge, about twelve "mild reservationists" like future Secretary of State Kellogg, and about a dozen "irreconcilables." This last group was headed by Senator Borah and the no less isolationist Senator Hiram Johnson of California, a fiery spellbinder.

The Lodge reservations finally broke the back of the treaty. They were all added by a simple majority vote, even though the entire pact would have to be approved by a two-thirds vote. The dozen or so Republican mild reservationists were not happy over the strong Lodge reservations, and if Wilson had deferred sufficiently to these men, he might have persuaded them to vote with the Democrats. Had they done so, the Lodge reservations could have all been voted down, and a milder version, perhaps acceptable to Wilson, could have been substituted.

As the hot summer of 1919 wore on, Wilson became increasingly impatient with the deadlock in the Senate. Finally he decided to take his case to the country, as he had so often done in response to his ingrained "appeal habit." He had never been robust, and his friends urged him not to risk breaking himself down in a strenuous barnstorming campaign. But Wilson, having made up his mind, was unyielding. He had sent American boys into battle in a war to end wars; why should he not risk his life in a battle for a League to end wars?

Wilson's spectacular tour met with limited enthusiasm in the

Middle West, the home of several million German-Americans. After him, like baying bloodhounds, trailed Senators Borah and Johnson, sometimes speaking in the same halls a day or so later, to the accompaniment of cries of ''Impeach him, impeach him!'' But on the Pacific Coast and in the Rocky Mountain area the enthusiasm for Wilson and the League was overwhelming. The high point—and the breaking point—of the trip came at Pueblo, Colorado, where Wilson, with tears streaming down his cheeks, pleaded for his beloved League of Nations.

That night Wilson's weary body rebelled. He was whisked back to Washington, where he suffered a stroke that paralyzed the left side of his body. For weeks he lay in bed, a desperately sick man. The Democrats, who had no first-rate leader in the Senate, were left rudderless. With the wisdom of hindsight, we may say that Wilson might better have stayed in Washington, providing the necessary leadership and compromising with the opposition, insofar as compromise was possible. A good deal of compromise had already gone into the treaty, and a little more might have saved it.

Senator Lodge, cold and decisive, was now in the driver's seat. His Fourteen Reservations, a sardonic parallel to Wilson's Fourteen Points, had been whipped into shape. Most of them now seem either irrelevant, inconsequential, or unnecessary; some of them merely reaffirmed principles and policies, including the Monroe Doctrine, already guaranteed by the treaty or by the Constitution.

But Wilson, who hated the sound of Lodge's name, would have no part of the Lodge reservations. They would, he insisted, emasculate the entire treaty. Yet the curious fact is that he had privately worked out his own set of reservations with the Democratic leader in the Senate, Gilbert M. Hitchcock, and these differed only in slight degree from those of Senator Lodge.

As the hour approached for the crucial vote in the Senate, it appeared that public opinion had veered a little. Although confused by the angry debate, it still favored the treaty—but with some safeguarding reservations. A stubborn Wilson was unwilling to accept this disheartening fact, or perhaps he was not made aware of it. Mrs. Wilson, backed by the President's personal physician, Dr. Cary Grayson, kept vigil at his bedside to warn the few visitors that disagreeable news might shock the invalid into a relapse.

In this highly unfavorable atmosphere, Senator Hitchcock had two conferences with Wilson on the eve of the Senate voting. He suggested compromise on a certain point, but Wilson shot back, ''Let Lodge compromise!'' Hitchcock conceded that the Senator would have to give ground but suggested that the White House might also hold out the olive branch. ''Let Lodge hold out the olive branch,'' came the stern reply. On this inflexible note, and with Mrs. Wilson's anxiety mounting, the interview ended.

The Senate was ready for final action on November 19, 1919. At the critical moment Wilson sent a fateful letter to the Democratic minority in the Senate, urging them to vote down the treaty with the hated Lodge reservations so that a true ratification could be achieved. The Democrats, with more than the necessary one-third veto, heeded the voice of their crippled leader and rejected the treaty with reservations. The Republicans, with more than the necessary one-third veto, rejected the treaty without reservations.

The country was shocked by this exhibition of legislative paralysis. About four fifths of the senators professed to favor the treaty in some form, yet they were unable to agree on anything. An aroused public opinion forced the Senate to reconsider, and Lodge secretly entered into negotiations with the Democrats in an effort to work out acceptable reservations. He was making promising progress when Senator Borah got wind of his maneuvers through an anonymous telephone call. The leading irreconcilables hastily summoned a council of war, hauled Lodge before them, and bluntly accused him of treachery. Deeply disturbed, the Massachusetts Senator said: "Well, I suppose I'll have to resign as majority leader."

"No, by God!" burst out Borah. "You won't have a chance to resign! On Monday, I'll move for the election of a new majority leader and give the reasons for my action." Faced with an upheaval within his party such as had insured Wilson's election in 1912, Lodge agreed to drop his backstage negotiations.

The second-chance vote in the Senate came on March 19, 1920. Wilson again directed his loyal Democratic following to reject the treaty, disfigured as it was by the hateful Lodge reservations. But by this time there was no other form in which the pact could possibly be ratified. Twenty-one realistic Democrats turned their backs on Wilson and voted Yea; 23 loyal Democrats, mostly from the rock-ribbed South, joined with the irreconcilables to do the bidding of the White House. The treaty, though commanding a simple majority this time of 49 Yeas to 35 Nays, failed of the necessary two-thirds vote.

Wilson, struggling desperately against the Lodge reservation trap, had already summoned the nation in "solemn referendum" to give him a vote in favor of the League in the forthcoming presidential election of 1920. His hope was that he could then get the treaty approved without reservations. But this course was plainly futile. Even if all the anti-League senators up for re-election in 1920 had been replaced by the pro-League senators, Wilson would still have lacked the necessary two-thirds majority for an unreserved treaty.

The American people were never given a chance to express their views directly on the League of Nations. All they could do was vote either for the weak Democratic candidate, Cox, who stood for the League, and the stuffed-shirt Republican candidate, Harding, who wobbled all over the map of the League arguments. If the electorate had been given an opportunity to express itself, a powerful majority probably would have favored the world organization, with at least some reservations. But wearied of Wilsonism, idealism, and self-denial, and confused by the wordy fight over the treaty, the voters rose up and swept Harding into the White House. The winner had been more anti-League than pro-League, and his prodigious plurality of 7,000,000 votes condemned the League to death in America.

What caused this costly failure of American statesmanship?

Wilson's physical collapse intensified his native stubbornness. A judicious compromise here and there no doubt would have secured Senate approval of the treaty, though of course with modifications. Wilson believed that in any event the Allies would reject the Lodge reservations. The probabilities are that the Allies would have worked out some kind of acceptance, so dire was their need of America's economic support, but Wilson never gave them a chance to act.

Senator Lodge was also inflexible, but prior to the second rejection he was evidently trying to get the treaty through—on his own terms. As majority leader of the Republicans, his primary task was to avoid another fatal split in his party. Wilson's primary task was to get the pact approved. From a purely political point of view, the Republicans had little to gain by engineering ratification of a Democratic treaty.

The two-thirds rule in the Senate, often singled out as the culprit, is of little relevance. Wilson almost certainly would have pigeonholed the treaty if it had passed with the Lodge reservations appended.

Wilson's insistence that the League be wedded to the treaty actually contributed to the final defeat of both. Either would have had a better chance if it had not been burdened by the enemies of the other. The United Nations, one should note, was set up in 1945 independently of any peace treaty.

Finally, American public opinion in 1919-20 was not yet ready for the onerous new world responsibilities that had suddenly been forced upon it. The isolationist tradition was still potent, and it was fortified by postwar disillusionment. If the sovereign voters had spoken out for the League with one voice, they almost certainly would have had their way. A treaty without reservations, or with a few reservations acceptable to Wilson, doubtless would have slipped through the Senate. But the American people were one war short of accepting leadership in a world organization for peace.

By 1919, when this Bronstrup cartoon appeared, Wilson was sinking rapidly in a whirlpool of adverse public opinion.

Colonel T. N. Dupuy

PEARL HARBOR: WHO BLUNDERED?

The Japanese attack on Pearl Harbor, aptly characterized in this
essay by the military historian Colonel Trevor N. Dupuy as "the
worst disaster in the military annals of the United States," was an
event so implausible, so shocking, and so enormous in its results
that it has been studied exhaustively—by politicians, by military
men, by plain citizens, and of course, by historians. "What happened"
was never difficult to determine; why it happened—who was
responsible for the unpreparedness of the American forces in Hawaii
—is a question that has excited the bitterest of controversies.

Colonel Dupuy's effort to untangle the events of late November
and early December, 1941, takes an unusual but interesting and
effective form. Superficially his essay appears almost a chronicle. He
describes day by day from November 25 to December 7 what was
going on in Washington, in Hawaii, and in the western Pacific, where
the Japanese attack force was steaming toward its destination. The
dramatic force of this approach is considerable, but alone it would
not produce a sound history of the affair. To it Dupuy adds both a
prologue, setting the stage and introducing the main characters in
the tragedy, and a conclusion, in which he weighs and balances the
evidence and offers his own explanation of what went wrong.

P recisely at 7:55 A.M. on Sunday, December 7, 1941, a most devastating Japanese aerial attack struck the island of Oahu, Territory of Hawaii. When it was all over, the battleships of our Pacific Fleet, moored by pairs in their Pearl Harbor base, had received a mortal blow. Our army air strength in Hawaii—the Japanese found its planes ranged neatly wing to wing on airfield ramps— was a tangled mass of smoking wreckage.

The worst disaster in the military annals of the United States had ushered us into World War II. As in most wars, the political and diplomatic background was so complex and confused as to defy definitive analysis—though this has not prevented historians and others from making the attempt. But as to the disaster itself, the military record is clear.

A well-planned and brilliantly executed surprise attack by Japanese carrier-based aircraft was launched against the major American bastion in the Pacific. The United States government, its senior military leaders, and its commanders in Hawaii had had sufficient information to be adequately warned that an attack was possible, and had had time to be prepared to thwart or to blunt the blow. The information was largely ignored; the preparations were utterly inadequate.

Someone had blundered. Who? And how?

At the moment of the attack four professional military men filled posts of vital importance. In Washington, General George C. Marshall, Chief of Staff, was responsible for the entire United States Army and all of its installations. In a nearby office sat his Navy counterpart, Admiral Harold R. Stark, Chief of Naval Operations. On the Hawaiian island of Oahu, Lieutenant General Walter C. Short commanded the Hawaiian Department, the Army's most vital overseas outpost. Commanding the United States Pacific Fleet was Rear Admiral Husband E. Kimmel; his headquarters was also on Oahu, overlooking the great Navy base at Pearl Harbor.

Marshall, product of the Virginia Military Institute, had a well-deserved reputation for brilliant staff work under Pershing in France in World War I. Later he had taken a prominent part in developing the Army's Infantry School at Fort Benning, Georgia. Short, a graduate of the University of Illinois, had entered the Army from civilian life in 1901. Early in 1941 he had been chosen by Marshall to command the Hawaiian Department.

Both Stark and Kimmel had graduated from the United States Naval Academy at Annapolis—Stark in 1903, Kimmel a year later. Both had risen to their high positions in the Navy following exemplary command and staff service at sea and on shore. Close personal friends, both were highly respected by their naval colleagues.

The thinking and attitudes of these four men were shaped by two decades of unanimous opinion among American soldiers and sailors that someday Japan would clash with the United States in a struggle for predominance in the vast Pacific Ocean. All accepted without question the basic elements of U.S. doctrine for the defense of the Pacific in such a war.

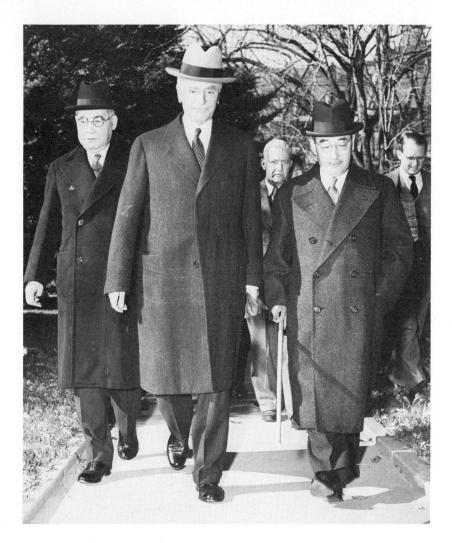

Saburo Kurusu (right) and Kichisaburo Nomura (left)
with Secretary of State Cordell Hull arriving at the White House
on November 17 for a conference with President Roosevelt.

The doctrine was that the United States Navy—and in particular its Pacific Fleet—was the essential element to American success in a Pacific war. Immobilization or destruction of that fleet would be the greatest damage Japan could inflict on the United States. Upon the Army lay the responsibility for furthering the offensive powers of the fleet by protecting its great Pearl Harbor base; by safeguarding the Panama Canal, the Navy's life line from the Atlantic to the Pacific; and by defending the advanced Philippine delaying position, which in military opinion was likely to be Japan's initial target.

Since 1939 the top military authorities of the nation, including President Franklin D. Roosevelt, had understood the almost inexorable logic of events that pointed to our eventual involvement either in the conflict which Hitler had begun in Europe or that in Asia between Japan and China—or both. And under Roosevelt's skillful guidance the nation, albeit grudgingly, was very slowly building up its military strength.

As 1941 rolled along, it became apparent, even to the man in the street, that the most pressing danger lay in the Far East. Our diplomatic relations with Japan were worsening; by November they appeared to be almost at the breaking point. The long-continued diplomatic bickering between the two nations on a variety of subjects had resulted in the arrival in Washington of a special envoy, Saburo Kurusu, who—with Ambassador Kichisaburo Nomura—had on November 20 presented the State Department with a document that was practically an ultimatum.

Japan would acquiesce to our government's demands that she withdraw from Indochina only upon "establishment of an equitable peace in the Pacific area" and, further, upon "supply to Japan [by the U.S. of] a required quantity of oil."

In 1940, our cipher experts had cracked the Japanese secret codes —a cryptoanalytical procedure known in the War Department as "Magic." Hence our government knew that the envoys had received instructions to press for American acceptance of this "final proposal" by November 25. The ambassadors had been warned that for reasons "beyond your ability to guess" this was essential, but that if the "signing can be completed by the 29th" the Imperial Japanese government would wait. "After that things are automatically going to happen."

It was also known through Magic radio intercepts that a large proportion of Japanese military strength—land, sea, and air—was concentrating in the Indochina and South China Sea areas. No evidence of aircraft carriers had been found, however, either in those areas or in the Japanese mandated islands. Intelligence agencies, monitoring Japanese radio traffic, considered it probable that the carriers were still in their home waters, but they were not certain.

On this basis Marshall, Stark, and their respective staffs concluded that the Japanese were preparing to strike in Southeast Asia; this threat, of course, included the Philippine Commonwealth. Accordingly our Army and Navy commanders in the Philippines and at Guam had been specifically warned. The commanders in Hawaii, Panama, Alaska, and on the West Coast were kept informed of important developments.

This was the situation as Marshall and Stark saw it early on November 25. From that time on events succeeded one another with increasing rapidity, both in Washington and in Hawaii. This is how they unfolded:

Washington, Tuesday, November 25

Marshall and Stark attended a "War Council" meeting with the President, Secretary of State Cordell Hull, Secretary of War Henry

L. Stimson, and Secretary of the Navy Frank Knox. Were the Japanese bluffing? Hull thought not; rejection of their terms would mean war. "These fellows mean to fight," he told the group. "You [Marshall and Stark] will have to be prepared."

Adequate preparation could not be guaranteed by either service chief. The great draft army was still only a partly disciplined mass. The Navy, better prepared for an immediate fight, was still far from ready for an extended period of combat. Marshall urged diplomatic delay. If the State Department could hold war off for even three months, the time gained would be precious, especially in the Philippines, where Douglas MacArthur's newly raised Commonwealth Army was only partly organized and equipped.

Perhaps the State Department's formula—*modus vivendi* they called it—which had been sent by cable to our British, Chinese, Australian, and Dutch allies for comment—would gain the needed time. This was a proposal for a three-month truce in Sino-Japanese hostilities, during which the United States, in return for Japan's withdrawal from southern Indochina, would make limited economic concessions to her.

It was evident to all concerned that otherwise hostilities were almost certain to break out within a few days. The President, noting Japan's proclivity for attacking without a declaration of war, impressed on all concerned that if war came, it must result from an initial blow by Japan. How, then, asked Roosevelt, could the United States permit this without too much danger to itself?*

That evening Stark wrote a lengthy warning to Kimmel in Hawaii, informing him that neither the President nor the Secretary of State "would be surprised over a Japanese surprise attack," adding that while "an attack upon the Philippines would be the most embarrassing

---

* The claim has been advanced—notably by Rear Admiral Robert A. Theobald in *The Final Secret of Pearl Harbor* (Devin-Adair, 1954)—that President Roosevelt abetted the Japanese surprise "by causing the Hawaiian Commanders to be denied invaluable information from decoded Japanese dispatches concerning the rapid approach of the war and the strong probability that the attack would be directed at Pearl Harbor." He did so, according to now-retired Admiral Kimmel in a recent interview with United Press International, to "induce the Japanese to attack Pearl Harbor and thus permit him to honor his secret commitments to Great Britain and the Netherlands with the full support of the American people."

The report of the Army Pearl Harbor Board, submitted to the Secretary of War on October 20, 1944, apportioned a share of the blame for the surprise to the War and Navy Departments and their top military officers in Washington. Even so, the service inquiries concluded that General Short and Admiral Kimmel had sufficient information to realize that war was imminent and had no excuse for inadequate security measures. They were not court-martialed, despite their requests, largely for political reasons. In this they were grievously wronged, for they had a right to be heard in their own defense. On the other hand, although I am not an apologist for the late President Roosevelt, it is simply ridiculous to suggest that he, who loved the Navy perhaps more than did any of our Presidents, would deliberately offer the Pacific Fleet as a sacrifice to entice Japan into war, and that this scheme was abetted by other responsible military men and statesmen. So many people would have known of such a nefarious plot that it would in fact have been impossible to muffle it.—T.N.D.

thing that could happen to us . . . I still rather look for an advance into Thailand, Indochina, Burma Road areas as the most likely.'' Marshall reviewed the incoming and outgoing messages to overseas commanders, and busied himself with the almost numberless duties of his most important task: preparing our Army for combat.

Honolulu, Tuesday, November 25

Kimmel and Short had more than a passing interest in the status of our negotiations with Japan. Admiral Kimmel had been kept informed of the increasingly strained relations by frequent frank and newsy letters from Admiral Stark. One of these, dated November 7, had said in part: ''Things seem to be moving steadily towards a crisis in the Pacific. . . . A month may see, literally, most anything . . . It doesn't look good.''

Admiral Kimmel undoubtedly was thinking of that letter when he reread the official radio message which he had received the day before, November 24:

> Chances of favorable outcomes of negotiations with Japan very doubtful . . . A surprise aggressive movement in any direction including attack on Philippines or Guam is a possibility. Chief of Staff has seen this dispatch, concurs and requests action addressees to inform senior Army officers their areas. Utmost secrecy necessary in order not to complicate an already tense situation or precipitate Japanese action.

Admiral Kimmel promptly sent a copy of the message to General Short. He had standing instructions to show such messages to the Army commander: the most critical messages from Washington were usually sent over Navy channels because the Army code was considered to be less secure. The Admiral saw no need for further action. After receiving a warning message on October 16 he had taken some measures for a partial alert and reported those promptly to Stark, who replied: ''OK on the disposition which you made.''

Admiral Kimmel and General Short had a cordial personal relationship, despite subsequent widespread but unfounded allegations to the contrary. They had frequently discussed, officially and personally, the possibility of a surprise Japanese attack and the measures to be taken to prepare for it and to thwart it if it should come. These plans had been approved in Washington. The Navy was responsible for long-range reconnaissance up to 700 miles, while the Army, with its land-based aircraft, was responsible for inshore reconnaissance for a distance up to twenty miles from shore. The Army's new radar would provide additional reconnaissance and air-warning service for a distance of up to 130 miles from Oahu. Periodically the commanders held joint maneuvers to test the plans and the readiness of their forces to carry them out.

They commanded large forces which might soon be called upon to fight, and it was essential that they maintain an intensive training schedule to assure the highest possible standard of combat efficiency.

This was a formidable task, since many of their officers and men were inexperienced and untrained, having only recently been brought into our rapidly expanding armed forces. At the same time, as outpost commanders, both Short and Kimmel were well aware of their responsibilities for assuring the security of the fleet and of the island of Oahu.

Moreover, each commander assumed the other knew his business; each assumed the other's command was running on a full-time status. Each felt—as shown by later testimony—that to probe into the other's shop would be an unpardonable and resented intrusion. As a result, the liaison essential to any sort of joint or concerted operation—the daily constant and intimate exchange of details of command operations between Army and Navy staffs—was almost nonexistent. Each commander, then, was working in a partial vacuum.

On the single island of Oahu were concentrated most of the 42,857 troops that comprised the units of General Short's department. Carrying out the intensive training schedule was the bulk of two infantry divisions, less one regiment scattered in detachments on the other islands of the group. Also on Oahu were most of the antiaircraft and coast defense units of the Coast Artillery Command, and more than 250 aircraft of the Army's Hawaiian air force. Some of these aircraft, aloft on routine training exercises, were being tracked by the inexperienced crews of six Army mobile radar units newly installed at different points on the island.

There was comparable activity at the great Pearl Harbor Navy Yard, on the southern coast of the island, close by the bustling metropolis of Honolulu. Quite a few vessels of the U.S. Pacific Fleet were in port. Here Kimmel, the fleet's commander in chief, had his headquarters, from which he and his staff closely supervised the intense training programs of their ships in Hawaiian waters. The fleet comprised eight battleships, two aircraft carriers (with a total of 180 planes), sixteen cruisers, forty-five destroyers, twelve submarines, and slightly more than 300 land-based aircraft. In addition another battleship, an aircraft carrier, four cruisers, and various smaller vessels were temporarily absent, many being in mainland yards for repairs.

The Navy Yard itself was the principal installation of the Fourteenth Naval District; both base and the district were commanded by Rear Admiral Claude C. Bloch, who was a direct subordinate of Kimmel both as base commander and as a Pacific Fleet staff officer—a setup which bred no little confusion and which was not helped by the fact that Bloch was Kimmel's senior in the service, though not in command. Kimmel properly held Bloch responsible for the functioning and local security of all the land-based installations of the fleet in Hawaii, while he himself devoted his principal attention to the readiness of the fleet to function offensively at sea. He considered Bloch to be Short's naval counterpart, so far as local protection of the fleet in Hawaii was concerned. Formal co-ordination of Army and Navy activities in Hawaii and nearby Pacific areas, however, was done at conferences—fairly frequent—between Kimmel and Short.

[*On November 25 (Washington date line), Vice Admiral Chuichi Nagumo's First Air Fleet—six aircraft carriers and 414 combat planes, escorted by two battleships, two heavy cruisers and one light, and nine destroyers—put to sea from Tankan Bay in the southern Kurile Islands. Eight tank ships trailed it. Screening the advance were twenty-eight submarines which had left Kure a few days earlier.*

This powerful naval striking force had long been preparing for a surprise attack on the United States Pacific Fleet at Pearl Harbor. It did not, however, have a final directive to carry it out. The First Air Fleet was to leave the Kurile Islands and steam slowly east into the North Pacific to await orders either to attack or, if negotiations with the United States reached a conclusion satisfactory to Japan, to return home.]

Washington, Wednesday, November 26

Before attending a meeting of the Army-Navy Joint Board, both General Marshall and Admiral Stark had learned that Secretary of State Hull, with the full approval of the President, had made a momentous decision.

During the evening of the twenty-fifth and the early hours of the twenty-sixth, the State Department received the comments of our allies on the *modus vivendi* reply to the Japanese ultimatum. The British, Australians, and Dutch gave lukewarm approval to the proposal for a three-month truce, though in a personal message to the President, Prime Minister Winston Churchill remarked pointedly, "What about Chiang Kai-shek? Is he not having a very thin diet?"

Chiang, in fact, had protested violently against the truce proposal, which, with its relaxation of economic pressure on Japan, could only work to the psychological and military disadvantage of China. The protest, as well as information gleaned from more intercepted messages indicating that the Japanese would accept nothing less than complete agreement to their demands of November 20, caused Secretary Hull to doubt the wisdom of the *modus vivendi*. Obviously, these concessions were inadequate to satisfy Japanese demands, yet, because they would seem like American appeasement they would strike a major blow to Chinese morale.

Hull therefore recommended a different reply, which the President approved. After a calm but firm restatement of the principles which had guided the American negotiations, the new note proposed, in essence: withdrawal of Japanese military forces from China and Indochina, recognition of the territorial integrity of those countries, unqualified acceptance of the National Government of China, and, finally, negotiation of a liberal U.S.-Japanese trade treaty once the other conditions had been met.

At 5 P.M. on November 26 Secretary Hull met with the two Japanese ambassadors and presented this reply to them. Special envoy Kurusu read the note, then commented that his government would "throw up its hands" and that the American position practically "put an end to the negotiations."

By frequent phone calls, Secretary Hull had kept both Stimson and Knox informed of these rapid developments, and the two service secretaries had passed on the information to their senior military subordinates. So it was that when they met at a Joint Board conference that same day, Marshall and Stark were well aware of the course of the events still in progress at the State Department. Agreeing that war was now almost certain, they both felt that it was incumbent upon them to remind the President once more of the dangerous weakness of the Army and the Navy and particularly the grave danger of disaster in the Philippines if war were to break out before further reinforcements of men and matériel could reach General MacArthur. They directed their subordinates to have ready for their signatures the next day a joint memorandum to the President which would urge avoidance of hostilities for as long as possible consistent with national policy and national honor.

Late in the afternoon General Marshall held a conference with Major General Leonard T. Gerow, Chief of the War Plans Division, to discuss what should be done the next day, November 27. Marshall had planned to be in North Carolina that day to observe the final phases of the largest maneuvers in the Army's peacetime history; he felt he should carry out that intention, despite his concern about a report that a large Japanese troop convoy had moved into the South China Sea. The two officers discussed the grave implications of the growing Japanese concentrations in the Southeast Asia region. Even though he intended to be back at his desk on the twenty-eighth, General Marshall authorized Gerow to send overseas commanders a warning in his name if further information next day—the twenty-seventh—should point to the possibility of a surprise Japanese attack.

Honolulu, Wednesday, November 26

Admiral Kimmel received a report from the radio intelligence unit in Hawaii of a strong concentration of Japanese submarines and carrier aircraft in the Marshall Islands. This implied, but did not definitely prove, that some Japanese carriers were there as well. This information was perhaps inconsistent with a somewhat more definite report from the Philippines saying that radio traffic indicated all known Japanese carriers to be in home waters. Neither Admiral Kimmel nor members of his staff saw any need to inform General Short of these reports.

Short, meanwhile, had received an official message directing him to send two long-range B-24 bombers—due from the mainland—to photograph and observe the Japanese bases of Truk in the Caroline Islands and Jaluit in the Marshalls, reporting the number and locations of all Japanese naval vessels. He was to make sure both planes were "fully equipped with gun ammunition." But neither mission was ever flown: only one B-24 reached Short, and it was not properly equipped.

[On the high seas, their bleak rendezvous at Tankan far astern, Nagumo's task force was steaming eastward. Radio silence was absolute.

High-grade fuel kept smoke to a minimum. No waste was thrown overboard to leave telltale tracks; blackout on board was complete. Only the Admiral and a handful of his staff knew their orders; the rest of the command buzzed with speculation like so many hornets.]

Washington, Thursday, November 27

General Gerow, summoned to Mr. Stimson's office, found Secretary Knox and Admiral Stark already there. The Secretary of War felt the time had come to alert General MacArthur in the Philippines. He told his listeners that Secretary Hull had warned him no peaceful solution was apparent. "I have washed my hands of it," Hull had said, "and it is now in the hands of you and Knox, the Army and the Navy."

Stimson added word of a telephone discussion with the President, who, agreeing that an alert order be sent out, desired all commanders to be cautioned that Japan must commit the first overt act of war. All four in Stimson's office then prepared drafts of alert messages to be sent to General MacArthur and Admiral Hart in the Philippines and to Army and Navy commanders in Hawaii, Panama, and on the West Coast.

Early in the afternoon Gerow sent out the warning:

Negotiations with Japan appear to be terminated to all practicable purposes with only the barest possibilities that the Japanese Government might . . . offer to continue.

The message then reiterated Mr. Roosevelt's desire that Japan commit the first overt act. But this, it was pointed out,

should not repeat not be construed as restricting you to a course . . . that might jeopardize your defense. *Prior to hostile Japanese action you are directed to undertake such reconnaissance and other measures as you deem necessary* [italics supplied], but these measures should be carried out so as not repeat not to alarm civil population or disclose intent. Report measures taken . . .

The message further directed that, should hostilities occur, commanders would undertake offensive tasks in accordance with existing war plans. It concluded with the caution that dissemination of "this highly secret information" should be limited to the essential minimum.

Stark's message to Navy commanders (as well as to our special naval observer in London, who was to advise the British) was sent at the same time; it opened bluntly: "This dispatch is to be considered a war warning." It related the end of negotiations and the expectation that "an aggressive move" might come within the next few days. Then, in contrast to the more general Army warning, it added the information that known military activities of the Japanese indicated they probably intended to launch "an amphibious expedition against either the Philippines, Thai or Kra peninsula or possibly Borneo." Like the Army warning, it directed execution of existing war plans in the event of hostilities. Naval commanders in the continental United States, Guam, and Samoa were cautioned to take antisabotage measures.

If read together, these two messages definitely pointed a finger at Southeast Asia as the expected enemy target. This, of course, in no way excuses any of the subsequent actions of our commanders in Hawaii, whose paramount responsibility was the security of their post. But it must have influenced their thinking.

Honolulu, Thursday, November 27

The official warnings from Washington confirmed to Short and Kimmel the seriousness of the international situation. Short, who noted that he was expected to report the measures he was taking, sent the following reply: "Report Department alerted to prevent sabotage. Liaison with the Navy."

The Hawaiian Department plans provided for three kinds of alert. Number 1, which was what Short had ordered, was to guard against sabotage and uprisings—long a preoccupation of all Hawaiian commanders because of the high proportion of Japanese in the Islands. Number 2 included security against possible isolated, external air or naval attacks. Number 3 was a full-scale deployment for maximum defense of the Islands, and particularly of Oahu—heart of the military organization. Only in the two higher stages of alert was ammunition to be distributed to the antiaircraft batteries; in Alert No. 1 all ammunition was to be kept stored in the dumps. Under Alert No. 1, planes would be parked closely for easy guarding; under the others they would be dispersed.

General Short felt he was confirmed in his concern over sabotage when his intelligence officer—or G-2—presented a message from the War Department G-2, warning that "subversive activities may be expected."

In obedience to the instruction to make such reconnaissance as he might "deem necessary," Short did, however, order his newly installed radar stations to operate daily from 4 A.M. to 7 A.M.; these were the dawn hours when surprise attack was most likely. Further reconnaissance, he felt, was the Navy's responsibility. He didn't know that Kimmel was having troubles of his own in attempting any sustained offshore reconnaissance. Nor was Kimmel aware that Short's radar was operating only on a curtailed basis.

Kimmel pondered over what steps he should take. Though he was already alerted to some extent, he knew that for the moment he could do little in the way of "defensive deployment" in his war plan tasks—most specifically, raids into the Japanese mandated islands. Should he then prepare for an attack against Oahu? The Washington message implied that this was not a probability. Even so, he didn't have sufficient planes for a 360 degree, distant reconnaissance from Oahu.

In compliance with instructions from Washington, Kimmel was sending some Marine planes to Wake and Midway islands. He decided that the two carrier task forces he was ordering to carry out this instruction could, en route, conduct long-range searches to the west, over the direct route from Japan to Oahu.

Task Force 8, under Vice Admiral William F. Halsey, including the carrier *Enterprise* and three cruisers, was leaving that day. In conference with Halsey before departure, Kimmel showed him the "war warning" message. Halsey asked how far he should go if he met any Japanese ships while searching. "Use your common sense," was Kimmel's reply. Halsey, it is understood, commented that these were the best orders he could receive, adding that if he found as much as one Japanese sampan, he would sink it. Kimmel, by making no further comment, apparently acquiesced.

Pending the arrival of Halsey at Wake, Kimmel sent orders to a patrol plane squadron based on Midway to proceed to Wake and return, searching ocean areas and covering a 525-mile area around Wake itself.

Kimmel felt that he had done all he could in that line without completely halting fleet training and exhausting the pilots of his relatively weak air command. But he did order immediate attack on any and all unidentified submarines discovered in the vicinity of Oahu and other fleet operating zones. Neither then nor later, apparently, did he check on the local security measures undertaken by Admiral Bloch's command, nor did he suggest any co-ordination between Bloch and Short.

[*Nagumo's force was steady on a course laid between the Aleutians and Midway Island, the carriers in two parallel rows of three each. Battleships and cruisers guarded the flanks, destroyers screened wide, and submarines were scouting far ahead.*]

Washington, Friday, November 28

General Marshall, back from his North Carolina inspection, was briefed by Gerow on the previous day's happenings. He read and approved the joint memorandum, already signed by Admiral Stark, which urged on the President the need for gaining time, particularly until troops—some already at sea and nearing Guam, others about to embark on the West Coast—could reach the Philippines. He also approved the warning message Gerow had sent to the overseas commanders.

At noon he attended the President's "War Council" meeting at the White House. The implications of a large Japanese amphibious force, known to be sailing southward through the South China Sea, were discussed. British Malaya, the Netherlands East Indies, and the Philippines were potential targets, the invasion of which would immediately involve us in war. But unless Congress should previously declare war, the United States could not attack this force. It was agreed that the President should send a message to Emperor Hirohito urging him to preserve peace, and that Mr. Roosevelt should also address Congress, explaining the dangers being created by this Japanese aggressive action. The President then left for a short vacation at Warm Springs, Georgia, directing his advisers to have the two documents prepared in his absence.

Marshall, back at his desk, thumbed through a sheaf of radio replies to the "war warning" message. Lieutenant General John L. DeWitt, commanding on the Pacific Coast, reported instituting a harbor alert at San Francisco and similar precautions in Alaska in liaison with naval authorities. He requested permission to direct air as well as ground deployment of his far-flung command. It was a long message, contrasting sharply with Short's succinct report of sabotage defense measures in Hawaii. But the Chief of Staff didn't pay much attention; it would be Gerow's job to handle any necessary responses. So Marshall initialed most of the messages and then forgot about them.

Short's message, however, was not initiated by Marshall. He would later testify he had no recollection of ever having seen it, although it bore the routine rubber stamp, "Noted by Chief of Staff."

As for Admiral Stark, he was pushing off a long message to Navy commanders on the West Coast, and to Admiral Kimmel, quoting the Army alert message of the twenty-seventh, including its admonition that Japan must commit the first "overt act."

Honolulu, Friday, November 28

Kimmel read Stark's long quote of the Army's alert message. He was particularly interested in its stress that "if hostilities cannot . . . be avoided the United States desires that Japan commit the first overt act." This appeared to confirm his decision of the previous day: limiting defensive deployment to one patrol squadron cruising from Wake to Midway and sending carrier task forces for local defense of those outposts.

Admiral Kimmel received several other interesting reports. The U.S.S. *Helena* reported contact with an unidentified submarine. An intelligence estimate based on radio intercepts indicated Japanese carriers were still in their own home waters. Another report on intercepted Japanese messages established a "winds code," by means of which Japan would notify its diplomatic and consular representatives abroad of a decision to go to war: "east wind rain" meant war with the United States; "north wind cloudy," war with Russia; "west wind clear," war with England and invasion of Thailand, Malaya, and the Dutch East Indies.

It was all very interesting. However, the Admiral never thought of mentioning any of these reports during his conference with General Short that day. They discussed mutual responsibility for security of Wake and Midway—in light of the mixed Army-Navy garrisons at both places. But neither thought of asking the other what action he had taken on the November 27 warnings, nor did either volunteer any information on matters he considered to be of interest to his own individual service only.

[*Admiral Nagumo's fleet spent the day in attempts to refuel in a plunging sea—an operation which, as it turned out, would continue for several days under almost heartbreaking conditions of bad weather.*]

Washington, Saturday, November 29

Both General Marshall and Admiral Stark received Magic copies of more intercepted Japanese messages. One of these from Premier Tojo in Tokyo to the ambassadors in Washington was quite ominous:

> The United States' . . . humiliating proposal . . . was quite unexpected and extremely regrettable. The Imperial Government can by no means use it as a basis for negotiations. Therefore . . . in two or three days the negotiations will be de facto ruptured. . . . However, I did not wish you to give the impression that the negotiations are broken off. Merely say to them that you are awaiting instructions. . . . From now on, do the best you can.

To Marshall and Stark this was clear evidence indeed that the Japanese were stalling for time only long enough to get their forces ready to attack in the Indonesia-Southeast Asia area. It seemed now only a question of time, as more reports streamed in about Japanese convoys moving into the South China Sea.

For a good part of the morning Stark and Marshall were working closely with Secretaries Knox and Stimson in preparing and revising drafts of the presidential messages to Congress and to Emperor Hirohito, in accordance with the agreement at the previous day's meeting of the War Council. Finally, about noon, the two secretaries were satisfied, and their proposed drafts were sent to Secretary Hull.

Late in the afternoon both read with considerable interest reports of a warlike speech which Premier Tojo had delivered that day (November 30, Tokyo time). The twenty-ninth had been the deadline established in the messages from Tokyo to the ambassadors. The speech, while warlike, failed to give any indication of Japanese intentions.

Honolulu, Saturday, November 29

Things were generally quiet on Oahu and in the outlying waters, as the Army and Navy both began a weekend of relaxation after five days of strenuous training. There was considerable bustle, however, at the Army's headquarters at Fort Shafter, as well as at Navy headquarters at nearby Pearl Harbor. General Short approved a message in reply to the latest sabotage warning from Washington, outlining in detail the security measures which had been taken. Admiral Kimmel received another message from Washington reminding him once more that he was to be prepared to carry out existing war plans in the event of hostilities with Japan. Thus, once again, the two commanders were reminded of the alert messages they had received on the twenty-seventh, and once again they found themselves satisfied with the actions they had then taken.

[*In the North Pacific Admiral Nagumo's fleet continued refueling.*]

Washington, Sunday, November 30

General Marshall, returning from his usual Sunday morning horse-back ride at Fort Myer, found another intercepted Japanese message awaiting him; the Foreign Ministry was cautioning its envoys in Washington to keep talking and "be careful that this does not lead to anything like a breaking-off of negotiations." He agreed with G-2's conclusion that the Japanese were stalling until their South China Sea assault was ready.

Stark, at his desk, was called that morning by Secretary of State Hull, gravely concerned about Premier Tojo's warlike speech. The Secretary told him he was going to urge the President's return from Warm Springs. A later call from Hull informed Stark that President Roosevelt would be back Monday morning; Stark must see the President and report on the naval developments in the Far East.

Honolulu, Sunday, November 30

General Short, in light of his instructions "not to alarm the civil population," must have been annoyed to read the Honolulu *Advertiser* headlines that morning: "Hawaii Troops Alerted." There wasn't anything he could do about it, however; even the limited nature of his Alert No. 1 would draw newspaper attention in a critical time such as this. He also read that "Leaders Call Troops Back in Singapore—Hope Wanes as Nations Fail at Parleys" and "Kurusu Bluntly Warned Nation Ready for Battle."

Kimmel ordered a squadron of patrol planes to Midway, to replace temporarily the squadron which he had ordered to reconnoiter about Wake. He was also interested in an information copy of a Navy Department message to Admiral Hart, commanding our Asiatic Fleet at Manila, directing him to scout for information as to an intended Japanese attack on the Kra Isthmus of Thailand, just north of Malaya.

Kimmel didn't think that war could be delayed much longer. He wrote on the top of a piece of paper the words—"Steps to be taken in case of American-Japanese war within the next twenty-four hours," an *aide-mémoire* of the orders he must issue to his fleet.

[*The Japanese First Air Fleet was still engaged in the arduous re-fueling job, while continuing its eastward course at slow speed.*]

Washington, Monday, December 1

A busy day. Stark learned from his intelligence staff that the Japanese Navy had changed service radio frequencies and call letters for all units afloat—a normal prewar step. He went to the White House with Secretary Hull and briefed the President.

In the afternoon both Stark and Marshall digested an unusual number of important Magic intercepts of Japanese messages. Japan's Foreign Minister was urging his ambassadors to prevent the United States "from becoming unduly suspicious," emphasizing that it was important to give the impression to the Americans that "negotiations are continuing." Tokyo also had ordered its diplomatic offices in London, Hong Kong, Singapore, and Manila "to abandon the use of code machines and to dispose of them." Japan's ambassador at Bangkok reported his intrigues to maneuver Thailand into a declaration of war on Great Britain.

But most significant was an exchange between Japan's ambassador to Berlin and his foreign office. The ambassador reported that Foreign Minister von Ribbentrop had given him Hitler's unequivocal assurance that "should Japan become engaged in a war against the United States, Germany, of course, would join the war immediately." Tojo promptly told the ambassador to inform the German government that "war may suddenly break out between the Anglo-Saxon nations and Japan through some clash of arms. . . . This war may come quicker than anyone dreams."

And how quickly would that be? This was the question which sprang immediately to the minds of Admiral Stark and General Marshall, the men responsible for readying the armed forces of the United States for the coming clash of arms. They had no way of knowing that the answer lay in a brief uncoded message picked up by several American radio intelligence intercept stations just a few hours earlier. "Climb Mount Niitaka," was the message. No significance could be attached to it, so it never came to the attention of Marshall or Stark. Nor would it have meant anything to either of them.

Honolulu, Monday, December 1

Kimmel and Short held another routine conference. Presumably they discussed at some length the grave international situation. Supplementing the cryptic but alarming official intelligence reports and warnings were the headlines blazoning the Honolulu newspapers.

But neither Kimmel nor Short in their conversation discussed local security precautions or a possible threat to Oahu. Politely but inconclusively they continued discussion of the divided responsibility at Wake and Midway. Kimmel never thought to mention to Short that he had received another Washington warning about the "winds code" and that he had also been informed of the change in Japanese military frequencies and call letters. It never occurred to Kimmel that Short might not have been told about either matter.

Routine training continued in Army posts. General Short was quite pleased that his limited alert—which the War Department had apparently approved—had not interfered noticeably with training programs.

[*"Climb Mount Niitaka!"*

Admiral Nagumo sucked in his breath as the message was laid before him this day. This was it; the prearranged code which meant "Proceed with attack."

Obedient to the signal flags broken out aboard the flagship, the gray ships came foaming about to a southeasterly course, vibrating to the thrust of increased propeller speed. Inside the steel hulls the mustered crews, learning the news, cheered, quaffed sake, and burned incense to the spirits of their ancestors.]

Washington, Tuesday, December 2

Additional Magic intercepts indicated further Japanese preparations for war, with the enemy's known offensive weight still massing in Southeast Asia.

Honolulu, Tuesday, December 2

Kimmel, discussing intelligence reports with his staff, noted the change in Japanese radio frequencies as related in the Navy Department's fortnightly intelligence summary, received late the previous day. The gist of it was that Tokyo was preparing for "operations on a large scale."

Then Kimmel called for intelligence estimates on the location of Japanese aircraft carriers. Captain Edwin T. Layton, his intelligence officer, gave estimated locations for all except Divisions 1 and 2— four carriers.

"What!" exclaimed Kimmel, "you don't know where [they] are?"

"No, sir, I do not. I think they are in home waters, but—"

Sternly, but with a suspicion of a twinkle in his eyes, Kimmel delivered himself of a masterpiece of unconscious irony.

"Do you mean to say they could be rounding Diamond Head and you wouldn't know it?"

The conference ended after a discussion on the difficulty of locating a force operating under sealed orders while preserving radio silence.

Short met Kimmel that day again. They continued debate over jurisdiction at Wake and Midway.

[*Nagumo's fleet was steadily driving south toward Oahu. In prearranged code—unintelligible to American Magic interceptors—Tokyo had confirmed the target date: "X-Day will be 8 December"— December 7, Honolulu time.*]

Washington, Wednesday, December 3

Along with the other recipients of Magic information, General Marshall and Admiral Stark noted but attached no particular significance to a pair of intercepted messages made available to them that day.

One, dated November 15, was already old; its translation had been deferred for several days in order to take care of messages considered more urgent. It referred to an earlier message directing the Japanese consulate at Honolulu to make periodic reports on the location of American warships in Pearl Harbor, and requested the Honolulu consulate to step up these reports to twice a week.

No particular importance was attributed to this by Admiral Stark or his senior naval intelligence officers, since the Japanese had long been making efforts to obtain information about the activities and number of ships in harbor at other naval bases on the West Coast and at Panama. The fact that the Japanese wanted more complete data, including exact locations of specific vessels in Pearl Harbor, was assumed to be merely an indication of their thoroughness in evaluating intelligence on America's main Pacific combat force.

The other message was a reply by Prime Minister Tojo to the suggestion of his ambassadors at Washington that peace could perhaps be preserved through a high-level conference—they had proposed former Premier Prince Konoye as the Japanese envoy and Vice President Henry Wallace or Presidential Assistant Harry Hopkins for the United States—at "some midway point, such as Honolulu." Tojo's response, that "it would be inappropriate for us to propose such a meeting," seemed a less significant indication of Japan's immediate intentions than the continuing reports of her movements in and near Indochina.

Honolulu, Wednesday, December 3

Admiral Kimmel noted the continuing and surprising lack of information on Japanese carriers contained in the latest daily radio intelligence summary, which stated that "carrier traffic is at a low ebb."

That day, too, he received Admiral Stark's letter of November 25. He agreed with Stark's view that "an attack on the Philippines" might be embarrassing, but that "an advance into Thailand, Indochina, Burma Road area [was] most likely."

In the afternoon Short and Kimmel conferred. They soon got into a grim discussion of what they could do to carry out assigned war plans when and if war broke out. Both were thinking, of course, of planned naval and air raids into the Marshall Islands and of security measures for Wake and Midway. There was no mention of like measures for Oahu. Nor did Admiral Kimmel think to mention to General Short his latest intelligence reports about the burning of Japanese codes or the missing aircraft carriers.

[*Nagumo's planners on the high seas were busy marking on their charts of Pearl Harbor the exact locations of six of the U.S. battle fleet—the* Pennsylvania, Arizona, California, Tennessee, Maryland, *and* West Virginia. *The data came from Honolulu, relayed by radio through Imperial Navy Headquarters in Tokyo.*]

Washington, Thursday, December 4

A mixed bag of Magic intercepts available to both Stark and Marshall gave clear indication of Japanese intentions to go to war. Instructions came to Ambassador Nomura to completely destroy one of the two special machines for secret coding, but to hold the other and its cipher key—which should be in his personal possession—"until the last minute." One intercepted message, considered to be relatively insignificant, was to the Japanese consul at Honolulu; he was to "investigate completely the fleet-bases in the neighborhood of the Hawaiian military reservation."

Stark and Marshall concerned themselves with routine activities.

Honolulu, Thursday, December 4

Admiral Kimmel conferred with two of his senior task-force commanders, scheduled to sail the next day on combined training-alert missions. One, under Vice Admiral Wilson Brown, was to proceed to Johnson Island, 700 miles southwest of Oahu, on a joint Navy-Marine bombardment and landing exercise. The other, under Rear Admiral T. H. Newton, included the carrier *Lexington*. This force was to go to Midway Island, fly off a squadron of Marine planes to reinforce the local garrison, and then rendezvous with Brown at Johnson Island. En route the *Lexington*'s planes would conduct routine scouting flights.

Kimmel's intention was that, should war break out, these forces would be available for raids into the Marshall Island group in accordance with existing war plans. Both task-force commanders understood their war-plan missions; both were aware in general of the tense international situation. Kimmel, therefore, felt he was under no obligation to inform either of Washington's November 27 "war warning" message.

The net naval situation on Oahu now was that the entire carrier force of the Pacific Fleet was either at sea or about to steam and that the approaches to the island from the west would be scouted for several days to come.

Kimmel felt that these steps would ensure a reconnaissance search of a large portion of the central Pacific Ocean, as extensive as his limited aircraft strength would permit. But, from the Hawaiian Islands north to the Aleutians, both sea and air were still bare of American reconnaissance.

Kimmel and Short did not meet that day.

[*Admiral Nagumo, watching the intermittent refueling being carried on during the day, was intrigued to learn from Honolulu, via Tokyo, that watchful Japanese eyes were "unable to ascertain whether air alert had been issued. There are no indications of sea alert. . . ."*]

Washington, Friday, December 5

Both War and Navy departments were busy compiling data for President Roosevelt on Japanese sea, land, and air strength concentrating in French Indochina and adjacent areas. In an intercepted Japanese message from Washington, Ambassador Nomura told Tokyo that in case of Japanese invasion of Thailand, joint military action by Great Britain and the United States "is a definite certainty, with or without a declaration of war." Another, from Tokyo, reiterated the previous instructions about destruction of codes and coding machines.

Admiral Stark, conferring with staff officers, decided no further warning orders need be sent to overseas naval commanders; the message of November 27 was adequate. All concurred.

Honolulu, Friday, December 5

General Short read with interest a cryptic message from G-2 in Washington to his intelligence officer, directing him to get in touch with the Navy immediately "regarding broadcasts from Tokyo reference weather." So Lieutenant Colonel George W. Bicknell, assistant G-2, gave the General all facts obtainable from his own office and from Kimmel's headquarters. Short was informed by Kimmel of the departure of the two naval task forces of Admirals Brown and Newton.

[*While pilots and squadron leaders on board Nagumo's fleet studied and restudied their coming roles, the ships—900 miles north of Midway and 1,300 miles northwest of Oahu—slid slowly down the North Pacific rollers, still far beyond the range of any American search plane.*]

Washington, Saturday, December 6

Reports of increasing Japanese concentration and movements in Indochina, South China, and the South China Sea absorbed Stark and Marshall, as well as all the other members of the War Cabinet from the President down. Mr. Roosevelt, the service chiefs were glad to learn, had decided that he would personally warn Emperor Hirohito that further aggressions might lead to war and urge the Japanese ruler that withdrawal of his forces from Indochina "would result in the assurance of peace throughout the whole of the South Pacific area."

Late in the afternoon Magic plucked out of the air thirteen parts of a fourteen-part memorandum from Tokyo to the Japanese envoys. This much of the message summarized negotiations from the Japanese viewpoint, concluding that the American note of November 26 was not "a basis of negotiations." The envoys were instructed to handle it carefully, since "the situation is extremely delicate."

Distribution of this intercept was curious. Decoding was completed after office hours. General Sherman A. Miles, Army G-2, saw no need to disturb either the Secretary of War, General Marshall, or General Gerow at their homes. (In passing it might be mentioned that one didn't disturb General Marshall at home without extremely good reason.) Some Navy people saw the message. Stark, who was at the theater, learned of it when he returned home and found that he was expected to call the White House. The President had received the intercept, as had the State Department. The details of the conversation are not known, but presumably the President told Stark, as he had earlier said to Harry Hopkins: "This means war!"

Honolulu, Saturday, December 6

In the daily radio intelligence summary received that morning from Washington, Admiral Kimmel was again struck by lack of information on the location of Japanese carriers. In other dispatches, however, there was considerable information about different kinds of Japanese activity. He received a copy of Admiral Hart's message reporting on the movement of the two convoys south of Indochina. And he received a message from Washington authorizing him, "in view of the international situation and the exposed position of our outlying Pacific Islands," to order the destruction of classified documents at these islands, "now or under later conditions of greater emergency." Neither the Admiral nor any member of his staff saw any need to pass on any information to the Army. Presumably General Short was getting it all through Army channels.

Carefully checking the reported locations of all fleet units and projecting their planned routes for the next twenty-four hours, Admiral Kimmel again made his daily revision of his personal check-list memorandum: "Steps to be taken in case of American-Japanese war within the next twenty-four hours."

Over at Fort Shafter, Army headquarters, the daily staff conference was as usual presided over by Colonel Walter C. Phillips, chief of staff. General Short did not normally attend these meetings. Bicknell, assistant G-2, who seems to have been on his toes those days, reported the Japanese consulate in Honolulu was busily burning and destroying secret papers, significant in light of similar reports throughout the world already noted in the intercepts. The chief of staff and G-2 reported this information later to General Short.

And so Oahu drifted into another weekend: a time of relaxation for both Army and Navy. Short, however, was interrupted by Bicknell early that evening at his quarters while he and his G-2—Colonel Kendall Fielder—and their wives were about to drive to a dinner dance.

Bicknell, with some sense of urgency, reported that the local FBI agent had passed to him and to Navy intelligence a transcript of a suspicious long-distance telephone message. A Japanese named Mori, talking to someone in Tokyo, mentioned flights of airplanes, searchlights, and the number of ships in Pearl Harbor, along with cryptic reference to various flowers—apparently part of some sort of code.

Both the FBI man and Bicknell were alarmed at the implications of this flower code. Neither Short nor Fielder, however, was disturbed. Short, before they hurried to the car where their wives awaited them impatiently, told Bicknell he was, perhaps, "too intelligence-conscious." In any event they could talk about it again in the morning.

The district intelligence officer of the Navy decided that the transcript should be studied further by a Japanese linguist and so put the FBI report away until Monday morning. Admiral Kimmel was not informed.

[Nagumo's fleet, the wallowing tankers now left behind, was churning southward at twenty-four-knot speed. By 6 A.M. next day it would be 230 miles north of Oahu with its planes thrusting skyward. And at dawn, five midget two-man submarines—disgorged from five large Japanese submarines gathered offshore that night—poked their way around Diamond Head, Pearl Harbor-bound.]

Washington, Sunday, December 7

By 8 A.M. the last part of the Japanese memorandum—Part Fourteen—had been intercepted, transcribed, and was ready for distribution. Both Army and Navy intelligence officers were slightly surprised at its mild tone: "The Japanese Government regrets . . . that it is impossible to reach an agreement through further negotiations."

Stark got it in his office. Marshall was taking his Sunday morning recreational ride at Fort Myer: the message would await his arrival —usually at about 11 A.M. All others concerned got it. Meanwhile two other messages had been intercepted by Magic, and Colonel Rufus Bratton, executive officer in G-2, was so upset by them he tried vainly to get them to the Chief of Staff.

One of the messages ordered the embassy to destroy immediately its one remaining cipher machine plus all codes and secret documents. The other read:

"Will the Ambassador please submit to the United States Government (if possible to the Secretary of State) our reply to the United States at 1 P.M. on the 7th, your time."

It will be remembered that General Marshall did not take kindly to interruptions in his off-duty hours. So, despite the limited area of his ride—an automobile or motorcycle from Fort Myer headquarters could have intercepted him in fifteen minutes at most—not until his return to his quarters at ten-thirty did Marshall learn that an important message was awaiting him. He reached his office in the Munitions Building at about 11:15, to find General Gerow, General Miles, and Colonel Bratton there. Bratton handed him the three intercepted messages—the memorandum, the instructions to destroy codes and papers, and the instruction to deliver the Japanese answer at 1 P.M. precisely. Marshall read quickly but carefully, as was usual with him. Then—

"Something is going to happen at one o'clock," he told the officers. "When they specified a day, that of course had significance, but not comparable to an hour."

He immediately called Stark, who had read all three messages. A warning should be sent at once to all Pacific commanders, Marshall felt. Stark hesitated; he felt all had already been alerted. Marshall stated that in view of the "one o'clock" item he would apprise Army commanders anyway.

Hanging up, he reached for a pencil and drafted his instruction to DeWitt, Western Defense Command; Andrews, Panama Command; Short, Hawaiian Command; and MacArthur, Philippine Command. It took him about three minutes. He read it to the group:

"The Japanese are presenting at 1 P.M. E.S.T. today, what amounts to an ultimatum. Also they are under orders to destroy their code machine immediately. Just what significance the hour set may have, we do not know, but be on alert accordingly."

As he was ordering Bratton to send it out at once, Stark telephoned back. Would Marshall please include in his dispatch the "usual expression to inform the naval officer?" Marshall quickly added the words "Inform naval authorities of this communication." He sent Bratton on his way, instructing him to return as soon as the message had been delivered to the message center.

Bratton was back in five minutes; he had delivered the message personally to the officer in charge of the message center, Colonel French.

Marshall, obviously more perturbed than any of those present had ever before seen him, asked Bratton how much time would be consumed in enciphering and dispatching the message. Bratton didn't know. So back he was rushed to find out.

Marshall, it developed, was pondering whether or not he should telephone a warning—especially to MacArthur. Time was running out; not much more than one hour remained. Marshall had a "scrambler" phone on his desk, which permitted secure long-distance conversations with similar phones in the headquarters of overseas commanders; eavesdroppers would hear only unintelligible gibberish. Marshall, however, must have had some private reservations as to the efficacy of the scrambler mechanism, and apparently feared that the Japanese might have some way of deciphering the conversation. A telephone call which could not be kept secret might precipitate Japanese action; it would almost certainly indicate we had broken their secret code. Would it be worth it?

Bratton reported back that the process would take about thirty minutes.

"Thirty minutes until it is dispatched, or thirty minutes until it is received and decoded at the other end?"

Business of rushing back to the message center again, while the big office clock ticked away. Bratton, charging back, announced that the message, decoded, would be in the hands of the addressees in thirty minutes. It was now precisely noon. In Hawaii it was only 6:30 A.M. Marshall, satisfied, made no further follow-up.

Had he done so he would have found out that Colonel French at the message center was having some troubles. To San Francisco, Panama, and Manila the warning sped without delay. But the War Department radio, so Colonel French was informed, had been out of contact with Hawaii since 10:20 that morning. French decided to use commercial facilities: Western Union to San Francisco, thence commercial radio to Honolulu. This was a normal procedure; usually it would mean but little further delay. French never dreamed of disturbing the Chief of Staff by reporting such trivia. So Marshall's warning was filed at the Army Signal Center at 12:01 P.M. (6.31 A.M. in Hawaii); teletype transmission to San Francisco was completed by 12:17 P.M. (6:47 A.M. in Hawaii), and was in the Honoulu office of RCA at 1:03 P.M. Washington time (7:33 A.M. in Hawaii). Since that was too early for teletype traffic to Fort Shafter, RCA sent it by motorcycle messenger. He would, as it turned out, be delayed through extraordinary circumstances.

Honolulu, Sunday, December 7

Extraordinary circumstances had become almost commonplace on and near Oahu as early as 3:42 A.M. At that hour the mine sweeper *Condor*, conducting a routine sweep of the harbor entrance, sighted a submarine periscope. This was a defensive area where American submarines were prohibited from operating submerged. The *Condor* flashed a report of the sighting to the destroyer *Ward*, of the inshore patrol. For two hours the *Ward* searched the harbor entrance in vain; meanwhile the *Condor* and another mine sweeper had entered the harbor at about 5 A.M.; for some reason the antisubmarine net, opened to permit the entrance of the mine sweepers, was not closed.

At 6:30 the U.S.S. *Antares*—a repair ship towing a steel barge—was approaching the harbor entrance when she sighted a suspicious object, which looked like a midget submarine. The *Antares* immediately notified the *Ward*. At 6.55 a Navy patrol plane sighted the same object and dropped two smoke pots on the spot. The *Ward* hastened to the scene, spotting the sub—her superstructure just above the surface—at 6:40, and promptly opened fire. At the same time the patrol plane dropped bombs or depth charges. The submarine keeled over and began to sink, as the *Ward* dropped more depth charges. Shortly after 6:50 the destroyer sent a coded message that it had attacked a submarine in the defensive sea area.

At about 7:40 Admiral Kimmel received a telephone call from the staff duty officer, reporting the *Ward*-submarine incident. Kimmel replied, "I will be right down." Quickly he completed dressing and left for his headquarters.

Meanwhile, the Army's six mobile radar stations on Oahu had

been on the alert since 4 A.M. in compliance with General Short's Alert
No. 1 instructions. At 7 A.M. five of these stations ceased operations, in
accordance with these same instructions. At the remote Opana station
at the northern tip of the island, Privates Joseph Lockard and George
Elliott kept their set on while waiting for the truck which was to pick
them up to take them to breakfast. Lockard, an experienced radar
operator, planned to use this time to give Elliott a bit more instruction.
At this moment an unusual formation appeared at the edge of the
screen; Lockard checked the machine, found it operating properly,
and at 7:02 A.M. concluded that a large number of aircraft, approximately 130 miles distant, was approaching Oahu from the north. For
fifteen minutes Lockard and Elliott observed the approach of the
formation, debating whether they should report it. Finally, at 7:20,
Lockard called the radar information center. The switchboard operator
informed him that the center had closed down twenty minutes before,
that everyone had left except one Air Corps officer, First Lieutenant
Kermet Tyler. Lockard reported the approaching flight to Tyler, who
thought for a moment; the flight was undoubtedly either a naval patrol,
a formation of Hickam Field bombers, or—most likely—a number of
B-17's due from the mainland. "Forget it," he told Lockard.

Twenty minutes later—about 7:50—there was a bustle of activity
on the decks of the ninety-four vessels of the Pacific Fleet in Pearl
Harbor. It was almost time for morning colors on each vessel, and
white-garbed sailors were briskly preparing for the daily flag-raising
ceremony. Except for one destroyer, moving slowly toward the entrance, each ship was motionless at its moorings.

At 7:55 boatswains' whistles piped, and the preparatory signal for
the colors ceremony was hoisted on each ship. At the same moment a
low-flying plane, approaching over the hills to the northeast, swooped
low over Ford Island, in the middle of the harbor. A bomb dropped on
the seaplane ramp, close by the eight battleships moored next to the
island. As the plane zoomed upward, displaying the red sun emblem of
Japan, it was followed closely by others. By 9:45 some 260 Japanese
planes had flashed that emblem over Oahu, and when the dreadful
110 minutes were over, 2,403 Americans—mostly sailors on the battleships—were dead or dying; 1,178 more had been wounded; the battle
force of the Pacific Fleet had been destroyed, with four battleships
sunk or capsized and the remaining four damaged, while several smaller
vessels were sunk or damaged severely. The Japanese lost twenty-nine
planes, five midget submarines, and less than a hundred men.

One small further incident is pertinent to our assessment of United
States leadership in high places just before Pearl Harbor.

The Nisei RCA messenger boy carrying General Marshall's message
speedily found himself involved in trouble. Not until 11:45 could he
thread his way through traffic jams, road blocks, and general confusion
to reach the Fort Shafter signal office, which was itself swamped in
traffic by this time.

Not until 2:58 P.M. Hawaiian time—9:58 that evening in bewildered
Washington—was the message decoded and placed on Short's desk.

Scene at Pearl Harbor during December 7, 1941 attack.

He rushed a copy to Admiral Kimmel, who read it, remarked—perhaps unnecessarily—that it was not of the slightest interest any more, and dropped it into the wastebasket.

It had been a pretty long thirty minutes.

Who was responsible?

No disaster of the magnitude of Pearl Harbor could have occurred without the failure—somewhere and somehow—of leadership. A total of eight separate official investigations searched for scapegoats, and found them. The disaster remained a political football long after the last three of these investigations. And much confusion and argument still exist.

Yet through this welter of discord, some facts and conclusions stand out. Today, nearly thirty years later, in another time of crisis, they hold important lessons.

It makes no difference, in assessing responsibility, that exceptional Japanese military skill, shrouded by deceit and assisted by almost incredible luck, accomplished its mission. Nor, indeed, does it matter that—as adjudicated in the always brilliant light of afterthought—Japan might well have inflicted defeat upon our Pacific Fleet and our Army forces in Hawaii regardless of how well alerted they may have been on December 7, 1941.

It makes no difference, so far as responsibility for the disaster itself was concerned, whether the war could have been prevented by wiser statesmanship or more astute diplomacy—though this would have required a wholehearted and unified national determination which did not exist in America in 1941 and the years before. It makes no difference that on December 7 the President and the Secretary of State—like the civilian Secretaries of War and Navy—had their eyes fixed on the Japanese threat in Southeast Asia. They had repeatedly warned the military men that war had probably become unavoidable.

What *does* matter is that the civilian statesmen—however deft or clumsy, shrewd, or shortsighted—performed their difficult tasks of diplomacy and of administration confident that the military men would carry out their professional responsibilities by doing everything humanly possible to prepare for a war so clearly impending. They had every right to expect that—within the limits of scanty means available—the Armed Forces would be ready for any contingency.

The confidence and expectations of civilian leadership and of the nation were tragically dashed that Sunday almost thirty years ago.

Military failures were responsible for Pearl Harbor.

In Washington the most important of these were the following:

1. The War Department staff, over which General Marshall presided, was at the time a complicated but "one-man" shop, where delegation of responsibility was the exception rather than the rule. When Marshall was absent, the operational wheels tended to freeze. This situation was to some extent due to cumbersome organization, to some extent due to the personality of the Chief of Staff.

2. General Marshall, in a letter to General Short on February 7, 1941, stressed that "the risk of sabotage and the *risk involved in a surprise raid by air and submarine* [italics supplied] constitute the real perils of the [Hawaiian] situation." Yet, although definitely warning General Short on November 27 of the threat of war, and ordering him to report the measures he would take in response, Marshall did not check up on those measures; moreover, he was unaware that Short had done no more than to take routine precautions against sabotage. And General Gerow, heading the War Plans Division of General Marshall's General Staff—as he testified later in taking full responsibility for this slip—had not made any provision for following up operational orders. The net result was that both Marshall and Short remained the whole time in blissful ignorance of a vital misinterpretation of orders.

3. Marshall and Admiral Stark—and indeed all members of their staffs who knew the situation—permitted themselves to be hypnotized by the concrete evidence of the aggressive Japanese build-up in Southeast Asia which threatened our Philippines outpost. This theme, it will be remembered, ran as background to nearly all the warnings sent Hawaii. Thus succumbing to the illusory diagnosis of "enemy probable intentions," both top commanders ignored the danger implicit in our inability to locate at least four Japanese carriers.

4. Finally, on December 7, having indicated his full realization of the significance of the "one o'clock" intercept—that less than two hours

now separated peace and war—and having decided not to use his "scrambler" telephone, Marshall failed to require surveillance and positive report on the delivery of his final warning.

These certainly were grave lapses in leadership. Yet in fairness, it should be noted that the consequences might not have been disastrous if all subordinate commanders had taken adequate security measures on the basis of the instructions, information, and warnings which they had received. To General Marshall's credit one must also chalk up his ability to profit by his mistakes. In less than three months after Pearl Harbor, he completely reorganized the War Department, decentralizing the mass of relatively minor administrative and executive matters that choked major strategical and tactical decisions. His newly created Operations Division of the General Staff—which he aptly termed his "command post"—ensured co-ordinated action and direction of Army activities in theaters of war all around the globe. On Oahu the situation was less ambiguous: military leadership at the top failed utterly.

Almost three decades later, with war clouds still lowering over most of the world, the story of the Pearl Harbor disaster has more significance than mere passing memorials to the brave men who lost their lives that day. If the lessons are heeded, our surviving descendants may never again have to commemorate another "day of infamy."

Charles L. Mee, Jr.

THE COLD WAR

During the latter stages of World War II, the American people were subjected to a barrage of propaganda designed to convince them that the Soviet Union was fighting democracy's battle against fascist tyranny (as indeed it was) and that the Russian dictator Joseph Stalin was somehow a benevolent grandfather who puffed amiably at an old pipe while dispensing shrewd bits of folk wisdom to millions of loyal and admiring followers (which was utterly preposterous). Then, almost before the echoes of the last shots of the war had faded, the United States and the Soviet Union were engaged in the first of that long series of crises and confrontations that are known as the Cold War. American historians have written about this conflict at great length, and in recent years many of them have argued that the Cold War was largely the responsibility of the United States. Apparently aggressive Soviet actions, these students insist, were in reality Russian attempts at self-protection. Stalin, if not the kindly character depicted in the early 1940's, was not an aggressor; he was primarily interested in protecting his nation from a possible invasion from the West.

What distinguishes the work of Charles L. Mee, Jr., from that of most other historians who are critical of American Cold War policy is that his interpretation is so nicely balanced. He understands the problems American leaders faced and has no illusions about the character of Soviet leadership. No one will be able to write the definitive history of the Cold War until the Russian archives are opened, but Mee's account is as definitive as possible at this time. Mee is a former editor of *Horizon* and the author of *Meeting at Potsdam*.

On April 12, 1945, Franklin Roosevelt died, and soon afterward Vyacheslav M. Molotov, the Russian foreign minister, stopped by in Washington to pay his respects to Harry Truman, the new President. Truman received Molotov in the Oval Office and, as Truman recalled it, chewed him out "bluntly" for the way the Russians were behaving in Poland. Molotov was stunned. He had never, he told Truman, "been talked to like that in my life."

"Carry out your agreements," Truman responded, "and you won't get talked to like that."

That's a good way to talk, if you want to start an argument . . .

In Europe, Germany surrendered to the Allies on May 8. On May 12, Prime Minister Winston Churchill sent Truman an ominous cable about the Russians: "An iron curtain is drawn down upon their front," Churchill said, and, moreover, "it would be open to the Russians in a very short time to advance if they chose to the waters of the North Sea and the Atlantic." On May 17, Churchill ordered his officers not to destroy any German planes. In fact, Churchill kept 700,000 captured German troops in military readiness, prepared to be turned against the Russians.

That, too, is a good way to behave, if you are looking for trouble . . .

Joseph Stalin said little: he did not advance his troops to the Atlantic, but he planted them firmly throughout eastern Europe and, in violation of previous agreements with the British and Americans, systematically crushed all vestiges of democratic government in Poland, Hungary, Czechoslovakia, Bulgaria, Rumania, Yugoslavia, and Finland. In truth, not quite: the Finns had managed to salvage a few bits and scraps of democratic usage for themselves. At dinner one night in the Kremlin, Andrei Zhdanov, one of Stalin's propagandists, complained that the Russians should have occupied Finland. "Akh, Finland," said Molotov, "that is a peanut."

And that, too, is a nice way to behave, if you are trying to stir up a fight . . .

Most people, most of the time, want peace in the world, and they imagine that most politicians, being human, share the same wishes. At the end of a war, presumably, the desire for peace is most intense and most widely shared. Lamentably, that is not always the case. At the end of World War II the Russians, as Churchill remarked, feared "our friendship more than our enmity."

The Russians had both immediate cause and long-standing historical reasons for anxiety.

"From the beginning of the ninth century," as Louis Halle, a former State Department historian, has written, "and even today, the prime driving force in Russia has been fear. . . . The Russians as we know them today have experienced ten centuries of constant, mortal fear. This has not been a disarming experience. It has not been an experience calculated to produce a simple, open, innocent, and guileless society." Scattered over a vast land with no natural frontiers for protection, as Halle remarks, the Russians have been overrun "generation after generation, by fresh waves of invaders. . . . Lying defenseless on the plain, they were slaughtered and subjugated and humiliated by the invaders time and again.''

Thus the Russians sought to secure their borders along eastern Europe. The czars attempted this, time and again: to secure a buffer zone, on their European frontier, a zone that would run down along a line that would later be called the Iron Curtain.

Yet, at the end of World War II, Stalin's fears were not just fears of outsiders. World War II had shown that his dictatorship was not only brutal but also brutally inept; he was neither a great military leader nor a good administrator; and the Russian soldiers returning from the Western Front had seen much evidence of Western prosperity. Stalin needed the Cold War, not to venture out into the world again after an exhausting war, but to discipline his restless people at home. He had need of that ancient stratagem of monarchs—the threat of an implacable external enemy to be used to unite his own people in Russia.

Churchill, on the other hand, emerged from World War II with a ruined empire irretrievably in debt, an empire losing its colonies and headed inevitably toward bankruptcy. Churchill's scheme for saving Great Britain was suitably inspired and grand: he would, in effect, reinvent the British Empire; he would establish an economic union of Europe (much like what the Common Market actually became); this union would certainly not be led by vanquished Germany or Italy, not by so small a power as the Netherlands, not by devastated France, but by Great Britain. To accomplish this aim, unfortunately, Churchill had almost nothing in the way of genuine economic or military power left; he had only his own force of persuasion and rhetoric. He would try to parlay those gifts into American backing for England's move into Europe. The way to bring about American backing was for Churchill to arrange to have America and Russia quarrel; while America and Russia quarreled, England would—as American diplomats delicately put it—''lead'' Europe.

Truman, for his part, led a nation that was strong and getting stronger. Henry Luce, the publisher of the influential *Time* and *Life* magazines, declared that this was to be the beginning of ''the American Century''—and such a moment is rarely one in which a national leader wants to maintain a status quo. The United States was securing the Western Hemisphere, moving forcefully into England's collapsing ''sterling bloc,'' acquiring military and economic positions over an area of the planet so extensive that the sun could never set on it.

The promise was extraordinary, the threat equally so. The United States did not practice Keynesian economics during the 1930's. It was not Roosevelt's New Deal that ran up the enormous federal deficit or built the huge, wheezing federal bureaucracy of today. War ran up the deficit; war licked the depression; war made the big federal government. In 1939, after a decade of depression, after the Civilian Conservation Corps, the Public Works Administration, the Civil Works Administration, the Agricultural Adjustment Act, the Social Security

Act, and all the rest of the New Deal efforts on behalf of social justice, the federal budget was $9 billion. In 1945 it was $100 billion.

American prosperity was built upon deficit spending for war. President Truman knew it, and maintained deficit spending with the Cold War. Eventually, with the Truman Doctrine and the Marshall Plan, the encouragement of American multinational companies, and a set of defense treaties that came finally to encompass the world, he institutionalized it. The American people might find this easier to damn if they had not enjoyed the uncommon prosperity it brought them.

In October, 1944, Churchill visited Stalin in Moscow. The need then, clearly, was for cooperation among the Allies in order to win the war—and it appeared at the time that the cooperativeness nurtured during the war could be continued afterward. Each had only to recognize the other's vital interests. Churchill commenced to outline those interests to be recognized for the sake of the postwar cooperation.

"I said," Churchill recalled, " 'Let us settle about our affairs in the Balkans. Your armies are in Rumania and Bulgaria. We have interests, missions, and agents there. Don't let us get at cross-purposes in small ways. So far as Britain and Russia are concerned, how would it do for you to have ninety per cent predominance in Rumania, for us to have ninety per cent of the say in Greece, and go fifty-fifty about Yugoslavia?' "

Churchill wrote this out on a piece of paper, noting, too, a split of Bulgaria that gave Russia 75 per cent interest, and a fifty-fifty split of Hungary. He pushed the piece of paper across the table to Stalin, who placed a check mark on it and handed it back. There was a silence. "At length I said, 'Might it not be thought rather cynical if it seemed we had disposed of these issues, so fateful to millions of people, in such an offhand manner? Let us burn the paper.' 'No, you keep it,' said Stalin."

Such casual and roughshod "agreements" could hardly be the last word on the matter; yet, they signified a mutual recognition of one another's essential interests and a willingness to accommodate one another's needs—while, to be sure, the smaller powers were sold out by all sides. At this same time, in October, 1944, and later on in January, 1945, Roosevelt entered into armistice agreements with Britain and Russia that gave Stalin almost complete control of the internal affairs of the ex-Nazi satellites in eastern Europe. As a briefing paper that the State Department prepared in the spring of 1945 for President Truman said, "spheres of influence do in fact exist," and "eastern Europe is, in fact, a Soviet sphere of influence."

In short, the stage was set for postwar peace: spheres of influence had been recognized; a tradition of negotiation had been established. Yet, the European phase of World War II was no sooner ended than symptoms of the Cold War began to appear. The Big Three no longer needed one another to help in the fight against Hitler, and the atomic bomb would soon settle the war against Japan.

Toward the end of May, 1945, Harry Hopkins arrived in Moscow to talk with Stalin, to feel out the Russians now that the war in Europe had ended, and to prepare the agenda for discussion at the Potsdam Conference that would be held in Germany in mid-July. The United States had a problem, Hopkins informed Stalin, a problem so serious that it threatened ''to affect adversely the relations between our two countries.'' The problem was, Hopkins said, Poland: ''our inability to carry into effect the Yalta Agreement on Poland.''

But, what was the problem? Stalin wanted to know. A government had been established there, under the auspices of the occupying Red Army, a government that was, naturally, ''friendly'' to the Soviet Union. There could be no problem—unless others did not wish to allow the Soviet Union to ensure a friendly government in Poland.

''Mr. Hopkins stated,'' according to the notes taken by his interpreter, Charles Bohlen, ''that the United States would desire a Poland friendly to the Soviet Union and in fact desired to see friendly countries all along the Soviet borders.

''Marshal Stalin replied if that be so we can easily come to terms in regard to Poland.''

But, said Hopkins, Stalin must remember the Declaration on Liberated Europe (signed at the Yalta Conference in February, 1945) and its guarantees for democratic governments; there was a serious difference between them; Poland had become the issue over which cooperation between Russia and America would flourish or fail.

Evidently Stalin could not understand this demand; apparently he could not believe that Americans were sincerely so idealistic. Did not America, after all, support a manifestly undemocratic dictatorship in Franco's Spain? ''I am afraid,'' Averell Harriman, the U.S. ambassador to the Soviet Union, cabled home to Truman, ''Stalin does not and never will fully understand our interest in a free Poland as a matter of principle. He is a realist in all of his actions, and it is hard for him to appreciate our faith in abstract principles. It is difficult for him to understand why we should want to interfere with Soviet policy in a country like Poland, which he considers so important to Russia's security, unless we have some ulterior motive.''

And indeed, Russia's sphere of influence was recognized, it seemed, only so that it might serve as a bone of contention. Poland, Czechoslovakia, Bulgaria, Rumania, Hungary, all became bones of contention. It is not clear that any one of the Big Three deeply cared what happened to these eastern European countries so long as the countries served as useful pawns. Hopkins insisted that Stalin must recognize freedom of speech, assembly, movement, and religious worship in Poland and that all political parties (except fascists) must be ''permitted the free use, without distinction, of the press, radio, meetings and other facilities of political expression.'' Furthermore, all citizens must have ''the right of public trial, defense by counsel of their own choosing, and the right of habeas corpus.''

Of course, Stalin said, of course, ''these principles of democracy are well known and would find no objection on the part of the Soviet

The Big Three at Potsdam: Joseph Stalin,
Harry Truman, and Winston Churchill.

Government.'' To be sure, he said, ''in regard to the *specific* [italics added] freedoms mentioned by Mr. Hopkins, they could only be applied in full in peace time, and even then with certain limitations.''

In the latter two weeks of July, 1945, the Big Three gathered at Potsdam, just outside of Berlin, for the last of the wartime conferences. They discussed the issues with which the war in Europe had left them, and with which the war in the Far East would leave them when it came to an end. They discussed spheres of influence, the disposition of Germany, the spoils of war, reparations, and, of course, eastern Europe.

At one of the plenary sessions of the Potsdam Conference, they outlined the spheres of influence precisely, clearly, and in detail during a discussion of the issue of ''German shares, gold, and assets abroad.'' To whom did these items belong? What, for instance, did Stalin mean when he said ''abroad''?

STALIN: ''. . . the Soviet delegation . . . will regard the whole of Western Germany as falling within your sphere, and Eastern Germany, within ours.''

Truman asked whether Stalin meant to establish "a line running from the Baltic to the Adriatic." Stalin replied that he did.

STALIN: "As to the German investments, I should put the question this way: as to the German investments in Eastern Europe, they remain with us, and the rest, with you. . . ."

TRUMAN: "Does this apply only to German investments in Europe or in other countries as well?"

STALIN: "Let me put it more specifically: the German investments in Rumania, Bulgaria, Hungary, and Finland go to us, and all the rest to you."

FOREIGN MINISTER ERNEST BEVIN: "The German investments in other countries go to us?"

STALIN: "In all other countries, in South America, in Canada, etc., all this is yours. . . ."

SECRETARY OF STATE JAMES BYRNES: "If an enterprise is not in Eastern Europe but in Western Europe or in other parts of the world, that enterprise remains ours?"

STALIN: "In the United States, in Norway, in Switzerland, in Sweden, in Argentina [general laughter], etc.—all that is yours."

A delegation of Poles arrived at Potsdam to argue their own case before the Big Three. The Poles, struggling desperately and vainly for their land, their borders, their freedoms, did not seem to understand that their fate was being settled for reasons that had nothing to do with them. They wandered about Potsdam, trying to impress their wishes on the Big Three. "I'm sick of the bloody Poles," Churchill said when they came to call on him. "I don't want to see them. Why can't Anthony [Eden] talk to them?" Alexander Cadogan, Permanent Undersecretary for Foreign Affairs, found the Poles at Eden's house late one night and "had to entertain them as best I could, and went on entertaining them—no signs of A. He didn't turn up till 11:30. . . . So then we got down to it, and talked shop till 1:30. Then filled the Poles (and ourselves) with sandwiches and whiskies and sodas and I went to bed at 2 A.M." Altogether, it had been an agreeable enough evening, although in general, Cadogan confided to his diary, he found the Poles to be "dreadful people. . . ."

Germany, too, provided a rich field for contention. The answer to the German question became a simple but ticklish matter of keeping Germany sufficiently weak so that it could not start another war and yet, at the same time, sufficiently strong to serve as a buffer against Russia, or, from Russia's point of view, against the Western powers. To achieve this delicate balance, the Big Three haggled at Potsdam over a complex set of agreements about zones of authority, permissible levels of postwar industry, allocation of resources of coal and food-stuffs, spoils of war reparations, and other matters. The country as a whole was divided into administrative zones in which Allied commanders had absolute veto powers over some matters, and, in other respects, had to defer to a central governmental council for measures to be applied uniformly to Germany.

Out of all these careful negotiations came the astonishing fact that

Germany was established as the very center and source of much of the anxiety and conflict of the Cold War. How this could have happened is one of the wonders of the history of diplomacy. The discussions and bargaining at Potsdam among Churchill, Truman, and Stalin, and among the foreign ministers, and on lower levels, among economic committees and subcommittees, is maddeningly tangled; but, once all of the nettlesome complexities are cleared away, the postwar arrangement for Germany can be seen with sudden and arresting clarity. The Big Three agreed to have a Germany that would be politically united—but, at the very same time, economically divided. They agreed, then, to create a country that could never be either wholly united nor entirely divided, neither one Germany nor two Germanies, but rather a country that would be perpetually at war with itself, and, since its two halves would have two patrons, would keep its two patrons in continuous conflict. Whether this postwar arrangement for Germany was intentional or inadvertent, it was certainly a diplomatic tour de force. In 1949, with the formation of the West German and East German governments, the contradictions of the Potsdam policy became overt.

Eastern Europe, Germany, and the atomic bomb were the three most striking elements of the early Cold War. It was while he was at the Potsdam Conference that President Truman received news that the test of the bomb at Alamogordo had been successful. By that time the bomb was no longer militarily necessary to end the war against Japan; the Japanese were near the end and were attempting to negotiate peace by way of their ambassador to Moscow. After the bomb was dropped, Truman would maintain that it had avoided the invasion of the Japanese mainland and so saved a million American lives. But was that true?

General Henry (Hap) Arnold, chief of the Army Air Forces, said, before the atomic device was dropped on Japan, that conventional bombing would end the war without an invasion. Admiral Ernest J. King, chief of U.S. naval operations, advised that a naval blockade alone would end the war. General Eisenhower said it was "completely unnecessary" to drop the bomb, and that the weapon was "no longer mandatory as a measure to save American lives." Even General George Marshall, U.S. chief of staff and the strongest advocate at that late hour for the bomb's use, advised that the Japanese at least be forewarned to give them a chance to surrender. Diplomats advised Truman that he need only have Russia sign his proclamation calling for Japanese surrender; the Russians had not yet declared war against Japan, and so the Japanese still had hopes that the Russians would help them negotiate peace; if Russia signed the proclamation, the Japanese would see that their last chance was gone and would surrender. None of this advice was followed.

After the war, the United States Strategic Bombing Command issued a study confirming the advice Truman had been getting before he gave the order to drop the atomic bomb: "Japan would have surrendered even if the atomic bombs had not been dropped, even if Russia had not entered the war, and even if no invasion had been planned or

contemplated.'' Then why was it dropped? Admiral William Leahy, Truman's top aide, was unable to offer the puzzled British chiefs of staff a better explanation than that it was ''because of the vast sums that had been spent on the project,'' although he commented that in using the bomb, the Americans ''had adopted an ethical standard common to the barbarians of the Dark Ages.''

However that may be, its use must have been chilling to Stalin; doubly chilling if Stalin realized that the United States had used the bomb even when it was not militarily necessary. Indeed, according to Secretary of State James Byrnes, that was the real reason why the bomb was used after all—''to make Russia,'' as he said, ''more manageable in Europe.'' Perhaps it is because that constituted a war crime— to kill people when it is not militarily necessary is a war crime according to international accord—that Truman insisted to his death, and in obstinate defiance of all other opinion, that it was militarily necessary.

The bomb may have been dropped, too, in order to end the war against Japan without Russian help. The Russians had promised to enter the war in the Far East exactly three months after the war in Europe ended—which it did on May 8, Truman's aim was not merely to end the war against Japan, but to end it before August 8.

When word reached Potsdam that the atomic bomb had been successfully tested, Truman was enormously pleased. When the news was passed along to Churchill, the prime minister was overcome with delight at the ''vision—fair and bright indeed it seemed—of the end of the whole war in one or two violent shocks.'' Churchill understood at once that ''we should not need the Russians,'' and he concluded that ''we seemed suddenly to have become possessed of a merciful abridgment of the slaughter in the East and of a far happier prospect in Europe. I have no doubt that these thoughts were present in the minds of my American friends.''

The problem was what to tell the Russians. Presumably, as allies of the Americans and British, they needed to be told of this new weapon in which Truman and Churchill placed such tremendous hopes. Yet, if the Russians were told, they might rush to enter the war against Japan and so share in the victory. ''The President and I no longer felt that we needed [Stalin's] aid to conquer Japan,'' Churchill wrote. And so Stalin must be told about the existence of the bomb—and at the same time he must not be told. In short, Truman and Churchill decided, Stalin must be informed so casually as not to understand that he was being informed of much of anything.

On July 24, after one of the sessions of the Potsdam Conference, Truman got up from the baize-covered table and sauntered around to Stalin. The President had left his interpreter, Charles Bohlen, behind and relied on Stalin's personal translator—signifying that he had nothing important to say, just idle, end-of-the-day chit-chat.

The August 6, 1945 bombing of Hiroshima—the first of two atomic bombings of Japan.

"I was perhaps five yards away," Churchill recalled, "and I watched with the closest attention the momentous talk. I knew what the President was going to do. What was vital to measure was its effect on Stalin. I can see it all as if it were yesterday."

"I casually mentioned to Stalin," Truman wrote in his memoirs, "that we had a new weapon of unusual destructive force. The Russian Premier showed no special interest. All he said was that he was glad to hear it and hoped we would make 'good use of it against the Japanese.'"

"I was sure," Churchill said, "that [Stalin] had no idea of the significance of what he was being told . . . his face remained gay and genial and the talk between these two potentates soon came to an end. As we were waiting for our cars I found myself near Truman. 'How did it go?' I asked. 'He never asked a question,' he replied."

According to the Russian General Shtemenko, the ploy worked: the Russian Army staff "received no special instructions" after this meeting. According to Marshal Georgi K. Zhukov, commander of the Russian zone of occupation in Germany, Stalin returned from the meeting and told Molotov about Truman's remarks. Molotov "reacted immediately: 'Let them. We'll have to talk it over with Kurchatov and get him to speed things up.' I realized they were talking about research on the atomic bomb."

Whatever the case, whether Stalin realized what he had been told at the time, or only in retrospect, the nuclear arms race began, in effect, at Potsdam, on July 24, 1945, at 7:30 P.M.

Distrust, suspicion, anxiety, fear—all were intensified at Potsdam, and to them were added harshness and provocation, from all sides. During the next few months the agreements that had been reached were violated, or used as the bases for accusations of duplicity and bad faith. Many of the questions raised at Potsdam had been postponed and delegated to a Council of Foreign Ministers that was established to deal with these questions, and new ones, as they arose. The first meeting of the council was set for September, 1945. James Byrnes, before he left Washington to attend the meeting, had chatted with Secretary of War Henry Stimson. "I found that Byrnes was very much against any attempt to cooperate with Russia," Stimson noted in his diary. "His mind is full of his problems with the coming meeting of foreign ministers and he looks to have the presence of the bomb in his pocket, so to speak, as a great weapon to get through the thing. . . ." The British Chancellor of the Exchequer, Rt. Hon. Hugh Dalton, asked Foreign Minister Ernest Bevin how things were going, once the meeting started. "Like the strike leader said," Bevin replied, "thank God there is no danger of a settlement."

Not everyone was so quick or so eager to encourage the start of the Cold War. Henry Stimson was very much the elder statesman in 1945; he had spent more than fifty years in assorted government positions, and he foresaw dread consequences in Truman's developing policies toward Russia. Stimson had long thought that America should be tough with the Soviet Union, but he now believed that toughness was turning into harshness and harshness into provocativeness. In a memo that he wrote Truman in the autumn of 1945, he focused his thoughts around one of the most vexing problems of the postwar world:

". . . I consider the problem of our satisfactory relations with Russia as not merely connected with but as virtually dominated by the problem of the atomic bomb. Except for the problem of the control of that bomb, those relations, while vitally important, might not be immediately pressing. . . . But with the discovery of the bomb, they became immediately emergent. These relations may be perhaps irretrievably embittered by the way in which we approach the solution of the bomb with Russia. For if we fail to approach them now and merely continue to negotiate with them having this weapon rather ostentatiously on our hip, their suspicions and their distrust of our purposes and notives will increase. . . .

"The chief lesson I have learned in a long life is that the only way you can make a man trustworthy is to trust him; and the surest way to make him untrustworthy is to distrust him and show your distrust."

Men like Stimson—and Henry Wallace, then Secretary of Commerce—were allowed, or forced, to resign. Others, those who tended to believe in an aggressive attitude toward Russia, were spotted, and promoted—young men such as John Foster Dulles and Dean Rusk. George Kennan, then in the American embassy in Moscow, was discovered after he sent a perfervid 8,000-word cable back to Washington:

Secretary of War Henry Stimson with Chief of Staff George C. Marshall in early 1945. Marshall later became Secretary of State and developer of the Marshall Plan—a key feature of the Cold War.

"We have here a political force committed fanatically to the belief that with U.S. there can be no permanent modus vivendi, that it is desirable and necessary that the internal harmony of our society be disrupted, our traditional way of life be destroyed, the international authority of our state be broken. . . ." In his memoirs, Kennan says that he now looks back on his cable "with horrified amusement." At the time, however, he was ideal for Truman's use, and he was recalled from Moscow and made chairman of the State Department's Policy Planning Committee, or as the *New York Times* called him, "America's global planner."

At Potsdam, the Big Three had all agreed to remove their troops from Iran. They set a deadline of March 2, 1946, and, as the deadline approached, the British announced that they would be leaving. The Russians, however, let it be known that they were somewhat reluctant to leave until they had made an agreement with the Iranians for an oil concession, and, regardless even of that agreement, Stalin rather thought he would like to withdraw only from central Iran and keep some troops in northern Iran. Not all these matters were immediately clarified and so, on March 1, 1946, Stalin announced that Russian soldiers would remain in Iran "pending clarification of the situation."

President Truman, meanwhile, invited Winston Churchill to deliver an address in March, 1946, at Fulton, Missouri: "A shadow has fallen upon the scenes so lately lighted by the Allied victory," said the former prime minister. "Nobody knows what Soviet Russia and its Communist international organization intends to do in the immediate future, or what are the limits, if any, to their expansive and proselytising tendencies. . . . From Stettin in the Baltic to Trieste in the Adriatic [the line, as Churchill neglected to mention, to which he and Truman had agreed at Potsdam], an iron curtain has descended across the Continent. Behind that line lie all the capitals of the ancient states of Central and Eastern Europe . . . in what I must call the Soviet sphere . . . . this is certainly not the Liberated Europe we fought to build up. Nor is it one which contains the essentials of permanent peace."

In Moscow, a well-rehearsed Russian reporter quizzed Stalin.

QUESTION: "How do you appraise Mr. Churchill's latest speech in the United States?"

STALIN: "I appraise it as a dangerous act, calculated to sow the seeds of dissension among the Allied states and impede their collaboration."

QUESTION: "Can it be considered that Mr. Churchill's speech is prejudicial to the cause of peace and security?"

STALIN: "Yes, unquestionably. As a matter of fact, Mr. Churchill now takes the stand of the warmongers, and in this Mr. Churchill is not alone. He has friends not only in Britain but in the United States of America as well."

During the winter of 1946–47, a succession of snowstorms hit Britain. Coal was already in short supply; factories had already closed for lack of fuel that winter. With the blizzards came rationing, first of electricity and then of food; finally heat was cut off. Britain, as Louis Halle wrote, "was like a soldier wounded in war who, now that fighting was over, was bleeding to death." The empire was at last dying.

In Washington, on February 21, 1947, a Friday afternoon, First Secretary H. M. Sichel of the British embassy delivered two notes to Loy Henderson at the State Department. Until that moment, Britain had been the principal support for the economy of Greece and the provider for the Turkish Army. The first of Sichel's notes said that Britain could no longer support Greece; the second said Britain could no longer underwrite the Turkish Army. "What the two notes reported," Halle observed, "was the final end of the *Pax Britannica.*"

The following week, on February 27, Truman met with congressional leaders in the White House. Undersecretary of State Dean Acheson was present at the meeting, and Truman had him tell the congressmen what was at stake. Acheson spoke for ten minutes, informing the legislators that nothing less than the survival of the whole of Western civilization was in the balance at that moment; he worked in references to ancient Athens, Rome, and the course of Western civilization and freedoms since those times. The congressmen were silent for a few moments, and then, at last, Senator Arthur Vandenberg of Michigan, a prominent Republican who had come to support an active foreign policy, spoke up. All this might be true, Vandenberg said; but, if the President wished to sell his program to the American people, he would have to "scare hell out of the country." It was at that moment that the Cold War began in earnest for the United States.

It would be nice to be able to say that one nation held back from the nattering and abusiveness, that one seemed reluctant to start a conflict with its former allies, that one tried to compose the differences that had predictably arisen at the end of the war, that this one was the first to make a provocative move or charge and that one was last—but in truth all three leaped into the fray with such haste and determination that the origins of the Cold War are lost in a blur of all three sides hastening to be first in battle.

It is difficult to know the effects the Cold War had upon the Russian people in these years. But America paid heavy costs. When a nation has an actively internationalist, interventionist foreign policy, political power in that country tends to flow to the central government, and, within the central government, to the executive branch. That there was, in recent times, the creation of an "imperial presidency" in the U.S. was no quirk or happenstance; it was the natural outgrowth of the Cold War. From the imperial presidency, from the disorientation of the constitutional system of checks and balances, Watergate, proteiform and proliferating spy organizations, the impotence and decadence of Congress—all these were almost inevitable. That is why George Washington, a profoundly sophisticated man, advised Americans to avoid foreign entanglements; and that is why Americans who prize their freedom have always been a peace-loving people.

In 1932 thousands of World War I veterans marched on Washington to demand payment of a cash bonus; this California group camped on the Capitol grounds.

Part Five
Great Depression and the New Deal

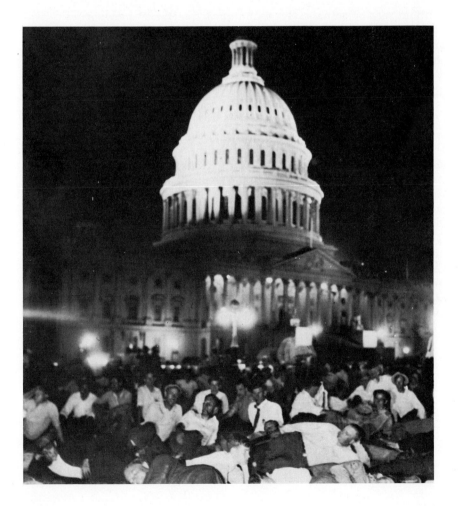

John Kenneth Galbraith

THE CAUSES OF THE GREAT CRASH

The following essay is an example of analytical history at its best. Without relying on narrative techniques, the Harvard economist John Kenneth Galbraith takes apart the economy of the 1920's and shows us how its weaknesses led to the Great Depression of the 1930's. In the course of doing so, he also "takes apart," in the colloquial sense of that expression, the Presidents of the 1920's and a number of their leading advisers.

The effectiveness and power of the essay depend upon a number of factors. One is Galbraith's mastery both of the facts he deals with and of the economic mechanisms of the society; he discusses few events that are not thoroughly familiar to students of the subject, but he has an unfailing eye for what is significant. Another is his gift for anecdote and the pithy phrase. As he says, the epigram that Elbert H. Gary of U. S. Steel "never saw a blast furnace until his death" is well known; but not everyone who writes about Gary knows enough to use it. Still a third is Galbraith's ability to state his own opinions without qualification and at the same time without passion, to make the kind of calm, reasoned judgments that are characteristic of a convinced but unprejudiced and intelligent mind. All these qualities explain why his books, such as *American Capitalism, The Affluent Society,* and *The Great Crash, 1929* (a fuller treatment of the subject of this essay), have been both popular and critical successes.

The decade of the twenties, or more exactly the eight years between the postwar depression of 1920–21 and the sudden collapse of the stock market in October, 1929, were prosperous ones in the United States. The total output of the economy increased by more than 50 per cent. The preceding decades had brought the automobile; now came many more and also roads on which they could be driven with reasonable reliability and comfort. There was much building. The downtown section of the mid-continent city—Des Moines, Omaha, Minneapolis—dates from these years. It was then, more likely than not, that what is still the leading hotel, the tallest office building, and the biggest department store went up. Radio arrived, as of course did gin and jazz.

These years were also remarkable in another respect, for as time passed it became increasingly evident that the prosperity could not last. Contained within it were the seeds of its own destruction. The country was heading into the gravest kind of trouble. Herein lies the peculiar fascination of the period for a study in the problem of leadership. For almost no steps were taken during these years to arrest the tendencies which were obviously leading, and did lead, to disaster.

At least four things were seriously wrong, and they worsened as the decade passed. And knowledge of them does not depend on the always brilliant assistance of hindsight. At least three of these flaws were highly visible and widely discussed. In ascending order, not of importance but of visibility, they were as follows:

First, income in these prosperous years was being distributed with marked inequality. Although output per worker rose steadily during the period, wages were fairly stable, as also were prices. As a result, business profits increased rapidly and so did incomes of the wealthy and the well-to-do. This tendency was nurtured by assiduous and successful efforts of Secretary of the Treasury Andrew W. Mellon to reduce income taxes with special attention to the higher brackets. In 1929 the 5 per cent of the people with the highest incomes received perhaps a quarter of all personal income. Between 1919 and 1929 the share of the one per cent who received the highest incomes increased by approximately one seventh. This meant that the economy was heavily and increasingly dependent on the luxury consumption of the well-to-do and on their willingness to reinvest what they did not or could not spend on themselves. Anything that shocked the confidence of the rich either in their personal or in their business future would have a bad effect on total spending and hence on the behavior of the economy.

This was the least visible flaw. To be sure, farmers, who were not participating in the general advance, were making themselves heard; and twice during the period the Congress passed far-reaching relief legislation which was vetoed by Coolidge. But other groups were much less vocal. Income distribution in the United States had long been unequal. The inequality of these years did not seem exceptional. The trade-union movement was also far from strong. In the early twenties the steel industry was still working a twelve-hour day and, in some jobs, a seven-day week. (Every two weeks when the shift changed a man worked twice around the clock.) Workers lacked the organization or the power to deal with conditions like this; the twelve-hour day was, in fact, ended as the result of personal pressure by President Harding on the steel companies, particularly on Judge Elbert H. Gary, head of the United States Steel Corporation. Judge Gary's personal acquaintance with these working conditions was thought to be slight, and this gave rise to Benjamin Stolberg's now classic observation that the Judge "never saw a blast furnace until his death." In all these circumstances the increasingly lopsided income distribution did not excite much comment or alarm. Perhaps it would have been surprising if it had.

But the other three flaws in the economy were far less subtle. During World War I the United States ceased to be the world's greatest debtor country and became its greatest creditor. The consequences of this change have so often been described that they have the standing of a cliché. A debtor country could export a greater value of goods than it imported and use the difference for interest and debt repayment. This was what we did before the war. But a creditor must import a greater value than it exports if those who owe it money are to have the wherewithal to pay interest and principal. Otherwise the creditor must either forgive the debts or make new loans to pay off the old.

During the twenties the balance was maintained by making new foreign loans. Their promotion was profitable to domestic investment houses. And when the supply of honest and competent foreign borrowers ran out, dishonest, incompetent, or fanciful borrowers were invited to borrow and, on occasion, bribed to do so. In 1927 Juan Leguia, the son of the then dictator of Peru, was paid $450,000 by the National City Company and J. & W. Seligman for his services in promoting a $50,000,000 loan to Peru which these houses marketed. Americans lost and the Peruvians didn't gain appreciably. Other Latin American republics got equally dubious loans by equally dubious devices. And, for reasons that now tax the imagination, so did a large number of German cities and municipalities. Obviously, once investors awoke to the character of these loans or there was any other shock to confidence, they would no longer be made. There would be nothing with which to pay the old loans. Given this arithmetic, there would be either a sharp reduction in exports or a wholesale default on the outstanding loans, or more likely both. Wheat and cotton farmers and others who depended on exports would suffer. So would those who owned the bonds. The buying power of both would be reduced. These consequences were freely predicted at the time.

The second weakness of the economy was the large-scale corporate thimblerigging that was going on. This took a variety of forms, of which by far the most common was the organization of corporations to hold stock in yet other corporations, which in turn held stock in yet other corporations. In the case of the railroads and the utilities, the purpose of this pyramid of holding companies was to obtain control of a very large number of operating companies with a very small investment in the ultimate holding company. A $100,000,000 electric utility, of which the capitalization was represented half by bonds and half by common stock, could be controlled with an investment of a little over $25,000,000—the value of just over half the common stock. Were a company then formed with the same capital structure to hold *this* $25,000,000 worth of common stock, it could be controlled with an investment of $6,250,000. On the next round the amount required would be less than $2,000,000. That $2,000,000 would still control the entire $100,000,000 edifice. By the end of the twenties, holding-company structures six or eight tiers high were a commonplace. Some of them—the utility pyramids of Insull and Associated Gas & Electric, and the railroad pyramid of the Van Sweringens—were marvelously complex. It is unlikely that anyone fully understood them or could.

In other cases companies were organized to hold securities in other companies in order to manufacture more securities to sell to the public. This was true of the great investment trusts. During 1929 one investment house, Goldman, Sachs & Company, organized and sold nearly a billion dollars' worth of securities in three interconnected investment trusts—Goldman Sachs Trading Corporation; Shenandoah Corporation; and Blue Ridge Corporation. All eventually depreciated virtually to nothing.

This corporate insanity was also highly visible. So was the damage. The pyramids would last only so long as earnings of the company at the bottom were secure. If anything happened to the dividends of the underlying company, there would be trouble, for upstream companies had issued bonds (or in practice sometimes preferred stock) against the dividends on the stock of the downstream companies. Once the earnings stopped, the bonds would go into default or the preferred stock would take over and the pyramid would collapse. Such a collapse would have a bad effect not only on the orderly prosecution of business and investment by the operating companies but also on confidence, investment, and spending by the community at large. The likelihood was increased because in any number of cities—Cleveland, Detroit, and Chicago were notable examples—the banks were deeply committed to these pyramids or had fallen under the control of the pyramiders.

Finally, and most evident of all, there was the stock market boom. Month after month and year after year the great bull market of the twenties roared on. Sometimes there were setbacks, but more often there were fantastic forward surges. In May of 1924 the New York *Times* industrials stood at 106; by the end of the year they were 134; by the end of 1925 they were up to 181. In 1927 the advance began in earnest—to 245 by the end of that year and on to 331 by the end of 1928. There were some setbacks in early 1929, but then came the fantastic summer explosion when in a matter of three months the averages went up another 110 points. This was the most frantic summer in our financial history. By its end, stock prices had nearly quadrupled as compared with four years earlier. Transactions on the New York Stock Exchange regularly ran to 5,000,000 or more shares a day. Radio Corporation of America went to 573¾ (adjusted) without ever having paid a dividend. Only the hopelessly eccentric, so it seemed, held securities for their income. What counted was the increase in capital values.

And since capital gains were what counted, one could vastly increase his opportunities by extending his holdings with borrowed funds—by buying on margin. Margin accounts expanded enormously, and from all over the country—indeed from all over the world— money poured into New York to finance these transactions. During the summer, brokers' loans increased at the rate of $400,000,000 a month. By September they totaled more than $7,000,000,000. The rate of interest on these loans varied from 7 to 12 per cent and went as high as 15.

This boom was also inherently self-liquidating. It could last only so long as new people, or at least new money, were swarming into the market in pursuit of the capital gains. This new demand bid up the stocks and made the capital gains. Once the supply of new customers began to falter, the market would cease to rise. Once the market stopped rising, some, and perhaps a good many, would start to cash in. If you are concerned with capital gains, you must get them while the getting is good. But the getting may start the market down, and this will one day be the signal for much more selling—both by those who are trying to get out and those who are being forced to sell securities that are no longer safely margined. Thus it was certain that the market would one day go down, and far more rapidly than it went up. Down it went with a thunderous crash in October of 1929. In a series of terrible days, of which Thursday, October 24, and Tuesday, October 29, were the most terrifying, billions in values were lost, and thousands of speculators—they had been called investors—were utterly and totally ruined.

This too had far-reaching effects. Economists have always deprecated the tendency to attribute too much to the great stock market collapse of 1929: this was the drama; the causes of the subsequent depression really lay deeper. In fact, the stock market crash was very important. It exposed the other weakness of the economy. The overseas loans on which the payments balance depended came to an end. The jerry-built holding-company structures came tumbling down. The investment-trust stocks collapsed. The crash put a marked crimp on borrowing for investment and therewith on business spending. It also removed from the economy some billions of consumer spending that was either based on, sanctioned by, or encouraged by the fact that the spenders had stock market gains. The crash was an intensely damaging thing.

And this damage, too, was not only foreseeable but foreseen. For months the speculative frenzy had all but dominated American life. Many times before in history—the South Sea Bubble, John

Cartoonist Forbell titled this 1929 drawing
"Club Life in America—The Stock Brokers."

Law's speculations, the recurrent real-estate booms of the last century, the great Florida land boom earlier in the same decade—there had been similar frenzy. And the end had always come, not with a whimper but a bang. Many men, including in 1929 the President of the United States, knew it would again be so.

The increasingly perilous trade balance, the corporate buccaneering, and the Wall Street boom—along with the less visible tendencies in income distribution—were all allowed to proceed to the ultimate disaster without effective hindrance. How much blame attaches to the men who occupied the presidency?

Warren G. Harding died on August 2, 1923. This, as only death can do, exonerates him. The disorders that led eventually to such trouble had only started when the fatal blood clot destroyed this now sad and deeply disillusioned man. Some would argue that his legacy was bad. Harding had but a vague perception of the economic processes over which he presided. He died owing his broker $180,000 in a blind account—he had been speculating disastrously while he was President, and no one so inclined would have been a good bet to curb the coming boom. Two of Harding's Cabinet officers, his secretary of the interior and his attorney general, were to plead the Fifth Amendment when faced with questions concerning their official acts, and the first of these went to jail. Harding brought his fellow townsman Daniel R. Crissinger to be his comptroller of the currency, although he was qualified for this task, as Samuel Hopkins Adams has suggested, only by the fact that he and the young Harding had stolen watermelons together. When Crissinger had had an ample opportunity to demonstrate his incompetence in his first post, he was made head of the Federal Reserve System. Here he had the central responsibility for action on the ensuing boom. Jack Dempsey, Paul Whiteman, or F. Scott Fitzgerald would have been at least equally qualified.

Yet it remains that Harding was dead before the real trouble started. And while he left in office some very poor men, he also left some very competent ones. Charles Evans Hughes, his secretary of state; Herbert Hoover, his secretary of commerce; and Henry C. Wallace, his secretary of agriculture, were public servants of vigor and judgment.

The problem of Herbert Hoover's responsibility is more complicated. He became President on March 4, 1929. At first glance this seems far too late for effective action. By then the damage had been done, and while the crash might come a little sooner or a little later, it was now inevitable. Yet Hoover's involvement was deeper than this—and certainly much deeper than Harding's. This he tacitly concedes in his memoirs, for he is at great pains to explain and, in some degree, to excuse himself.

For one thing, Hoover was no newcomer to Washington. He had been secretary of commerce under Harding and Coolidge. He had also been the strongest figure (not entirely excluding the President) in both Administration and party for almost eight years. He had a clear view of what was going on. As early as 1922, in a letter to Hughes, he expressed grave concern over the quality of the foreign loans that were being floated in New York. He returned several times to the subject. He knew about the corporate excesses. In the latter twenties he wrote to his colleagues and fellow officials (including Crissinger) expressing his grave concern over the Wall Street orgy. Yet he was content to express himself—to write letters and memoranda, or at most, as in the case of the foreign loans, to make an occasional speech. He could with propriety have presented his views of the stock market more strongly to the Congress and the public. He could also have maintained a more vigorous and persistent agitation within the Administration. He did neither. His views of the market were so little known that it celebrated his election and inauguration with a great upsurge. Hoover was in the boat and, as he himself tells, he knew where it was headed. But, having warned the man at the tiller, he rode along into the reef.

And even though trouble was inevitable, by March, 1929, a truly committed leader would still have wanted to do something. Nothing else was so important. The resources of the Executive, one might expect, would have been mobilized in a search for some formula to mitigate the current frenzy and to temper the coming crash. The assistance of the bankers, congressional leaders, and the Exchange authorities would have been sought. Nothing of the sort was done. As secretary of commerce, as he subsequently explained, he had thought himself frustrated by Mellon. But he continued Mellon in office. Henry M. Robinson, a sympathetic Los Angeles banker, was commissioned to go to New York to see his colleagues there and report. He returned to say that the New York bankers regarded things as sound. Richard Whitney, the vice-president of the Stock Exchange, was summoned to the White House for a conference on how to curb speculation. Nothing came of this either. Whitney also thought things were sound.

Both Mr. Hoover and his official biographers carefully explained that the primary responsibility for the goings on in New York City rested not with Washington but with the governor of New York State. That was Franklin D. Roosevelt. It was he who failed to rise to his responsibilities. The explanation is far too formal. The future of the whole country was involved. Mr. Hoover was the President of the whole country. If he lacked authority commensurate with this responsibility, he could have requested it. This, at a later date, President Roosevelt did not hesitate to do.

Finally, while by March of 1929 the stock market collapse was inevitable, something could still be done about the other accumulating disorders. The balance of payments is an obvious case. In 1931 Mr. Hoover did request a one-year moratorium on the inter-Allied (war) debts. This was a courageous and constructive step which came directly to grips with the problem. But the year before, Mr. Hoover, though not without reluctance, had signed the Hawley-Smoot tariff. "I shall approve the Tariff Bill. . . . It was undertaken as the result of pledges given by the Republican Party at Kansas City. . . . Platform promises must not be empty gestures." Hundreds of people— from Albert H. Wiggin, the head of the Chase National Bank, to Oswald Garrison Villard, the editor of the *Nation*—felt that no step could have been more directly designed to make things worse. Countries would have even more trouble earning the dollars of which they were so desperately short. But Mr. Hoover signed the bill.

Anyone familiar with this particular race of men knows that a dour, flinty, inscrutable visage such as that of Calvin Coolidge can be the mask for a calm and acutely perceptive intellect. And he knows equally that it can conceal a mind of singular aridity. The difficulty, given the inscrutability, is in knowing which. However, in the case of Coolidge the evidence is in favor of the second. In some sense, he certainly knew what was going on. He would not have been unaware of what was called the Coolidge market. But he connected developments neither with the well-being of the country nor with his own responsibilities. In his memoirs Hoover goes to great lengths to show how closely he was in touch with events and how clearly he foresaw their consequences. In his *Autobiography*, a notably barren document, Coolidge did not refer to the accumulating troubles. He confines himself to such unequivocal truths as ''Every day of Presidential life is crowded with activities'' (which in his case, indeed, was not true); and ''The Congress makes the laws, but it is the President who causes them to be executed.''

At various times during his years in office, men called on Coolidge to warn him of the impending trouble. And in 1927, at the instigation of a former White House aide, he sent for William Z. Ripley of Harvard, the most articulate critic of the corporate machinations of the period. The President became so interested that he invited him to stay for lunch, and listened carefully while his guest outlined (as Ripley later related) the ''prestidigitation, double-shuffling, honey-fugling, hornswoggling, and skulduggery'' that characterized the current Wall Street scene. But Ripley made the mistake of telling Coolidge that regulation was the responsibility of the states (as was then the case). At this intelligence Coolidge's face lit up and he dismissed the entire matter from his mind. Others who warned of the impending disaster got even less far.

And on some occasions Coolidge added fuel to the fire. If the market seemed to be faltering, a timely statement from the White House—or possibly from Secretary Mellon—would often brace it up. William Allen White, by no means an unfriendly observer, noted that after one such comment the market staged a 26-point rise. He went on to say that a careful search ''during these halcyon years . . . discloses this fact: Whenever the stock market showed signs of weakness, the President or the Secretary of the Treasury or some important dignitary of the administration . . . issued a statement. The statement invariably declared that business was 'fundamentally sound,' that continued prosperity had arrived, and that the slump of the moment was 'seasonal.' ''

Such was the Coolidge role. Coolidge was fond of observing that ''if you see ten troubles coming down the road, you can be sure that nine will run into the ditch before they reach you and you have to battle with only one of them.'' A critic noted that ''the trouble with this philosophy was that when the tenth trouble reached him he was wholly unprepared. . . . The outstanding instance was the rising boom and orgy of mad speculation which began in 1927.'' The critic was Herbert Hoover.

Plainly; in these years, leadership failed. Events whose tragic

March 4, 1929: President Coolidge (left) and President-Elect Hoover drive from the White House to Hoover's inauguration at the Capitol.

culmination could be foreseen—and was foreseen—were allowed to work themselves out to the final disaster. The country and the world paid. For a time, indeed, the very reputation of capitalism itself was in the balance. It survived in the years following perhaps less because of its own power or the esteem in which it was held, than because of the absence of an organized and plausible alternative. Yet one important question remains. Would it have been possible even for a strong President to arrest the plunge? Were not the opposing forces too strong? Isn't one asking the impossible?

No one can say for sure. But the answer depends at least partly on the political context in which the Presidency was cast. That of Coolidge and Hoover may well have made decisive leadership impossible. These were conservative Administrations in which, in addition, the influence of the businessman was strong. At the core of the business faith was an intuitive belief in *laissez faire*—the benign tendency of things that are left alone. The man who wanted to intervene was a meddler. Perhaps, indeed, he was a planner. In any case, he was to be regarded with mistrust. And, on the businessman's side, it must be borne in mind that high government office often nurtures a spurious sense of urgency. There is no more important public function than the suppression of proposals for unneeded action. But these should have been distinguished from action necessary to economic survival.

A bitterly criticized figure of the Harding-Coolidge Hoover era was Secretary of the Treasury Andrew W. Mellon. He opposed all action to curb the boom, although once in 1929 he was persuaded to say that bonds (as distinct from stocks) were a good buy. And when the depression came, he was against doing anything about that. Even Mr. Hoover was shocked by his insistence that the only remedy was (as Mr. Hoover characterized it) to ''liquidate labor, liquidate stocks, liquidate the farmers, liquidate real estate.'' Yet Mellon reflected only in extreme form the conviction that things would work out, that the real enemies were those who interfered.

Outside of Washington in the twenties, the business and banking community, or at least the articulate part of it, was overwhelmingly opposed to any public intervention. The tentative and ineffective steps which the Federal Reserve did take were strongly criticized. In the spring of 1929 when the Reserve system seemed to be on the verge of taking more decisive action, there was an anticipatory tightening of money rates and a sharp drop in the market. On his own initiative Charles E. Mitchell, the head of the National City Bank, poured in new funds. He had an obligation, he said, that was ''paramount to any Federal Reserve warning, or anything else'' to avert a crisis in the money market. In brief, he was determined, whatever the government thought, to keep the boom going. In that same spring Paul M. Warburg, a distinguished and respected Wall Street leader, warned of the dangers of the boom and called for action to restrain it. He was deluged with criticism and even abuse and later said that the subsequent days were the most difficult of his life. There were some businessmen and bankers—like Mitchell and Albert Wiggin of the Chase National Bank—who may have vaguely sensed that the end of the boom would mean their own business demise. Many more had persuaded themselves that the dream would last. But we should not complicate things. Many others were making money and took a short-run view—or no view—either of their own survival or of the system of which they were a part. They merely wanted to be left alone to get a few more dollars.

And the opposition to government intervention would have been nonpartisan. In 1929 one of the very largest of the Wall Street operators was John J. Raskob. Raskob was also chairman of the Democratic National Committee. So far from calling for preventive measures, Raskob in 1929 was explaining how, through stock market speculation, literally anyone could be a millionaire. Nor would the press have been enthusiastic about, say, legislation to control holding companies and investment trusts or to give authority to regulate margin trading. The financial pages of many of the papers were riding the boom. And even from the speculating public, which was dreaming dreams of riches and had yet to learn that it had been fleeced, there would have been no thanks. Perhaps a President of phenomenal power and determination might have overcome the Coolidge-Hoover environment. But it is easier to argue that this context made inaction inevitable for almost any President. There were too many people who, given a choice between disaster and the measures that would have prevented it, opted for disaster without either a second or even a first thought.

On the other hand, in a different context a strong President might have taken effective preventive action. Congress in these years was becoming increasingly critical of the Wall Street speculation and corporate piggery-pokery. The liberal Republicans—the men whom Senator George H. Moses called the Sons of the Wild Jackass— were especially vehement. But conservatives like Carter Glass were also critical. These men correctly sensed that things were going wrong. A President such as Wilson or either of the Roosevelts (the case of Theodore is perhaps less certain than that of Franklin) who was surrounded in his Cabinet by such men would have been sensitive to this criticism. As a leader he could both have reinforced and drawn strength from the contemporary criticism. Thus he might have been able to arrest the destructive madness as it became recognizable. The American government works far better—perhaps it only works— when the Executive, the business power, and the press are in some degree at odds. Only then can we be sure that abuse or neglect, either private or public, will be given the notoriety that is needed.

Perhaps it is too much to hope that by effective and timely criticism and action the Great Depression might have been avoided. A lot was required in those days to make the United States in any degree depression-proof. But perhaps by preventive action the ensuing depression might have been made less severe. And certainly in the ensuing years the travail of bankers and businessmen before congressional committees, in the courts, and before the bar of public opinion would have been less severe. Here is the paradox. In the full perspective of history, American businessmen never had enemies as damaging as the men who grouped themselves around Calvin Coolidge and supported and applauded him in what William Allen White called "that masterly inactivity for which he was so splendidly equipped."

Poverty makes strange bedfellows: in Everett
Shinn's depression drawing of a breadline,
former businessmen and bums queue up.

David J. Rothman

THE POOR IN THE GREAT DEPRESSION

In this essay, David J. Rothman of Columbia University carries
the story of how Americans have dealt with the problem of poverty
in the twentieth century down to the 1930's. The tale, inspiring
in the sense that it reveals how American reformers have struggled
to help the poor, is also discouraging in that despite all efforts the
problem of poverty was not eliminated. Even more disturbing is
the fact that with all our fantastic expansion and new technology,
poverty continues to exist among us today.

The years of the progressive era marked a major shift in public attitudes and policies toward the poor. Beginning in the 1890's and culminating in the administrations of Theodore Roosevelt and Woodrow Wilson, a new and more complex understanding of the origins of dependency spread through the nation, together with a host of fresh alternatives to institutionalization. The innovations were the work of clergymen like Washington Gladden and Walter Rauschenbusch, who preached a new social gospel; of social workers like Robert Hunter, Jane Addams, and Robert Woods, who practiced community work in their settlement houses; of sociologists like Margaret Byington and Crystal Eastman, who provided the first sophisticated and detailed studies of the causes and conditions of poverty; and of popularizers like Jacob Riis, who wrote newspaper articles and books to arouse the American conscience. Taken together, these groups influenced the thinking and responses of ordinary citizens and political leaders.

The new view toward poverty rested first on an understanding of the shortcomings of the economy—the periodic unemployment that forced many laborers below the subsistence line, the prevalent low wages that did not allow even the thrifty among them to accumulate savings. ("Many, many thousand families," wrote Robert Hunter in *Poverty* [1904], "receive wages so inadequate that no care in spending, however wise it may be, will make them suffice for the family needs.") It also was sensitive to the debilitating effects of slums, the crowded and unsanitary tenements through which disease rapidly spread, particularly tuberculosis, robbing households of their main providers. ("Penury and poverty," declared Jacob Riis in *How the Other Half Lives* [1890], "are wedded everywhere to dirt and disease.") It emphasized the dangers inherent in work itself—the inevitable accidents that occurred when managers neglected to install safety devices; when employees were crowded into sweatshops that were firetraps; when laborers, after ten or twelve hours on the job, grew fatigued and careless. (We must do something, pleaded Crystal Eastman in *Work Accidents and the Law* [1910], to insure that modern industry is conducted "without the present wholesale destruction of the workers.") Critics recognized, too, the general misery of life for those at the bottom of society, a misery that drove them to the tavern to gain a temporary respite from their troubles. And they understood how generation after generation would remain trapped in poverty: families, hard pressed to make ends meet, would put young children out to work, depriving them of the education necessary to take skilled jobs. In brief, these reformers taught Americans to think of the needy as the laboring poor who, as Robert Hunter put it, "live miserably . . . [and] know not why. They work sore, and yet gain nothing."

To some degree these conclusions almost forced themselves upon social observers. Forays into the urban slums, whether to bring the gospel to the unchurched or to ameliorate their need, taught ministers and charity workers that the poor were victims not of immorality but of forces beyond their control. The deeper sociologists probed, the more apparent it became that the moralism traditionally characterizing American attitudes toward poverty explained only a fraction of the problem. Ten million Americans, it was reliably estimated in 1904 —an eighth of the population—earned less than subsistence incomes, and clearly the great majority of them were feeling the effects of social and economic dislocations. When newly graduated college students went into the ghettos to learn about the poor and to offer their help, whether at Chicago's Hull House or New York's Henry Street Settlement, they too immediately recognized the many disadvantages that the poor could not escape. To all these commentators it was obvious that America had become, once and for all, an urban and industrial nation, with a frontier that was now practically settled and, given successive waves of immigrants, a surplus of labor. The emphasis of earlier reformers on personal reformation and rehabilitation now seemed largely irrelevant, and the isolation of the poor in an almshouse an inadequate response.

The new outlook on poverty also reflected special fears and hopes for American society. The majority of the urban poor (and it was the city's needs that monopolized attention) were also immigrants. To reformers, the newcomers represented both a major threat to the national well-being and an unusual opportunity to do good. Two intimately related problems demanded resolution: the immigrant had to be assimilated into American life, and his standard of living had to be improved. The prospect of failure was haunting, for progressives were deeply suspicious of the aliens, disturbed by many of their idiosyncratic customs (from their strange modes of dress to worshipping in Roman Catholic churches), and frightened that they might act on foreign principles (be it a slavish obedience to Rome or a dedicated allegiance to European socialism). And yet, these critics were also confident that American society had the resources to counter these threats. They pinned their hopes on the opportunities for all men to climb the ladder of success and for all families to enjoy an unprecedented material well-being. Once the several barriers that penned the immigrant into his ghetto poverty were removed, once ambitious and energetic foreigners enjoyed the full chance to succeed, then the nation's stability and security would be assured.

Still, the reformers themselves, and many more of their countrymen, could not completely escape a moralistic view of poverty. The equation of the immigrant with the poor kept alive the conviction that vice helped generate dependency. After all, one had only to walk through an ethnic ghetto to discover the omnipresence of taverns, beer halls, dance halls, and houses of prostitution. Even Robert Hunter, as sympathetic an observer as once can find in this period, maintained the older distinction between the worthy and the unworthy poor. "There is unquestionably," he conceded, "a poverty which men deserve, and by such poverty men are perhaps taught needful lessons. It would be unwise to legislate out of existence . . .

Among the earliest "social workers," as we would use the term, was the visiting nurse. This nurse is talking with a tenement family of the 1890's.

that poverty which penalizes the voluntarily idle and vicious." And progressives, like others before and after them, could not altogether reconcile the presence of poverty with their deep sense of the munificence of American life. A ton of condescension entered their rhetoric, reflecting a certain disdain not only for the "wretched refuse" of European shores but also for those who had not been clever or ambitious enough to profit in the land of opportunity.

Despite such doubts, reformers did put an end to the almshouse monopoly, establishing new procedures that kept at least some of the poor within the community. The persons who benefited immediately were widows with small children—the group least suspect among the needy. In 1909 President Roosevelt convened the White House Conference on the Care of Dependent Children and happily publicized its major findings. "Poverty alone should not disrupt the home," he announced. "Parents of good character, suffering from temporary misfortune, and above all deserving mothers . . . deprived of the support of the normal breadwinner, should be given such aid as may be necessary to enable them to maintain suitable homes for the rearing of their children.'' To this end, Illinois in 1911 passed a widow's pension bill, and by the close of World War I nearly every industrial state had followed its example. The worthy widow and her children would no longer suffer separation and incarceration in almshouses and orphan asylums.

Reformers also moved to protect the lower classes both on the job and in their communities, to enable them to enjoy more of the advantages of industrialism. They enacted accident insurance to compensate injured laborers and regulated the number of hours women and children could work. They passed stringent building and fire codes to offset the most glaring dangers of slum living. They also tried to rescue the children of the poor from their parents' fate, enacting compulsory school laws and establishing a minimum age (ranging from twelve to sixteen) for factory work.

There was an enormous amount progressives did not do. They paid little attention to the plight of the black, his economic or social disabilities, and they almost completely ignored the rural poverty of tenant farmers, sharecroppers, and migrant laborers. They neither enacted health-care programs nor extended government pension provisions to the general work force. Although proposals for unemployment compensation and retirement benefits were heard between 1890 and 1914 (and indeed, several European countries were already administering them), no such advances were made here. Even the innovations that did occur were carefully circumscribed. Widow's pensions were limited to only the most deserving, so that mothers whose husbands had deserted them were not eligible, nor those with illegitimate children. As a result the majority of the poor still had to rely upon the limited funds of private charities, or turn to public relief for some coal or wood, or suffer a stint in the almshouse. Nevertheless, the progressives did signal a new departure. In attitude and practice, it was they who first broke with tradition.

Few advances in policy or thought occurred during the 1920's. In fact, given the severe tensions that pervaded the nation, it is noteworthy that the moderate advances of the progressives were not eradicated. This was the decade when the K.K.K. and the temperance movement and immigration restriction reached the zenith of their power and appeal, and antialien, antiurban sentiments also led to a resurgence of harsh and critical judgments on the poor, especially those who were first- or second-generation immigrants. If only they would stop drinking, gambling, and paying obeisance to Rome, the argument went, if only they would become full-fledged Americans, then poverty would disappear. To be sure, a few social critics who did not embrace these prejudices continued to circulate among themselves analytic studies of the poor in the best reformist tradition. Some explored the most efficient methods for organizing a national old-age assistance and pension program; others undertook the first investigations of conditions in black ghettos and among tenant farmers. And an occasional state legislature did manage to widen the eligibility requirements for widows' pensions. But in all, the 1920's was not an auspicious time to innovate, and the public achievement against poverty was not impressive.

The one significant change in this period affecting the poor was the organization and professionalization of social work. The good-hearted but casual home visitor to the needy, who dispensed a little cash and a lot of homilies, gave way to the college- and university-trained full-time social worker. The founding ideology of the discipline looked both to helping the poor adjust to society and to encouraging society to offer more help. But not surprisingly, in the 1920's it was the poor who had to do all the accommodating. Casework lost sight of social reform, focussing instead on teaching the lower classes to cope with their situation, to budget more carefully, to be more industrious, to emulate those above them. Part of the severity of this vision reflected the inhospitable climate of public opinion. But it also reflected the impact of Freudian theory and the eagerness of social workers to become professionals. Using psychological therapy as a way to establish and exert their expertise, social workers insisted that many of the difficulties confronting the poor resulted from their emotional problems. The needy were not the victims of vice but of maladjustment, and careful and sympathetic counselling would teach them to achieve. But the net result of this new doctrine was to couch in modern terminology some very traditional ideas. The poor remained essentially responsible for their difficulties. Reformation and rehabilitation returned to the center of the stage, now rationalized in updated language. The "unworthy" poor had become the "emotionally deprived" poor. Hence, by the close of this decade, public programs and attitudes had rigidified. The nation was not well equipped to confront the phenomenon of the Great Depression.

Suddenly, the poor had more than enough company. The crash of 1929 sparked the most massive economic dislocation in our history, at its peak leaving 25 per cent of the work force unemployed. Poverty was no longer the exclusive fate of the ghetto immigrant or the migrant farmer but of blue-collar workers laid off the assembly line and white-collar workers dismissed from brokerage houses. The problem had unexpectedly become national.

At first, both powerful and ordinary Americans denied the magnitude of the crisis, insisting that recovery was imminent. Herbert Hoover, wedded to an older American credo and fearful of undermining the country's moral fiber, refused to involve the federal government in relief. "I am opposed," he declared in 1931, "to any direct or indirect government dole. . . . Our people are providing against distress from unemployment in true American fashion." But true American fashion meant that local governments and private charities had to carry all of the burden, and by 1932 they were without the resources. Cities lacked funds and the taxing power to raise them. The Red Cross distributed bags of flour and the community chest armfuls of coal. Distress was everywhere apparent: migrants pitched camps at one water spot and then another, their life's possessions piled on the back of a broken-down truck. The urban poor pasted together shacks in shantytowns in the parks and along the river banks. Those with some savings cut corners, awaiting a bank's foreclosure or a landlord's eviction. Often unable to clothe their families decently, they kept their children out of school and shunned their neighbors.

New Deal legislation alleviated some of this misery. Less bound by tradition, Franklin D. Roosevelt plunged the national government into the business of relief. By 1936, with the passage of the Social Security Act and the establishment of the Works Progress Administration, Washington was providing the states with relief funds and the unemployed with jobs. New Deal legislation did alter permanently the character of public programs. To meet immediate problems, the unemployable (the aged, blind, and very young) received, after passing a means test, direct relief at home; at the same time, federally sponsored projects made jobs available for destitute but able-bodied workers. Unemployment compensation, funded by a tax on employers, provided incomes for the temporarily unemployed; and retirement pensions, paid for by employee contributions, gave the aged a new measure of security. The almshouse became a thing of the past, abolished through the effects of these innovations.

Still, the New Deal investment in relief fell considerably short of the nation's need. Afraid to violate the sanctity of the balanced budget or the prerogatives of the states, and committed first and foremost to work relief, President Roosevelt insisted on funding relief through the states but would not set national standards. (Thus, the poor in Mississippi received about one third the support of those in Massachusetts.) The sums allotted to the aged were far below subsistence—nineteen dollars a month when forty dollars would barely do. WPA regulations required men to leave the rolls after eighteen months, no matter how grim their economic condition. Social security was not to take effect until 1942—and even then the pension sums were too small to support recipients. The states were no more generous. California, for example, packed migrant workers and the young unmarried unemployed off to work camps that bordered on penal colonies. The states also tried to seal their borders by reviving stringent residence laws.

Despite the magnitude of the problem and the unprecedented government response, a very traditional attitude toward poverty persisted through the Depression. The new leadership continued to preach many ancient axioms, and the average citizen retained older beliefs. F.D.R. himself denigrated direct relief, keeping alive the term "dole." To some degree this was a conscious strategy to swell public support for the millions expended on W.P.A. But it also reflected his inner conviction that relief corrupted and weakened the recipient. Those on relief, or who tottered on the brink, felt an acute sense of dread and guilt, a painful reluctance to take what they still defined as charity. Hence, just when one might have anticipated a public furor over real suffering, when widespread turmoil and vicious riots might have broken out, the nation remained remarkably quiescent. Most Americans remained silent, suffering alone.

In essence, poverty demoralized rather than activated the country. The unemployed insisted on blaming themselves for their misery, defining their problems as internal, not external. If only they looked harder or put up a better front, they would find a job. Instead of joining with others in faulting the system, they became immobilized and isolated. One after another they passionately and honestly told the interviewers that before taking relief they would "rather be dead and buried." Years later, when good times returned, they still vividly recalled these feelings. "I didn't want to go on relief," one small businessman remembered. "Believe me, when I was forced to go to the office of relief, the tears were running out of my eyes. I couldn't bear myself to take money from anybody for nothing." Their actions did not belie their words. Of nearly one thousand unemployed in New Haven, Connecticut, less than one quarter had asked for relief after being without a job for over a year.

Desperation also took more comic or pathetic turns in the Depression. The board game called Monopoly swept the country. If one could not eke out a living in the real world, one could accumulate a paper fortune in a fantasy one. Dale Carnegie's *How to Win Friends and Influence People* became a best seller with an overt message of doubtful relevance: confidence, grace, personal style, and sensitive shrewdness would bring success. Its latent message was also obvious: failures had only their own personalities to blame. Soap operas, which fastened themselves on the radio public in the 1930's, provided a catalogue of troubles for the listener to compare with his own. But the serials usually blamed failure on personal and emotional inadequacy, rarely on external and social events.

Public-opinion polls during the Depression accurately gauged the degree of persistence and change in American attitudes toward poverty and the poor. There can be no doubt of the popularity of the federal involvement in relief among all the sectors of society. In March, 1939, a Roper poll indicated that three-quarters of the American public affirmed the government's obligation to relieve all persons who had no other means of subsistence. Yet, at the same time, a majority of the public continued to think of the poor in hostile and pejorative terms. Relievers could get jobs, they believed, if only they tried. The New Deal did institute new and important and widely supported relief programs, but the welfare recipient remained a target of suspicion, disparaged by himself and others. Even the Great Depression could not wipe away the stigma of poverty. . . .

Allan Nevins

THE PLACE OF FRANKLIN D. ROOSEVELT IN HISTORY

This essay brings together a great historian and a great subject. Allan Nevins' estimation of Franklin D. Roosevelt is complicated. He says as much about Roosevelt's weaknesses as about his strengths. He looks at Roosevelt through the eyes of the President's friends and his enemies; he refers to his personal observations of the man and also makes the broadest of generalizations, based on his amazing understanding not only of the whole course of American history but of much of the history of the western world. He tells us funny stories that reveal Roosevelt in moments of relaxation and quotes from formal state papers which show him center stage at crucial points in his career. Above all, like a great conductor interpreting a symphony, he is at every stage absolute master of his subject and his materials, devoting exquisite care to every detail yet never forgetting that each separate passage contributes vitally to the total effect.

That effect is, in a word, sunny. Nevins, despite his awareness of Roosevelt's limits and defects, admired the man because of what he calls his "effective greatness," which he believed was produced by qualities of spirit rather than of intellect or even of moral fiber.

Seldom has an eminent man been more conscious of his special place in history than was Franklin D. Roosevelt. He thought of history as an imposing drama and himself as a conspicuous actor. Again and again he carefully staged a historic scene: as when, going before Congress on December 8, 1941, to call for a recognition of war with Japan, he took pains to see that Mrs. Woodrow Wilson accompanied Mrs. Roosevelt to the Capitol, thus linking the First and Second World Wars. As governor and as President, he adopted for the benefit of future historians the rule that every letter addressed to him, however insignificant, and copies of every document issued from his office, should be preserved. This mass of papers, mounting into the millions, soon became almost overwhelming. It might have been added, with some difficulty, to the many other official collections in the Library of Congress. But, with a strong sense of his special place in history, Roosevelt wanted a memorial all his own, a place of resort for scholars, connected uniquely with his name and his administrations. He announced the gift of his papers to the nation; his mother gave sixteen acres of land for a building at Hyde Park; some 28,000 donors subscribed $400,000 for an edifice; and Congress made the Roosevelt Library a federal institution.

In this Library at Hyde Park, as a token of his place in history, he took an almost naïve pride. I well recall the dinner he gave early in 1939 to the trustees and a select number of historians to discuss plans for its management. It took place at the Mayflower Hotel in Washington; he was wheeled up an inclined ramp to his place at a central table; he waved joyously to everyone; he enjoyed his stewed mulligatawny turtle—a favorite dish—his companions, his sense of launching another original enterprise. In a long informal speech he talked of certain predecessors: of Lincoln, of Grover Cleveland, whom he had known, and of his cousin Theodore Roosevelt; he dwelt on Woodrow Wilson's sense of history—Wilson in 1917 had forbidden young Roosevelt, then Assistant Secretary of the Navy, to bring warships up from Cuban waters to the United States lest future historians should accuse him of making a provocative gesture on the eve of our first war with Germany. I well recall, too, the still more interesting occasion when he laid the cornerstone of the Hyde Park Library on November 19, 1939. Trustees, historians, and editors lunched with him; he gaily drove his own specially equipped car to the site; he chatted blithely with everyone; and he watched the cornerstone slip into place with a gratified smile.

Today his grave lies close by that Library, and by the family home that has become a national shrine, visited by hundreds of thousands every year. To the collections there shelved, multitudes of scholars annually repair, for they are open to all. Roosevelt's own deposits, including letters, documents, books, pamphlets, films, photographs, speeches, and museum pieces, have exceeded a total of fifty million items; and to them are being added the papers of Cabinet officers and other official associates. The career of no other American President has so vast a documentation for history.

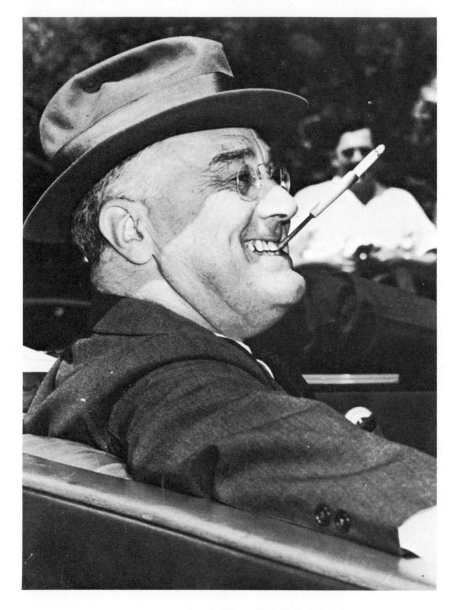

*An ebullient F.D.R. holding an outdoor press
conference at Warm Springs, Georgia, in 1939.*

Is it too soon to estimate the place of Franklin D. Roosevelt in the
stream of American and world events? It is never too soon for such a
task. History is not a remote Olympian bar of judgment, but a controversial arena in which each generation must make its own estimate of
the past. We have every right to fix the historical position of Roosevelt
as we see it today, knowing that it will be reassessed from the vantage

point of a longer perspective and fuller knowledge in 1975, and re-estimated again in 2065. That it will be a great place we may already be certain. A statue to Roosevelt has been reared in Oslo. When a statue was proposed in London, five-shilling subscriptions were opened one morning; they were closed that night with the sum oversubscribed; had they been kept open a few days money would have poured in for five statues. Streets have been named for him around the world. Fifty American historians, interrogated by Arthur M. Schlesinger, Sr., of Harvard, have all but unanimously agreed that in the roster of Presidents Lincoln stands first, Washington second, and Franklin D. Roosevelt third. Hearing of that verdict, Winston Churchill declared that in impact upon world history Roosevelt unquestionably stood first.

We have this advantage in attempting the task, that a great part of the necessary evidence is already at hand. Never before in human annals has so huge a volume of reminiscences, autobiographies, impressions, letters, official documents, and other data bearing on one man been issued within twenty years of his death. The thirteen volumes of Roosevelt's official papers edited by Judge Samuel I. Rosenman and the four volumes of personal letters edited by Elliot Roosevelt; the memoirs of Cordell Hull, Harry Hopkins, Henry Morgenthau, Harold Ickes, Henry L. Stimson, James Farley, Edward J. Flynn, Mrs. Franklin D. Roosevelt, Frances Perkins, Grace Tully, Hugh Johnson, Dwight Eisenhower, Omar Bradley, and a hundred others; the mass of comment by Washington reporters and war correspondents who watched history being made; the procession of European histories and memoirs so impressively headed by Winston Churchill's volumes —this already forms a corpus too great for one student to explore fully in a lifetime. But while we shall have immense fresh accretions of detail, it is unlikely that we shall receive any startling new ''revelations,'' any facts that will offer a basis for sweeping revisions of judgment.

In dealing with every commanding figure of history, a fundamental question presents itself: To what extent did greatness inhere in the man, and to what degree was it a product of the situation? If great men have their stars, as Napoleon said he did, it is often because a national or world crisis favors greatness. The reason why fifty American historians did not wholly agree with Winston Churchill upon Roosevelt's rank among the nation's Presidents is, I think, simple. Washington had indisputable greatness in himself. ''The first, the last, the best, the Cincinnatus of the West,'' as Lord Byron called him, he was great in character, great in traits of leadership, great in insight and wisdom. Lincoln had an even more manifest and appealing personal greatness. His public utterances, from the House Divided address to the Gettysburg Address, his state papers, from the First Inaugural to the final pronouncements on Reconstruction, attest a rare intellectual power. The wisdom of his principal public acts, his magnanimity toward all foes public and private, his firmness under adversity, his elevation of spirit, his power of strengthening the best purposes and suppressing the worst instincts of a broad, motley democracy, place him in the front rank of modern statesmen.

But with Franklin D. Roosevelt we feel no such assurance of tran-scendent personal eminence. We feel that he lacked the steadfast elevation of character exhibited by George Washington. We find in him distinctly less intellectual power than in Jefferson, Lincoln, or perhaps Woodrow Wilson. We conclude, in short, that his tremendous place in history was in lesser degree the product of his special per-sonal endowments, and in larger degree the handiwork of his stormy times, than that occupied by George Washington or Abraham Lincoln.

That Roosevelt had remarkable intellectual gifts is plain; but these gifts fell short of the highest distinction. He possessed a quick, re-sourceful, and flexible mind. This fact is illustrated on an elevated level by his ability to deal with fifty important issues in a day, making shrewd decisions on each; by his power in wartime of efficiently co-ordinating departments, industries, and armies, of gaining the team-work of generals, admirals, and business leaders, as no other President has ever done. He organized the national energies with unique success. His intellectual proficiency is illustrated on a lower plane by almost any of the press conferences recorded in Judge Rosenman's volumes; by his deft tact in handling two-score quick-witted newspapermen, evading some questions, dissecting the fatuity of others, using a few to touch a needed chord of publc opinion, and responding to many with concise, expert answers. Like his cousin Theodore Roosevelt, he had an insatiable curiosity about books, about men, about events. It was linked with an unquenchable zest for experience; the zest expressed in his famous wartime message to Churchill, "It is fun to be in the same century with you."

He had a talent for quick parliamentary hits. He could make his enemies ridiculous by a few pungent words, as in the happy rhyth-mical phrase about "Martin, Barton, and Fish" that, recited over the radio, exposed these three reactionary congressmen to a continental gale of laughter in 1940; or by a lambent flare of humor, as in his speech of 1944 picturing the Scottish unhappiness of his dog Fala over an accusation of extravagance. He had flashes of daring imagina-tion. He had a remarkable gift of rapid improvisation, as he showed in all the recurrent crises of his twelve crowded years in office. In part this consisted of his ability to use other men's thought; "he is the best picker of brains who ever lived," his intimates used to say. His power of application was remarkable even among our overworked Presidents. He had an average working day of fourteen hours (Truman later boasted of sixteen), and he told Governor James M. Cox: "I never get tired."

But of pre-eminent intellectual talent he had little. I recall Walter Lippmann saying in the second administration: "He has never written a real state paper." In a sense that is true. No paper signed by him equals Washington's Farewell Address, Lincoln's great papers, Theodore Roosevelt's first annual message, or Woodrow Wilson's nobler productions. Nearly all his speeches were in fact largely written for him by others. Robert Sherwood describes a typical scene: Judge

As this 1938 cartoon from the Columbus Dispatch *suggests, Roosevelt was exceedingly interested in assuring himself a place among the outstanding Presidents of American history.*

Rosenman, Harry Hopkins, and Sherwood gathered about a table discussing the material for an imminent presidential address, and threshing it over and over until Judge Rosenman impatiently flung down a pencil with the words, ''There comes a time in the life of every speech when it's got to be *written!*'' Roosevelt wrote no books; he was probably incapable of matching such a work as Theodore Roosevelt's *The Winning of the West.* He threw out no such immortal epigrams as Churchill's sentence challenging Britons to face a future of ''blood, sweat, and tears.'' His best phrases, like ''the forgotten man'' and ''the new deal,'' were borrowed from other men.

A capacity for abstract thought was largely omitted from his equipment. The idea once current that he had a special intimacy with Maynard Keynes was obviously erroneous, for he was simply incapable of following a mind so analytical, an intellect so subtle, as that of Lord Keynes. When John Gunther asked one of Roosevelt's friends, ''Just how does the President think?'' he met the reply: ''The President never *thinks.*'' Like Theodore Roosevelt, he was primarily a man of action. His mental processes, as many friends have said, were intuitive rather than logical. He reacted rather than reflected. A President is not necessarily too busy to do abstract thinking. Newton D. Baker, who held a minor post in Grover Cleveland's administration and a major office under Woodrow Wilson, once observed to me that while Cleveland shouldered his way through difficulties like a buffalo charging a thicket, Wilson ''dissolved his problems by an acid process of thought.'' This acid process was beyond Roosevelt. All that is told us of his reading suggests that it was rather adolescent: either escapist, like the detective stories carried on every long trip; or attached to a hobby, like naval history; or journalistic. His humor lacked the philosophic overtones of Lincoln's, or even the saltiness of Harry Truman's; it too was somewhat adolescent. It was usually the humor of the quip, as when he said to his secretary, Grace Tully, over-addicted to punctuation, "Grace, how often do I have to tell you not to waste the taxpayer's commas?" Or it was the humor of the wisecrack, as when he remarked to the six New England governors who startled him in 1933 by suddenly appearing at the White House in a body: "What, all six of you? You're not going to secede from the Union, are you?"

We all know what Lord Bacon said makes a ready man; and intellectually, the talkative Roosevelt was a ready leader—perhaps the readiest of all the world's leaders in his exigent time. This power to act quickly, shrewdly, and earnestly was a gift that served the nation and the free world with unforgettable dexterity and force. Honoring this princely capacity, we can afford to give minor weight to the fact that his mind, compared with that of Woodrow Wilson, sometimes appears superficial, and that he possessed no such intellectual versatility as Thomas Jefferson—to say nothing of Winston Churchill.

In respect to character, similarly, he had traits of an admirable kind; but we must add that even in combination, they fell short of a truly Roman weight of virtue. He held sincere religious convictions, and it was no mere gesture that led him to take his Cabinet, on the morn of his first inauguration, to divine service at St. John's. "I think," writes Mrs. Roosevelt in *This I Remember*, "he actually felt he could ask God for guidance and receive it. That was why he loved the Twenty-third Psalm, the Beatitudes, and the thirteenth chapter of First Corinthians." He was one of the unflinching optimists of his time. Having conquered a prostrating illness and horrible physical handicap, he felt an inner faith in man's power to conquer anything. When his aides made estimates of American industrial capacity, he raised them; when the Combined Chiefs of Staff set down dates for the various goals in the invasion of Europe, he revised them forward. Because of his religious faith and his ingrained optimism, he possessed an unfailing serenity. In the stormiest of hours his nerve was never shaken.

On his first day in the Presidency in 1933, with the banks of the nation closed down and the country almost prostrate with anxiety, he found his desk at six o'clock in the afternoon quite clear. He pressed a button. Four secretaries appeared at four doors to the room. "Is there anything more, boys?" he inquired. "No, Mr. President," they chorused. And Roosevelt remarked with his happy smile: "This job is a cinch!"

Equally admirable were his idealism, his consciousness of high objectives, and his frequent nobility of spirit. He was willing to sacrifice himself for the public weal. When in 1928 Alfred E. Smith, the Democratic presidential candidate, asked him to run for governor of New York, he was told by physicians that if he kept out of public life another year or two, he could regain the use of his left leg, while if he did not he would be incurably lame; but he answered the call of duty. His concern for the poor, the friendless, the unfortunate, was more keenly humane than that of any leader since Lincoln. "I see one-third of a nation," he said in his Second Inaugural, "ill-housed, ill-clad, ill-nourished''—and meant to do something about it. Moderately rich himself, he disliked those who were too rich. The steel magnate Eugene Grace, who took a bonus of a million dollars a year without the knowledge of his stockholders, aroused his bitter scorn. ''Tell Gene he'll never make a million a year again!'' was the angry message he sent the man. Frances Perkins, who had known him as a rather arrogant, snobbish young man before his seizure by infantile paralysis, and who knew him as a battler for social justice afterward, believed that this physical ordeal taught him sympathy for the afflicted and underprivileged.

Yet, we must add, these impressive virtues were flawed by certain grievous defects. He had flashes of insincerity which sometimes impaired the confidence even of close friends. Henry L. Stimson mentions in his memoirs the fact that, having found out Roosevelt in a quite needless bit of duplicity, for several years he avoided all contact with him. Henry A. Wallace committed to paper an account of Roosevelt's double-dealing (as Wallace saw it) in handling the Vice Presidential nomination in 1944. Other men have penned different stories. Even the President's defenders could not deny that his treatment of that critical problem showed a certain irresponsibility, to be excused perhaps by the fact that he was already more ill than he realized. Because of this instability, Roosevelt was ready at times to abandon principle for expediency. Cordell Hull has described how unfortunate were the results of such an abandonment in the Neutrality Acts. And Mrs. Roosevelt writes: ''While I often felt strongly on various subjects, Franklin frequently refrained from supporting causes in which he believed, because of political realities. There were times when this annoyed me very much. In the case of the Spanish Civil War, for instance, we had to remain neutral, though Franklin knew quite well he wanted the democratic government to be successful. But he also knew he could not get Congress to go along with him. To justify his action, or lack of action, he explained to me, when I complained, that the League of Nations had asked us to remain neutral. . . . He was simply trying to salve his own conscience. It was one of the many times I felt akin to a hair shirt.''

Edward J. Flynn writes flatly: ''The President did not keep his word on many appointments.'' There exists no question that he promised to make Louis Johnson Secretary of War, and broke the promise. All statesmen have to adjust principle to events and to public sentiment, and are sometimes compelled to revoke promises. But Roosevelt was at times indefensibly evasive even with intimates like Flynn and Louis Johnson, and lacked straightforwardness. It can be said, too, that he often followed a Machiavellian technique in administration. He liked, for example, to put two or three men in positions of conflicting authority, so that they worked at loggerheads, with himself as ultimate arbiter. It was in part his fault that Sumner Welles and Cordell Hull made the State Department for several years a maelstrom of rival policies and ambitions—although this is a complex story; it was in part his fault that Jesse Jones and Henry Wallace engaged at one time in a feud which sadly injured both the administration and the country.

Other unhappy traits might be copiously illustrated. Roosevelt could seem dismayingly casual about everything from a political speech to some of the issues at Yalta. He could be reprehensibly secretive; he kept the minutes of the Teheran Conference from Secretary of State Hull, and withheld from the American people the concession he made at Yalta to Russia on votes in the United Nations Assembly. He was pettily vindictive toward some opponents, as Raymond B. Moley and James Farley testify in detail, and his attempted purge of certain southern leaders in 1938 is far from the happiest chapter in his career. All in all, we must repeat our conclusion that his character lacked the symmetry, harmony, and weight found in that of Washington and of Lincoln.

Yet without the highest inner greatness Roosevelt had an effective greatness of action, in relation to his time, which will cause him to be remembered as happily as any American leader. It is significant that Churchill, intellectually so much superior, always treated him with manifest deference, as a lesser man bowing to a greater. Was this simply because Roosevelt headed the more powerful state? I think not. We must here face what seems to me a salient fact of history. A leader who puts second-rate qualities of intellect and character into first-rate application to the needs of his time may be a greater man than the leader who puts first-rate qualities into a second-rate application. Roosevelt signally illustrates this aphorism. He had, to begin with, the gift of address: a gift for doing the right thing at just the right time. He had, in the second place, the greater gift of being able to put his personal forces into harmony with the best forces of his era.

Roosevelt's effective greatness included an unrivalled power of matching the urgent crisis with the adequate act; a power of timing an impressive measure to meet a desperate need. Take the first days of 1933, after his election. Never in a period of peace—never since the days of British invasion in 1814, or Confederate victory in 1863—had the nation been in such straits. Between twelve and fifteen million men were out of work. Five million families, one seventh of the population, were supported by public relief or private charity. Since the beginning of the depression, 4,600 banks had failed. Travellers through the broad industrial belt from Chicago to New York seemed to pass nothing but closed factory gates. Half the automobile plants of Michigan had shut down. Along the Great Lakes, path of the largest marine commerce of the world, ships had almost ceased to move. In the iron beds of the Mesabi and Vermilion ranges scarcely a shovel dipped into the richest ores of the globe; in the copper mountain at Butte scarcely a drill was at work. The looms of southern textile factories were cobwebbed. On railway sidings locomotives gathered rust in long rows; behind them huddled passenger and freight cars in idle hundreds, their paint fading. Middle-western farmers gazed bitterly at crops whose market value was less than the cost of harvesting; on the high plains, ranchers turned cattle loose to graze at will because it did not pay to send them to the stockyards. In Pennsylvania and New England desperate men and women offered to work for anything, and some did work for a dollar a week.

Worst of all was the fear which gripped the nerves of the nation. To observers who travelled across the country in trains almost empty, through factory districts with hardly a wisp of smoke, the helpless populations sent up an almost audible cry of anger, bewilderment, and panic. The day before Roosevelt took office the crisis gathered to a climax. By midnight of March 3 the closing of all remaining banks had been or was being ordered in every state. Never before had a change of Presidents taken place against a background so dramatic. The people, awakening on March 4 to read that their financial system was prostrate, gathered at noon by millions about their radios to listen in anguish, in anxiety, but in hope, to the voice of their new national leader.

There ensued four of the most brilliantly successful months in the history of American government. Roosevelt's first words promised energy: "I assume unhesitatingly the leadership of this great army of our people, dedicated to a disciplined attack upon our common problems." He improvised a series of policies, and mobilized an administrative machine, with a vigor that would have done credit to any wartime executive. Within thirty-six hours he had taken absolute control of the currency and banking system, and called Congress in extraordinary session. He forthwith launched an aggressive attack along half a dozen fronts; upon banking problems, industrial prostration, farm distress, unemployment, public works, the burden of public and private debt. One reporter wrote that the change in Washington was like that from oxcart to airplane. Congress labored for ninety-nine days under the President's all-but-complete sway. Almost his every wish was obeyed by immediate votes. One staggered member said of the program: "It reads like the first chapter of Genesis."

And as Roosevelt took these steps his courage, his resourcefulness, his blithe optimism, infected the spirit of the people; he gave Americans new confidence and the *élan* of a new national unity. When he gaily signed his last bills and departed for a brief sail up the Atlantic coast as skipper of a 45-foot sailing boat, the nation realized that it had turned from stagnation to a bright adventure. As the President put it, we were "on our way."

Nor was this an isolated spasm of leadership; for each recurrent crisis found the same resourcefulness called into effective play. When France fell, when the British Commonwealth stood alone against the deadliest foe that modern civilization had known, Americans gazed at the European scene in fear, in gloom, in perpexity. With a sense of dumb helplessness, tens of millions put their intensest feeling into the hope for Britain's survival. Those tens of millions never forgot the morning of September 3, 1940, when they read the headlines announcing that Roosevelt had told a startled Congress of the transfer of fifty destroyers to embattled Britain; a defiance of Hitler, a defiance of home isolationists, a first long stride toward ranging America against the Fascist despots. Nor could lovers of world freedom ever forget the dramatic steps that followed hard upon British victory over Hitler's air force and upon Roosevelt's re-election: the Four Freedoms speech of January 6, 1941; the introduction of the Lend-Lease Bill four days later, a measure which completely transformed American foreign policy; the establishment of naval and military posts in Greenland and Iceland; the proclamation of an unlimited national emergency; the seizure of all Axis ships and Axis credits; the Atlantic Charter meeting with Churchill off Newfoundland; the establishment of convoys for American ships carrying aid to Britain; and, in the background, the stimulation of American production to an unprecedented flow of guns, tanks, shells, and airplanes, with factories roaring day and night for the defense of democracy.

These years 1940–41 were, as we see now, among the greatest crises in modern history. They were met with an imagination, boldness, and ingenuity that can hardly be overpraised. Parochialism, timidity, or fumbling might have been fatal; even a pause for too much reflection might have been fatal. We knew then that Roosevelt was determined to face the exigency with an intrepidity worthy of the republic. But his intention was even more courageous than we supposed. For we know now that Harry Hopkins told Churchill in London early in 1941: "The President is determined that we shall win the war together. Make no mistake about it. He sent me here to tell you that at all costs and by all means he will carry you through."

Roosevelt's second quality of effective greatness was his ability to vindicate the American method of pragmatic experiment, of practical *ad hoc* action, step by step. He was essentially a Jeffersonian. He belonged to the school which, following the historic Anglo-American bent of mind, is attached to facts rather than ideas, to the enlargement of precedents rather than the formulation of dazzling visions. Like all Anglo-American statesmen, he disliked sweeping generalizations of an intolerant, exclusive nature. He loved experimental advance, and was wont to say that if he were right sixty per cent of the time, he would be satisfied. Like Jefferson, he was willing to scrap a theory the moment a brute fact collided with it; he trusted experience, and distrusted flights into the empyrean. His so-called revolution, though unprecedentedly broad and swift, was like Jefferson's "revolution"; it was simply a combination of numerous practical changes, the main test of which was whether or not they worked.

The Rooseveltian changes did work. They did transform American life and the American outlook in two distinct ways. They converted a nation of aggressive individualists into a social-minded nation accepting the principles of the welfare state. They changed an isolationist or largely isolationist nation into one committed to world partnership and world leadership. The New Deal in home affairs was empirical, not ideological. The emergency program I have sketched was a stopgap affair put together to tide over a crisis, and as Mrs. Roosevelt once put it, "give us time to think." It succeeded. Taken as a whole, the New Deal passed through two phases. In the first, 1933–35, the government tried scarcity economics, reducing factory production, farm output, and hours of work, and doing what it could to cut off the American economy from the outside world. In the second and better phase, 1935–50, it tried full employment, full production, enlarged distribution of goods, and freer international trade. This led directly toward the acceptance of Cordell Hull's ideal of co-operative internationalism. American participation in world affairs after 1938 similarly passed through two phases. In the first, all the nation's energies were devoted to the defeat of the Axis. In the second, Roosevelt, Hull, Welles, and Stettinius moved step by step to construct a new world order, an enduring fabric of the United Nations. In home and foreign affairs alike action was always direct, experimental, and pragmatic.

It gave America a new social order at home, and a new orientation in global affairs. It worked; it is still working. But because it never approached a sweeping ideological revolution of the Marxist or totalitarian type, it was the despair of certain impractical theorists *pur sang*.

For example, readers of that brilliant but extraordinarily half-informed and error-streaked book, Harold Laski's *The American Democracy*, will find an almost incredible analysis of what the author regards as Mr. Roosevelt's fundamental failure. This was his failure to smash the old America completely, and build a quite new America on the theories that pleased Mr. Laski. The author draws an illuminating comparison between Lenin and Roosevelt. Lenin, it appears, made a marvelously precise and correct analysis of the maladies of modern society and economics; and he applied it with revolutionary courage. Roosevelt, on the other hand, was never converted—he never learned that "the foundations of the Americanism he inherited were really inadequate to the demands made upon its institutional expression." In particular, writes Laski, he failed to see that he should destroy "private ownership of the means of production"; that is, that the state should take over all mines, factories, transport, workshops, and farms. Roosevelt, as a result of his faulty analysis, unhappily failed to carry through a real revolution. What was the upshot? In Russia, admits Laski, life became nearly intolerable. The price of revolution proved "almost overwhelming"—starvation of millions, wholesale executions, vast concentration camps, the extinction of freedom. In America, Laski admits, life was immensely improved. Industrial production became enormous; farm output grew tremendous; the standard of living steadily rose. But theory (says Mr. Laski) is everything. Lenin with his ideology was right; Roosevelt with his practical experimentalism was a failure!

This view of the matter would be emphatically rejected by all but a handful of Americans, including those who do not admire Roosevelt. Like Jefferson, like Lincoln, like Wilson, he was innovator and conservator at once; he made daring new additions to the American fabric, but he kept the best of the old structure. While he converted

Americans to the new ideal of social security, he strengthened their old faith in individual opportunity. He proved again that America needs no ideological revolution. He vindicated our traditional method of solving problems one at a time by pragmatic trial and error. As one journalist wrote: "One remembers him as a kind of smiling bus driver, with that cigarette holder pointed upward, listening to the uproar from behind as he took the sharp turns. They used to tell him that he had not loaded his vehicle right for all eternity. But he knew that he had stacked it well enough to round the next corner, and he knew when the yells were false, and when they were real, and he loved the passengers."

Roosevelt's third and most important quality of effective greatness lay in his ability to imbue Americans, and to some extent even citizens of other lands, with a new spiritual strength. Well into the twentieth century, most men in the New World had shared a dream of ever-widening adventure, a sense of elated achievement. They had dared much in coming to the new continent, and still more in mastering it. They were optimistic, self-confident, exuberant. The heavy costs of the First World War, the disillusionments of its aftermath, the pressure of complex new social problems, and above all the staggering blows of the Great Depression darkened our horizons. We had entered the Shadow Belt which Bryce predicted in his book on *The American Commonwealth*. From that zone of gloom, that numbed consciousness of frustration and failure, Roosevelt lifted Americans on the wings of his great new adventures—the alphabetical adventures of the AAA, the NRA, the TVA; above all, on the wings of the greatest adventure in our history, the effort to rescue democracy from totalitarianism, and to organize the world to safeguard freedom.

For a few years Americans had felt lost, bewildered, paralyzed. Roosevelt carried them to a Moabite peak whence once more they saw promised lands. They threw off their frustrations; he gave them a feeling that they were participating in a life far wider than their everyday parochial concerns. His self-confidence, his enthusiasm, his happy faculty of obliterating old failures by bold new plans, taught them that they were not imprisoned in a dead past but were helping build a living future. In the three centuries 1607–1907 Americans had triumphantly mastered their physical environment. Just so, in the next century to come, they would master their social and economic environment at home, and join other nations in a mastery of the world environment. As the storm thickened after 1940, Roosevelt's rich voice grew more urgent—"bidding the eagles of the West fly on." Here at last, he seemed to say, is a task worthy of you; tyranny like Hell is not easily conquered. Lincoln had once used a phrase which haunts his countrymen. "Thanks to all," he exclaimed after Gettysburg and Vicksburg, "thanks to all: for the great republic—for the principle it lives by and keeps alive—for man's vast future—thanks to all." A sense of man's vast future, a hope of shaping it for the better, never left Roosevelt's cheerful heart.

It is not often realized to what a degree the spirit of adventure kindled at home under the New Deal was carried over into world affairs when the United States faced the Axis menace. The defeatism of Hoover's day was gone. A hundred and sixty million citizens had been morally prepared to undertake unprecedented tasks. They grumbled; they cursed the hard luck of their grim era; they shuddered over the mounting costs—the colossal debt, the wasted resources; but they never doubted their ability to put the job through. That change in temper was primarily Roosevelt's accomplishment. It threw open, temporarily, the portals of a wider world. The change from oxcart was a spiritual, not a material, change. Never in our history have the emotion and resolution of the American people been so completely fused as when, as the first waves of American and British troops stormed across the Normandy beaches, Roosevelt sat at the radio leading the nation in prayer.

Effective greatness—that is Roosevelt's title to a high place in the world's history. Intellect and character are not enough; to them must be added personality, energy, and an accurate sense for the proper timing of action. Roosevelt was not an intellectual giant; but what of the personality that made the Arkansas sharecropper and the Harlem Negro feel they shared all the destinies of the republic? His character did not awe men by its massive strength; but what of the gifts that made him so efficient in harmonizing labor, capital, and agriculture at home, and getting discordant nations to pool their wartime efforts? He lacked the iron traits of Cromwell—but how incomparably more successful he was! He did not have the powerful grasp of Bismarck, but how much more beneficent was his career! In time his specific achievements may be blurred, but the qualities of his spirit will be remembered. For centuries Americans will think of him as one of those spirits who ride in front; we shall see his jaunty figure, his gaily poised head, still in advance of us. We shall hear his blithe voice in his words just before his death at Warm Springs on April 12, 1945:

"The only limit to our realization of tomorrow will be our doubts of today. Let us move forward with strong and active faith."

Part Six
Modern America

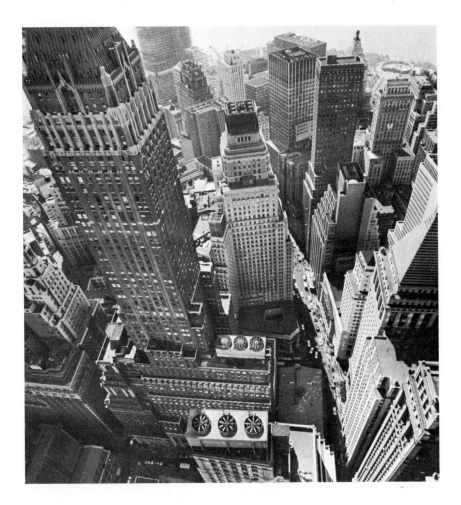

Daniel P. Moynihan

THE AMERICAN CITY: CONTINUITY AND CHANGE

Current concerns always produce "new" history; they lead us to reconsider the past in our search for an understanding of the present. This essay by Daniel P. Moynihan illustrates this principle perfectly. Moynihan has devoted most of his adult life to what may generally be called urban problems—as a government official, as a university professor, and as a writer. He served in the United States Department of Labor from 1961 to 1965, rising to the post of Assistant Secretary. He then became a professor at Harvard and director of Harvard and M.I.T.'s Joint Center for Urban Studies, then Special Assistant for Urban Affairs to President Nixon, then United States Ambassador to India. He is currently Unted States Senator from New York. His book *Beyond the Melting Pot,* written with Nathan Glazer, has been a major force in shaping liberal attitudes toward the problems of ethnic minorities in America.

In the following pages Moynihan takes a hard look at American cities today. His essay bristles with references to modern social science studies of urban life. But in attempting to place urban problems in perspective, he refers repeatedly to history, showing how present-day difficulties are similar to—and different from—those of earlier times. He ends on a note of uncertainty. Avoiding the easy tendency of many historians to justify social evils by "proving" that they have always existed, he concludes by admitting "we do not know" the prescription for curing America's sick cities. But surely, if urban problems are ever to be solved or even mitigated, it will be by considering them in the thoughtful, learned, yet modest way that Moynihan here employs.

There is to be encountered in a Benjamin Disraeli novel a gentleman described as a person "distinguished for ignorance" as he had but one idea and that was wrong. It is by now clear that future generations will perforce reach something of the same judgment about contemporary Americans in relation to their cities, for what we do and what we say reflect such opposite poles of judgment that we shall inevitably be seen to have misjudged most extraordinarily either in what we are saying about cities or in what we are doing about them. We are, of course, doing very little, or rather, doing just about what we have been doing for the past half century or so, which can reflect a very great deal of activity but no very considerable change. Simultaneously, and far more conspicuously, we are talking of crisis. The word is everywhere: on every tongue; in every pronouncement. The President has now taken to sending an annual message to Congress on urban subjects. In 1968 it was bluntly titled *The Crisis of the Cities*. And indeed, not many weeks later, on Friday, April 5, to be exact, he was issuing a confirming proclamation of sorts:

> Whereas I have been informed that conditions of domestic violence and disorder exist in the District of Columbia and threaten the Washington metropolitan area, endangering life and property and obstructing execution of the laws, and the local police forces are unable to bring about the prompt cessation . . . of violence and restoration of law and order. . . .

The excitement is nothing if not infectious. In a recent joint publication, *Crisis: The Condition of the American City,* Urban America, Inc. and the League of Women Voters noted that during 1967 even the Secretary of Agriculture devoted most of his speeches to urban problems. At mid-1968, the president of the University of California issued a major statement entitled, "What We Must Do: The University and the Urban Crisis." The bishops of the United States Catholic Conference came forth with their own program, entitled "The Church's Response to the Urban Crisis." At its 1968 convention the Republican party, not heretofore known for an obsession with the subject, adopted a platform plank entitled "Crisis of the Cities," while in an issue featuring a stunning black coed on the cover, *Glamour* magazine, ever alert to changing fashions, asked in appropriate form the question many have posed themselves in private—"The Urban Crisis: What Can One Girl Do?"

Academics who have been involved with this subject might be expected to take some satisfaction that the alarums and jeremiads of the past decades seem at last to have been heard by the populace, and yet even those of us most seized with what Norman Mailer has termed the "middle-class lust for apocalypse" are likely to have some reservations about the current enthusiasm for the subject of urban ills. It is not just a matter of the continued disparity between what we say and what we do: it is also, I suspect, a matter of *what* we are saying, and the manner of our saying it. A certain bathos comes through. One thinks of Sean O'Casey's Captain Boyle and Joxer in that far-off Dublin tenement: no doubt the whole world was even then in a "state of chassis" but precious little those two could or would do about it, save use it as an excuse to sustain their own weakness, incompetence, and submission to the death wishes of the society about them. One wonders if something not dissimilar is going on in this nation, at this time. Having persistently failed to do what it was necessary and possible to do for urban life on grounds that conditions surely were not so bad as to warrant such exertion, the nation seems suddenly to have lurched to the opposite position of declaring that things are indeed so very bad that probably nothing will work anyway. The result either way is paralysis and failure. It is time for a measure of perspective.

I take it Lewis Mumford intended to convey something of this message in his most recent book, *The Urban Prospect*, which he begins with a short preface cataloguing the ills of the modern city with a vigor and specificity that command instant assent from the reader. Exactly! one responds. That is precisely the way things are! Mumford is really "telling it like it is." (A measure of *négritude* has of late become the mark of an authentic urban-crisis watcher.) One reads on with increasing recognition, mounting umbrage, only to find at the end that this foreword was in fact written for the May, 1925, edition of *Survey Graphic*. Things have changed, but not that much, and in directions that were, in a sense, fully visible to the sensitive eye nearly a half century ago. To be sure, at a certain point a matter of imbalance becomes one of pathology, a tendency becomes a condition, and for societies as for individuals there comes a point when mistakes are no longer to be undone, transgressions no longer to be forgiven. But it is nowhere clear that we have reached such a point in our cities.

Continuity and change. These are the themes of all life, and not less that of cities. However, as in so many aspects of our national experience, Americans seem more aware of, more sensitive to modes of change than to those of continuity. This is surely a survival from the frontier experience. There has not, I believe, ever been anything to match the rapidity, nay, fury with which Americans set about founding cities in the course of the seventeenth, eighteenth, and nineteenth centuries. Only just now is the historical profession beginning to catch up with that breathless undertaking. Before long we are likely to have a much clearer idea than we do now as to how it all began. But it is still possible at this early state, as it were, to identify a half dozen or so persistent themes in the American urban experience which seem to evolve from earlier to later stages in a process that some would call growth, and others decay, but in a manner that nonetheless constitutes change.

The first theme is that of violence. Through history—the history, that is, of Europe and Asia and that great bridge area in between—cities have been, nominally at least, places of refuge, while the countryside has been the scene of insecurity and exposure to misfortune and wrongdoing. Obviously the facts permit of no generalization, but there is at least a conceptual validity, a persistence over time, of the association of the city with security. In the classical and feudal world, to be without the gates was to be in trouble. Writing of the destruction of Hiroshima and Nagasaki, the critic George Steiner evokes the ancient certainty on this point, and suggests the ways in which it lives on.

> In these two cities, the consequences have been more drastic and more specialized. Therein lies the singularity of the two Japanese communities, but also their symbolic link with a number of other cities in history and with the role such cities have played in man's consciousness of his own vulnerable condition—with Sodom and Gomorrah, visited by such fiery ruin that their very location is in doubt; with Nineveh, raked from the earth; with Rotterdam and Coventry; with Dresden, where in 1944, air raids deliberately kindled the largest, hottest pyre known to man. Already, in the "Iliad," the destruction of a city was felt to be an act of peculiar finality, a misfortune that threatens the roots of man. His city smashed, man reverts to the unhoused, wandering circumstance of the beast from which he has so uncertainly emerged. Hence the necessary presence of the gods when a city is built, the mysterious music and ceremony that often attend the elevation of its walls. When Jerusalem was laid waste, says the Haggada, God Himself wept with her.

Little of this dread is to be encountered in the United States, a society marked by the near absence of internal warfare once the major Indian conflicts were over. Warfare, that is to say, between armies. We have, on the other hand, been replete with conflict between different groups within the population, classified in terms of race, class, ethnicity, or whatever, and this conflict has occurred in our cities, which in consequence have been violent places.

An account of the draft riots in New York City in 1863 strikes a surpassingly contemporary note.

> Nothing that we could say, could add to the impressiveness of the lesson furnished by the events of the past year, as to the needs and the dangerous condition of the neglected classes in our city. Those terrible days in July—the sudden appearance, as if from the bosom of the earth, of a most infuriated and degraded mob; the helplessness of property-holders and the better classes; the boom of cannon and rattle of musketry in our streets; the skies lurid with conflagrations; the inconceivable barbarity and ferocity of the crowd toward an unfortunate and helpless race; the immense destruction of property—were the first dreadful revelations to many of our people of the existence among us of a great, ignorant, irresponsible class,

During New York's draft riots in 1863, looters did not hesitate to put homes to the torch.

who were growing up here without any permanent interest in the welfare of the community or the success of the Government—the *proletaires* of the European capitals. Of the gradual formation of this class, and the dangers to be feared from it, the agents of this Society have incessantly warned the public for the past eleven years.

—Eleventh Annual Report
Children's Aid Society, New York

In some degree this violence—or the perception of it—seems to have diminished in the course of the 1930's and 1940's. James Q. Wilson, a professor of government at Harvard, has noted the stages by which, for example, the treatment of violence as an element in American politics steadily decreased in successive editions of V. O. Key's textbook on American politics that appeared during the latter part of this period. It may be that depression at home and then war abroad combined to restrict opportunity or impulse. In any event, there was a lull, and in consequence all the more alarm when violence reappeared in the mid-1960's. But it was only that: a reappearance, not a beginning.

Yet with all this it is necessary to acknowledge a transformation howsoever subtle and tentative. The tempo of violence seems to have speeded up, the result, more or less direct, of change in the technology of communications, which now communicate not simply the fact but also the spirit of violent events, and do so instantaneously. More ominously, there appears to have been a legitimation of violence, and

Four Detroit policemen drag a handcuffed man during the riot of July 24, 1967.

a spread of its ethos to levels of society that have traditionally seen themselves, and have been, the repositories of stability and respect for, insistence upon, due process. It is one thing to loot clothing stores —Brooks Brothers was hit in 1863—to fight with the police, to seize sections of the city and hold out against them. It is another thing to seize university libraries, and that is very much part of the violence of our time, a violence that arises not only among the poor and disinherited, but also among the well-to-do and privileged, with the special fact that those elements in society which normally set standards of conduct for the society as a whole have been peculiarly unwilling, even unable, to protest the massive disorders of recent times.

A second theme is migration. The American urban experience has been singular in the degree to which our cities, especially those of the North and East, have been inundated by successive waves of what might be called rural proletarians, a dispossessed peasantry moving— driven from—other people's land in the country to other people's tenements in the city. American cities have ever been filled with unfamiliar people, acting in unfamiliar ways, at once terrified and threatening. The great waves of Catholic Irish of the early nineteenth century began the modern phase of this process, and it has never entirely stopped, not so much culminating as manifesting itself at this time in the immense folk migration of the landless southern Negro to the northern slum. In small doses such migrations would probably have been easily enough absorbed, but the sheer mass of the successive migrations has been such as to dominate the life of the cities in their immediate aftermath. The most dramatic consequence was that popular government became immigrant government: in the course of the nineteenth century, great cities in America came to be ruled by men of the people, an event essentially without precedent in world history —and one typically deplored by those displaced from power in the course of the transformation. Let me cite to you, for example, a schoolboy exercise written in 1925 by a young Brahmin, the bearer of one of Boston's great names, on the theme "That there is no more sordid profession in the world than *Politics.*"

> The United States is one of the sad examples of the present form of government called democracy. We must first remember that America is made up of ignorant, uninterested, masses, of foreign people who follow the saying, "that the sheep are many but the shepards are few." And the shepards of our government are wolves in sheeps clothing. From Lincoln's Gettysburg address let me quote the familiar lines "a government of the people, for the people, and by the people." In the following lines I shall try and show you how much this is carried out in modern times.
>
> Let us take for example the position of our mayors. They are elected by majority vote from the population in which they live. Let us take for a case Mayor Curley of Boston. He tells the Irish who make up the people of Boston that he will lower their taxes, he will make Boston the greatest city in America. He is elected by the Irish mainly because he is an Irishman. He is a remarkable politician: he surrounds himself by Irishmen, he bribes the Chief Justice of the court, and although we know that the taxes that we pay all find a way into his own pocket we cannot prove by justice that he is not a just and good mayor.

But such distaste was not wholly groundless. The migrant peasants did and do misbehave: as much by the standards of the countryside they leave behind, as of the urban world to which they come. The process of adapting to the city has involved great dislocations in personality and manners as well as in abode. From the first, the process we call urbanization, with no greater specificity than the ancient medical diagnosis of "bellyache" or "back pain," has involved a fairly high order of personal and social disorganization, almost always manifesting itself most visibly in a breakdown of social controls, beginning with the most fundamental of controls, those of family life. The Children's Aid Society of New York was founded in response to the appearance of this phenomenon among the immigrant Irish. Let me quote from their first annual report:

> It should be remembered, that there are no dangers to the value of property or to the permanency of our institutions, so great as those from the existence of such a class of vagabond, ignorant, ungoverned children. This "dangerous class" has not begun to show itself, as it will in eight or ten years, when these

boys and girls are matured. Those who were too negligent or too selfish to notice them as children, will be fully aware of them as men. They will vote. They will have the same rights as we our-selves, though they have grown up ignorant of moral principle, as any savage or Indian. They will poison society. They will perhaps be embittered at the wealth, and the luxuries, they never share. *Then let society beware, when the outcast, vicious, reckless multitude of New York boys, swarming now in every foul alley and low street, come to know their power and* use *it!*

Mumford in his new book speaks of precisely the same phenomenon:

One of the most sinister features of the recent urban riots has been the presence of roaming bands of children, armed with bottles and stones, taunting and defying the police, smashing windows and looting stores. But this was only an intensification of the window-breakings, knifings, and murders that have for the past twenty years characterized "the spirit of youth in the city streets."

And note the continuity of his last phrase, which alludes, of course, to Jane Addams' book *The Spirit of Youth and the City Streets*, in which she describes just those conditions at the turn of the century in terms that William James declared "immortal" and which, we must allow, were hardly ephemeral.

Yet here, too, technology seems to have been playing us tricks, accentuating and exacerbating our recent experience. The newest migrants come upon an urban world that seems somehow to need them less, to find them even more disturbing and threatening, and to pro-vide them even less secure a place in the scheme of things than was ever quite the case with those who preceded them. I take this to be almost wholly a function of changing employment patterns consequent upon changing technology. But this very technology has also provided an abundance of material resources—and a measure of social con-science—so that people who are not especially needed are still provided for: by 1968, after seven years of unbroken economic ex-pansion, there were 800,000 persons living on welfare in New York City, with the number expected to reach 1,000,000 in 1969. In part this is a phenomenon of birth rates. One person in ten, but one baby in six today is Negro. The poor continue to get children, but those children no longer succumb to cholera, influenza, and tuberculosis. Thus progress more and more forces us to live with the consequences of social injustice. In a more brutal age the evidence soon disappeared!

A third theme of the American urban experience has been the great wealth of our cities. Those who have moved to them have almost in-variably improved their standard of life in the not-very-long run. Nor has this been wholly a matter of the consumption of goods and services. "City air makes men free," goes the medieval saying, and this has not been less true for industrial America. The matter was settled,

Urban traffic congestion has a long history.
This is New York's Fifth Avenue in 1921.

really, in an exchange between Hennessey and Dooley at the turn of the century. The country, said that faithful if not always perceptive patron, is where the good things in life come from. To which the master responded, "Yes, but it is the city that they go to." Technology is at the base of this process. The standard of life in American cities rises steadily, and there are few persons who do not somehow benefit. And yet this same technology—wealth—takes its toll. More and more we are conscious of the price paid for affluence in the form of manmade disease, uglification, and the second- and third-order effects of innovations which seem to cancel out the initial benefits.

Nathan Keyfitz, a sociologist at the University of Chicago, has nicely evoked the paradox implicit in many of the benefits of technology. Plenty encourages freedom. It also encourages density. Density can be managed only by regulation. Regulation discourages freedom. The experienced, conditioned city dweller learns, of course, to live with density by maintaining, as Keyfitz puts it, "those standards of reserve, discretion, and respect for the rights of others" that keep the nervous system from exhausting itself from the overstimulus available on any city street. The traditional assertion of Manhattan apartment dwellers that they have never met their neighbors across the hall is not a sign of social pathology: to the contrary, it is the exercise of exemplary habits of social hygiene. Borrowing the meter from George Canning's account of the failings of the Dutch, the rule for the modern cliff dweller might be put as follows:

> *In the matter of neighbors,*
> *The sound thing to do,*
> *Is nodding to many*
> *But speaking to few.*

It may be speculated, for example, that a clue to the transformation of the roistering, brawling, Merrie England of tradition into that somber land where strangers dare not speak to one another in trains lies *in the fact of the trains.* Technology—in this case the steam engine that created the vast nineteenth-century complexes of London and Manchester—brought about urban densities which required new forms of behavior for those who wished to take advantage of technology's advances and yet retain a measure of internal balance. The British, having been first to create the densities, were first to exhibit the telltale *sang-froid* of the modern urban dweller.

It may also be speculated that the "disorganized" life of the rural immigrants of today arises in some measure at least from an inability to control the level of stimulus: to turn down the radio, turn off the television, come in off the streets, stay out of the saloons, worry less about changing styles of clothes, music, dance, whatever. Lee Rainwater, a professor of sociology at the University of Washington, has provided us with painful accounts of the feeling of helplessness of the mothers of poor urban families in the face of the incursions from the street: the feeling, literally, that one cannot simply close one's door in the housing project and refuse to allow family, friends, neighbors, and God knows who else to come and go at will. This makes for lively neighborhoods, which from a distance seem almost enviable. But also for very disturbed people.

When such groups became large enough, when densities become ominous, government regulation becomes necessary, or at least all but invariably makes its appearance, so that even for the disciplined urbanite, technology at some point begins to diminish freedom. Keyfitz writes:

> George Orwell's *1984* is inconceivable without high population density, supplemented by closed circuit television and other devices to eliminate privacy. It exhibits in extreme form an historical process by which the State has been extending its power at the expense of the Church, the Family, and the Local Community, a process extending over 150 years.

There are few bargains in life, especially in city life.

A fourth theme of the American urban experience is mobility. Cities are not only places where the standards of life improve, but also very much—and as much now as ever—they are places where men rise in social standing. Otis Dudley Duncan and Peter M. Blau in their powerful study, *The American Occupational Structure*, have made this abundantly clear. American cities are places where men improve their position, as well as their condition. Or at least have every expectation that their sons will do so. The rigidities of caste and class dissolve, and opportunity opens. Yet this has never been quite so universally agreeable an experience as one could be led to suppose from the accounts of those for whom it has worked. In the city men first, perhaps, come to know success. There also men, especially those from the most caste-ridden rural societies, first come to know failure. It seems to me that this is a neglected aspect of the urban experience. I would argue that the rural peasant life of, let us say, the Irish, the Poles, the Slavs, the Italians, the Negro Americans who have migrated over the past century and a half was characterized by a near total absence of opportunity to improve one's position in the social strata, but also it was characterized by the near impossibility of observing others improve theirs. Rarely, in either absolute or relative terms, did individuals or families of the lowest peasant classes experience decline and failure: that in a sense is the law of a non-contingent society. Only with arrival in the city does that happen, and I would argue that for those who lose out in that competition, the experience can be far more embittering than that brought on by the drab constancy of country life.

Again technology—again television, for that matter—plays its part. Stephan Thernstrom in *Poverty and Progress* has noted that the immigrant workers of nineteenth-century New England, earning $1.50 a day when they had work, nonetheless managed in surprising numbers to put aside some money and to buy a piece of property and respectability before their lives were out, despite the fact that their incomes rarely permitted them to maintain what the social workers of the time calculated to be the minimum standard of living. The difference, Thernstrom notes, was that for the migrants a minimum standard of living was potatoes. Period. So long as they did not share the expectations of those about them—even the small expectations of social workers—they were not deprived. But advertising and television, and a dozen similar phenomena, have long since broken down that isolation, and the poor and newly arrived of the American city today appear to be caught up in a near frenzy of consumer emotions: untouched by the disenchantment with consumption of those very well off, and unrestrained by the discipline of household budgets imposed on those in between. The result, as best such matters can be measured, is a mounting level of discontent, which seems to slide over from the area of consumption as such to discontent with levels of social status that do not provide for maximum levels of consumption. Thus, even those who seem to be succeeding in the new urban world feel they are not succeeding enough, while others are suffused with a sense of failure.

A fifth theme of the American urban experience relates not to the experience of the poor and the newly arrived so much as to that of the well-to-do and the comparatively well settled: the persistent, one almost says primal, distaste for the city of educated Americans. In *The Intellectual Versus the City*, Morton and Lucia White point out that "enthusiasm for the American city has not been typical or predominant in our intellectual history. Fear has been the more common reaction." Fear, distaste, animosity, ambivalence. "In the beginning was the farm." or so the Jeffersonian creed asserts. And the great symbol —or perhaps *consummation* would be the better term—of this belief was the agreement whereby in return for the Jeffersonian willingness to have the federal government accept the debts acquired by states during the Revolutionary War, the capital of the new nation would be transferred from the city of New York to a swamp on the banks of the Potomac. Do not suppose that that agreement has not affected American history. New York remains the capital of the nation, as that term is usually understood, in the sense of the first city of the land. It is the capital of finance, art, theatre, publishing, fashion, intellect, industry . . . name any serious human endeavor other than politics, and its center in the United States will be found in New York City. In years of hard-fought presidential primaries, it is even for many purposes the political capital of the nation. But the seat of government is in Washington, which is only just beginning to respond to the fact that for half a century now ours has been a predominantly urban society.

Once again technology seems to be interacting with a pre-existing tendency. As the American city came more and more to be the abode of the machine, the alarm of American intellectuals, if anything, was intensified. And to a very considerable degree legitimated, for surely machines have given a measure of reality to alarums that were previously more fantasy than otherwise. To this has been added an ever more persistent concern for social justice, so that American intellectuals of the present time now conclude their expanding catalogues of the horrors of urban life with ringing assertions that the cities must be saved. But it is to be noted that this comes almost as an afterthought: the conviction that in the cities will be found the paramount threat to the life of the Republic has changed hardly at all. But at long last what they have been saying may be beginning to be true.

A sixth theme of the American urban experience, and the last with which I shall deal, has been and continues to be the singular ugliness of the average American city. That there are great and stunning exceptions is as much a matter of accident as anything. The essential fact is that for all the efforts to sustain and assert a measure of elite concern for urban aesthetics—of the kind one associates with historical preservation societies—and for all the occasional bursts of energy within the urban planning profession, the American city remains an ugly place to live, pretty much because we like it that way. A measure, no doubt, of this persisting condition can be attributed to the business and propertied interests of the nation that have resisted municipal expenditure, notably when it passed through the hands of egalitarian city halls. But it is more than that. Somehow, somewhere, in the course of the development of democratic, or demagogic, tradition in this nation the idea arose that concern for the physical beauty of the public buildings and spaces of the city was the mark of —what?—crypto-deviationist antipeople monumentalism—and in any event an augury of defeat at the polls. The result has been a steady deterioration in the quality of public buildings and spaces, and with it a decline in the symbols of public unity and common purpose with which the citizen can identify, of which he can be proud, and by which he can know what he shares with his fellow citizens. For the past seven years, as an example, I have been involved with efforts to reconstruct the center of the city of Washington, an attempt that begins with the assertion of the validity and viability of L'Enfant's plan of the late eighteenth century. In this effort we have had the tolerant to grudging co-operation of a fairly wide range of public and private persons, but let me say that we have had at no time the enthusiasm of any. And now I fear we may have even less, since of late there has arisen the further belief that to expend resources on public amenities is in effect to divert them from needed areas of public welfare. The very persons who will be the first to demand increased expenditures for one or another form of social welfare will be the last to concede that the common good requires an uncommon standard of taste and expenditure for the physical appointments of government and the public places of the city.

This attitude was perhaps unintentionally evoked by the respected Episcopal bishop of New York who in 1967 announced that in view of the circumstances of the poor of the city he would not proceed with the completion of the Cathedral of St. John the Divine, the largest such building ever begun, situated on a magnificent site overlooking the flat expanse of Harlem. Why? Meaning no disrespect, is it the plan of the church to liquidate its assets and turn them over to the poor? How much would that come to per head? But even so, would not the completed cathedral be an asset? If men need work, could they not be given jobs in its construction? The French—*toujours gai*, as mehitabel would have it—built Sacre Coeur as an act of penance for the excesses of the Commune. Could not the Episcopalians build St. John the Divine—a perfect symbol of rebirth—as a gesture of penance for all that Brahmin disdain which, in one form or another, to use Max Ways's phrase, taught us to despise our cities until they became despicable? If the phenomenon of ugliness, the last of my urban themes, can be thought to have arisen from more or less abstract qualities of American society, in the present and foreseeable future its principal cause is visible, concrete, and ubiquitous, which is to say it is the automobile. More than any other single factor it is the automobile that has wrecked the twentieth-century American city, dissipating its strength, destroying its form, fragmenting its life. So pervasive is the influence of the automobile that it is possible almost not to notice it at all. Indeed, it is almost out of fashion to do so: the men who first sought to warn us have almost ceased trying, while those who might have followed have sought instead formulations of their own, and in that manner diverted attention from the essential fact that in the age of the automobile cities, which had been places for coming together, have increasingly become machines for moving apart, devices whereby men are increasingly insulated and isolated one from the other.

A coda of sorts that has persisted through the elaboration of the themes of this paper has been the recent role of technology in accentuating and in a sense exacerbating long-established tendencies. The

impact of technology on human society—on all forms of life—is the
pre-eminent experience of the modern age, and obviously of the city
as well. But only of late, one feels, has any very considerable appreciation developed that a change in quantity becomes after a point a
change in quality, so that a society that begins by using technology
can end by being used by it, and in the process, somehow, lose such
control of its destiny as past human societies can be said to have had.
Technology being so outwardly rational, it has been assumed by many
that those who have been concerned about its directions have not
really understood it. People easily come to fear what they do not
understand, and it has been suspected, not always without foundation,
that a certain amount of criticism of technology has been a latter-day
form of rick burning.

One begins to think that this may not be so. Take the family automobile: a simple, easily enough comprehended (or seemingly so), un-
threatening, and convenient product of folk technology rather than
of modern science. Who would imagine any great harm coming from
the automobile? Yet consider a moment. With its advent, everyday
citizens, for the first time in human history, came into possession of
unexampled physical energy: the powers of the gods themselves became commonplace. And from the very outset, violence ensued. It
is said, for example, that when there were only four gasoline-powered
vehicles in Missouri, two of them were in St. Louis and managed to
collide with such impact as to injure both drivers, one seriously. Thus
was introduced a form of pathology that was to grow steadily from
that year to this. Today, something between one quarter and two thirds
of the automobiles manufactured in the United States end up with
blood on them. Indeed so commonplace and predictable have collisions
become that the U.S. Court of Appeals for the Eighth Circuit recently ruled that a crash must be considered among the "intended
uses" of a motor vehicle, and the manufacturers accordingly responsible to provide for such contingency in their design.

It becomes increasingly clear that the major environment, or, if
you will, vehicle, in which incidents of uncontrolled episodic violence
occur within the population is that of the automobile. Whether access
and exposure to this environment have increased the incidence of such
episodes, or whether the urban environment now largely created and
shaped by the automobile has generally increased the violence level
is uncertain at best (there has, of course, been a great decline in
violence directed toward animals), but with the number of deaths and
injuries at the present ongoing rates, and the number of vehicles in
use approaching the one-hundred-million mark, it is a matter worth
pondering.

Crashes are but one form of pathology. Each year in the United
States automobiles pour eighty-six million tons of carbon monoxide,
oxides of nitrogen and sulfur, hydrocarbons, lead compounds and
particulates into the air we breathe. Recently my younger son came
home with a button that announced, "Clean air smells funny." Dr.
Clare C. Patterson of the California Institute of Technology put it

another way in testimony before a congressional committee: "The average resident of the United States is being subject to severe chronic lead insult," originating in lead tetraethyl. Such poisoning can lead to severe intellectual disability in children: so much that Patterson feels it is dangerous for youth to live long periods of time near freeways.

But that is only the beginning, hardly the end of the impact of this particular form of technology on the society at this time. In consequence of the management of the automobile traffic system by means of traditional rules of the road, the incidence of armed arrest of American citizens is the highest of any civilization in recorded history. In 1965, for example, the California highway patrol alone made one million arrests. Indeed so commonplace has the experience become that a misdemeanor or felony committed in a motor vehicle is no longer considered a transgression of any particular consequence, and to be arrested by an armed police officer is regarded as a commonplace. That is precisely what Orwell told us would happen, is it not?

There are some 13,600,000 accidents a year, with some thirty million citations for violations issued each twelve months. And at this point, ineluctably, technology begins to have an effect on the most fundamental of civil institutions, the legal system itself. Largely in consequence of the impact of traffic-crash litigation, it now takes an average of 32.4 months to obtain a civil jury trial for a personal injury case in the metropolitan areas of the nation. In Suffolk County, New York, it is 50 months. In the Circuit Court of Cook County, serving Chicago, it is 64 months. This past winter in Bronx County, New York, the presiding judge of the appellate division announced he was suspending civil trials altogether while he tried to catch up with criminal cases. The courts are inundated; the bar is caught up, implicated and confused; the public knows simply that somehow justice is delayed and delayed. All of which is a consequence of this simplest form of technology, working its way on the institutions of an essentially pretechnological society.

It sometimes happens that a work of art appearing at a particular moment in time somehow simultaneously epitomizes and reveals the essential truths of the time. In a most astonishing and compelling way this has happened for the American city, and it has done so, most appropriately, on Forty-second Street in Manhattan, in the persona of the Ford Foundation headquarters, designed by Kevin Roche, John Dinkeloo & Associates—a great firm, successor to Eero Saarinen & Associates whose first large commission was, of course, the General Motors Technical Center outside Detroit. Saarinen, and now Roche, have gathered a group of artist/technicians whose work, from the Dulles Airport at Chantilly, Virginia, to the Trans World Airlines Terminal at Kennedy Airport and the Columbia Broadcasting headquarters in New York City, has evoked the power and purpose of the age of technology as perhaps no other organization has.

Here in the Ford Foundation headquarters is expressed the very highest purposes of modern technological power: compassionate and

potent concern for the betterment of man's lot. The building is everything a building could be: a splendid work place, a gift to the city in
the form of a public park, a gift to the world simply as a work of
imagination and daring. If it is a reproach of sorts to the public and
private builders of the nation who by and large show little of either,
it is a gentle reproach, more show than tell. In that favored form of
foundation giving, it is a kind of demonstration project: an example
of what can, and what therefore in an age of technology must, be
done.

The exterior of the building is quiet and unassertive: it is not *that*
big a building, and it seeks rather to understate both its size and importance. No-nonsense shafts of Cor-ten steel rise from the ground,
here and there sheathed with a blue-brown granite and interspersed
with large rectangular glass panels. Rather in the mode of a cathedral,
the portals do not so much impart as suggest the experience to come.
It is only on entering—Chartres, say, or Vézelay—and encountering
the incomparable space, shaped and reserved for a single purpose only,
that one leaves off observing the building and begins to be shaped
by it: the eye rises, the mind turns to last things. So with the Ford
Foundation headquarters. One passes through revolving doors to enter
a garden. Truly a garden, a small park, like nothing anywhere else
to be encountered, a third of an acre, lush and generous, climbing a
small hill that follows the terrain of Manhattan at this point, illu-
minated by the now vast windows that climb nine stories toward
heaven itself, and there only to be met by a glass roof. Water moves
slightly in a pool—a font? Attendants move quietly, and are helpful.
One notices that vegetation sprouts from beams and ledges on the
third and fourth and even the fifth floors. One is awestruck by the
wealth and power of the foundation, and the sheer authority of its
intent to do good. Only the gray-white light is not quite what it should
be: as in those French and German cathedrals whose stained glass
was lost to war or revolution or Protestantism.

But this is only the entering light. As in any such edifice, there is
a light within. In this case a very monstrancelike golden-brown glow
that shines forth from the offices of the foundation executives, who
from the floor of the park are to be seen at their work behind glass
panels formed and reticulated by the same rusted beams that frame
the colorless glass of two sides of the building. (Cor-ten steel seals
itself by rusting and need not be painted.) At this point one perceives
readily enough that the building has been built as a factory. Not
precisely as a factory—any more than the Gothic Revival built office
buildings precisely as medieval monasteries—but rather to evoke the
style and somehow the spirit of a great plant. The huge, heavy lateral
beams, from which elsewhere would be suspended the giant hoists that
roam back and forth amidst the clatter and roar; the sawtooth roof;
the plant managers' eyrie hung from the ceiling, keeping an eye on
everything; the perfectly standardized, interchangeable fixtures in
each office; the seriousness and competence of it all, even the blue-
black, somehow oily granite of the cheerless rest rooms (No Loitering

*The Ford Foundation building
at night, as seen from
New York's 42nd Street.*

in the Can) magically, stunningly, triumphantly, evoke the style and
spirit of the primeval capitalist factory. Cor-ten. Red. Rouge. River
Rouge. Of course! And why not, for $16,000,000 of Henry Ford's
money? He was that kind of man. Knew how to make automobiles and
obviously liked to. Else he could hardly have done it so well. All black,
just as the Ford Foundation headquarters is all brown. Same principle.
So also the panopticon effect of the exposed offices wherein the pre-
sumptively interchangeable officers at their perfectly interchangeable
desks labor at their good works in full view of management and
public alike. (The public serving, perhaps, as the visitors to Jeremy
Bentham's prospective model prison: a "promiscuous assemblage of
unknown and therefore unpaid, ungarbled and incorruptible inspectors"?) Critics, at least in the first reviews, seem to have missed
most of this, but no matter: the architecture needs no guidebook: the
intellectual and aesthetic effect is not to be avoided, even when the
intent is least perceived. All in all it is just as McGeorge Bundy proclaimed it in the 1968 annual report of the foundation: "Kevin
Roche's triumph."

But it is more than that. Or rather, there is more than is to be
perceived at one time. A great work of art has levels of meaning at
once various and varying. Standing in the park, gazing upward, following the factory motif, the mind is of a sudden troubled. Something
is missing. Noise. Factories are places of noise. Of life. Clatter. Roar.

A daytime view, looking out from the two-hundred-foot-square interior garden.

There is no noise here. Only quiet. The quiet of the . . .? The mind oscillates. It is a factory, all right. But a *ruined* factory! The holocaust has come and gone: hence the silence. The windows have blown out, and only the gray light of the burned-out world enters. The weather has got in, and with it nature now reclaiming the ravaged union of fire and earth. The factory floor has already begun to turn to forest. Vegetation has made its way to ledges halfway up the interior. The machine tools are gone. Reparations? Vandalism? Who knows. But the big machines will no longer be making little machines. Gone too is the rational, reforming, not altogether disinterested purpose of the panopticon. One is alone in the ominous gloom of a Piranesi prison, noting the small bushes taking hold in the crevices of the vast ruined arches.

Is it the past or the future that has taken hold of the mind? Certainly the ruined steel frame is a good enough symbol of the twentieth century so far. (Where had one last seen that color? Of course. Pingree Street in Detroit after the riot. A year later there it was again, on Fourteenth Street in Washington: the fiery orange-red of the twisted steel shopping centers' framing after the looting and arson has passed.) Or is it the future? There is a *sur réal* quality that comes of standing in the ruined half of the building, watching the life going on behind the glass walls of the intact half, seemingly oblivious to the devastation without. Can ruin advance slowly like rot? No. Yes. Did the automobile start all this? No. Surely it is all this that started automobiles. One quarter to two thirds of which end up with blood on them. Blood. Red. Rouge. River Rouge.

Enough.

But then why has the American architect Joseph Stein built the Ford Foundation headquarters in New Delhi immediately adjacent the Lodi Tombs, symbols of death sensual to the point of necrophilia? Did not Bentham remark that he could legislate wisely for all India from the recesses of his study? There's a panopticon in your future.

No. Enough.

And yet it comes together in a way. "*Le siècle de la machine,*" Le Corbusier wrote in 1924, "*a réveillé l'architecte.*" Not least because the machine destroys so much of that experience of community that the architect seeks to create. A biographer describes Eero Saarinen's purpose thus: "What . . . [he] wished to renew, maintain, and improve was the organic expression of the *civitas* which he found weakened or destroyed virtually everywhere in modern civilization, with one significant exception—the university campus." And so Roche built a ruined machine-for-making-machines as the headquarters of a great philanthropic foundation whose principal concerns have been to support the universities of the nation, and to seek to strengthen the community life of its cities.

The research of James Q. Wilson and Edward C. Banfield at Harvard University is now beginning to produce results surprisingly similar to the visions of the architect/artist. As Wilson puts it, "After a decade or more of being told by various leaders that what's wrong with our large cities is inadequate transportation, or declining retail sales, or poor housing, the resident of the big city is beginning to assert his own definition of that problem—and this definition has very little to do with the conventional wisdom on the urban crisis." Wilson and his colleague asked one thousand Boston homeowners what *they* thought to be the biggest urban problem of this time.

> The "conventional" urban problems—housing, transportation, pollution, urban renewal, and the like—were a major concern of only 18 per cent of those questioned, and these were expressed disproportionally by the wealthier, better-educated respondents. Only 9 per cent mentioned jobs and employment, even though many of those interviewed had incomes at or even below what is often regarded as the poverty level. *The issue which concerned more respondents than any other was variously stated—crime, violence, rebellious youth, racial tension, public immorality, delinquency. However stated, the common theme seemed to be a concern for improper behavior in public places.*
>
> What these concerns have in common, and thus what constitutes the "urban" problem for a large percentage (perhaps a majority) of urban citizens, is *a sense of the failure of community.*

And yet cities, by definition, destroy community. Or is it only when they are too big, too unsettled, that they do this? Is it only when social conditions are allowed to arise which lead inevitably to assaults on the private communities that experienced city dwellers create for themselves, which in turn lead to more collective regulation and, in consequence, less of the self-imposed decision to behave properly and as expected, which is the essence of community?

We do not know. "Them what gets the apple gets the worm," goes an old folk saying. Is that what the Ford Foundation building represents: a shining exterior, rotting from within? A civilization whose cancerous growth has already devoured half its offspring, and is moving toward the unthinking, untroubled other half? We shall see. Hopefully, in the meantime we shall also think about it a bit. Mumford, unfailingly, has sorted out the levels of immediacy and difficulty of the current crisis.

> To go deeper into this immediate situation we must, I suggest, distinguish between three aspects, only one of which is open to immediate rectification. We must first separate out the problems that are soluble with the means we have at hand: this includes such immediate measures as vermin control, improved garbage collection, cheap public transportation, new schools and hospitals and health clinics. Second, those that require a new approach, new agencies, new methods, whose assemblage will require time, even though the earliest possible action is urgent. And finally there are those that require a reorientation in the purposes and ultimate ideals of our whole civilization—solutions that hinge on a change of mind, as far-reaching as that which characterized the change from the medieval religious mind to the modern scientific mind. Ultimately, the success of the first two changes will hinge upon this larger—and, necessarily, later —transformation. So, far from looking to a scientifically oriented technology to solve our problems, we must realize that this highly sophisticated dehumanized technology itself now produces some of our most vexatious problems, including the unemployment of the unskilled.

But something more than thinking will be required. A certain giving of ourselves with no certainty of what will come of it. It is the only known way, and imperfectly known at that.

Attend to Mrs. Boyle at the end of *Juno and the Paycock*, pleading for the return of a simpler life, a life before all things had become political, before all men were committed, before all cities somehow seemed in flames:

> Sacred Heart o' Jesus, take away our hearts o' stone, and give us hearts o' flesh! Take away this murdherin' hate, an' give us Thine own eternal love!

Richard Rhodes

THE AMERICAN FARM: CHANGE AND REVOLUTION

We think of our century as preeminently an industrial age and
the United States as the world's leading producer of manufactured
goods. Steadily, almost since the birth of the Republic, a shrinking
proportion of the American people have been engaged in farming,
and in recent decades the actual number of farmers has declined
precipitously. Yet agricultural output has soared since 1945,
and the United States is still by far the most important producer
of food on earth.

How farming has changed in the lifetime of one person of our
day is the subject of Richard Rhodes' essay. In part the essay
is more autobiography than history, for Rhodes has
participated in some of the changes he describes. Yet he has
drawn upon much more than his own experience, and thus his
work is clearly within the historical genre. Rhodes is the author
of *The Inland Ground: An Evocation of the American Middle West.*

The fences have come down all across Missouri. Fields in Iowa are no longer necessarily rectangular; within their Jeffersonian boundaries, many follow the lay of the land. In flat western Kansas they are often circular to accommodate the center-pivot self-propelled pipes that irrigate them. Where cotton reigned in the South, cattle now are fed, and soybeans, which once were spurned as useless everywhere in rural America or were plowed under for green manure, darken the fields of summer. Corn, wheat, cattle, and hogs change shape and variety, go hybrid with vigor; lamb is scarce as lobster; poultry are hardly farmed any more—one might say they are factoried.

In the nearly two decades since I marked the beginning of adolescence by moving from Kansas City streets to a Missouri farm, American farming has changed radically and permanently. It has not been swallowed by corporations, has not become "agribusiness," not yet—the overwhelming majority of profitable farms today are father-son operations, father-son partnerships, or family corporations—but it has become lean and specialized, capital-intensive and cost-effective, the work of fewer men and women than ever before, the work of systems increasingly scientific and of massive machines. And proudly, without exaggeration, the wonder of the world, a blessing we need not blush to count. "Over the past 200 years," wrote Earl O. Hardy, Curtiss Distinguished Professor at Iowa State University, in a special food and agriculture edition of *Scientific American* in 1976, "the U.S. has had the best, the most logical and the most successful program of agricultural development anywhere in the world."

The farm where I moved when I was twelve, 360 rich acres outside Independence, Missouri, was also a boys' home. A pioneer cattleman and banker named Andrew Drumm, who drove hogs across the Central Valley of California to feed the miners of the Gold Rush and who ranched his way to wealth in the Cherokee Strip, established it in his will. He meant for boys who needed a home to work their way through school and he intended those boys to know intimately the sources of the food and fiber that sustained their civilization. The Drumm Institute for Boys was a thriving, diversified farm when I arrived there in the summer of 1949. With forty boys to preserve from mischievous leisure, it was also deliberately labor-intensive, and therefore persistent with practices already becoming antique. Our chickens never left the chicken house, for example, and that was technology avant-garde in 1949; but we milked our cows by hand, having so many hands available, and with oak-handled, copper-plated hoes we hoed our field crops as few farmers any longer could afford to do. So Drumm's practices were modern, but its technology was not, and I take it now as a model, somewhat enlarged, for the old family farm, a model against which to compare the high technologies of today. . . . Changes were coming even to boy-powered Drumm. I left for college then, about the time someone discovered that soybeans were a mighty crop, worth something more than plowing under to fertilize the corn. I remember farming as romantic, and to a former city boy it was, but it was also hard, hot work.

The Drumm Institute is surrounded by suburbs now, and not much farming gets done there any more, but farming has changed everywhere in America. It has changed in response to economic necessity. That "most successful program of agricultural development" that Heady refers to has been a program, a long-standing government policy, of government-supported overproduction. Overproduction has meant that supply has frequently exceeded demand, and the results of that imbalance have been cheap food for American consumers and marginal profits for farmers. In 1971, before inflation boosted the figure, Americans spent only an average 15.7 per cent of their disposable income for food. Compare the U.S.S.R. at 30.0 per cent, Europe at 26.0 per cent, the developing countries at 65.0 per cent. Somehow, in the public mind, however, the cheap food never reaches the supermarket, and farmers are forever defending themselves against charges of profiteering. Retail food prices are high because the cost of processing raw farm products is high, not because the farmers of America are getting rich. They aren't: profits from farming over the long haul have averaged no more than three or four per cent, which is why corporate farming hasn't dominated agriculture in the United States except in certain specialized industries such as citrus fruits and broiler and egg production.

Low and frequently nonexistent profits and the rising cost of labor demanded increased efficiency and increased productivity of American farmers. With the help of intense scientific research—a legacy of the land-grant college system established after the Civil War—they delivered both. The number of farms has declined; their average size has gone up. The United States had 6,400,000 farms in 1920. By the mid-1970's only 2,800,000 were left. Between 1959 and 1974 the average acreage per farm increased from 288 to 385, and the most successful farms were far larger; today, in the Midwestern corn belt, one man, alone with his machinery, may farm 600 to 800 acres.

A million workers left the farm for the city between 1950 and 1955. Machinery took their place. To get maximum return for his machinery investment, a farmer had to farm more land. In the mid-1960's the average investment per farm in land and equipment was $55,300. By the mid-1970's that investment had swollen to $148,600. Few could afford to enter farming—if you have $150,000 to invest, why invest it in sixteen-hour days for a profit of four per cent?—which is why so many profitable farms today are operated by fathers and sons.

But without increased productivity, farm expansion would have been disastrous. In this case, productivity can be taken literally: the farmer farmed more acres, but he also found ways to get more production from every acre he farmed. Herbicides largely replaced mechanical cultivation, and that kept down labor costs, but because herbicides reduced weed competition, they also increased yield. The same was true of pesticides. In neither case was the farmer simple-mindedly enamored of chemicals, a tool of the diabolical oil interests. He was trying to get the job done and still make a living. Fertilizer increased productivity more directly by increasing yield, and between 1950 and 1972, fertilizer use in the United States expanded by 276 per cent.

Increased agricultural productivity has taken many forms, not all of them petrochemical. Hybridization has been among the most important. As far back as the 1930's, American agricultural scientists were aware that crossbreeding two distantly related strains of animal or plant resulted in a phenomenon they called heterosis and farmers called hybrid vigor. Distant crosses suppressed undesirable genetic recessives; hybrids were stronger than their parents, grew faster, were more resistant to disease. Hybridization alone can add 10 to 15 per cent to the growth rate of cattle. Properly fertilized and cultivated, hybrid corn can yield one hundred bushels or more to the acre compared to its parents' thirty-five or fifty. Hybrid corn and hybrid soybeans now dominate the corn belt, and after years of difficult research, hybrid wheat today begins to come on line. The cattle industry, traditionally the most conservative sector of agriculture, resisted hybridization until the late 1960's. Then a few entrepreneurs began importing the semen of ''exotic'' European breeds of cattle—animals themselves were barred because of the relentless U.S. quarantine of animals from countries that harbored hoof-and-mouth disease—and breeding up purebred exotics for crossing with Herefords and Aberdeen Angus, the most populous American breeds. The Charolais came from France, the Chianina from Italy, the Simmental from Switzerland. All the exotics were large dual-purpose breeds the Europeans had developed for milk and work as well as for beef, and they added growth and feed-conversion efficiency and sheer size—longer rib-eyes, as the exotic breeders like to say—to domestic breeds short on milk and stunted by years of breeding small. A purebred Hereford calf may weigh sixty pounds at birth; a Hereford-Simmental calf is likely to weigh ninety or ninety-five. Other factors being equal, the Hereford calf won't ever catch up. Eventually hybrid crosses will dominate the cattle industry as they already dominate the grain, poultry, and swine industries.

All these changes have altered the *look* of farming, though the difference may not be obvious from the road. Diversified farming, the kind of farming we practiced at Drumm, is a thing of the past. A wheat farmer in eastern Kansas grows two crops, wheat and soybeans, planting the soybeans after he harvests his wheat in June. He buys his meat and milk and eggs and vegetables at the supermarket, as you and I do, and probably lives in an air-conditioned house (tractors and combines also come with air conditioning, as well as with heaters, eight-track stereos, and two-way or CB radios). In western Kansas, where the rainfall is sparse enough to require fallowing the wheat fields in alternate years to allow the underground water to build up, he may have converted from wheat farming to growing irrigated soybeans by drilling a well and investing in a center-pivot irrigation system. You can see such fields while flying west to California, great circles of green on the brown buffalo plains, and won't see them again this

side of the Middle East, the only other place where they have so far been installed.

An Iowa farmer may plant corn and soybeans, but he almost certainly runs no cattle or hogs. Farming today is specialized. Its technology requires it; the farmer's heavy investment in machinery requires it; maximum productivity requires it; fixed costs and narrow profits require it. Where corn grows best, corn is grown; where wheat grows best (or rather, where nothing else survives without irrigation), wheat is grown. There are a few counties in Iowa devoted almost exclusively to popcorn, which is why, in grain country, with no animals to confine, so many of the fences are down.

The raising of animals has changed even more dramatically than the cultivation of grains. Here the change is evident and radical: more slowly in some industries, more rapidly in others, all the animals are being moved indoors for all or part of their life cycles. The production of broilers, which is to say the production of young chickens destined for the frying pan, has become a factory operation. With automated

(Left) A modern, air-conditioned tractor. Tractors are no longer designed just to do the job, comfort for the operator is a feature.

(Below) A chicken factory. In today's broiler housing the environment is closely regulated by controlled use of heat and ventilation, along with automated systems for feeding and watering.

air-exchange systems, automated water supplies, automated food supplies, and automated waste disposal, one man now raises seventy-five
thousand birds from delivery at one day of age to slaughter at eight
weeks. I raised broilers indoors at Drumm for a 4-H project; even
with antibiotic feed it took me nine weeks to get them to weight in 1954.
A poultry "farmer" no longer needs a farm. He needs a building, a
feed mixer or a loading dock, a sewage aeration system and adjacent
lagoon, and crucially, a back-up power supply. If his operation is
large enough, he also needs a slaughter-house.

Domestic animals were seldom treated as pets on the old family
farms, since sooner or later they would be killed and eaten; increasingly
today they are being treated as biochemical factories, fed scientifically
balanced diets mixed with vitamins and antibiotics, confined in moni-
tored housing to direct all their energy to growth, killed younger, and
packaged in close proximity to the farm. The packing houses in Kansas
City and Omaha and Chicago have all but closed down. There are
cattlemen in Kansas who not only run breeding herds but fatten the
calves in enormous feed lots, slaughter them, and ship from their
ranches the sorted, graded, retail cuts of meat that the cattle industry
calls "boxed beef." Why, after all, ship waste on expensive lines of
transportation?

Devotees of organic food and others abhor these high-pressure
efficiencies and, because of pesticides and the injection of hormones,
fear for human health, and those of us who remember home-grown
vegetables and meat notice the decline of flavor, not to say of taste. So
much criticism has been leveled against the practices of modern farming that it seems fair to present here the opposite side of the argument.
Many such practices are indirectly the result of government policy
designed to hold down the cost of food, policy that has been remarkably
successful in the United States: chicken may be bland, but it's also the
best bargain in town, and to ask for a return to the twelve-week, yard-
scratching, worm-fattened chicken of yesteryear is at least romantic. . . . Eggs are often tasteless, beef too soft (but much leaner than
it used to be, as is pork), milk and butter as good or better than they
once were—but you know the litany. American consumers might be
better served by a two-tiered agricultural economy, one that supplied
high-priced, organic, old-fashioned vegetables and meats to those who
are willing to pay the difference and mass-produced foods to those who
can't or won't. Something like that seems to be happening to the
market, at least in large cities: Kansas City, where I live, has more
than one organic supermarket, and gourmet frozen foods in nearly
every store. To paraphrase the slogan of the A & P ("Price and
Pride"), it's a question of price *versus* pride. What it *isn't* is a conspiracy to deprive the American people of nutritious food. It's a
pocketbook issue, for the farmer as well as for the consumer, and one
notes that half the beef slaughtered in the United States now goes to
hamburger, and a major portion of the chicken to chicken pies and
the boxes and buckets of the Colonel and his imitators.

I saw the future of what my vocational-agriculture instructor called "animal husbandry" at the Farmland Industries Demonstration Farm south of Leavenworth, Kansas. There, not only laying hens but also hogs and dairy cattle are confined indoors, and beef cattle in sheltered concrete lots. The confinement of dairy cattle intrigued me, because herding the cows in from pasture was one of my duties at Drumm. Farmland's research animals, big raw-boned Guernseys, never leave the barn and its attached open-air lot. A manager feeds them hay and a diet of grain and protein pellets; their energy goes to milk production, not to grazing, and they produce more milk than ordinary cows. At a spotless milking station, the milk flows through glass tubing into a stainless-steel cooler, later to be pumped untouched into a refrigerated truck for delivery to the dairy. There was nothing surreal about the dairy barn; it even boasted the obligatory cat, black with white paws.

Hog production at Farmland is even more automated. Sows farrow indoors in pens too narrow to allow them to turn around, which helps prevent them from stepping on their pigs. At weaning, the pigs go into a special building where they feed *ad lib* on a diet of protein pellets. The floor of their pen is assembled from metal slats; below the floor aerated water flows through a wide trough, liquefying and oxygenating their manure; beyond the building is a sewage lagoon. Sewage disposal is a major expense of livestock production today. At

A modern milking station. The cows are being attached to the milking machines.

Drumm we walked the pasture watching where we set down our feet, a habit I still haven't shaken.

Barrows—castrated males—go to another building, similarly arranged, for fattening. Gilts—female pigs—go to indoor pens for eventual breeding. The boar lives there too, in a pen of his own, his presence and his odors stimulating the gilts to sexual maturity. The gilts are sorted by size to reduce dominance battles. They are fed fully, but only once a day; their hunger, and subsequent activity, gives them squealing exercise. They eat not in a common trough, as has been the usual lot of swine, but in individual stalls, to assure that each gets her full ration of feed. They are bred by artificial insemination, but not with frozen semen. Boar semen, I am told, doesn't freeze very well.

The farmers I know aren't much different from the farmers I knew when I was a child. They are better educated, they are more professional, they are more efficient, and of course they produce more food. They are still, most of them, hard-working, and individualistic, and down to earth. One elderly acquaintance, a wheat farmer in central Kansas, farms more than two thousand acres with the help of his two partner-sons. He's built a new brick house, suburban and air conditioned, across the yard from the old white frame house he once occupied—it now serves as bunkhouse for the summer hired men; and massive white tanks for storing the pressure-liquefied fertilizing gas called anhydrous ammonia line his lane. He uses older combines because, he says, it takes several years to get to know all their chains and gears and lubrication points, to break them in as once he broke in horses. Two thousand acres is a monumental load of wheat—at, say, thirty-five bushels to the acre, that's seventy thousand bushels to combine and truck and dry and store—and when it's ripe it has to be combined out within two weeks, because rain won't hold off longer than that, and rain will ruin the grain. Those two weeks are bone-grinding, eighteen-hour days. My friend's wife drives out to the field twice a day with a church supper of meats and salads and casseroles laid on in the capacious trunk of her Cadillac, and father and sons and hired help chow down in shifts. They truck the wheat in to a five-binned, three-storied complex of storage buildings near the family house, test its moisture content, augur it into the bins, and dry it to quality. Then it is trucked on to town, or stored at home, depending on the fluctuations of the market. In the winter, man and wife take cruises, visit Japan, or fly around the world.

A farmer I met in southeastern Nebraska, a young man of thirty-two, works eight hundred acres on his own, with occasional help from his father. His land is scattered across the county, forty acres here, eighty acres there, and one man couldn't farm it if tractors hadn't been designed with higher road speeds. Our tractors at Drumm, in what we called "road gear," could muster fifteen miles an hour on the straightaway; his roars by at twenty-five. He grows corn and soybeans; he works long days; he lives in an old farmhouse with his wife and two children; and despite his heavy investment in land and equipment, amounting to several hundred thousand dollars, he earned only six thousand dollars last year, and that only by not counting the value of his labor. He and his local bank are old friends; he'd like to farm more acres and increase his income, but even with heavy machinery to help him, it isn't physically possible, and hired hands are scarce as hen's teeth so close to Omaha.

A southern-Kansas farmer and rancher illustrates another extreme of modern farming. His father was so cash poor that he never in his life paid any income tax, and when the rancher started out on his own, he wasn't, at first, much better off. He heard somewhere that New York florists craved a certain kind of New Mexican wood for ''driftwood'' arrangements, and for years, whenever he was short on cash, he would drive his pickup truck down to New Mexico, gather a load of the wood, haul it to Manhattan's wholesale florist district, and sell it out of the back of his truck. In the meantime he was building a purebred breeding herd of white French Charolais cattle, the first of the profitable new breeds of exotic cattle to reach the United States in any numbers in the late 1960's. Then some Canadian ranchers began importing the Swiss Simmental, and the rancher went into Simmental trading on the side. At one time or another, in the early 1970's, more than twenty-five thousand head of Simmental passed through his ranch, animals worth, in the inflated market of those best years in the history of American farming, anywhere from two to twenty-five thousand dollars apiece. Now the rancher owns twelve hundred acres of good Kansas prairie, and spends his spare time wildcatting for oil. He is perhaps more entrepreneur than farmer; the business of breeding cattle has been so notoriously unprofitable since 1975 that only the entrepreneurs have survived.

I could mention other changes in farming: embryo transplantation, which transfers embryos from a prize cow to lesser common cows, who bear the genetically superior calves as their own, enabling the prize cow to produce as many as forty or fifty calves a year; fields arranged by watersheds with a distinctly European look; hens confined in crowded cages, their eggs rolling on conveyor belts into automatic crating machines; the search for a featherless chicken; the installation of irrigation systems, even in such relatively moist states as Missouri, to reduce the farmer's dependence on the vagaries of the weather; cattle and hog feed lots confining as many as a hundred thousand head; the possibility, still distant, that recombinant DNA research will create varieties of wheat and corn genetically transformed into legumes, producing their own nitrogen in nodules on their roots. Optimists may call such changes miracles, romantics may call them heartless and degenerate; they are stages in the evolution of American farming, and they promise the humane possibility of feeding a populous world.

Larry L. King

LYNDON B. JOHNSON AND VIETNAM

President Lyndon B. Johnson was the kind of politician people tend to tell tall stories about. He always had a strong—some would say an overpowering—personality. When he was placed by fate and an assassin's bullet in a position of enormous power, he came to project a larger-than-life image, to seem a kind of elemental, irresistible force that no mere mortal could successfully resist. He swiftly pushed through economic and social reforms that had appeared to paralyze his predecessor in the White House, the popular John F. Kennedy.

Although he could certainly be devious, Johnson was not a very subtle person and when, during the Vietnam war, he decided that the national honor and the safety of what he called the free world required that the United States pursue the conflict to victory, he devoted all his energies to the task. Of course he failed. Why he failed and how he reacted to failure is the subject of this article by Larry L. King. The account is one of the most graphic and tragic portraits we have of Johnson, or for that matter of any President. King is the author of a number of novels and also of *Confessions of a White Racist.* He was active in the 1960 and 1964 presidential campaigns and is currently working on a biography of President Johnson.

He was an old-fashioned man by the purest definition. Forget that he was enamored of twentieth-century artifacts—the telephone, television, supersonic airplanes, spacecraft—to which he adapted with a child's wondering glee. His values were the relics of an earlier time; he had been shaped by an America both rawer and more confident than it later would become; his generation may have been the last to believe that for every problem there existed a workable solution: that the ultimate answer, as in old-time mathematics texts, always reposed in the back of the book. He bought the prevailing American myths without closely inspecting the merchandise for rips or snares. He often said that Americans inherently were "can-do" people capable of accomplishing anything they willed; it was part of his creed that Americans were God's chosen: why otherwise would they have become the richest, the strongest, the freest people in the history of man? His was a God, perhaps, who was a first cousin to Darwin: Lyndon B. Johnson believed in survival of the fittest, that the strong would conquer the weak, that almost always the big 'uns ate the little 'uns.

There was a certain pragmatism in his beliefs, a touch of fatalism, even a measure of common sense. Yet, too, he could be wildly romantic. Johnson truly believed that any boy could rise to become President, though only thirty-five had. Hadn't he—a shirt-tailed kid from the dusty hard-scrabble precincts of the Texas outback—walked with kings and pharaohs while reigning over what he called, without blushing, the Free World? In his last days, though bitter and withering in retirement at his rural Elba, he astonished and puzzled a young black teen-ager by waving his arms in windmill motions and telling the youngster, during a random encounter, "Well, maybe someday all of us will be visiting *your* house in Waco, because you'll be President and your home will be a national museum just as mine is. It'll take a while, but it'll happen, you'll see. . . ." Then he turned to the black teen-ager's startled mother: "Now, you better get that home of yours cleaned up spick-and-span. There'll be hundreds of thousands coming through it, you know, wanting to see the bedroom and the kitchen and the living room. Now, I hope you get that dust rag of yours out the minute you get home."

Doris Kearns, the Harvard professor and latter-day L.B.J. confidante, who witnessed the performance, thought it to be a mock show: "almost a vaudeville act." Dr. Johnson peddling the same old snake oil. Perhaps. Whatever his motives that day, Lyndon Johnson chose his sermon from that text he most fervently believed throughout a lifetime; his catechism spoke to his heart of American opportunity, American responsibility, American good intentions, American superiority, American destiny, American infallibility. Despite a sly personal cynicism—a suspicion of others, the keen, cold eye of a man determined not to be victimized at the gaming tables—he was, in his institutional instincts, something of a Pollyanna. There *was* such a thing as a free lunch; there *was* a Santa Claus; there *was*, somewhere, a Good Fairy, and probably it was made up of the component parts of Franklin Roosevelt, Saint Francis, and Uncle Sam.

These thoroughly American traits—as L.B.J. saw them—comprised the foundation stone upon which he built his dream castle; he found it impossible to abandon them even as the sands shifted and bogged him in the quagmire of Vietnam. If America was so wonderful (and it *was;* he had the evidence of himself to prove it), then he had the obligation to export its goodness and greatness to the less fortunate. This he would accomplish at any cost, even if forced to "nail the coonskin to the wall." For if Lyndon B. Johnson believed in God and greatness and goodness, he also believed in guts and gunpowder.

All the history he had read, and all he had personally witnessed, convinced him that the United States of America—if determined enough, if productive enough, if patriotic enough—simply could not lose a war. As a boy his favorite stories had been of the minutemen at Lexington and Concord, of the heroic defenders of the Alamo, of rugged frontiersmen who'd at once tamed the wild land and marauding Indians. He had a special affinity for a schoolboy poem proclaiming that the most beautiful sight his eyes had beheld was "the flag of my country in a foreign land." He so admired war heroes that he claimed to have been fired on "by a Japanese ace," though no evidence supported it; he invented an ancestor he carelessly claimed had been martyred at the Alamo; at the Democratic National Convention in 1956 he had cast his state's delegate votes for the Vice-Presidential ambitions of young John F. Kennedy, "that fighting sailor who bears the scars of battle."

On a slow Saturday afternoon in the 1950's expansive and garrulous in his posh Senate majority-leader quarters, Johnson discoursed to a half dozen young Texas staffers in the patois of their shared native place. Why—he said—you take that ragtag bunch at Valley Forge, who'd have given them a cut dog's chance? There they were, barefoot in the snow and their asses hanging out, nothing to eat but moss and dead leaves and snakes, not half enough bullets for their guns, and facing the soldiers of the most powerful king of his time. Yet they sucked it up, wouldn't quit, lived to fight another day—and won. Or you take the Civil War, now: it had been so exceptionally bloody because you had aroused Americans fighting on *both* sides; it had been something like rock against rock, or like two mean ol' pit bull-dogs going at each other with neither of them willing to be chewed up and both of 'em thinking only of taking hunks out of the other. He again invoked the Alamo: a mere handful of freedom-loving men standing against the Mexican hordes, knowing they faced certain death, but they'd carved their names in history for all time, and before they got through with ol' General Santa Anna he thought he'd stumbled into a nest of stinging scorpions or bumble-bees.

Fifteen years later Johnson would show irritation when Clark Clifford suggested that victory in Vietnam might require a sustaining commitment of twenty to thirty years. No—L.B.J. said—no, no, the thing to do was get in and out quickly, pour everything you had into

the fight, land the knockout blow: hell, the North Vietnamese *had* to
see the futility of facing all that American muscle. If you really
poured it on 'em, you could clean up that mess within six months. We
had the troops, the firepower, the bombs, the sophisticated weaponry,
the oil—everything we needed to win. Did we have the resolve? Well,
the Texas Rangers had a saying that you couldn't stop a man who
just kept on a-coming. And that's what we'd do in Vietnam, Clark, just
keep on a-coming . . .

Always he talked of the necessity to be strong; he invoked his
father's standing up to the Ku Klux Klan in the 1920's, Teddy Roosevelt's carrying that big stick, F.D.R.'s mobilizing the country to beat
Hitler and Tojo. He liked ol' Harry Truman—tough little bastard
and his own man—but, listen, Harry and Dean Acheson had lost control when they failed to properly prosecute the Korean War. They lost
the public's respect, lost control of General MacArthur, lost the backing of Congress, lost the *war* or the next thing to it. Next thing you
know, they got blamed for losing China and then there was Joe Mc-
Carthy accusing them of being soft on communism and everybody
believed it. Well, it wouldn't happen to him, nosir. *He* hadn't started
the Vietnam war—Jack Kennedy had made the first commitment of
out-and-out combat troops, don't forget—but *he* wouldn't bug out no
matter how much the Nervous Nellies brayed. Kennedy had proved
during the Cuban missile crisis that if you stood firm then the Reds
would back down. They were playground bullies, and he didn't intend
to be pushed around any more than Jack Kennedy had. When a bully
ragged you, you didn't go whining to the teacher but gave him some of
his own medicine.

Only later, in exile, when he spoke with unusual candor of his
darker parts, did it become clear how obsessed with failure Lyndon
Johnson always had been. As a preschool youngster he walked a country
lane to visit a grandfather, his head stuffed with answers he knew would
be required ("How many head of cattle you got, Lyndon? How much
do they eat? How many head can you graze to the acre?") and fearing
he might forget them. If he forgot them, he got no bright-red apple but
received, instead, a stern and disapproving gaze. L.B.J.'s mother, who
smothered him with affection and praise should he perform to her
pleasure, refused to acknowledge his presence should he somehow dis-
please or disappoint her. His father accused him of being a sleepyhead,
a slow starter, and sometimes said every boy in town had a two-hour
head start on him. Had we known these things from scratch, we might
not have wondered why Lyndon Johnson seemed so blind for so long to
the Asian realities. His personal history simply permitted him no
retreats or failures in testings.

From childhood L.B.J. experienced bad dreams. As with much else,
they would stay with him to the grave. His nightmares were of being
paralyzed and unable to act, of being chained inside a cage or to his
desk, of being pursued by hostile forces. These and other disturbing
dreams haunted his White House years; he could see himself stricken

and ill on a cot, unable even to speak—like Woodrow Wilson—while, in an adjoining room, his trusted aides squabbled and quarreled in dividing his power. He translated the dreams to mean that should he for a moment show weakness, be indecisive, then history might judge him as the first American President who had failed to stand up and be counted.

These deep-rooted insecurities prompted Lyndon Johnson always to assert himself, to abuse staff members simply to prove that he held the upper hand, to test his power in small or mean ways. Sometimes, in sending Vice President Hubert Humphrey off on missions or errands with exhortations to "get going," he literally kicked him in the shins. "Hard," Humphrey later recalled, pulling up his trouser leg to exhibit the scars to columnist Robert Allen. Especially when drinking did he swagger and strut. Riding high as Senate majority leader, Johnson one night after a Texas State Society function, at the National Press Club in Washington—in the spring of 1958—repaired to a near-by bar with Texas Congressmen Homer Thornberry and Jack Brooks. "I'm a powerful sumbitch, you know that?" he repeatedly said. "You boys realize how goddamn *powerful* I am?" Yes, Lyndon, his companions uneasily chorused. Johnson pounded the table as if attempting to crack stout oak: "Do you know Ike couldn't pass the Lord's Prayer in Congress without me? You understand that? Hah?" Yes, Lyndon. "Hah? Do you? Hah?" An observer thought he never had seen a man more desperate for affirmations of himself.

Johnson always was an enthusiastic Cold Warrior. He was not made uncomfortable by John Foster Dulles' brinkmanship rhetoric about "rolling back" communism or of "unleashing" Chiang Kai-shek to free the Chinese mainland. He was, indeed, one of the original soldiers of the Cold War, a volunteer rather than a draftee, just as he had been the first member of Congress to rush to the recruiting station following Pearl Harbor. Immediately after World War ii he so bedeviled House Speaker Sam Rayburn about his fears of America dismantling its military machine that Rayburn appointed him to the postwar Military Policy Committee and to the Joint Committee on Atomic Energy. L.B.J. early had a preference for military assignments in Congress; he successfully campaigned for a seat on the House Naval Affairs Committee in the 1930's and, a decade later, the Senate Armed Services Committee. He eventually chaired the Senate Preparedness Committee and the Senate Space Committee. Perhaps others saw the exploration of outer space in scientific or peaceful terms. Johnson, however, told Senate Democrats that outer space offered "the ultimate position from which total control of the earth may be exercised. Whoever gains that ultimate position gains control, total control, over the earth."

Lyndon Johnson was a nagger, a complainer, a man not always patient with those of lesser gifts or with those who somehow inconvenienced him in the moment. Sometimes he complained that the generals knew nothing but "spend and bomb"; almost always, however, he went along with bigger military spending and, in most cases, with more bombing or whatever other military action the brass proposed. This was his consistent record in Congress, and he generally affirmed it as President.

On November 12, 1951, Senator Johnson rattled his saber at the Russians:

> We are tired of fighting your stooges. We will no longer sacrifice our young men on the altar of your conspiracies. The next aggression will be the last. . . . We will strike back, not just at your satellites, but at you. We will strike back with all the dreaded might that is within our control, and it will be a crushing blow.

Even allowing for those rhetorical excesses peculiar to senatorial oratory, those were not the words of a man preoccupied with the doctrine of peaceful coexistence. Nor were they inconsistent with Johnson's mind-set when he made a public demand—at the outbreak of the Korean War, in June, 1950—that President Truman order an all-out mobilization of all military reserve troops, national guard units, draftees, and even civilian manpower and industry. In a Senate debate shortly thereafter Senator Johnson scolded colleagues questioning the Pentagon's request for new and supplementary emergency billions: "Is this the hour of our nation's twilight, the last fading hour of light before an endless night shall envelop us and all the Western world?"

His ties with Texas—with its indigenous xenophobic instincts and general proclivities toward a raw yahooism—haunted him and, in a sense, may have made him a prisoner of grim political realities during the witch-hunting McCarthy era. "I'm damn tired," he said, "of being called a Dixiecrat in Washington and a Communist in Texas"; it perfectly summed up those schizophrenic divisions uneasily compartmentalizing his national political life and the more restrictive parochial role dictated by conditions back home. He lived daily with a damned-if-I-do-and-damned-if-I-don't situation. Texas was a particularly happy hunting ground for Senator Joe McCarthy, whose self-proclaimed anticommunist crusade brought him invitation after invitation to speak there; the Texas legislature, in the 1950's controlled beyond belief by vested interests and showing the ideological instincts of the early primates, whooped through a resolution demanding that Senator McCarthy address it despite the suggestion of State Representative Maury Maverick, Jr., that the resolution be expanded to invite Mickey Mouse. Both Johnson's powerful rightist adversaries and many of his wealthy Texas benefactors were enthusiastic contributors to the McCarthy cause.

Privately Johnson groused to intimates of McCarthy's reckless showboat tactics and particularly of the Texas-directed pressures they brought down on him: why, Joe McCarthy was just a damn drunk, a blowhard, an incompetent who couldn't tie his own shoelaces, probably the biggest joke in the Senate. But—L.B.J. reminded those counseling him to attack McCarthy—people believed him, they were so afraid of the Communists they would believe anything. McCarthy was as strong as horseradish. There would come a time when the hysteria died down, and then McCarthy would be vulnerable; such a fellow was certain to hang himself in time. But right now anybody openly challenging McCarthy would come away with dirty hands and with his heart broken. "Touch pitch," he paraphrased the Bible, "and you'll be defiled." By temperament a man who coveted the limelight and never was bashful about claiming credit for popular actions, Johnson uncharacteristically remained in the background when the U.S. Senate voted to censure McCarthy in late 1954. Though he was instrumental in selecting senators he believed would be effective and creditable members in leading the censure effort, Johnson's fine hand was visible only to insiders.

Johnson believed, however—and probably more deeply than Joe McCarthy—in a worldwide, monolithic Communist conspiracy. He believed it was directed from Moscow and that it was ready to blast America, or subvert it, at the drop of a fur hat. L.B.J. never surrendered that view. In retirement he suggested that the Communists were everywhere, honeycombing the government, and he told surprised visitors that sometimes he hadn't known whether he could trust even his own staff. The Communists (it had been his first thought on hearing the gunshots in Dallas, and he never changed his mind) had killed Jack Kennedy; it had been their influence that turned people against the Vietnam war. One of L.B.J.'s former aides, having been treated to that angry lecture, came away from the Texas ranch with the sad and reluctant conclusion that "the Old Man's absolutely paranoid on the Communist thing."

In May, 1961, President Kennedy dispatched his Vice President to Asia on a "fact-finding" diplomatic trip. Johnson, who believed it his duty to be a team player, to reinforce the prevailing wisdom, bought without qualification the optimistic briefings of military brass with their charts and slides "proving" the inevitable American victory. "I was sent out here to report the *progress* of the war," he told an aide, as if daring anyone to give him anything other than good news. Carried away, he publicly endowed South Vietnam's President Ngo Dinh Diem with the qualities of Winston Churchill, George Washington, Andrew Jackson, and F.D.R. Visiting refugee camps, he grew angry at Communist aggressions "against decent people" and concluded: "There is no alternative to United States leadership in Southeast Asia. . . . We must decide whether to help to the best of our ability or throw in the towel . . . [and] . . . pull back our defenses to San Francisco and a 'Fortress America' concept." He believed then—and always would—in the "domino theory" first stated by President Eisenhower. Even after announcing his abdication, he continued to sing the tired litany: if Vietnam fell then the rest of Asia might go, and then Africa, and then the Philippines . . .

When Lyndon Johnson suddenly ascended to the Presidency, however, he did not enter the Oval Office eager to immediately take the measure of Ho Chi Minh. Although he told Ambassador Henry Cabot

Lodge that "I am not going to be the President who saw Southeast Asia go the way China went," he wanted, for the moment, to keep the war—and, indeed, all foreign entanglements—at arm's length. His preoccupation was with his domestic program; here, he was confident, he knew what he was doing. He would emulate F.D.R. in making people's lives a little brighter. To aides he eagerly talked of building schools and houses, of fighting poverty and attaining full employment, of heating the economy to record prosperity. The honeymoon with Congress—he said—couldn't last; he had seen Congress grow balky and obstinate, take its measure of many Presidents, and he had to assume it would happen again. Then he would lean forward, tapping a forefinger against someone's chest or squeezing a neighboring knee, and say: "I'm like a sweetheart to Congress right now. They love me because I'm new and courting 'em and it's kinda exciting, like that first kiss. But after a while the new will wear off. Then Congress will complain that I don't bring enough roses or candy and will accuse me of seeing other girls." The need was to push forward quickly: pass the Civil Rights bill in the name of the martyred John F. Kennedy, then hit Capitol Hill with a blizzard of domestic proposals and dazzle it before sentiment and enthusiasms cooled. Foreign affairs could wait.

Lyndon Johnson at that point had little experience in foreign affairs. Except for showcase missions accomplished as Vice President, he had not traveled outside the United States save for excursions to Mexico and his brief World War II peregrinations. He probably had little confidence in himself in foreign affairs; neither did he have an excessive interest in the field. "Foreigners are not like the folks I am used to," he sometimes said—and though it passed as a joke, his intimates felt he might be kidding on the level.

Ambassadors waiting to present their credentials to the new President were miffed by repeated delays—and then angrily astonished when L.B.J. received them in groups and clumps, seemingly paying only perfunctory attention, squirming in his chair, scowling or muttering during the traditional ceremonies. He appeared oblivious to their feelings, to their offended senses of dignity. "Why do *I* have to see them?" the President demanded. "They're Dean Rusk's clients, not mine."

Defense Secretary Robert McNamara was selected to focus on Vietnam while L.B.J. concocted his Great Society. McNamara should send South Vietnam equipment and money as needed, a few more men, issue the necessary pronouncements. But don't splash it all over the front pages, don't let it get out of hand, don't give Barry Goldwater Vietnam as an issue for the 1964 campaign. Barry, hell, he was a hip shooter; he'd fight Canada or Mexico—or, at least, give that impression—so the thing to do was sit tight, keep the lid on, keep all Vietnam options open. Above all, "Don't let it turn into a Bay of Pigs." Hunker down; don't gamble.

The trouble—Johnson said to advisers—was that foreign nations

*President Johnson with Defense Secretary McNamara at the
White House after one of McNamara's inspection trips to Vietnam.*

didn't understand Americans or the American way; they saw us as
"fat and fifty, like the country-club set"; they didn't think we had
the steel in our souls to act when the going got rough. Well, in time
they'd find out differently. They'd learn that Lyndon Johnson was not
about to abandon what other Presidents had started; he wouldn't
permit history to write that he'd been the only American President to
cut and run; he wouldn't sponsor any damn Munichs. But for right
now—cool it. Put Vietnam on the back burner and let it simmer.

But the Communists—he later would say—wouldn't permit him to
cool it. There had been that Gulf of Tonkin attack on the United States
destroyer *Maddox*, in August of 19-and-64, and if he hadn't convinced
Congress to get on record as backing him up in Vietnam, why, then, the
Reds would have interpreted it as a sign of weakness and Barry Goldwater would have cut his heart out. And in February of 19-and-65,
don't forget, the Vietcong had made that attack on the American
garrison at Pleiku, and how could he be expected to ignore that? There
they came, thousands of 'em, barefoot and howling in their black
pajamas and throwing homemade bombs: it had been a damned insult,
a calculated show of contempt. L.B.J. told the National Security
Council: "The worst thing we could do would be to let this [Pleiku]
thing go by. It would be a big mistake. It would open the door to a
major misunderstanding." Twelve hours later American aircraft—for

the first time—bombed in North Vietnam; three weeks later L.B.J. ordered continuing bombing raids in the north to "force the North Vietnamese into negotiations"; only a hundred and twenty days after Pleiku, American forces were involved in a full-scale war and seeking new ways to take the offensive. Eight Americans died at Pleiku. Eight. Eventually fifty thousand plus would die in Asia.

Pleiku was the second major testing of American will within a few months, in L.B.J.'s view. Then in the spring of 1965 rebels had attacked the ruling military junta in the Dominican Republic. Lives and property of U.S. citizens were endangered, as Johnson saw it, but —more—this might be a special tactic by the Reds, a dry run for bigger mischief later on in Vietnam. The world was watching to see how America would react. "It's just like the Alamo," he lectured the National Security Council. "Hell, it's like you were down at that gate, and you were surrounded, and you damn well needed somebody. Well, by God, I'm going to go—and I thank the Lord that I've got men who want to go with me, from McNamara right down to the littlest private who's carrying a gun."

Somewhat to his puzzlement, and certainly to his great vexation, Lyndon Johnson would learn that not everybody approved of his rushing the Marines into the Dominican Republic, and within days building up a twenty-one-thousand-man force. Attempting to answer criticism, he would claim thousands of patriots "bleeding in the streets and with their heads cut off," paint a false picture of the United States ambassador cringing under his desk "while bullets whizzed over his head," speak of howling Red hordes descending on American citizens and American holdings, and, generally, open what later became known as the Credibility Gap.

By now he had given up on his original notion of walking easy in Vietnam until he could put the Great Society across. Even before the three major testings of Tonkin Gulf, the Dominican Republic, and Pleiku, he had said—almost idly—"Well, I guess we have to touch up those North Vietnamese a little bit." By December, 1964, he had reversed earlier priorities: "We'll beat the Communists first, then we can look around and maybe give something to the poor." Guns now ranked ahead of butter.

Not that he was happy about it. Though telling Congress "This nation is mighty enough, its society is healthy enough, its people are strong enough to pursue our goals in the rest of the world while still building a Great Society here at home," he knew, in his bones, that this was much too optimistic an outlook. He privately fretted that his domestic program would be victimized. He became touchy, irritable, impatient with those who even timorously questioned America's increasing commitment to the war. Why should I be blamed—he snapped—when the Communists are the aggressors, when President Eisenhower committed us in Asia in 1954, when Kennedy beefed up Ike's efforts? If he didn't prosecute the Vietnam war now, then later Congress would sour and want to hang him because he hadn't—and would gut his domestic programs in retaliation. He claimed to have "pounded President Eisenhower's desk" in opposing Ike's sending two hundred Air Force "technicians" to assist the French in Indochina (though those who were present recalled that only Senators Russell of Georgia and Stennis of Mississippi had raised major objections). Well, he'd been unable to stop Ike that time, though he *had* helped persuade him against dropping paratroopers into Dien Bien Phu to aid the doomed French garrison there. And after all that, everybody now called Vietnam Lyndon Johnson's war. It was unfair. "The only difference between the Kennedy assassination and mine is that I am alive and it [is] more torturous."

Very well; if it was his war in the public mind, then he would personally oversee its planning. "Never move up your artillery until you move up your ammunition," he told his generals—a thing he'd said as Senate majority leader when impatient liberals urged him to call for votes on issues he felt not yet ripe. Often he quizzed the military brass, sounding almost like a dove, in a way to resemble courtroom cross-examinations. He forced the admirals and generals to affirm and reaffirm their recommendations as vital to victory. Reading selected transcripts, one might make the judgment that Lyndon Johnson was a most reluctant warrior, one more cautious than not. The evidence of Johnson's deeds, however, suggests that he was being a crafty politician —making a record so that later he couldn't be made the sole scapegoat. He trusted McNamara's computers, perhaps more than he trusted men, and took satisfaction when their print-outs predicted that X amount of bombing would damage the Vietcong by Y, or that X number of troops would be required to capture Z. Planning was the key. You figured what you had to do, you did it, and eventually you'd nail the coonskin to the wall.

He devoutly believed that all problems had solutions: in his lifetime alone we'd beaten the Great Depression, won two world wars, hacked away at racial discrimination, made an industrial giant and world power of a former agrarian society, explored outer space. This belief in available solutions led him, time and again, to change tactics in Vietnam and discover fresh enthusiasm for each new move; he did not pause, apparently, to reflect upon why given tactics, themselves once heralded as practical solutions, had failed and had been abandoned. If counterinsurgency failed, you bombed. If bombing wasn't wholly effective, then you tried the enclave theory. If *that* proved disappointing, you sent your ground troops on search-and-destroy missions. If, somehow, the troops couldn't find the phantom Vietcong in large numbers (and therefore couldn't destroy them), you began pacification programs in the areas you'd newly occupied. And if *this* bogged down, you beefed up your firepower and sent in enough troops to simply outmuscle the rice-paddy ragtags: napalm 'em, bomb 'em, shoot 'em. Sure it would work. It always had. Yes, surely the answer was there somewhere in the back of the book, if only you looked long enough . . .

He sought, and found, assurances. Maybe he had only a "cow-college" education, perhaps he'd not attended West Point, he might not have excessive experience in foreign affairs. But he was surrounded by good men, what David Halberstam later would label "the best and the brightest," and certainly these were unanimous in their supportive conclusions. "He would look around him," Tom Wicker later said, "and see in Bob McNamara that [the war] was technologically feasible, in McGeorge Bundy that it was intellectually respectable, and in Dean Rusk that it was historically necessary." It was especially easy to trust expertise when the experts in their calculations bolstered your own gut feelings—when their computers and high-minded statements and mighty hardware all boiled down to reinforce your belief in American efficiency, American responsibility, American destiny. If so many good men agreed with him, then what might be wrong with those who didn't?

He considered the sources of dissatisfaction and dissent: the liberals—the "red-hots," he'd often sneeringly called them, the "pepper pots"—who were impractical dreamers, self-winding kamikazes intent on self-destruction. He often quoted an aphorism to put such people in perspective: "Any jackass can kick down a barn, but it takes a carpenter to build one." He fancied, however, that he knew all about these queer fellows. For years, down home, Ronnie Dugger and his *Texas Observer* crowd, in L.B.J.'s opinion, had urged him to put his head in the noose by fighting impossible, profitless fights. They wanted him to take on Joe McCarthy, slap the oil powers down, kick Ike's rear end, tell everybody who wasn't a red-hot to go to hell. Well, he'd learned a long time ago that just because you told a fellow to go to hell, he didn't necessarily have to go. The liberals didn't understand the Communists. Bill Fulbright and his bunch—the striped-pants boys over at the State Department and assorted outside pepper pots—thought you could *trust* the Communists; they made the mistake of believing the Reds would deal with you honorably when—in truth—the Communists didn't respect anything but force. You had to fight fire with fire; let them know who had the biggest guns and the toughest heart.

Where once he had argued the injustice of Vietnam being viewed as "his" war, Lyndon Johnson now brought to it a proprietary attitude. This should have been among the early warnings that L.B.J. would increasingly resist less than victory, no matter his periodic bombing halts or conciliatory statements inviting peace, because once he took a thing personally, his pride and vanity and ego knew no bounds. Always a man to put his brand on everything (he wore monogrammed shirts, boots, cuff links; flew his private L.B.J. flag when in residence at the L.B.J. ranch; saw to it that the names of Lynda Bird Johnson and Luci Baines Johnson and Lady Bird Johnson —not Claudia, as she had been named—had the magic initials L.B.J.), he now personalized and internalized the war. Troops became "my" boys, those were "my" helicopters, it was "my" pilots he prayed

*An unusual wall arrangement in the Johnson
home; an example of L.B.J.'s unembarrassed style.*

might return from their bombing missions as he paid nocturnal calls
to the White House situation room to learn the latest from the battle-
fields; Walt Rostow became ''my'' intellectual because he was hawkish
on L.B.J.'s war. His machismo was mixed up in it now, his manhood.
After a cabinet meeting in 1967 several staff aides and at least one
cabinet member—Stewart Udall, Secretary of the Interior—remained
behind for informal discussions; soon L.B.J. was waving his arms and
fulminating about his war. Who the hell was Ho Chi Minh, anyway,
that he thought he could push America around? Then the President
did an astonishing thing: he unzipped his trousers, dangled a given
appendage, and asked his shocked associates: ''Has Ho Chi Minh got
anything like that?''

By mid-1966 he had cooled toward many of his experts: not be-
cause they'd been wrong in their original optimistic calculations so
much as that some of them had recanted and now rejected *his* war.
This Lyndon Johnson could not forgive: they'd cut and run on him.
Nobody had deserted Roosevelt, he gloomed, when he'd been fighting
Hitler. McGeorge Bundy, deserting to head the Ford Foundation, was

no longer the brilliant statesman but merely "a smart kid, that's all." Bill Moyers, quitting to become editor of *Newsday*, and once almost a surrogate son to the President, suddenly became "a little puppy I rescued from sacking groceries"—a reference to a part-time job Moyers held while a high-school student. George Ball, too, was leaving? Well, he'd always been a chronic beller-acher. When Defense Secretary McNamara doubted too openly (stories of his anguish leaked to the newspapers), he found it difficult to claim the President's time; ultimately he rudely was shuttled to the World Bank. Vice President Hubert Humphrey, privately having second thoughts, was not welcomed back to high councils until he'd muffled his dissent and shamelessly flattered L.B.J. Even then Johnson didn't wholly accept his Vice President; Hubert, he said, wasn't a real man, he cried as easily as a woman, he didn't have the weight. When Lady Bird Johnson voiced doubts about the war, her husband grumbled that *of course* she had doubts; it was *like* a woman to be uncertain. *Has Ho Chi Minh got anything like that?*

Shortly after the Tet offensive began—during which Americans would be shocked by the Vietcong temporarily capturing a wing of the American embassy in Saigon—the President, at his press conference of February 2, 1968, made such patently false statements that even his most loyal friends and supporters were troubled. The sudden Tet offensive had been traumatic, convincing many Americans that our condition was desperate, if not doomed. For years the official line ran that the Vietcong could not hang on: would shrink by the attritions of battle and an ebbing of confidence in a hopeless cause; stories were handed out that captured documents showed the enemy to be of low morale, underfed, ill-armed. The Vietcong could not survive superior American firepower; the kill ratio favored our side by 7-to-1, 8-to-1, more. These and other optimisms were repeated by the President, by General Westmoreland, by this ambassador or that fact-finding team. Now, however, it became apparent that the Vietcong had the capability to challenge even our main lair in Asia—and there to inflict serious damage as well as major embarrassments.

It was a time demanding utmost candor, and L.B.J. blew it. He took the ludicrous position that the Tet offensive (which would be felt for weeks to come) had abysmally failed. Why, we'd known about it all along—had, indeed, been in possession of Hanoi's order of battle. Incredible. To believe the President one had also to believe that American authorities had simply failed to act on this vital intelligence, had wittingly and willingly invited disaster. The President was scoffed at and ridiculed; perhaps the thoughtful got goose bumps in realizing how far Lyndon Johnson now lived from reality. If there was a beginning of the end—of Johnson, of hopes of anything remotely resembling victory, of a general public innocence of official razzmatazz —then Tet, and that press conference, had to be it.

Even the stubborn President knew it. His Presidency was shot, his party ruined and in tatters; his credibility was gone; he could speak only at military bases, where security guaranteed his safety against

*President Johnson during television speech in which
he announced that he would not seek reelection.*

the possibility of mobs pursuing him through the streets as he had
often dreamed. The nightmare was real now. Street dissidents long
had been chanting their cruel ''Hey, Hey, L.B.J. / How Many Kids
Did You Kill Today''; Senator Eugene McCarthy soon would capture
almost half the vote in the New Hampshire primary against the unpopular President. There was nothing to do but what he'd always
sworn he would not do: quit. On March 31, 1968, at the end of a
televised speech ordering the end of attacks on North Vietnam in the
hope of getting the enemy to the negotiation table, Johnson startled the
nation by announcing: ''. . . I do not believe that I should devote an
hour or a day of my time to any personal partisan causes or to any
duties other than the awesome duties of this office—the Presidency of
your country. Accordingly, I shall not seek, and I will not accept, the
nomination of my party for another term . . .''

''In the final months of his Presidency,'' former White House aide
Eric Goldman wrote, ''Lyndon Johnson kept shifting in mood. At
times he was bitter and petulant at his repudiation by the nation; at
times philosophical, almost serene, confidently awaiting the verdict of
the future.'' The serenity always was temporary; he grew angry with
Hubert Humphrey for attempting to disengage himself from the

Johnson war policy and, consequently, refused to make more than a token show of support for him. He saw Richard Nixon win on a pledge of having "a secret plan" to end the war—which, it developed, he did not have.

In his final White House thrashings—and in retirement—Lyndon Johnson complained of unfinished business: he had wanted to complete Vietnam peace talks, free the crew of the *Pueblo*, begin talks with the Russians on halting the arms race, send a man to the moon. But the war—he would say in irritation—the war had ruined all that; the people hadn't rallied around him as they had around F.D.R. and Woodrow Wilson and other wartime Presidents; he had been abandoned—by Congress, by cabinet members, by old friends; no other President had tried so hard or suffered so much. He had a great capacity for self-pity and often indulged it, becoming reclusive and rarely issuing a public statement or making public appearances. Doris Kearns has said that she and others helping L.B.J. write his memoirs, *The Vantage Point*, would draft chapters and lay out the documentation—but even then Lyndon Johnson would say no, no, it wasn't like that, it was like *this;* and he would rattle on, waving his arms and attempting to justify himself, invoking the old absolutes, calling up memories of the Alamo, the Texas Rangers, the myths and the legends. He never seemed to understand where or how he had gone wrong.

John Brooks

MODERN AMERICAN SOCIETY

In this essay John Brooks attempts to combine two of the most difficult forms of historical writing. He seeks to describe and explain the broad trends that give periods of time their character, and to do this for the most recent past. The first task requires both encyclopedic knowledge and the capacity to distinguish among thousands of events, hundreds of fads, and dozens of trends. The second calls for the most acute judgment and insight reached without the historian's most useful tool—hindsight. That Brooks has carried this tour de force off brilliantly is demonstrated by the fact that he wrote this article barely five years ago. Readers now have at least a modicum of hindsight on the year 1970 and thus cannot help but be impressed by the soundness of his analysis of a time we all remember. That he recognized what was happening in the late 1960's is clear to us now; it was not so obvious at that time.

This essay, as Brooks, who is on the staff of the *New Yorker*, notes, was an outgrowth of his book, *The Great Leap: The Past Twenty-Five Years in America.* He has also written *Once in Golconda: A True Dream of Wall Street*, other books about modern high finance, and *Telephone.*

Something very strange has happened in the United States very recently. Traditional attitudes and values that have prevailed and come down from generation to generation in all but unbroken succession since the founding of the republic have suddenly been overturned or are in the process of being overturned. Traditional American ways of looking at things—including the traditional way of looking at our own past—have suddenly been reversed. A startling discontinuity, as stark as a geologic fault, has occurred in our cultural history since 1964.

It is a temptation, and one constantly yielded to by social commentators, to look upon these things (like the geologic fault) as having simply *happened*—as having occurred without human volition or control. The environment has changed, it is said; no wonder people and their attitudes change. The process is made to appear as inexorable as changes in the phase of the moon.

What has "happened" in America has been largely the doing of the older half of our present population—those born before the Second World War. Through their ingenuity and enterprise and with the help of their equally ingenious and enterprising predecessors of the generations before, the members of the present older generation have changed the country so radically that the old conditions under which the old values obtained are simply not there any more. True enough, the change was brought about (in traditional American fashion) entirely without planning, and, indeed, its social effects have by and large not been felt by the generation responsible. Not really understanding what it has wrought (still quaintly anthropomorphizing computers, for example) and being beyond the age when long-held attitudes and values are easily surrendered, the older half of the country mostly clings to the old ideas. In the meantime the younger half, those born since the war, have grown up in a whole new world and, in a triumph of environment over heredity, have become a new breed. The fathers, clever enough to invent computers, jet planes, moon ships, antibiotics, and weapons of race suicide, are not wise enough to know their own sons, who are now shaping the values of America and will soon *be* America.

A quarter century ago next month, with V-J Day, the United States emerged from the war into modern times. In the subsequent twenty years, while the nation's adults, the prewar generation, were unwittingly removing from their own and their children's lives the physical underpinnings of the old national faiths and attitudes, they were also continuing—in fact, accelerating—the long process of social amelioration that had gone on, though not uninterruptedly, since not long after the Civil War. The first postwar quarter century was one of outstanding social as well as material progress.

About five years ago, I undertook a study of social change in the United States over the twenty-five years between the outbreak of the Second World War in 1939 and the mid-sixties. I found, among other things, that the great corporations, considered so gigantic and sinister in 1939, had become many times more gigantic and—in the pretty-well-substantiated public view—a good deal less sinister. (In the late thirties the Temporary National Economic Committee had reported with awe that General Motors, perhaps the archetypical American corporation, had assets of one billion dollars; less than two decades later General Motors would have *annual profits after taxes* of one billion dollars. It would meanwhile have abandoned its former rather surly attitude toward society and become a corporation as enlightened as most in its social attitudes.) The gross national product over the period had gone from 90 billion to 630 billion dollars a year; the federal budget had swollen from around nine billion to over one hundred billion; national income per capita had risen from nine hundred to well over three thousand dollars, while the national population (in sharp contradiction to the glum demographic predictions of 1939 that the nation faced a people shortage) had risen from 130,000,000 to over 190,000,000. Taxes and other forces had brought about a vast and generally beneficent redistribution of national wealth. Computer technology, in 1939 just a gleam in a few scientists' eyes, was already on the way to bringing about a new era in science and technology and, more obviously at first, in business methods; and the initial fears that computers would throw millions of people out of their jobs were beginning to prove unfounded. Poverty had by no means been eliminated, but by almost any fair-minded standard it had been sharply reduced; indeed, my calculations showed that by the standards applied in 1964, Franklin D. Roosevelt's one third of a nation ill fed, ill housed, and ill clothed in the thirties had been a gross understatement.

I found that over the period under study there had been a vast tidal migration from farms to cities. Thirty-one million Americans, or a quarter of the population, were farmers in 1939; only thirteen million, or less than 7 per cent, were still on the farms by 1964. The effect of this influx on the cities and on the new urbanites themselves, despite crime and overcrowding and suburbia and urban sprawl, had not proved to be all bad. I found a tremendous rise in formal education: the average American was an elementary-school graduate in 1939, a high-school graduate by 1964; 15 percent of college-age Americans attended college in 1939, well over 40 per cent in 1964.

Further, I argued that anti-Semitism, a strong and ominous thread in our national warp in 1939, had ceased by 1964 to be an important factor—permanently, I patriotically supposed. On the question of Negro rights and privileges the evidence of progress, though more equivocal, was nevertheless present. In 1964, in the nation's capital city, where in 1939 no black man had been suffered to eat in a public restaurant used by whites or to register in any hotel, Congress was passing a wide-ranging civil rights act, and the next year it would pass a far wider-ranging one. A long, painful campaign for civil rights in the South, beginning with the Supreme

Court's first desegregation decision in 1954, had caught the national imagination and that of our Texan President himself, and as a result of increased black-voter registration Negroes were being elected to office at many levels in most parts of the country. Economically, to be sure, the average black man was only slightly better off in relation to the average white man than he had been in 1939. Formerly his income had been somewhat less than half of the white man's; now it was slightly more than half. But in 1964 the country seemed to have the will to tackle even this anomaly. One felt, buoyantly, that with the political liberation of the Negro virtually accomplished, his economic liberation was next on the agenda.

In its foreign affairs I said that the United States, which with the end of the war had assumed free-world leadership for the first time, had handled this generally unwanted responsibility fairly well in spite of some spectacular bungling. There were, despite moral arguments advanced in their behalf, such egregious disasters as the Bay of Pigs, the ill-starred U-2 reconnaissance flight, the unfortunate (but then not yet overwhelmingly tragic) miscalculation of our involvement in Vietnam. But there was also the nuclear test-ban treaty of 1963, the relief programs all over the world, and, of course, the Marshall Plan, which through its backers' statesmanlike vision of where enlightened self-interest lay, had done so much to set flattened Europe back on its feet.

In sum, my research convinced me that "the quarter-century ... had seen such rapid and far-reaching changes in many aspects of American life as are not only unprecedented in our own national experience, but may well be unprecedented in that of any nation other than those that have been suddenly transformed by . . . war or plague." And I concluded that while the enormous material gains of the quarter century had unquestionably had their moral costs, the moral loss was far less clear than the material gain. America could not patly be said to have "sold its soul for mediocrity."

So I wrote then. Between then and now, over the past five years, many but not all of the trends I noted have continued. Economic growth has gone on to the point where most economists believe that 1971 will be the year when our gross national product will pass the all but inscrutable figure of a trillion dollars a year. Our 1964 federal budget is now almost doubled. Poverty, more and more in the news, is nevertheless still decreasing in fact.

On the other hand the migration from farms to cities has slowed sharply. Anti-Semitism in a new form has made an ominous appearance among Negro militants. Racial integration of schools has failed tragically, as shown by the fact that the beginning of 1970—sixteen years after the Supreme Court's desegregation decision—less than one fifth of southern Negro pupils and hardly more than one fourth of northern and western Negro pupils were attending predominantly white schools. The stagnation of black economic status is shown by the persistence of two familiar statistics—black income still just over half that of whites, black unemployment still double that among whites.

But statistics are not all. There exist also national moods, and they rather than statistics reflect attitudes and values. There are fashions in statistics; appropriate ones can be found to fit any mood, to buttress any conventional wisdom, and it can be argued that the moods give birth to the figures rather than vice versa. At any rate, some time recently, probably in 1965, the national mood reversed itself as dramatically as a manic-depressive patient goes from the heights to the depths, and I see my study as having been completed in the last, climactic days of a period of national euphoria.

The trigger for the mood change is harder to identify. Many would equate it with the hateful trigger of Lee Harvey Oswald's mail-order gun in Dallas in November, 1963, and contend that the accomplishments of 1964 and early 1965 were the result of accumulated momentum—that, indeed, the productive phase of the Kennedy administration was actually the year and a half after John Kennedy's death. Others would choose the Watts riots of August, 1965, the first time the murderous and suicidal rage and despair of urban blacks outside the South was revealed; perhaps the largest number would choose the escalation of the Vietnam war, which began with the bombing of North Vietnam that February. At all events the change occurred, and the nation went into the valley of a shadow from which it has not yet emerged as this is written.

In terms of inner change, of change in American attitudes and American values, these last five years have surely been the crucial ones in the quarter century since V-J Day. And these changes, which I propose to examine here as cheerfully as possible, seem of such a magnitude that every American except the very young, the very empty, and the very enclosed must now, to some extent, feel himself a foreigner in his native land.

Better than statistics, as a starting point for a study of moods, are words. The 1947 *Britannica Book of the Year* gave a list of words that, according to its authorities, "became prominent or were seemingly used for the first time" in either 1945 or 1946. Predictably enough, some of the listed words were of only ephemeral usefulness and have vanished without leaving a trace; for example, *athodyd* (a ramjet engine), *cuddle seat* (a contrivance for carrying small children, both word and device introduced by Australian war brides), and *Huff-Duff* (a navigation aid for ships and planes that was quickly superseded). But a surprising number of the new coinages survive, and a listing of some of them gives a remarkable picture of the preoccupations of the time: *atomic cloud, be-bop, buyers' strike, existentialism, fact finder* (as in a labor dispute), *fissionable, gray market, iron curtain, operation* (as in Operation This-or-That), *push-button* (as a metaphorical adjective), *shock wave, sitter* (for babysitter), *truth serum, U.N., UNESCO.*

Fact finder, fissionable, sitter: talismans of the time, casting strange shafts of light into the future. It was a time of getting settled. That, of course, meant more than veterans coming home; it also meant industrial workers demanding the raises that had been deferred by wartime controls, and therefore strikes. In November, 1945, there began a series of crippling strikes in key industries. Meanwhile, as the government vacillated on price controls, meat disappeared from grocery shelves for days at a time because of speculative withholding by suppliers. None of these inconveniences held back the business of nest building. The year 1946 stands out as the all-time record year for marriages in the nation's history, not only relative to population but in absolute numbers—2,291,000 marriages all told, or almost 700,000 more than in 1945, and almost twice as many as there had been in the deep Depression years before the war. The first nest in 1946 was usually an apartment rather than a house; material shortages held up the beginning of the great postwar home-building boom, but even so, construction of one-family dwellings tripled between 1945 and 1946. And whatever their nature, the new nests were quickly fruitful. The national birth rate went up 20 per cent in 1946 over 1945 (that November, New York City actually ran out of birth certificates) and another 10 per cent in 1947 over 1946, as the celebrated postwar baby boom got under way.

So the ex-serviceman, in college on the GI Bill, with his pregnant wife struggling to make a palatable dinner on short meat rations in their barracks apartment, was earnestly trying to sop up the knowledge that would get him a civilian job, with no thought farther from his mind than questioning, much less protesting against, the social framework or the institution in which he worked. Nest-building time is not a time for rebellion. Also in 1946 the government was paring back its budget from 1945's one hundred billion to sixty billion dollars, and the next year it would spend less than forty billion; the infant United Nations was trying out its unsteady legs at the optimistically named Lake Success on Long Island; there were four lynchings in the South; the Bikini bomb tests were appalling us, and the Cold War was taking shape; radio was still the great national diversion, with Jack Benny first in the Hooperatings, Fibber McGee and Molly second, and—incredible as it now seems—Amos 'n Andy seventh. And while all these quaint happenings were in process, the word *existentialism* was coming into the American language.

Of such was the nest-building mood, the nation's first in the postwar period. There have been five more since then that I can distinguish: the Korean-war mood, the McCarthy mood, the Eisenhower-prosperity mood, the Kennedy go-go mood, and finally the present one of paralysis, gloom, and reappraisal.

Beginning with the North Korean invasion of South Korea on June 25, 1950, the Korean war was a time of nightmare. There was a kind of *déja vu* about finding ourselves again embroiled in a war when we had just settled down to peace, and for thousands of veterans of the Second World War who had signed up for the reserves without thinking twice about it (I remember, for example, that when I was separated from the Army at Fort Dix, New Jersey, in 1945, they encouraged reserve enlistment by letting you out one day sooner if you signed up), it meant an actual return to combat. It was a new kind of war—not even officially called a war, but rather a ''police action''— as frustrating as an unpleasant dream, that we could not win and apparently were not *supposed* to win. (We would learn more about that kind of war later.) The rumors we heard, later confirmed, that American prisoners were being subjected to a new and horrifying form of mental torture called brainwashing were literally the stuff of a nightmare. So was the vision of an endless mass of humanity, bent on killing and seemingly unconcerned about being killed, that was embodied in the phrase ''human wave,'' used to describe the Chinese Communist hordes that streamed south across the Yalu River in November, 1950. Finally, during the two years that the armistice talks dragged on at Panmunjom while the shooting continued, there was the nightmare sense of trying to wake up to a pleasanter reality and being unable to do so.

Shaken but relieved, the country finally awoke with the signing of the armistice on July 27, 1953—but awoke merely, as sometimes happens, from one level of nightmare to another. The time of the paid informer and the false witness had already come. As early as 1948 Whittaker Chambers had first made his charges of Communist spying against Alger Hiss, the apparently exemplary young statesman who had been a framer of the United Nations charter, and the Dreyfus case of modern America was launched. In 1949 eleven leaders of the U.S. Communist Party had been sent to prison; the following year Judith Coplon and Dr. Klaus Fuchs had been convicted of spying, the latter with reference to vital atomic secrets, and the young Senator Joseph McCarthy, seeing his chance, had made his famous series of accusations that there were 205 (or 57 or 81 or 10 or 116) Communists in the State Department. With that, the hounds of fear and distrust slipped their leashes, and by the time of the Korean armistice Senator McCarthy had made the nightmarishly irrational term ''Fifth Amendment Communist'' into a household expression; hardly any professional in the country could feel his job or his way of life safe from the random malice of almost anyone, and constitutional guarantees against just this sort of mischief were becoming all but meaningless.

That nightmare almost drove us crazy—perhaps came closer than we care to admit, even now. But finally our underlying national health asserted itself, and we awoke at last, this time definitively, in December, 1954, when the Senate censured McCarthy and McCarthyism went into decline. Small wonder, after such horrors, that the next mood should have been a recessive one, one of huddling in our shells and comforting ourselves with material things while remaining heedless of the mess we were making. The essence of the Eisenhower mood was long-deferred self-indulgence. It was a time of soaring stockmarket prices and soaring participation in the boodle. The members of the middle class, the hugely expanding group that dominated the country, were becoming capitalists at last and were doing very well at it. It was a time of rocketing corporate profits and resulting fat dividends —at the cost of inflation and polluted air and water. It was a time of greatly increased leisure for millions—at the cost of littered roadsides and tamed and uglified national parks and forests. It was a time of more and more automobiles for more and more people—at the cost of traffic jams, more air pollution, eyesore automobile graveyards, and neglected public transportation. It was a time of bursting cities and proliferating suburbs—at the cost of increasingly neglected slums full of explosive anger quietly ticking away. It was a time when we thought of our "race problem" as being mainly a political matter confined to the South; when, in foreign policy, we fatalistically hid behind the dangerously provocative shield of "massive retaliation" and "brinkmanship" (and meanwhile were sowing the seeds of our Asian disaster); when college students kept a low profile, politically and otherwise, so as not to jeopardize their chances of flowing smoothly onto the production line to affluence right after graduation; and when—not so paradoxically as it may seem at first glance—the federal budget grew year by year and social security and other public benefits were greatly widened. The Eisenhower era is not to be compared too closely to that of Coolidge in terms of free enterprise's running wild. In the earlier time the country had been all too truly committed to unrestricted free enterprise, but by the late fifties, despite Fourth of July paeans to the "American system" as fulsome as ever, the notion of cradle-to-grave security *for most people* had been thoroughly accepted and, indeed, assimilated into the system. The mood was heedless hedonism.

Next, in abrupt reaction, came the Kennedy years with their quite opposite mood of responsibility and hope. It is tempting now to think of those years as a golden age, though if we look closely we find they were scarcely that in practical terms; after all, Kennedy's domestic legislative defeats—on civil rights, on tax reform, on Medicare—far outweighed his victories, and he died leaving unsolved most of the problems he had inherited, including, of course, Vietnam. But his successful conclusion of the 1962 Cuban missile crisis, along with the limited nuclear test-ban treaty that followed the next summer, did much to allay the fear of nuclear war that had overhung the country all through the postwar period up to then. Much more important, he and his administration, through the almost magically inspiring quality of their very style, succeeded in regenerating the old American faith, not in the perfection of man or his nation but in their perfectability. No one despaired under Kennedy; somehow everything seemed possible. "I have a dream that one day this nation will rise

Where did *it all go wrong? With the assassination of John F. Kennedy in Dallas, 1963, during the course of this parade or . . .*

up, [and] live out the true meaning of its creed . . ." Martin Luther King, Jr., said at the interracial March on Washington in August, 1963—a fitting epitome of the Kennedy mood, in a climax that no one could know came near the end of the last act.

Then everything went wrong. With Kennedy's death that November began an age of assassination; within five years probably the two most admired black men in the country, King and Malcolm X, and almost certainly the most admired white man, John Kennedy's brother Robert, would be dead from the same horrifying and dispiriting cause. During the same period more and more Negro leaders turned against King's dream, rejecting the American creed for a cynical, angry separatism; the hopeless war in Vietnam was escalated, and revelations about its conduct led many Americans to a similarly escalating sense of horror, disillusion, and shame; political colloquy at home became violent rather than reasonable; Americans achieved the technical masterwork of flying to the moon and back while failing to accomplish the technically simple one of giving all their citizens proper food and clothing. The sixth postwar mood was, and is, one of violence, disillusion, and doubt verging on despair such as has not been felt since the time of the Civil War.

*With the burning and looting of black ghettoes such
as Watts in Los Angeles in 1965 or ...*

It is my thesis, then, that while material change has generally been
steady, continuous, and for the most part beneficient over the postwar
period, the past five years or so have seen an explosive—and morally
equivocal—increase in the rate of change in values and attitudes. It
is in these last five years that most of our moral history since V-J Day
has been written, and it is since 1965 that many Americans have come
to feel like expatriates in America. In support of the thesis, let me
tick off a few current American attitudes—now accepted widely
enough among the influential, especially in the communications media,
to constitute what might be called leadership opinion, if not national
consensus—that would have been unthinkable not only on V-J Day
but on the day of John Kennedy's death as well.

The attitude toward military affairs, and in particular toward our
own military, has to a large extent undergone a reversal. My own
generation, the one whose coming of age coincided with U.S. entry
into the Second World War, had thought itself pacifist; we had been
brought up on Dos Passos' *Three Soldiers* and Hemingway's *A Farewell to Arms* and the Nye investigation with its implication that wars
are fought for the profits of munitions makers. But it turned out that

With the escalation of the war in Vietnam by the United States bombing of the North in 1965 and 1966? These North Vietnamese children are wearing wicker helmets to protect them against United States bomb splinters. Where did it all go wrong?

our pacifism was only skin-deep; when the call to arms came, it found us full of sanguine enthusiasm. We wanted to be in it, and quickly, and we hurried to the recruiting offices; we thought of draft-dodging as contemptible and conscientious objection as respectable but, to say the least, highly eccentric. After Pearl Harbor a uniform, even that of an ordinary soldier or sailor, was a clear-cut asset in the pursuit of girls.

In the postwar period up until recently a uniform was neutral, considered neither glamorous nor unappealing. Not so now. There are no American "heroes" of Vietnam (not that there has been no actual heroism), and the sporadic efforts of the military to create some have failed utterly. On the contrary, among the heroes to today's youth, or a significant segment of it, are the evaders who are hiding out illegally in Canada or Sweden. Idealistic young people casually and openly discuss and choose among the legal and illegal ways of avoiding induction, and many of them consider the act of draft avoidance or evasion to be a *moral* one. As for the sexual aspect: the son of some friends of mine, living in a conservative eastern community, complained soon after he was drafted that girls who had formerly gone out with him would no longer do so. The old taunt of "Why aren't you in uniform?" has become the opposite: "Why aren't you in Sweden or in jail?" Soldiers on leave these days wear mufti.

Again, certain broad, vague expressions of patriotic sentiment that in 1945 would have been considered commendable and in 1963 at least harmless have now become specifically distasteful to many as indicative of "extremist" beliefs. To a liberal—and liberals, on political record, are something like half of our voters—the display of a bumper sticker reading "Honor America" now suggests that the owner of the car is a full-fledged reactionary, ready to jail dissenters against the war and to use atomic weapons in its prosecution. "Support Your Local Police," which until a few years ago might have been an advertisement for a cake-sale benefit, now suggests racial prejudice. Even more to the point, display of the American flag itself in many unofficial settings has come to have disturbing implications. I confess, with some reluctance, that a flag decal posted in the window of a car or a barbershop now arouses in me feelings of hostility toward the owner. It would emphatically not have done so in 1945.

True enough, the practice called flag-waving has been in bad repute in sophisticated American circles for generations. But the expression was metaphorical, usually referring to overly florid oratory. That the display of the flag itself should come to suggest extremist political and social views is surely an anomaly without precedent. Try to imagine any other democratically ruled nation in which such a condition exists—or ever has existed.

The reason behind these changes is hardly obscure. On V-J Day we were triumphantly concluding a war in which the moral imperative had been clear to just about everyone. On the one hand our territory had been attacked in the Pacific, and on the other a barbaric aggressor who clearly represented a threat to us as well as to our allies was at large in Europe. Now we are engaged in a military adventure in a distant country in which I believe tortuous logic is required to find the threat to ourselves and in which, threats aside, the moral imperative is certainly not clear to many millions. Is the change, then, only temporary and expedient—like, say, the 1930's pacifism of my generation? I rather think not.

The computer revolution, filtering through from technology to culture, has recently come to change ways of thinking, perhaps more than we usually realize. Norman Macrae, deputy editor of the British *Economist*, commented after a recent U.S. visit on "the greater air of professionalism which runs through all ranks of American society; the greater instinct among ordinary individuals to say 'Now here is a problem, how can I solve it by a systematic approach?' '' We have learned that computers can not only imitate the human brain (play chess, choose marriage partners) but can in many ways far exceed it (retrieve material from huge library collections or scan the contents of a fat telephone book in a fraction of a second; predict election results in an instant; put men on the moon). Is it not logical, then, that we should try to improve our minds by making them as much like computers as possible? The young executive or computer programmer who has learned the meaning and value of the systems approach to problems tries to apply it in every area of his personal life—in choosing schools for his children, in mowing his lawn, in pleasing his wife. It may well be that the current cult of irrationality is partly a reaction against this computer-spawned mimicry of mechanical thinking in everyday life.

Whether or not television and its concomitants in mass communications and world travel have done what Marshall McLuhan says they have—destroyed the ''linear'' habit of thinking imposed by the printed page and returned the whole world to the instinctual communication methods of the primitive tribal village—they have, it seems evident enough, changed our living and thinking habits in the direction of passive receptivity. I suggest that, with the first generation of television children now coming of age, we are just beginning to feel the force of this change.

While the Negro-rights movement has passed through its various stages—full integration of the armed forces (1948), the fight for integration of schools and public facilities (1954 *et seq.*), and finally ''black power''—white attitudes toward aid to the Negro cause have gone through a spectrum of changes. In 1945 the majority of us, to judge from our actions, still clung to the thought that such aid through federal intervention was unnecessary or inappropriate. During the civil-rights decade beginning in 1954 most of us permitted ourselves to think of such aid as morally commendable on our part— that is to say, to think of it as having at least a component of charity. Now, in the black-power era when integration as a goal and the possible perfectability of American society are being increasingly rejected by the more militant black leaders, it has been borne in on more and more of us that giving things to minorities is and always was at best mere political expediency and at worst blackmail. Such ideas were unthinkable for nearly everyone in 1945; for all but a few in 1964. President Johnson, it is interesting to note, was very much in the avant-garde of American thought in 1965 when he said at Howard University, ''You do not wipe away the scars of centuries by saying, 'Now, you are free to go where you want, do what you desire, and choose the leaders you please.' You do not take a man who, for years, has been hobbled by chains, liberate him, bring him to the starting line of the race, saying, 'You are free to compete with the others. . . .' '' Might not those words—had they not been spoken by an American President—serve as a black-power slogan?)

Along with the change in white attitudes toward blacks is a profound and unsettling change in the attitude of liberals toward our national history. Blacks and others, mainly blacks, have persuaded liberals that ours is in crucial ways a racist society, and that it always has been. Formerly we thought of the American past, broadly, in terms of rural individualism, fanatical independence, and anti-intellectualism combined with visceral folk wisdom and an inherent sense of fairness—thought of it, that is, in a way that was both affectionate and patronizing. We minimized or dismissed particular instances of racism (lynchings, the Scottsboro case, or the wartime detention camps for Nisei) as being confined to a particular geographical area or attibutable to the bad judgment of particular leaders. Now, for many Americans, almost any tintype glimpse of the American past—the village band concert with its handful of tentatively smiling black faces in the back row, the political rally with no black faces anywhere—suggests racism. To a degree our history has been poisoned for us. And I believe that the consequences of this, in the light of our current national demoralization, can hardly be overemphasized at this time in America's life.

Our leaders themselves have become demoralized to an extent surely without precedent since the Civil War. ''We know our lakes are dying, our rivers growing filthier daily, our atmosphere increasingly polluted,'' John Gardner, former Cabinet member and more recently head of the Urban Coalition, said not long ago. ''We are aware of racial tensions that could tear the nation apart. We understand that oppressive poverty in the midst of affluence is intolerable. We see that our cities are sliding toward disaster. . . . But we are seized by a kind of paralysis of the will.'' Does not such language, in the nation of Fourth of July oratory, and coming from not just an Establishment figure but to some *the* Establishment figure of the present moment, represent a clear break with the past, even the very recent past?

Naturally, the demoralization of the leaders is felt among the people. ''Most people no longer seem to care—if, indeed, they know—what is happening to their country,'' Richard Harris wrote late last year in *The New Yorker* magazine. ''Exhausted by the demands of modern life and muddled by the fearful discord tearing at society, they seem to have turned their common fate over to their leaders in a way that would have been inconceivable five years ago.'' But when the leaders talk of paralysis of the will, who will lead?

I come now to recent changes in attitudes and values among the young, where we may find a key to what is happening to the country. To review briefly, then, the most obvious manifestations of these changes:

Youth on the campus has discovered its previously unsuspected and therefore untested power to change its environment and the conditions of its life. From the Berkeley revolt (1964) to the one at Columbia (1968) to the one at Harvard (1969) we have seen the content of such campus uprisings gradually broaden from demands for the right to use dirty words to demands for changes in the course of study, insistence on sexual and other forms of personal freedom, demands for revision of admissions policies, and ultimatums about the reorganization of entire curricula. The rebels have developed their own jargon—largely mindless and question-begging like all political jargon: in pursuit of "restructuring" (getting their own way) the dissidents resort to "confrontation" (violence or the threat of it), make "nonnegotiable demands" (refuse to engage in reasonable discussion), and, if they get what they want, sometimes complain with what seems to be a certain disappointment that they have been "co-opted" (yielded to). A comical aspect of their behavior is that they frequently ask those in authority to help them revolt against that very authority; they want, for example, to be offered formal courses in the techniques of campus disruption as well as guerrilla warfare. (A university president told me recently of a student delegation that had come to ask him, not without an attractive diffidence, that he help them by giving them the benefit of his political experience. "What they wanted me to help them rebel against was *me*," he commented.) But campus revolts are not a joke. They are evidence of an idea completely new in the United States, poles apart from the passive orthodoxy of the silent generation of a decade earlier, that teaching authority is not absolute but fluid and malleable, that the young can move the sun and the moon in their heavens if they try, that their universe in spite of its ordered surface is basically anarchic. And the authorities, by yielding to them again and again, have confirmed their most disturbing suspicions.

Recent statistics compiled by the Urban Research Corporation of Chicago give a striking picture of how widespread campus revolts have been. Covering 232 campuses over the first half of 1969, the study showed that during that period 215,000 students, or about one tenth of all those enrolled at the institutions studied, actively participated in a total of nearly three hundred major protests—all in just six months. Before the fact that only one student in ten was active in the uprisings is taken to indicate that the youth revolt is just the phenomenon of a small but visible minority, we would do well to consider that historically the passive sympathizers with new movements have usually far outnumbered the activists.

The young have turned against careers in business, particularly in big and long-established business, to such an extent that some campus recruiters have expressed concern as to where the managers of the future will come from—although up to now there have been enough exceptions to keep the business schools from being depopulated and the lower ranks of corporate management from being undermanned.

They have made a cult of irrationality, what with astrology, Oriental occultism, and above all the use of drugs. (*"We* never needed drugs to drive us crazy," the middle-aged social commentator David T. Bazelon once told me.) This tendency runs deep and wide, cutting across economic, social, and intellectual lines among the young. The sheltered, conservatively brought-up white southern darling and the would-be hippie son of liberal northern suburbanites yearn alike for the experience of New York City's East Village, and the young Harvard intellectual is almost as likely as the high-school dropout to express or imply hostility to the traditional intellectual materials, abstract ideas, and rational comment. Curiously, the defense of irrationality is often put—persuasively—on rational grounds: that logical thought in foreign policy led to Vietnam, that logical thought in economic development led to pollution, and so on.

The young are apparently in the process of radically redefining sex roles. The question of which forces (the Pill, the obscenity explosion in the media set off by the courts' anticensorship decisions, or the general air of permissiveness in the land) have brought about a radical change in sexual customs among both the young and their elders, remains undecided. No one really knows. What is much clearer, and perhaps more interesting, is that the traditional aggressiveness of the young American male about his maleness, which has so often led to anti-intellectualism, Babbittry, and cultural self-deprivation in general—for example, the American he-man's hostility to most of the arts on grounds that they are effete—seems to have been emphatically reversed. The short hair and pointedly different clothing that he always used to set himself unmistakably apart from girls are more and more being abandoned in favor of long hair, fur coats, beads, and other adornments that were formerly considered feminine. The American male's dread of appearing to be unmanly seems to be lessening. More significantly, one is struck by the new sense of community that boys and girls feel. The growing insistence of the young on coeducation is not just a matter of having sex available but one of principle, growing out of a new conviction that the sexes are not so different as American culture has decreed them to be and that the old segregation is therefore absurd.

The symptoms I have been recording are, of course, parts of a syndrome, and one that may be viewed in two diametrically opposed ways. Looked at in a favorable light, the new youth are gentle, loving, natural, intuitive, opposed only to war and obsession with money, to hypocrisy and the other agreed-upon weaknesses of modern society as organized by their elders. In a different perspective they represent progressive-school permissiveness and self-indulgence run wild: their causes are merely self-serving (opposition to the draft, for example), their attitudes are self-righteous ("Just because you are growing older do not be afraid of change," they gravely lecture their parents and teachers), their manners are deplorable or nonexistent, their minds are flabby, their herding together indicates fear of standing alone, and the manner of their protests sometimes appears ominously antidemocratic. Macrae of *The Economist* goes so far as to say that some of the actions of black-power and radical white students during the winter of 1968–69 "invited the most direct comparison with the way that Hitler's brownshirts operated in the Weimar Republic." On the other hand Ralph Nader's consumer-protection crusade, which clearly appeals strongly to the brightest and most idealistic among the young, might fairly be described as passionately *pro*democratic in that its aim is to save that most characteristic democratic institution, the business corporation, from its own shortcomings. Paradoxes and contradictions, then; and it is quite possible— indeed, perhaps it is inevitable—for a liberal of the previous generation to see the young in both lights at the same time.

For such an observer, analysis is more profitable than judgment. Consider, then, the vital statistics. The median age of the American population as present is a bit under twenty-eight years. Half of us, roughly speaking, were born before the middle of World War II and half since it. Half of us were of an age to be percipient before V-J Day, and half were not. The distinction is not arbitrary, because it was with the end of the war that the new era, the modern world, began. The time has come when "over thirty" means precisely "born before the war." Only the younger half of the American people have never known the world of traditional values as it was without the disrupters of those values—television, computers, jet travel, space travel, the threat of nuclear extinction. Only the younger half truly belong to the new world—that is, accept it instinctively, without mental or emotional effort, because they have not any old world to compare it with.

And consider this: the five postwar moods before the present one were conjoined as well as consecutive—each had its roots in reaction to the previous one, as have the moods of most nations through most of past history. Wartime family disruptions led logically and naturally to early postwar domesticity. The Cold War, which really began in 1945 at Yalta, bore its bitter fruit five years later in Korea. Armed conflict with our former allies, the Communists, led logically to the era of suspicion. The eventual relaxation of that crisis cleared the way for the Eisenhower years of self-indulgence. And the new energy and responsibility of the Kennedy term was clearly enough a reaction to that. In such a linear way did our history unfold for almost two decades.

And then—snap! The chain of events seemed to be broken. Suddenly we flew off in directions that seemed to be neither a continuation of nor a reaction of anything that had gone before. Disillusion with uniform and flag did not appear to be rooted in reaction to any particular superpatriotism of the preceding period; mechanized thinking was not new, but the existence, indeed the ubiquitous presence, of actual thinking machines was; the new youth rebellion could be seen as a reaction to youth passivity a decade earlier, but the breadth and depth of the response was so far out of proportion to the challenge as to make such an explanation seem entirely inadequate. The present American mood, then, in many of its aspects, has had no precedents or antecedents; it represents almost a clear break; it seems to have come out of the blue. Meanwhile, let us remember, it has not been accompanied by sharp breaks in or reversals of the broad ameliorative trends that have marched through the whole postwar period. There are no jolts or breaks around 1964 or 1965 in the charts of social progress. The nation seems to have changed its mind, or to be in the process of changing its mind, on many of the most basic matters for no immediately discernible material reason. And this occurs precisely at the time when the new post-V-J Day generation is coming of age.

Can this conjunction of facts be more than coincidental? Indeed, must it not be? If so, then the new generation, the generation that is in tune with the new world because it never knew the old one, appears, for better or worse, as the basic force behind the new, unprecedented American attitudes. As for the statistical charts, their relatively smooth continuance through this period of violent cultural upheaval may be explained by the fact that the charts and the things recorded in the charts—matters of business, government, philanthropy—remain in the hands of the old postwar generation. It does not really live in the new world it has made, yet it still nervously holds all the levers of national power.

One who accepts such an analysis is Margaret Mead. In her recent book, *Culture and Commitment: A Study of the Generation Gap*, she declares that "our present situation is unique, without any parallel in the past," and that—not just in the United States but world-wide—the human race is arriving through the youth revolt at an entirely new phase of cultural evolution. Putting her argument in a context of rigorous anthropological study rather than in the familiar one of parlor sociology, she describes the new phase as a "prefigurative" society: one in which the traditional handing down of knowledge and belief from the elder generation to the younger is being reversed and in which "it will be the child and not the parent or grandparent that represents what is to come." No longer anywhere in the world, Dr. Mead says, can the elders, born before the Second World War, know and understand what the children know and understand: "Even very recently the elders could say, 'You know, I have been young and you never have been old.' But today's young people can reply, 'You never have been young in the world I am young in, and you never can be.' " The prefigurative society she sees emerging is, Dr. Mead says, the first one in human history.

It is a persuasive case, and, fitted together with the vital statistics I have cited, it leads to a persuasive explanation of why changes in our values and attitudes, after years of poking along like a donkey cart in a time of great transformation in our material situation, have recently taken off as steeply as a jet plane. So it comes about that the elders—whether they conservatively wring their hands over the new changes or liberally try to understand, absorb, and temper them—feel like expatriate visitors in their own country. Like expatriates, we of the prewar generation are inclined to spend our days wavering between wonder, exasperation, apprehension, disgust, and superiority toward what we see around us. Again, like expartriates, we tend to cling together in enclaves, to propitiate our sense of loneliness by finding islands of our own within the new world that conform as closely as possible to the old one. The turned-on headlights of daytime drivers that have been so familiar a sight in many parts of the country in recent months are supposed to mean support of our Vietnam policy, but they mean more than that. They are a symbol by which the loneliest of the lonely expatriates reassure themselves that they are not wholly alone; they are the club ties of the American Club in Samarkand.

Even if the analysis is right, all of this is, of course, a change still in process, and indeed still in an early stage of process, rather than an accomplished fact. The "silent majority" apparently still *is* a majority—of poll respondents and of voters—and even if it were not, traditional methods of succession to power have survived up to now to the extent that the older generation would still hold business and government power and might be expected to continue to do so for some years to come. Even among the young themselves Dr. Mead's prefigurative culture is still very far from universal. There are whole campuses in "middle America" where a long-haired boy is an object of derision, where revolt against university authority never crosses anyone's mind, where books and magazines containing four-letter words are missing from the library shelves, and where "God Bless America" is sung without irony.

But such attitudes among the postwar generation seem to represent cultural lag. They are scarcely the wave of the future. It is those older than the nation's median age who make up the bulk of the silent majority. In purely actuarial terms, this majority is living on borrowed time; it is a majority under a death sentence.

What happens next?

One line of thought holds that the strange new attitudes and values are attributable not to the influence of youth but to the Vietnam war and the disruptions, frustrations, and loss of morale attendant upon it—its ability, as James Reston of the *New York Times* has written, to "poison everything." This interpretation is reassuring to the prewar generation because it implies that when the war is over everything will revert to the way it was before. But those born in the years immediately after V-J Day, who were entering college when the Vietnam war was escalated and are leaving it now, and who have lived only in the strange new world, can scarcely be expected to go back where they have never been. I am convinced that Vietnam is not the root cause of our current malaise and that if there had been no

Vietnam the young would have found plenty of other reasons to dissociate themselves violently from their elders and their elders' regime. Certainly the end of the war, when it blessedly comes, will mark the end of our current paralysis and the beginning of a seventh and more hopeful postwar mood; but I expect it to be a mood not of returning to the familiar but of pushing forward to something new and unknown. In the traditional American cultural pattern youth has always been allowed its fling with the tacit understanding between youngsters and elders that after graduation the youngsters would ''put away childish things'' and ''settle down.'' The wild young buck who had been proud of his capacity for beer and beer-inspired pranks would sink quickly into sober, hard-working domesticity, and the pretty blonde who had found it amusing to flirt with Communism while in college would become his meekly Republican, upwardly mobile bride. It is impossible for me to imagine the post-V-J Day generation following this familiar pattern. One can, for example, visualize their male hairstyle going from shoulder length to shaved heads—but not to crew cuts; one can visualize their politics doing a flip-flop to dangerously radical rightist positions—but not to traditional conservatism or traditional liberalism.

How, then, can they be expected to react to being older and to assuming power and responsibility instead of defying them? Will they, in their turn, be ''prefigured'' by the new younger generation that will consist of their children? How will they run the Ford Foundation? the Institute for Advanced Study? the Bureau of the Census? Will they continue the broad liberal trends initiated by the older generation that they now revile—trends toward more social-minded corporations, better-distributed wealth, more general education, less pervasive bigotry? Will they bring to reality *The Economist's* prophecy that ''the United States in this last third of the twentieth century is the place where man's long economic problem is ending''? Will, say, the affairs of General Motors be managed by men (or women) wearing long hair and beads and smoking pot during sales conferences? Or will there be no General Motors?

The fact that it sounds like material for a musical-comedy skit indicates how little we know what to expect. Adolf A. Berle said recently, speaking of economic and social affairs in the United States, ''We are beginning to evolve a new ball game.'' Whether we like it or not the rules of the new game will not be our rules. They will be devised by those born since V-J Day.

Epilogue

Arthur M. Schlesinger, Jr.

AMERICA:
EXPERIMENT OR DESTINY?

It is fitting that we end this excursion through American history
with a question. History leads to a present we can never wholly
understand and points to a future we can discern only in barest
outline. Serious historians, however, never attempt to predict the
future and deal with contemporary affairs rarely and usually very
tentatively. Therefore, although Professor Arthur M. Schlesinger,
Jr., of the City University of New York has been a maker of history
as a close adviser to President John F. Kennedy, and a recorder
of very recent events—as in his book *A Thousand Days* —he has
in this article asked a question about the past—about "the
meaning of the American experience." Such broad-gauged,
interpretive works as this are the most difficult historians can
attempt, and it takes one of Schlesinger's intellectual powers to
carry off the task successfully. Readers of such efforts, however,
need not possess the depth of knowledge that goes into writing
them in order to appreciate and profit from them. Ask yourself
after reading the following essay and thinking about its
relation to the other essays in the collection: "What *is* the meaning
of the American experience?"

Nearly two centuries after Crèvecoeur propounded his notorious question—"What then is the American, this new man?"—Vine Deloria, Jr., an American Indian writing in the Bicentennial year on the subject "The North Americans" for *Crisis*, a magazine directed to American blacks, concluded: "No one really knows at the present time what America really is." Surely few observers were more entitled to wonder at the continuing mystery than those who could accurately claim the designation Original American. Surely no audience had more right to share the bafflement than one made up of descendants of slaves.

But we are all baffled by the meaning of the American experience. All any of us can do is descry a figure in the carpet—realizing as we do that contemporary preoccupations define our own definitions. My effort here will be to suggest two themes that seem to me to have subsisted in subtle counterpoint since the time when English-speaking white men first began the invasion of America. Both have dwelt within the American mind and struggled for its possession through the course of our history. Their competition will doubtless continue for the rest of the life of the nation. This essay aims to present these rival themes and to propose some points about the relationship between the divergent outlooks and the health of the republic.

I will call one theme the tradition and the other the countertradition, thereby betraying at once my own bias. The tradition, as I prefer to style it, sprang initially from historic Christianity as mediated by Augustine and Calvin. The Calvinist ethos was suffused with convictions of the depravity of man, of the awful precariousness of human existence, of the vanity of mortals under the judgment of a pitiless and wrathful deity. Harriet Beecher Stowe recalled the atmosphere in *Oldtown Folks:* "The underlying foundation of life . . . in New England, was one of profound, unutterable, and therefore unuttered, melancholy, which regarded human existence itself as a ghastly risk, and, in the case of the vast majority of human beings, an inconceivable misfortune."

So terrible a sense of the nakedness of the human condition turned all of life into an unending and implacable process of testing. "We must look upon our selves," said William Stoughton, the chief justice of the court that condemned the Salem witches, "as under a *solemn divine Probation;* it hath been and it is a Probation-time, even to this whole People. . . ." So had it been at all times for all people. Most had failed the test. Were the American colonists immune to the universal law?

In the Calvinist view, all secular communities were finite and problematic; all flourished and all decayed; all had a beginning and an end. For Christians this idea had its *locus classicus* in the attempt to solve the problem of the decline and fall of Rome—a problem that transfixed the serious historical minds of the West. . . . By the time the revolutionaries came to Philadephia in 1776, the flames of Calvinism were already burning low. Hell was dwindling into an epithet. Still, for the fathers of the republic as for the fathers of the church, the history of Rome remained the example from which they thought to learn the most about human possibilities.

From different premises, Calvinists and classicists reached the same conclusion about the fragility of human striving. Antiquity haunted the Federal imagination. The Founding Fathers had embarked on a singular adventure—the adventure of a *republic*. "The Roman republic," Alexander Hamilton wrote in the *Federalist*, "attained to the pinnacle of human greatness." In this conviction the first generation of the American republic designed its buildings, wrote its epics, named the upper chamber of its legislature, signed its greatest political treatise "Publius," sculpted its heroes in togas, organized the Society of the Cincinnati, and instructed the young. There was plausibility in the parallel. There was also warning. For the grandeur that was Rome had come to an inglorious end. Could the United States of America hope to do better?

The Founding Fathers passionately ransacked the classical historians for ways to escape the classical fate. But the classical indoctrination reinforced the Calvinist judgment that this was probation-time for America. For the history of antiquity did not teach the inevitability of progress. It proved rather the perishability of republics, the subversion of virtue by power and luxury, the transience of glory, the mutability of human affairs. The apprehension of the mortality of states was a vital element in the sensibility of Philadelphia in 1787. Not only was man vulnerable through his propensity to sin, but republics were vulnerable through their propensity to corruption. The dread of corruption, as Professor Bernard Bailyn has demonstrated, was readily imported from England to the colonies. History showed that, in the unceasing contest between corruption and virtue, corruption had always—at least up to 1776— triumphed.

The Founding Fathers had an intense conviction of the improbability of their undertaking. Such assets as they possessed came in their view from geographical and demographic advantage, not from divine intercession. Benjamin Franklin ascribed the inevitability of American independence to such mundane factors as population increase and vacant lands, not to providential design. But even these assets could not be counted on to prevail against history and human nature.

Hamilton said in the New York ratifying convention, "The tendency of things will be to depart from the republican standard. This is the real disposition of human nature." If Hamilton be discounted as a temperamental pessimist or a disaffected adventurer, his great adversaries were not always more sanguine about the republic's future. "Commerce, luxury, and avarice have destroyed every republican government," Adams wrote Benjamin Rush in 1808. ". . . We mortals cannot work miracles; we struggle in vain against the constitution and course of nature." "I tremble for my country," Jefferson had said in the 1780's, "when I reflect that God is just." Though he was trembling at this point—rightly and presciently—over the problem of slavery, he also trembled chronically in the nineties over the unlikely prospect of "monarchy." In 1798 he saw the Alien and Sedition Acts as tending to drive the states "into revolution and blood, and [to] furnish new calumnies against republican government, and new pretexts for those who wish it to be believed, that man cannot be governed but by a rod of iron."

This pervasive self-doubt, this urgent sense of the precariousness of the national existence, was no doubt nourished by European assessments of the American prospect. For eminent and influential Europeans regarded the New World, not as an idyl of Lockean felicity— "in the beginning, all the world was America"—but as a disgusting scene of degeneracy and impotence.

In the middle of the eighteenth century, the famous Buffon lent the weight of scientific authority to the proposition that life in the Western Hemisphere was consigned to biological inferiority. American animals were smaller and weaker; European animals shrank when transported across the Atlantic, except, Buffon specified, for the fortunate pig. As for the natives of the fallen continent, they too were small and weak, passive and backward.

No one made this case more irritatingly and perseveringly than Abbé Raynal in France. His much-reprinted work, *Philosophical and Political History of the Settlements and of the Commerce of Europeans in the Two Indies*, first published in 1770, explained how European innocence was under siege by American depravity. America, Raynal wrote, had "poured all the sources of corruption on Europe." The search for American riches brutalized the European intruder. The climate and soil of America caused the European species, human as well as animal, to deteriorate. "The men have less strength and less courage . . . and are but little susceptible of the lively and powerful sentiment of love"—a comment that perhaps revealed Raynal in the end more as a Frenchman than as an abbé.

The Founding Fathers were highly sensitive to the proposition that America was a mistake. Franklin, who thought Raynal an "ill-informed and evil-minded Writer," once endured a monologue by the diminutive abbé on the inferiority of the Americans at his own dinner table in Paris. "Let us try this question by the fact before us," said Franklin, calling on his guests to stand up and measure themselves back to back. "There was not one American present," wrote Jefferson, who was also there, "who could not have tost out of the Windows any one or two of the rest of the Company."

Though the Founders were both indignant and effective in their rebuttal, the nature of the attack could hardly have increased their confidence in the future of their adventure. The European doubt, along with the Calvinist judgment and the classical pessimism, made them acutely aware of the chanciness of an extraordinary enterprise. From the fate of the Greek city-states and the fall of the Roman Empire, they drew somber conclusions about the prospects of the American republic. They had no illusions about the inviolability of America to history, nor about the perfectibility of man, Americans or others. The Constitution, James Bryce has well said, was "the work of men who believed in original sin, and were resolved to leave open for transgressors no door which they could possibly shut."

We have all applied the phrase "end of innocence" to one or another stage of American history. This is surely an amiable flourish—or a pernicious delusion. No people who systematically enslaved black men and killed red men could be innocent. No people reared on Calvin and Tacitus, on Jonathan Edwards and the *Federalist*, could be innocent. No nation founded on invasion, conquest, and slaughter could be innocent. No state established by revolution and thereafter rent by civil war could be innocent. The Constitution was hardly the product of immaculate conception. The Founding Fathers were not a band of saints. They were brave and imperturbable realists who committed themselves, in defiance of the available lessons of history and theology, to a monumental gamble.

This is why Hamilton, in the third sentence of the first *Federalist*, formulated the issue as he did. The American people, he wrote, had the opportunity "by their conduct and example, to decide the important question, whether societies of men are really capable or not of establishing good government from reflection and choice, or whether they are forever destined to depend for their political constitutions on accident and force." So Washington defined it in his first Inaugural Address: "The preservation of the sacred fire of liberty and the destiny of the republican model of government are justly considered, perhaps, as *deeply*, as *finally*, staked on the experiment intrusted to the hands of the American people." The Founding Fathers saw the American republic not as a consecration but as the test against history of a hypothesis.

Washington's early successors, with mingled anxiety and hope, reported on the experiment's fortunes. In his last message to Congress, James Madison permitted himself "the proud reflection that the American people have reached in safety and success their fortieth year as an independent nation." "Our institutions," said James Monroe in his last message, "form an important epoch in the history of the civilized world. On their preservation and in their utmost purity everything will depend." Washington, said Andrew Jackson in his own Farewell Address, regarded the Constitution "as an experiment" and "was prepared to lay down his life, if necessary, to secure to it a full and a fair trial. The trial has been made. It has succeeded beyond the proudest hopes of those who framed it." "The present year," Martin Van Buren said in 1838, "closes the first half century of our Federal institutions. . . . It was reserved for the American Union to test the advantages of a government entirely dependent on the continual exercise of the popular will." "After an existence of near three-fourths of a century as a free and independent Republic," said Polk in the next decade, "the problem no longer remains to be solved

whether man is capable of self-government.'' Sixty years after the
Constitution, Zachary Taylor pronounced the United States of America
''the most stable and permanent Government on earth.''

How is one to account for this rising optimism? It was partly a
tribute, reasonable enough, to survival. It was partly the spread-
eagleism and vainglory congenial to a youthful nationalism. It was
no doubt also in part admonitory exhortation, for the Presidents of the
middle period must have known in their bones that the American
experiment was confronting its fiercest internal trial. No one understood more profoundly the chanciness of the adventure than the young
man who spoke in 1838 on ''The Perpetuation of our Political Institutions'' before the Young Men's Lyceum of Springfield, Illinois.
Over most of the first half century, Abraham Lincoln said, America
had been felt ''to be an undecided experiment; now, it is understood
to be a successful one.'' But success contained its own perils; ''with
the catching, end the pleasures of the chase.'' As the memory of the
Revolution receded, the pillars of the temple of liberty were crumbling
away. ''That temple must fall, unless we . . . supply their places with
other pillars, hewn from the solid quarry of sober reason.'' The conviction of the incertitude of life informed his Presidency—and explained its greatness. His first message to Congress asked whether all
republics had an ''inherent and fatal weakness.'' At the Gettysburg
cemetery he described the great civil war as ''testing'' whether any
nation conceived in liberty and dedicated to the proposition that all
men are created equal ''can long endure.''

This was, then, a dominant theme of the early republic—the idea of
America as an experiment, undertaken in defiance of history, fraught
with risk, problematic in outcome. But a countertradition was also
emerging—and, as the mounting presidential optimism suggests, with
accumulating momentum. The countertradition, too, had its roots in
the Calvinist ethos.

Historic Christianity embraced two divergent thoughts: that all
people were immediate unto God; and that some were more immediate
than others. At first, Calvin had written in the *Institutes,* God ''chose
the Jews as his very own flock.'' Then, with what Edwards called ''the
abolishing of the *Jewish dispensation,*'' the wall was ''broken down to
make way for the more extensive success of the gospel.'' The chosen
people thereafter were the elect as against the reprobate. The age that
sent the Calvinists to New England also saw a revival of the primitive
millennialism of the first century. The New Englanders felt they had
been called from hearth and home to endure unimaginable rigor and
ordeal in a dangerous land; so they supposed someone of importance
had called them, and for important reasons. ''God hath covenanted
with his people,'' said Increase Mather, ''that sanctified afflictions shall
be their portion. . . . *Without doubt, the Lord Jesus hath a peculiar
respect unto this place, and for this people.*''

It was not only that they were, in Winthrop's words, as a City upon a
Hill, with the eyes of all people upon them. It was that they had been

despatched to New England, as Edward Johnson said, by a Wonder-working Providence because "this is the place where the Lord will create a new Heaven, and a new Earth." The "Lord Christ" intended "to make his *New England* Souldiers the very wonder of this Age." The fact that God had withheld America so long—until the Reformation purified the church, until the invention of printing spread the Bible among the people—argued that He had been preparing it for some ultimate manifestation of His grace. God, said Winthrop, having "smitten all the other Churches before our eyes," had reserved America for those whom He meant "*to save out of this generall callamitie,*" as he had once sent the ark to save Noah. The new land was certainly a part, perhaps the climax, of redemptive history; America was divine prophecy fulfilled.

The achievement of independence gave new status to this theory. The Reverend Timothy Dwight, Jonathan Edwards' grandson, called Americans "this chosen race." "God's mercies to New England," wrote Harriet Beecher Stowe, daughter of one minister, wife of another, foreshadowed "the glorious future of the United States . . . commissioned to bear the light of liberty and religion through all the earth and to bring in the great millennial day, when wars should cease and the whole world, released from the thralldom of evil, should rejoice in the light of the Lord." "We Americans," wrote the youthful Herman Melville, "are the peculiar, chosen people—the Israel of our time; we bear the ark of the liberties of the world. . . . Long enough have we been skeptics with regard to ourselves, and doubted whether, indeed, the political Messiah had come. But he has come in *us.*"

The belief that Americans were a chosen people did not imply a sure and tranquil journey to salvation. As the Bible made amply clear, chosen people underwent the harshest trials and assumed the most grievous burdens. The rival propositions—America as experiment, America as destiny—thus shared a belief in the process of testing. But one proposition tested works; the other, faith. So Lincoln and Mrs. Stowe agreed from different standpoints in seeing the Civil War as the climactic test. Northern victory, however, strengthened the conviction of providential appointment. "Now that God has smitten slavery unto death," Mrs. Stowe's brother Edward wrote in 1865, "he has opened the way for the redemption and sanctification of our whole social system."

It was a short step from the Social Gospel at home to Americans carrying the Social Gospel to the world. In 1898 the Reverend Alexander Blackburn, who had been wounded at Chickamauga, spoke of "the imperialism of righteousness"; and from Blackburn to the messianic demagoguery of Albert J. Beveridge was only another short step: "God has not been preparing the English-speaking and Teutonic peoples for a thousand years for nothing but vain and idle self-contemplation. . . . And of all our race He has marked the American people as His chosen nation to finally lead in the regeneration of the world."

So the impression developed that in the United States of America the Almighty had contrived a nation unique in its virtue and magnanimity, exempt from the motives that governed all other states. "America is the only idealistic nation in the world," said Woodrow Wilson on his pilgrimage to the West in 1919. ". . . The heart of this people is pure. The heart of this people is true. . . . It is the great idealistic force of history. . . . I, for one, believe more profoundly than in anything else human in the destiny of the United States. I believe that she has a spiritual energy in her which no other nation can contribute to the liberation of mankind. . . ."

In another forty years the theory of America as the savior of the world received the furious imprimature of John Foster Dulles, another Presbyterian elder, and from there roared on to the horrors of Vietnam. So the hallucination brought the republic from the original idea of America as exemplary experiment to the recent idea of America as mankind's designated judge, jury, and executioner. Nor are we yet absolutely clear that the victor in the Bicentennial election may not believe that nations, like Presidents, may be born again.

Why did the conviction of the corruptibility of men and the vulnerability of states—and the consequent idea of America as experiment—give way to the myth of innocence and the delusion of a sacred mission and a sanctified destiny? The original conviction was rooted in realistic conceptions of history and of human nature—conceptions that waned as the republic prospered. The intense historical-mindedness of the first generation did not endure. "The Past," Melville said in *White Jacket*, "is dead, and has no resurrection; but the Future is endowed with such a life that it lives to us even in anticipation." The new nation was largely populated by people torn from, fleeing from, or in revolt against their own histories. "Probably no other civilised nation," said the *Democratic Review* in 1842, "has . . . so completely thrown off its allegiance to the past as the American."

We find ourselves now, for all the show-business clatter of the Bicentennial celebrations, an essentially historyless people. Businessmen agree with the elder Henry Ford that history is bunk. The young no longer study history. Intellectuals turn their backs on history in the enthusiasm for the ahistorical behavioral "sciences." As the American historical consciousness has thinned out, the messianic hope has flowed into the vacuum. Experiment has given ground to destiny as the premise of national life.

So the theory of the elect nation, the redeemer nation, the happy empire of perfect wisdom and perfect virtue, almost became the official creed. Yet, while the countertradition prospered, the tradition did not quite expire. Some continued to regard it all as the deceitful dream of a golden age, wondering perhaps why the Almighty should have chosen the Americans. "The Almighty," Lincoln insisted at his second Inaugural, "has His own purposes." He clearly knew what he was saying, because he wrote soon thereafter to a fellow ironist, Thurlow

Weed: "Men are not flattered by being shown that there has been a difference of purpose between the Almighty and them. To deny, it, however . . . is to deny that there is a God governing the world."

After the war, Walt Whitman, once the supreme poet of democratic faith, suddenly perceived a dark and threatening future. The experiment was in jeopardy. These States no longer a sure thing, were caught up in a "battle advancing, retreating, between democracy's convictions, aspirations, and the people's crudeness, vice, caprices." America, Whitman apprehended, might well "prove the most tremendous failure of time." "'Tis a wild democracy," Emerson said in his last public address; "the riot of mediocrities and dishonesties and fudges." A fourth generation of Adamses raised particularly keen doubts whether Providence in settling America had after all opened a grand design to emancipate mankind. Henry Adams began as a connoisseur of political ironics; later he became a sort of reverse millennialist, convinced that science and technology were rushing the planet toward an apocalypse unredeemed by a Day of Judgment. "At the rate of increase of speed and momentum, as calculated on the last fifty years," he wrote in 1901, "the present society must break its damn neck in a definite, but remote, time, not exceeding fifty years more." The United States, like everything else, was finished. In the end Adams too abandoned experiment for destiny; but destiny for him was not only manifest but malign. "No one anywhere," he wrote a few weeks before the outbreak of the First World War, ". . . expects a future."

William James, the philosopher, retained the experimental faith, abhorring the fatalisms and absolutes implied by "the idol of a national destiny . . . which for some inscrutable reason it has become infamous to disbelieve in or refuse." We are instructed, James said, "to be missionaries of civilization. . . . We must sow our ideals, plant our order, impose our God. The individual lives are nothing. Our duty and our destiny call, and civilization must go on. Could there be a more damning indictment of that whole bloated idol termed 'modern civilization'?" All this had come about too fast "for the older American nature not to feel the shock." One cannot know what James meant by "the older American nature"; but he plainly rejected the supposition that American motives were, by definition, pure; and that the United States enjoyed a divine immunity to temptation and corruption. Like the authors of the *Federalist*, James was a realist. "Angelic impulses and predatory lusts," he precisely wrote, "divide our heart exactly as they divide the heart of other countries."

So the warfare between realism and messianism, between experiment and destiny, continued to our own day. If some political leaders were messianists, the perception of America as an experiment conducted by mortals of limited wisdom and power without divine guarantee informed the practical intelligence of others. The second Roosevelt saw life as uncertain and the national destiny as problematic. The republic was still an experiment and "demands bold, persistent experimentation. It is common sense to take a method and try it: If it fails, admit it frankly and try another. But above all, try something.'' Roosevelt's realism kept American participation in the Second World War closer to a sense of national interest than of world mission. In a later time John Kennedy argued that antimessianic case: ''We must face the fact that the United States is neither omnipotent nor omniscient—that we are only 6 per cent of the world's population—that we cannot impose our will upon the other 94 per cent of mankind—that we cannot right every wrong or reverse each adversity—and that therefore there cannot be an American solution to every world problem.'' ''Before my term has ended,'' he said in his first annual message, ''we shall have to test anew whether a nation organized and governed such as ours can endure. The outcome is by no means certain.''

This evoked the mood of the Founding Fathers. But the belief in national righteousness and providential destiny remains strong—a splendid triumph of dogma over experience. One cannot but feel that this belief has encouraged our recent excesses in the world and that the republic has lost much by forgetting what James called ''the older American nature.'' For messianism is an illusion. No nation is sacred and unique, the United States or any other. All nations are immediate unto God. America, like every country, has interests, real and fictitious; concerns, generous and selfish; motives, honorable and squalid. Providence has not set Americans apart from lesser breeds. We too are part of history's seamless web.

Yet we retain one signal and extraordinary advantage over most nations—an entirely secular advantage, conferred upon us by those quite astonishing Founding Fathers. For they bequeathed us standards by which to set our course and judge our performance—and, since they were exceptional men, the standards have not been rendered obsolete even by the second law of thermodynamics. The Declaration of Independence and the Constitution establish goals, imply commitments, and measure failures. The men who signed the Declaration, said Lincoln, ''meant to set up a standard maxim for a free society, which should be familiar to all, and revered by all; constantly looked to, constantly labored for, and even though never perfectly attained, constantly approximated, and thereby constantly spreading and deepening its influence, and augmenting the happiness and value of life to all people of all colors everywhere.''

We can take pride in our nation, not as we pretend to a commission from God and a sacred destiny, but as we struggle to fulfill our deepest values in an inscrutable world. As we begin our third century, we may well be entering our golden age. But we would be ill advised to reject the apprehensions of the Founding Fathers. Indeed, a due heed to those ancient anxieties may alone save us in the future. For America remains an experiment. The outcome is by no means certain. Only at our peril can we forget the possibility that the republic will end like Gatsby in Scott Fitzgerald's emblematic fable —Gatsby who had come so long a way and whose ''dream must have seemed so close that he could hardly fail to grasp it. He did not know that it was already behind him, somewhere back in that vast obscurity beyond the city, where the dark fields of the republic rolled on under the night.

"Gatsby believed in the green light, the orgastic future that year by year recedes before us. It eluded us then, but that's no matter— tomorrow we will run faster, stretch out our arms farther. . . . And one fine morning—

"So we beat on, boats against the current, borne back ceaselessly into the past."